HISTORY

OF THE

ORGANIZATION

OF THE

Methodist Episcopal Church, SOUTH.

BY A. H. REDFORD, D.D.

Nashville, Tenn.:
PUBLISHED BY A. H. REDFORD, AGENT,
FOR THE M. E. CHURCH, SOUTH.
1871.

STEREOTYPED AND PRINTED AT THE SOUTHERN METHODIST PUBLISHING HOUSE,
NASHVILLE, TENNESSEE.

TO THE MEMORY

OF THE

Deceased Bishops of the Methodist Episcopal Church, South,

THE LATE VENERABLE

JOSHUA SOULE, D.D.; JAMES OSGOOD ANDREW, D.D.; WILLIAM CAPERS, D.D.; AND HENRY BIDLEMAN BASCOM, D.D.;

THIS VOLUME IS RESPECTFULLY DEDICATED, BY

The Author.

PREFACE.

More than a quarter of a century has elapsed since the organization of the Methodist Episcopal Church, South. The men who were prominent in the General Conference of 1844, the extrajudicial legislation of which body resulted in the division of the Methodist Episcopal Church in the United States into two separate and distinct ecclesiastical organizations, with but few exceptions, have passed away. The names of Olin, Bangs, Finley, Elliott, Collins, Hamline, and of Bascom, Winans, Longstreet, Capers, Smith, and Fowler, no longer appear on the roll of the Conferences where, for so many years, they were the bulwarks of the Church. Bishop Morris, the senior Bishop of the Methodist Episcopal Church, (North,) alone remains of the men who composed the College of Bishops at that period. No longer able to go in and out before his brethren, he enjoys a serene old age, and is joyful in contemplation of the heavenly inheritance. His colleagues have passed over the river, and entered upon "the rest that remaineth to the people of God." The names of Hedding and Waugh will ever be dear to the memory of Methodism in the North; while those of Soule and Andrew, whose graves are yet damp with the tears of the Church, will always be cherished with a sacred fondness by the Methodist Episcopal Church, South.

Since the division of the Methodist Episcopal Church in the United States, a new generation has come upon the scene, who are not familiar with the circumstances that led to the separation. The object of this work is to place in a permanent and enduring form the proceedings of the General Conference of 1844, so far as they bear upon this question, together with all the official documents and papers necessary to a full understanding of the reasons by which the Southern Delegates in that body were governed in the declaration they made that "a continuance of the jurisdiction of that General Conference over the Conferences they represented, was inconsistent with the success of the ministry in the slaveholding States."

The success that has attended the Methodist Episcopal Church, South, since it became an independent organization, is cause of thanksgiving to Almighty God. The approving smiles of Heaven have rested upon it, indicating not only the propriety but the necessity of the separation.

A. H. REDFORD.

NASHVILLE, TENN., April 4, 1871.

CONTENTS.

CHAPTER I.

CHAPTER II.

CHAPTER III.

CHAPTER IV.

HISTORY OF THE ORGANIZATION

OF THE

M. E. CHURCH, SOUTH.

CHAPTER I.

The General Conference of 1844—The Compromise-law of 1816—The peaceful relations under this law between the Northern and Southern portions of the Church—The prosperity of the Church—Occasional agitations on the subject of Slavery—Petitions to the General Conference of 1844—Committee on Slavery—The Appeal of Francis A. Harding—Speech of Dr. Wm. A. Smith—Speech of John A. Collins—State of feeling in the South—The decision of the Baltimore Conference in the case of Harding affirmed—Sketch of William A. Smith.

THE General Conference which assembled in the city of New York in 1844, on the first day of May, will be ever memorable in the annals of American Methodism. The strength and influence of the Church represented by that body—its territorial extent spreading over a country reaching from British America on the North to the Gulf of Mexico on the South, and from the Atlantic Ocean on the East to the very verge of civilization on the Western frontier; the importance of the questions which occupied the attention of the Conference, together with the extrajudicial legislation in the cases of Francis A. Harding, an appellant from the Baltimore Conference, and Bishop James O. Andrew, of the State of Georgia, which resulted in the division of the "Methodist Episcopal Church in the United States" into two separate and distinct organizations, invested this General Conference with an interest and importance that cannot be claimed for any session that preceded it.

From the time of the organization of the Methodist Episcopal Church in America, the question of slavery had occupied the attention of both Annual and General Conferences. In 1816, a law was enacted, known as the Compromise-law of the Church, on this subject, which declared slaveholders ineligible to any official station in the Church, where "the laws of the State in which they live will admit of emancipation, and permit the liberated slave to enjoy freedom."

From 1816 to 1844, this compromise-law was recognized by the Church, and, with the exception of a few restless persons who occasionally appeared on the tapis, no dissatisfaction was expressed either North or South. While, without this spirit of accommodation, it would have been impossible for Methodism to obtain a foothold in the South, yet, under it, the Church had grown and prospered. Between the two sections the greatest harmony prevailed, each rejoicing in the prosperity of the other. The ecclesiastical history of the North and South was one history, and the achievements of the Church were the common property of the entire Connection.

Under this compromise-law the General Conference had met quadrennially for twenty-eight years, enjoying peace, fraternal confidence, and Christian love: under it, the Church, North and South, East and West, enjoyed a prosperity and power for the accomplishment of good, and attained to a position occupied by no other body of Christians on this continent. The light of her countenance and the brightness of her smiles were felt alike in homes of opulence and in the cottages of the poor, and from hearts gladdened by its blessings, from cabin and from palace, praises were continually ascending to Heaven.

The General Conference of 1844 was looked to by the Church with feelings of uncommon interest. During the quadrennial term that preceded it, the increase in the membership had been greater than during any four years previous, and the impression was general, if not universal, that the session would be unusually harmonious. The Southern portion of the Church was willing to submit to the law as it existed and had been executed, and it was not believed that the North desired to introduce any new terms of membership.

At no period since the introduction of Methodism into this country, had so great a calm been enjoyed. Scarcely an adverse breeze was stirring. Christian confidence and fraternal intercourse pervaded the whole Church. It was the calm, however, that precedes the tempest.

The question of slavery and abolition had been discussed in the councils of the nation, and political demagogues were courting political preferment, by appealing to the prejudices and inflaming the passions of the people on this subject; and these discussions occasionally disturbed the tranquillity of the Church. It was not, however, believed in the South that there would be any serious agitation in the General Conference of this or kindred questions.

Just previous to the convening of the General Conference, however, petitions on the subject of slavery were gotten up in several of the Northern Conferences. On the third day of the session, a petition from the Providence Conference was presented, which called at once to the floor several members of the body. It was moved by Mr.

Slicer, of the Baltimore Conference, "that it lie on the table until a committee should be appointed to whom to refer it." To this Mr. Crowder, of Virginia, objected, and called for its reading. In this opinion Mr. Drake, of Mississippi, concurred, and the motion was withdrawn, and the memorial was read.

Mr. Collins, of Baltimore, then moved "that the memorial be referred to a committee of one from each Annual Conference, to be called a Committee on Slavery." Dr. Capers, of South Carolina, objected to raising any such committee, as well as to the reference of the memorial, and "moved that the motion to refer lie on the table." This, however, was lost. On the motion to raise the committee, a spirited debate was elicited, in which Mr. Collins, of Baltimore, Dr. Capers, of South Carolina, Mr. Dow, of New Hampshire, and Mr. Early, of Virginia, took a part. The motion to lay on the table was lost, and the memorial was referred to a committee to be composed of one from each Annual Conference.

The petition from the Providence Conference was not the only one that was presented and referred. New England, Maine, New Hampshire, Black River, Pittsburgh, Rock River, Ohio, and other Conferences, also presented petitions on the same subject, which were referred to the Committee on Slavery.

On the 6th of May, Dr. W. A. Smith, of Virginia, offered the following resolution:

"*Resolved,* That the committee to whom the memorials on slavery are referred, be, and hereby are, requested to report directly on the points, the alleged facts and arguments, submitted by the memorialists, and present their report as soon as practicable."

Dr. Smith supported this resolution by a speech remarkable for its clearness and force, eliciting an animated discussion, in which Crandall and Adams, of New England, Dow and Cass, of New Hampshire, Slicer, of Baltimore, and Green, of Tennessee, were prominent.

On the 7th of May, the subject of slavery came before the General Conference in a more imposing form. The Rev. Francis A. Harding, a member of the Baltimore Conference, had become connected by marriage with slavery, and having failed to manumit these slaves, had been suspended, and had appealed from the decision of the Baltimore Conference. The case had been referred to a committee of the Baltimore Conference, with the following result:

"The committee reported that Mr. Harding had become possessed of five slaves: one named Harry, aged fifty-two; one woman, named Maria, aged fifty; one man, named John, aged twenty-two; a girl, named ——, aged thirteen; and a child, aged two years; and recommended the following preamble and resolution for adoption:

"'Whereas, the Baltimore Conference cannot, and will not, tolerate slavery in any of its members—

"'*Resolved*, That Brother Harding be required to execute a deed of manumission, and have the same enrolled in the proper court, and give to this Conference, during this present session, a pledge that this shall be done during the present year.'

"Brother Harding having stated the impossibility, with his views, of his compliance with this resolution, Mr. Collins moved for his suspension until he gave sufficient assurance of his compliance.

"The matter was again referred to a committee of five, for farther investigation, who reported that they had entirely failed to induce Brother Harding to comply with the wishes of the Conference.

"Brothers Collins and Emory moved the following resolution, which was adopted:

"'*Resolved*, That Brother Harding be suspended until the next Annual Conference, or until he assures the Episcopacy that he has taken the necessary steps to secure the freedom of his slaves.'"

Although the question of slavery had frequently been brought before the General Conference, yet on no previous occasion had it assumed such a commanding aspect as now. The Baltimore Conference had previously acted with the South in resisting the encroachments of abolitionism, and had wielded a potent influence in arresting its tide. The action of that body in the case of Mr. Harding had been extrajudicial, and from their decision he had very properly appealed to the General Conference, where he had the right to expect protection. Bishop Soule was in the chair when the appeal was presented, and remarked that "the question will arise, according to the Discipline, whether the General Conference will admit this appeal." On motion, the appeal was admitted, upon which Bishop Soule called upon the appellant to state the ground of his appeal.

The discussion in the case of Mr. Harding was quite protracted. It commenced on the 7th of May, and was concluded on the 11th. Dr. William A. Smith, of Virginia, conducted the appeal on the part of Mr. Harding, while John A. Collins, of Baltimore, had charge of the case on the part of the Baltimore Conference.

The speeches delivered on that occasion by these distinguished gentlemen, were equal to their reputation.

The speech of Dr. Smith, so masterly in argument, so replete with proof, and so overwhelmingly convincing, merits preservation. Dr. Smith said:

I appear before the General Conference, at the instance of the appellant, to state his case to the best of my ability. In entering upon this duty, especially as the case involves the question of slavery, it is proper that I should make some preliminary remarks personal to myself.

I am aware, from the use that has been made of my name within the last few years in various journals, in different sections of the country, it is reasonable to suppose that I entertain personally hostile feelings toward those who differ from me. I wish to disavow it. My own opinions on the subject have been made up for years. But these opinions have never been permitted with me, so far as I am competent to understand myself, to originate unchristian feelings to any honest man who differs with me. I have always held myself to be, and now do, an antislavery man—not, however, an abolitionist in any sense of the word. And in this I differ not from my Methodist brethren in the ministry and out of it. The sense which I attach to antislavery will, in the course of the observations I shall make on the merits of this case, be explained. In the present case I do not know if I am not called upon to represent an abolitionist, though a Southern man myself. I do not symbolize with the brother on the subject of slavery. I differ with him almost as widely as I do from any abolitionist, North or East. And I do, sir, with the more cheerfulness enter upon the defense of this case, being actuated by a sense of justice, because I believe, whatever may have been the design, (and I have not a solitary doubt that the design was a good one,) this brother has been wronged, and deeply wronged, by the decision in his case.

I learn from the journals of the Baltimore Conference, and from his own statement, that he entered as a probationer in the ministry in 1839, and in 1843 was ordained, in the regular course, an Elder in the Methodist Episcopal Church. On the 8th of February, in 1844, he became connected by marriage with Miss Swan, in the State of Maryland. At the session of the Conference in March last he was called up for examination, and from the journal of that body I learn his Presiding Elder stated that, by his late marriage, he had become connected with slavery. The Conference appointed a committee to investigate the subject. That committee reported. Their report you have heard read; it requires him to pledge himself that, during the year, he would execute a deed securing to the slaves their liberty. These slaves belonged to his wife by the demise of her parents. Let that be distinctly remembered. I understand that Brother Harding, for specific reasons, refused to comply with the decision of the Conference. It is due to him to state, that I could have wished the journals of the Conference had been kept as the rule requires they should be kept; that all the questions and all the answers put to the accused had been matter of record. This, however, is not the case. The proceedings of the Conference alone, so far as regards the resolutions moved and adopted, make up the journals of that Conference, and by consequence we have not the legal, authorized testimony, required by the Book of Discipline. I must, therefore, sir, rely for the facts that are important to a due consideration of this case, upon the correct and honest memory of the representatives of the Baltimore Conference. I therefore say that if, in relating any thing of importance, not on the records of the Conference, I should be found in their judgment in error—for it is not my purpose to misrepresent the history of this case—they will point out the error. I understand from the individual himself, and from some members of that Conference, that when the decision was read, he refused at once to comply with the demand of the Conference on the following grounds:—

First. That by the nature of the laws of the State of Maryland he did not become the owner of the slaves. They were held by his wife by descent from her parents, and that he had therefore no right to execute the deed required by the Conference.

Secondly. That if it were not so, the laws of the State of Maryland do not permit the liberated slave to enjoy liberty, and that, therefore, under the rule of Discipline, he was not required to comply with the condition. He maintained, therefore, that the pledge was impracticable, and contrary to the rule of Discipline; and, thirdly, that it would be in its practical results inhuman. And why? Because the demand, if carried out by him, without the consent of these slaves, would separate parents from children and other friends, which, without their consent, he, as a conscientious man, could not consent to do.

But while he thus refused a compliance with the proposed condition, he nevertheless tendered to the Conference the following pledge, in his own name and that of his wife, that he would have them removed to the colony in Africa, or to any free State in the Union, where they might be permitted to enjoy their freedom, at any time when he could do so with their consent. But pledge himself to fulfill the condition made by the Conference, with or without their consent, and thus sever the dearest ties on earth, he, as a humane and conscientious man, could not consent to do. I am now relating what the journals of the Baltimore Conference should have shown. Let the Conference understand that I am repeating the pledges made by this brother in my own language;

but I submit it to the delegation whether I give substantially the pledges he gave. If not, correct me on the spot, and do not leave me to labor in the dark.

Mr. Griffith. I understand you to say that he gave a pledge to remove them to any free State. I have no recollection of such a pledge. If tendered, it would have been accepted, as perfectly satisfactory.

Mr. Gere. Brother Griffith may not have heard the pledge, but he did, more than once, make that pledge in the presence of the Conference.

Mr. Collins. I attended to this case with great particularity, and had something to do with it. If Brother Harding ever made such a pledge, it did not reach my ears. And when he said that, with the consent of his wife and the slaves, he would send them to Liberia, I asked him if that consent could be obtained, and he answered in the negative.

Mr. Gere. Brother Collins is correct in saying that consent could not be obtained; but I clearly recollect the point spoken to. He would have preferred sending them to Liberia; but when the Conference desired it, he said he would permit them to go to any free State.

Mr. Slicer. I have no recollection of his agreeing to their going to a free State; but I do distinctly recollect that he put the issue of their freedom on their consent to go to Liberia.

Mr. Collins. On the basis of two *ifs*. *If* his wife and *if* his slaves consented, neither of which could he promise for.

Mr. Davis. What is stated by Brother Slicer is correct. He did say, that if these colored persons were willing to go to Liberia, and if his wife would consent, he should be willing that they should go.

Dr. Smith. Brother Gere, do you recollect distinctly whether Brother Harding said as you have stated?

Mr. Gere. I think those were the words, to the best of my recollection.

Mr. Drake said he thought oral testimony ought not to be taken.

Bishop Soule. I have admitted it at Brother Smith's instance.

Dr. Smith. What redress would there be without this? The laws require that the Annual Conference shall keep a record of every question and answer, both great and small. Has that been done?

Mr. Collins. This small matter may be disposed of at once. Brother Harding admitted the fact. We wanted no testimony, and we took none. Brother Harding was testimony against himself.

Bishop Soule. I take it for granted that you have no other proper testimony but what is presented to you in those journals; that there was not a witness called—no testimony given. You have heard the whole of the matter so far as it is on the records, and it is, I presume, to supply this defectiveness that he calls for those points from the delegates.

A member made some observation, and Bishop Soule answered that Dr. Smith would call for any witness he might want.

Dr. Smith. I do not know, sir, that I would care to meet every member of this Conference on the subject. I know that it is not admissible, but still I have, myself, no particular objection to it. I feel obliged by the reference made to Discipline. What is the meaning of Discipline? That your journal should contain every thing—

Mr. Collins. It does.

Dr. Smith (emphatically). Stick a peg there. A resolution is passed at the Baltimore Conference, requiring the appellant to submit to certain conditions. He refuses. Does the journal state under what circumstances? And do not the merits of the case rest on the circumstances? Why, sir, the course pursued shows that the matter rests just there. One says, if Mr. Harding had refused with such a declaration, there would have been no dispute about it. In the judgment of all who had taken any interest in the merits of this case, it turned on the manner and circumstances of his refusal. Then why not record it? It proves a defectiveness in the journal. Upon that journal we rely for the prosecution, and they upon it for the defense. But behold you, sir, on the very point at issue it is silent! Who shall suffer the wrong here? The appellant or the Baltimore Conference? Who are in the wrong that the journal is thus defective? I leave it to this Conference to decide, every man in his own mind. I am, sir, entitled to the oral testimony in the absence of the correct record which it was the duty of that Annual Conference to furnish us with. And that testimony goes to sustain us. What is the testimony? "I clearly remember," says Brother Gere, "as clearly as if I had heard it this morning, that Brother Harding said, over and over again, that with the consent of the servants, he stood pledged, and pledged his wife, to send them to Liberia; or, with their consent, to let them go to any free State in the Union."

Mr. Collins. If you understood his wife to be pledged, you are certainly mistaken.

Mr. Gere, on being appealed to, said that, as distinctly as he could remember, the words were, "I pledge on my own behalf, and that of my wife, that, if they consent, they shall go to a free State."

Mr. Hildt. I think Brother Gere must be mistaken. Conference was deeply interested in this subject, and I think every member would pay attention; and I do not recollect that Mr. Harding at any time said that he was willing, with the consent of his wife, that the slaves should go to a free State.

Dr. Smith. Well, if there were twenty present who did not hear it, that is no proof that it did not take place. Brother Collins was involved in the matter, and the other brethren had their feelings warmly enlisted, and it is no wonder that they did not hear all that Brother Harding said on this subject. I think you will find that they were so enlisted to carry out their own purposes—honest as they felt they were—that they urged the brother to comply with their condition, intending to investigate the propriety of it hereafter. You cannot suppose they would take a course of this kind unless their feelings were excited, and so excited that they did not hear what is in the clear and distinct remembrance of the brother himself, and of many more, if we had them all here. Others not recollecting it, is no proof that it did not take place. But I have positive proof that he did make this declaration. Its not appearing on the record is not our fault, but the fault of the Conference, and we are entitled to the positive testimony. I shall, therefore, assume that Brother Harding said, that, with the consent of these servants, they should be sent to any State where they could enjoy their freedom. The Conference, however, we learn, adopted the report of the committee, notwithstanding the pledges given by Mr. Harding —a report binding him to make the required pledge of manumission. Near the close of the Conference his case was called up, and he again required to comply with the decision of the Conference. He again refused. At this stage of the proceedings Brother Steele moved a resolution to locate him. This was ruled out. (No, from Mr. Collins.)

Mr. Harding. There was a resolution proposed by Brother Steele to have me located, and it was ruled out by the President.

Dr. Smith. And ruled out by the President?

Mr. Collins. I think it was withdrawn.

Mr. Harding. Brother Steele made the motion, and Bishop Waugh ruled it out.

Mr. Sargent. I was not the Secretary of the Baltimore Conference at the last session, but I had a seat adjoining Brother Steele when he made the motion to locate him. He did withdraw the motion, and at my suggestion.

Dr. Bangs. It must be very unpleasant to the speaker to be interrupted, but I wish to speak to a point of order in reference to oral testimony. Must not the speaker confine himself to the record? If the journal is not complete, the case can be quashed or nonsuited, and sent back. It is competent for him to make that appeal, but I insist that it is not in order to travel out of the record.

Dr. Smith. I could not show that the record is incomplete without reference to oral testimony.

Mr. Early. What brother cannot see that he is opening and amplifying his case? Will not the Baltimore Conference have the right to do the same in reply? Are you constantly to stop him, and confine him to the record? Permit them both to amplify, and let them correct him at the proper time.

Bishop Soule. I should not have permitted one of these queries to be put only at the instance of the speaker, who requested at the outset, that, if he erred, the delegation would set him right on the spot, to save time and labor in the premises.

Dr. Smith. Well, sir, by the testimony of the brethren, a resolution was moved to locate, which, by suggestion, was withdrawn. I wish the Conference not to forget that; it may appear that this point has a great deal to do with the final issue. Brother Collins then moved the suspension of the appellant, and Brother Slicer moved for a committee farther to investigate the case. The committee was appointed. They met, and appellant appeared before that committee, and submited the following paper from William D. Merrick, of Maryland, United States Senator from the first Congressional

District, touching the legal points involved in the case:

"At the request of Mr. Harding, I have to state that, under the laws of Maryland, no slave can be emancipated to remain in that State, nor unless provision be made by the person emancipating him for his removal from the State, which removal must take place, unless for good and sufficient reason the competent authorities grant permission to the manumitted slave to remain.

"There has lately (winter of 1843) been a statute enacted by the State Legislature, securing to married females the property (slaves of course included) which was theirs at the time of their marriage, and protecting it from the power and liabilities of their husbands.

(Signed) "Wm. D. Merrick."

This was read before the committee, but they were so occupied in "laboring" with the brother, to bring him to terms of submission, that it seems they entirely overlooked the opinion of this gentleman, and laying aside the legal view which illustrated the whole case, proceeded to make up their report, saying that they had failed to reduce the brother to terms, though the record shows that they were appointed to *investigate* the case. Yet they report about bringing him to terms. The Conference, then, on motion of Brothers Collins and Emory, resolved to suspend the appellant from his ministerial standing until the next session of Conference, or such time as he should give satisfaction to the Episcopacy that he had secured the manumission of the slaves. From this decision, sir, Brother Harding gave notice of his intention to appeal, and is now before the General Conference in prosecution of his design. I have thus gone through the statement of the case as I find it in the journals, and from oral testimony, because of the defectiveness of the journal itself.

The ground on which I rest this appeal is briefly this:

First. The appellant violated no rule of Discipline in refusing to comply with the condition of the Baltimore Conference. Secondly. But on the contrary, the rule of the Church makes provision in his favor. Thirdly. And, therefore, his suspension is unauthorized, and should be reversed.

If it be the pleasure of the Conference for me to proceed in the investigation of this subject, I propose to do so; but if they think it would be more in order for the defense to respond, I am ready and willing to give place that they may do so. I do not wish to forestall, and ask no right more than to state the case, and the grounds of our appeal.

Mr. Morgan said, in reference to Mr. Gere's statement, that there had been two cases before the Baltimore Conference involving the question of slavery—those of Mr. Harding and Mr. Hansberger. Mr. Harding did consent to send his slaves to Liberia, if their consent and that of his wife could be obtained; but the other was willing to emancipate his, provided certain arrangements could be made.

Dr. Smith. The ground we take is, that the appellant violated no rule of Discipline; on the contrary, the rules of the Church make provision in his favor, and, therefore, his suspension by the Baltimore Conference is unauthorized, and should be reversed. Because, under the law of Maryland, in which State he married, he did not come, by his marriage, to be the owner of the property which fell to his wife. As, therefore, he was not the owner of a single slave, he could not manumit one. The Conference required an impossibility. In proof thereof I will read an opinion of Judge Key. I suppose that this Conference would have no hesitation about receiving the opinion of that gentleman. He says:

"The Reverend Mr. Harding having married Miss Swan, who, at the time of her marriage, was entitled to some slaves, I am requested to say, whether he can legally manumit them or not? By an act of Assembly, no person can manumit a slave in Maryland; and by another act of our Assembly, a husband has no other or farther right to his wife's slaves than their labor, while he lives. He can neither sell nor liberate them. Neither can he and his wife, either jointly or separately, manumit her slaves, by deed, or otherwise. A reference to the Acts of Assembly of Maryland will show this. EDMUND KEY.

"Prince George county, April 25, 1844."

I would also refer to the Laws of the State of Maryland, Chap. 293:

"Section 1. *Be it enacted by the General Assembly of Maryland,* That from and after the passage of this act, any married woman may become seized or possessed of any property, real or of slaves, by direct bequest, demise, gift, purchase, or distribution, in her own name, and as of her own property; *provided,* the same does not come from her husband after coverture."

Now, sir, by this late act of Maryland, a woman can become an owner of property in her own name, though married.

"Sec. 2. *And be it enacted,* That hereafter, when any woman possessed of a property in slaves shall marry, her property in such slaves, and their natural increase, shall continue to her, notwithstanding her coverture, and she shall have, hold, and possess the same as her separate property, exempt from any liability for the debts or contracts of the husband."

Now, from this section, we perceive that the

property of a woman does not pass to the husband, as by the original law, and as is probably the case in other States of the Union.

"Sec. 3. *And be it enacted,* That when any woman during coverture shall become entitled to, or possessed of slaves, by conveyance, gift, inheritance, distribution, or otherwise, such slaves, together with their natural increase, shall inure and belong to the wife in like manner as is above provided as to slaves which she may possess at the time of marriage.

"Sec. 4. *And be it enacted,* That the control and management of all such slaves, the direction of their labor, and the receipts of the productions thereof, shall remain to the husband agreeably to the laws heretofore in force. All suits to recover the property or possession of such slaves shall be prosecuted or defended, as the case may be, in the joint names of the husband and wife; in case of the death of the wife, such slaves shall descend and go to her children and their descendants, subject to the use of the husband during life, without liability to his creditors; and if she die without leaving children living, or descendants of such children living, they shall descend and go to the husband."

From these we learn that, were a husband, marrying a woman with slaves, to manumit those slaves, any person who might inherit property from his wife might make him pay for every one so manumitted, because of the injury done to them by such an act of manumission.

"Sec. 5. *Be it enacted,* That the slaves owned by a *feme-covert* under the provisions of this act, may be sold by the joint deed of the husband and wife, executed, proved, and recorded agreeably to the laws now in force in regard to the conveyance of real estate of *feme-coverts,* and not otherwise.

"Sec. 6. *And be it enacted,* That a wife shall have a right to make a will and give all her property or any part thereof to her husband, and to other persons with the consent of the husband subscribed to said will; *provided always,* that the wife shall have been privately examined by the witnesses to her will, apart and out of the presence and hearing of her husband, whether she doth make the same will freely and voluntarily, and without being induced thereto by fear or threats of or ill usage by said husband, and says she does it willingly and freely; *provided,* that no will under this act shall be valid unless made at least sixty days before the death of the testatrix."

It is perfectly manifest that the opinion of Judge Key is correct, and that the appellant in this case did not possess the right of property in any one of these five slaves that his wife held by the demise of her parents. The Baltimore Conference said, "Manumit your slaves," thus requiring that appellant to dispose of property that did not belong to him; to set at liberty those in whom he had no right, and over whom he had no control whatever. Why, they might with equal propriety tell him to unhorse the first Methodist minister he found on the highway, and turn the horse loose beyond the power of his proper owner, or to manumit the slaves of every man in the State as a condition of holding his membership in their body. Mr. Harding had as much right to the horse, bridle, and saddle-bags of his brethren as to the slaves in question, and just as much right to every slave in the State as to these, and could with as much propriety execute a deed of manumission on their behalf. I say, then, that without doubt the Baltimore Conference required of him to do that which it was impossible for him to do. I am at a loss to know how that Conference could commit such an error. It really is so marvelous that I am utterly at a loss to account for it.

Secondly. If the doctrine I have just laid down could in any sense be held as doubtful, though I cannot see how it can possibly be so held, and it should therefore be said that he had property in the slaves of his wife, then the rule of Discipline, Sec. 10, pages 209, 210, makes provision in his favor.

"We declare that we are as much as ever convinced of the great evil of slavery: therefore no slaveholder shall be eligible to any official station in our Church hereafter, where the laws of the State in which he lives will admit of emancipation, and permit the liberated slave to enjoy freedom."

Now we maintain that, under this provisional exception to the general rule of our Church, he was not required to manumit these slaves, because he could not legally effect that manumission, even if they belonged to him, in that State. Such also is expressly the meaning of the second answer:

"When any traveling preacher becomes an owner of a slave or slaves, by any means, he shall forfeit his ministerial character in our Church, unless he execute, if it be practicable, a legal emancipation of such slaves, conformably to the laws of the State in which he lives."

This is a different phraseology expressing the same idea, and has been so decided by the General Conference. A legal emancipation! What is the common-sense meaning of this? Such an emancipation as will put the slave in possession of his freedom in that State. Now could the appellant give them such liberty? I hold in my hand an extract from the Laws of Maryland on this subject, from "Dorsey's Laws of Maryland," in 1831.

"*And be it enacted,* That it shall hereafter be the duty of every clerk of a county in this State, whenever a deed of manumission shall be left in his office for record, and of every register of wills in every county of this State, whenever a will manumitting a slave or slaves shall be admitted to probate, to send, within five days thereafter, (under a penalty of ten dollars for each and every omission so to do, to be recovered before any justice of the peace, one-half whereof shall go to the informer, and the other half to the State,) an extract from such deed or will, stating the names, number, and ages of the slave or slaves so manumitted, a list whereof, in the case of the will so proved, shall be filed therewith by the executor or administrator, to the Board of Managers for Maryland for removing the people of color of said State; and it shall be the duty of said Board, on receiving the same, to notify the American Colonization Society, or the Maryland State Colonization Society, thereof, and to propose to such Society that they shall engage, at the expense of said Society, to remove said slave or slaves so manumitted to Liberia; and if the said Society shall so engage, then it shall be the duty of the said Board of Managers to have the said slave or slaves delivered to the agent of such Society, at such place as the said Society shall appoint for receiving such slave or slaves, for the purpose of such removal, at such time as the said Society shall appoint; and in case the said Society shall refuse so to receive and remove the person or persons so manumitted and offered, or in case the said person or persons shall refuse so to be removed, then it shall be the duty of the said Board of Managers to remove the said person or persons to such other place or places beyond the limits of this State as the said Board shall approve of, and the said person or persons shall be willing to go to, and provide for their reception and support such place or places as the Board may think necessary, until they shall be able to provide for themselves, out of any money that may be earned by their hire, or may be otherwise provided for that purpose; and in case the said person or persons shall refuse to be removed to any place, beyond the limits of this State, and shall persist in remaining therein, then it shall be the duty of said Board to inform the sheriff of the county wherein such person or persons may be, of such refusal, and it shall thereupon be the duty of said sheriff forthwith to arrest, or cause to be arrested, the said person or persons so refusing to emigrate from this State, and transport the said person or persons beyond the limits of this State; and all slaves shall be capable of receiving manumission for the purpose of removal as aforesaid, with their consent, of whatever age, any law to the contrary notwithstanding." (Chap. 281, Sec. 3.)

We find a supplement to this law in 1832.

"Chap. 145, Sec. 1.—*Be it enacted by the General Assembly of Maryland,* That whenever the Board of Managers, appointed under the act to which this is a supplement, shall inform the sheriff of any county of the refusal to remove any person or persons therein mentioned, and shall provide a sum sufficient to defray the removal of said person or persons beyond the limits of the State, every sheriff then failing to comply, within the term of one month, with the duties prescribed in the third section of the act aforesaid, shall forfeit fifty dollars for every person he shall neglect so to remove, to be recoverable in the County Court of his county by action of debt on indictment.

"Sec. 2. *And be it enacted,* That nothing herein contained shall be construed to repeal any part of the act to which this is a supplement."

The foregoing is a copy, corrected by myself, from the acts referred to, as published in "Dorsey's Laws of Maryland." George H. Moore,
Ass't Librarian N. Y. Hist. Society.

May 6, 1844.

Now from these laws it is perfectly manifest that if there be a State to which the provisional exception of the Discipline applies, it is the State of Maryland. The laws of Virginia are not by any means so strict. The brethren from Virginia will agree with me, that they are by no means so strict. And no one can read these laws without concluding that it is very difficult to manumit slaves there, so that they can enjoy their liberty there; that it is indeed impossible, so far as the laws of the State are concerned. And if they *are* free *there,* it is because the laws of the State are not executed. It will be remembered, that it was in conformity with the law of the State that this brother stated his readiness to make a pledge; and the issue is that he would not pledge himself to do that which the laws forbade him to do, while he was willing to do what the laws of the State allowed, provided the slaves had belonged to him. This, then, is the issue between the appellant and the Baltimore Conference. He stated that he was ready to do that which the law provided for under the circumstances. The question will be, in the mind of every candid hearer, shall the vote of this General Conference side with the Baltimore Conference in demanding from this brother that he *should submit to their conditions without authority from the rules of the Church,* in the face of the very laws of that State that gave him birth, and afforded him protection in his rights and privileges? Or, shall their decision be in favor of the appellant, who stated that he was ready, and did pledge himself to fulfill the only condition in his power, by sending the slaves to Liberia, or to remove them beyond the limits of the State?

The third point in the general argument is, this

construction of the Discipline has already received the sanction of the General Conference. I allude to the case of the Westmoreland local preachers four years ago. The Conference will bear in mind that certain members of our Church in the State of Virginia appealed over and over again to the Baltimore Conference, as licensed local preachers, for ordination. The Baltimore Conference as often responded, "We will not ordain you, because you hold slaves." The applicants said, as citizens of Virginia, they were not bound to give up their slaves, because the laws of their State would not allow them to enjoy freedom; therefore they could not actually give them freedom, and that this clause of Discipline made provision for their case. The Baltimore Conference maintained a different doctrine, as you very well know. The discussion was painfully protracted. It involved a great deal of feeling within the bounds of the Baltimore Conference. The complainants first went to the General Conference at Cincinnati in 1836, and asked to be united to the Virginia Conference, but the Baltimore friends opposed. They were clever fellows, and could not be spared, though, according to the doctrines held by the Baltimore Conference, they were practically sinners. But now they were very clever fellows! I know, sir, that an unworthy motive could not enter the bosom of the members of the Baltimore Conference on a subject of the kind; but because of the unfortunate and unfriendly aspect of the case, it was believed in Virginia, much to the discredit of the Baltimore Conference, that it was because of the loaves and fishes. Well, sir, failing in their application to the Cincinnati Conference of 1836, they came up to the General Conference at Baltimore in 1840, and asked them to vindicate their rights by settling this issue. The General Conference referred the memorial to an able committee, of which Dr. Bascom was chairman—a committee fully competent to respond to the memorial. Their report was submitted to the General Conference, and adopted by them. The whole of it has been published. It contains an able and conclusive argument vindicating the construction put upon the clause of the Discipline by the memorialists, and concludes with the following resolution:

"*Resolved*, by the delegates of the several Annual Conferences, in General Conference assembled, That under the provisional exception of the general rule of the Church on the subject of slavery, the simple holding of slaves, or mere ownership of slave property, in States or Territories where the laws do not admit of emancipation, and permit the liberated slave to enjoy freedom, constitutes no legal barrier to the election or ordination of ministers to the various grades of office known in the ministry of the Methodist Episcopal Church, and cannot, therefore, be considered as operating any forfeiture of right in view of such election or ordination."

This, sir, was adopted by the General Conference. And if language can settle any point on earth, the language of this resolution goes to settle the construction we have put on this rule of Discipline, viz., that the brethren holding slaves in those States that do not permit the liberated slave to enjoy freedom, are not, under the Discipline of our Church, required to emancipate their slaves.

Now, sir, I beg to call the attention of the Conference to this point. This action of the General Conference was intended finally to settle the long-contested issue between the Baltimore Conference and certain members of the Church, and does it not settle it fairly and unequivocally? I appeal to this Conference, if it were to be looked for that an Annual Conference, cherishing due respect for the decisions of the General Conference, should proceed within four years after the passage of this very resolution to trample it under their feet, and act on another construction of the rule of Discipline, defining the terms of membership, and thus throw overboard one of their own body? Was this to be expected? So far as I feel myself entitled to any judgment in this matter, I say it was not! The act was wrong, and we had a right, under the circumstances, to expect that the Baltimore Conference would not thus have disregarded the decision of the General Conference. I take it upon me to say, that the decision referred to settled that point; and the appellant was not required under the laws of the State of Maryland, and under that decision upon our laws of Discipline, to manumit these slaves, because the act would not secure their freedom. I need not stop to notice, that, though that law was passed, and that report and resolution adopted for the government of the Baltimore Conference, they have never ordained these men.

Mr. Collins. That's the fact. It was no law; it was only a resolution.

Dr. Smith. We maintain, therefore, that the refusal to comply with the demand of the Baltimore Conference was no violation of the rules of Discipline; and also, that, as a conscientious and humane man, Mr. Harding could do no more than he proposed to do. It is admitted by all the delegation that he was ready to send every one of these slaves, with their consent, to Liberia. What more could he do, as a humane man? Should he send them there without their consent? Should he separate parents and children, and their friends, without their consent, and compel them to find refuge in the bosom of Africa? Should he have done so? He was willing so to do, *with* their consent, and I ask what more could humanity ask or Christianity require? Let me at this point briefly examine the requisitions made upon him. They wanted him to hold two of the slaves in perpetual bondage. Did you mark that? Yes! the decision of that Conference required him to hold two of the slaves in perpetual bondage—one till he was twenty-eight, and two till they were twenty-three! Now, sir, I beg leave to ask what Eastern man, consistently with his principles, can vote to sustain the Baltimore Conference in this instance? Stick to your principles, abide by them, and you cannot sustain them in their action! On the other hand, Harding, on the principle of the most ultra Eastern member here, pledges himself to let them go to Africa or any free State. What more could he do? What more would the laws permit him to do? And what Eastern man will fail to sustain him in this? He intended this, and does now intend it, so far as he has a right to control his movements on the subject.

My third general ground is, that the spirit of our Discipline does not, any more than the letter of it, justify the Baltimore Conference in their suspension of this brother. The spirit of the Discipline is a vague term, but I may explain. I mean, then, that the general design and tendency of the rules of our Discipline on the subject of slavery do not justify that Conference in their course. I hold that the rules of our Discipline on this subject are exclusively conservative. The whole Discipline is conservative, and I claim to be a conservative myself. I stand by Methodist Discipline; and if any man claims to be conservative, and will not stand on the same broad platform, I deny that he is one, and will contest it every inch. I repeat, our Discipline is conservative. Hear it: "What shall be done for the extirpation of the evil of slavery? Ans. 1. We declare that we are as much as ever convinced of the great evil of slavery." I believe it—with all my heart I subscribe to it. And I can repeat that language with a feeling that none, except those from the South, like circumstanced, can possibly do. I say it is an evil, because I feel it to be an evil. And who cannot say the same that has trod the soil of the South? It is an evil. The Discipline declares the truth, the whole truth, and, so far as it relates to the case, nothing but the truth; and a truth which, from our connection with the subject, we are not ashamed to own, nor afraid to proclaim on the house-tops, here or elsewhere. Is not this enough? What more can the brethren ask? What more would they ask from the South as a sacrifice on the altar of union than this broad, unqualified declaration? This, sir, is unquestionably conservatism. But, sir, it is not such conservatism as is represented by the cabs of your city, always, when the horse is taken out, letting down on one side. No, sir, that is not the principle of conservatism, for conservatism always involves principles appropriate to two sides. On the other hand, I should say that while the Discipline deprecates the evil of slavery, it requires the members of the Church within those States to conform their action to the rules or laws of those States in which they live. This is assuming the doctrine that though slavery is an evil, and a great evil, it is not necessarily a sin. There's the other side of the question. And is it not clearly so? Now, we of the South take both sides of the question—it is a great evil, *it is not necessarily a sin;* and we ask no more of you. But we maintain that it is not a sin, and we demand this concession on your part. They are conservatives who take both sides, and not those who are one-sided in their doctrine, practice, and votes.

To recur to the principles or position we have just laid down: we say that slavery is an evil, and that Southern people know and feel it to be an evil. Who knows how much the shoe pinches but he who wears it? And who more than we who have been compelled to submit to it, from our cradle to the present moment; and on whom the wrong has been inflicted by these very brethren of the North—the North, who refuse to help us in this our calamity? Who know it so well to be an evil as they who, but a few years ago, were ready to take legislative action on the subject? In 1831, so rife was the popular feeling and the popular sentiment on this subject, that there is not a doubt—so sorely did we in Virginia feel the evil—that long before this day some act of gradual manumission would have passed but for that which, after all, may prove to have been the *happy* interference of Northern abolitionists. I know this is strange ground for you to hear me take, but which I think I shall make as clear as the light of heaven to the mind of every candid hearer in this Conference. We felt the evils and groaned under them so deeply, and so heartily did we long to get rid of them, that from the debates in 1831, in the Virginia Legislature, and the popular sentiment expressed in the pulpit and through the press, no doubts were entertained that the State was about to adopt immediate measures for its gradual extirpation. Eighteen thousand dollars per annum were appropriated to advance the colonization interest only as an intimation that any reasonable claim for colonization upon the treasury of Virginia should be honored. Why was it not carried out? Why, just at this juncture, when the bow of promise was beginning to span the heavens, and the long-prayed-for hour was about to come upon us in all its glory, behold this dark cloud rises in the North and East, and though but the size of a man's hand in the beginning, it increased and passed over the whole North! It flung the dark shadows of its coming events over the moral hemisphere of the South, and mantled all in sackcloth and mourning! The tide of colonization was arrested—it rolled back, and the friends of the cause were left to mourn over their disappointments. And yet, in the face of all this, results have shown that while God never can direct any thing that is wrong, yet his hand was in this matter, in permitting the error, or the wickedness—I will not say which—to bring about a good result. At that very time your agents in Liberia, resident colored men, wrote back: "Stay your hand. If you are not more select in the choice of those you send here, we shall be reduced to a heathen state. Send us colonists, but send us select men. Do n't send us corn-field hands—they are not fit for freedom."

This, sir, was a wise and a sage remark; not the result of profound philosophical investigation, it is true, but the spontaneous promptings of practical observation. And what is the principle on which it operates? Why, that in forming a colony, you can pour into it a heterogeneous mass, only so far as it can be received into the body politic, and impart strength and vigor to the body. But if, instead of imparting strength, they give their own character to the body, the consequences will be certain ruin and destruction. I will give you an illustration. I hesitate not to say, and many will sustain me in declaring, that if the amount of vice and ignorance from Catholic Europe, and particularly Ireland, now poured like a flood into the bosom of this vast republic, had swept into the infant colonies of Jamestown or Plymouth Rock, never would you have seen this fair republic spring up, striking its roots deep in the soil, and spreading its branches from Maine to Mississippi, and from the Atlantic almost to the Pacific Ocean. But now, since this country has grown up to maturity, and taken the elevation and power of a great State, we can take in these vast crowds, and yet our political and moral character remains unharmed. The firm bases of our civil institutions are unmoved; the deep foundations of social and civil life have not been reached; and we are privileged to cherish the hope that time, in its rapid roll, will but strengthen and perpetuate our civil and religious liberty, while we continue to be an asylum for the ignorance, vice, infidelity, and what is worse than all combined, the Popery of Europe. Now, had *Liberia* been so colonized, it would have been ruined. Such a mass as Virginia was rapidly pouring into it would have reduced it to its original heathen condition. What prevented such a result? The abolition excitement, and nothing else. Thanks to them, then, that we have a colony

3

on the coast of Africa to spread itself out, and yet become an asylum for every freed slave if he pleases to go there; and I pray God that he may speed the happy day. I am aware that our abolition brethren never intended this, and therefore they may be compared to an enemy who plunges a dagger into your side, but which only opens some dangerous abscess. And you are mistaken if you think I have any animosity against abolition brethren. I believe God will use them as instruments, bad or good as they may be.

Now, sir, I have enlarged for a purpose which cannot fail to have been perceived. I ask, again, who are the conservatives? Those who maintain one side of the Discipline, that slavery is a great evil, but will not concede the principle that it is not necessarily a sin? or, are they the conservatives who take both sides of the book? Such is a conservative, and all who symbolize with him. I have heard a different doctrine from a very unexpected quarter. The case has been put with the abolitionists proper standing at one extreme, the Southern portion of the Church standing at the other extreme, distinguished by holding this doctrine, that slavery is a great political and social blessing. Sir, did you ever hear that doctrine advocated by a Southern minister of the Methodist Church in your life? I declare to you I never heard such a doctrine before. Forty-one years have passed over my head, twenty of which have been devoted to the service of the Methodist Episcopal Church, as a Southern minister, preaching to the master and the slave; and never in my life did I hear that doctrine until I heard it imputed to Southern brethren on the floor of this Conference, from a man, too, who claimed to be a conservative—a middle man, standing between the two extremes, like a mediator, putting his hands on both, and bidding them be reconciled. If I understand it rightly, the Discipline is conservative, because it occupies the middle ground between the two; and so stand the Southern men. The difference between us and either extreme, is just the difference between plain right and plain wrong. There is a clear, bold, vigorous line of demarkation. The partition wall betwixt right and wrong is as high as heaven, and it must be scaled before an entrance can be made from the right to the wrong. If you belong to us, take the ground of the Discipline and law. You make an imaginary extremity, and then assume to yourselves to be middle men. Now on this broad platform the Southern Church stands: Slavery is a great evil, but beyond our control; yet not necessarily a sin. We must then quietly submit to a necessity which we cannot control or remedy, endeavoring to carry the gospel of salvation to both masters and slaves.

Ultra antislavery men deny the great principles assumed, and maintain the doctrine that slavery is necessarily a sin under all circumstances. And now for the application of the whole subject to the case in hand. I regret to declare that it is my honest conviction, that all the action of the Baltimore Conference in this case symbolizes with the principles of ultra abolitionism. The Discipline of the Church, I have shown, clearly recognizes this brother in the relation in which he stands to slavery. The Laws of Maryland do not make him the possessor of slaves. And yet the action of the Baltimore Conference requires him to manumit them—the slaves that he never owned. A legal opinion was given in and confirmed, and yet they persisted in their demand! How could they do that on the principle of the conservative character of our Discipline? They could not, yet they did it, clearly on the doctrine that slavery is a sin under all circumstances.

The first argument brought by the advocates of this position is, that slavery is wrong in the abstract. What is slavery? Why, in its very nature it is a concrete act. What is it when taken abstractly? Why, it is the act taken away from all its circumstances. Take away from slavery all its circumstances, and how will any man predicate right or wrong of such a thing? It is neither right nor is it wrong, abstracted from its circumstances. But perhaps, in common parlance, slavery in the abstract is the simple overt act of slavery, which is inseparable from circumstances. Yet we will take it so, though it is a sort of hair-splitting business. It is then the government of man by physical force. Is it any thing more? Can it possibly be any thing less? And will you undertake to say that the government of man by physical force is wrong? Government by physical force! Why, the inhabitants of Sing Sing Prison are detained there by physical force, and without their consent. And will you undertake to say that such control of man by physical force is wrong? I imagine, sir, that no one will say that. What is true of an abstraction in this sense? Why, that it is right or wrong, according to its circumstances, as with murder. Murder itself is wrong. Murder in the abstract is neither right nor wrong. Taking life is right or wrong, according to its circumstances. And if the abstract or overt act of taking life be done according to the established laws of the country, or in self-defense, it is taking life on a correct principle. If done contrary to law or with malice aforethought, it is murder, and therefore wrong. And so with slavery. It is right or wrong, to be justified or condemned, according to its circumstances.

A second argument on the abstract question is, that what is wrong in the beginning can never become right by continuance. Applied to slavery, it is this. It was wrong to bring these slaves from Africa, and it can never be right to detain them here. This is false in principle and in practice; for if there be no prescription in politics by which things once wrong become right, then all the claims and possessions of the present generation are wrong, and to this day founded in injustice and oppression. And wherefore? Because there is scarcely a government now on the earth that has not had its origin in robbery, oppression, and wrong, more or less; and if these can never change, why the possessions of man all over the world remain held in crime to this day! Take, for example, the Norman conquest of England—as lawless a sweep of robbery as any that ever darkened the pages of history—and if this doctrine be correct, there is not a legal claim in existence in England to one foot of her soil. Take, sir, the conquest of your own country—save my own native State, and I am proud to make an exception in her favor—the Indian is the original owner of the soil from which he was driven; of the soil that gave him birth; and at this very day, the land where sleep his fathers, back to unknown generations, this land is *his,* not yours; and if the principle laid down is just, give him back the rights he once enjoyed, and the land that was his dear and social home.

But, we say, that it is indispensable to the well-being of human society, that there be principles of prescriptive right acknowledged and acted upon, and that the original wrong should ultimately become right, when the redress of that wrong would inflict a greater evil than the original wrong. So slavery may have had its origin in wrong, cruelty, oppression, and robbery; yet if the redress of that wrong would be a greater evil than the wrong itself, then it is to be assumed as right. And it remains with the opposition to show that the wrongs can be redressed without interfering more prejudicially with the institutions of society. Does any one doubt that the patriarch Abraham was a slave-holder, or that slavery existed among the Jews, and that, too, under the Divine sanction, and by Divine appointment? Of that we are assured on the authority of God's word. But, then, we are sure that the Divine Being could neither appoint nor sanction any thing that was in itself independently and absolutely wrong. It must, therefore, have been right, under the peculiar circumstances of Abraham and of the Jewish nation. And what was right in one instance may be right in another. What were the circumstances under which slavery was in these cases we know not—no man knows—but we are bound to allow the fact.

What was true on the subject of slavery in the days of the apostles? In Greece, at that time, there were about ninety slaves to every four hundred freemen; that is, about one-fifth of the whole population were slayes; and Rome was at that time the greatest slave-market in the world, where millions were bought and sold under the reign of the Cesars. Now the system of slavery in those days was the most unhallowed that is recorded on the pages of history; and they must know little indeed of American slavery who put it on a footing with that of Greece and Rome. Now, if in the days of Christ it passed unreproved, though existing in a bold and palpable form—if there were no warning epistles written to the Churches on the subject at the instance of the apostles, surely it is fair to conclude that it is not "necessarily a sin." They could not but be cognizant of its existence, since St. Paul himself recognizes the relation of master and servant, or slave, on the same principles that he did the civil government. This was an absolute monarchy. The lives of his subjects were at the disposal of the sovereign; St. Paul was in the hands of the civil power, and do n't you suppose that he saw and felt the evils of so despotic a government? And so with slavery. The particular authority of the master over the slave was a great evil, yet Paul acknowledged both the civil government and the system of slavery. He required all Christians to submit to the civil authority, offensive as it was; and he required all masters to treat their slaves as became masters, and slaves to be obedient to their masters. What did he intend by all this? Why, that it was his duty as a minister to preach, and watch, and labor, and thus bring about that state of things in society that would best indicate the necessity for a different form of government, and a different state of society. As a private citizen, he might have fallen out with the government, as a matter concerning his own personal and private feelings; but as a minister of the Church, he felt it his duty to pursue that course which would make a different form of government as practicable as it is at all times desirable. So we of the South see in slavery an evil; but in the circumstances we feel justified in our course, and, indeed, cannot avoid it. And we feel that we should be doing an infinitely greater wrong by altering the condition of the slaves, under present and existing circumstances. Our duty as a Church and as ministers is to labor by preaching to bless both master and servant—go preach among them—get master and servant both converted—and thus bring about a different state of things, and then a different state of society will be practicable as well as desirable; and thus, and thus only, can we occupy the broad, conservative platform of our Discipline.

They affirm of slavery in the South, that its origin was wicked—that the slaves were first acquired at the expense of our brother's blood. Admit it all. Yet the hand of God is above, and it is his to overrule every thing for good. Go with me to the Southern plantation, where our missionaries have been preaching for years. Come with me through the length and breadth of this land! Converse with the slaves on the subject of religion, and you will find thousands "clothed and in their right minds"—happy in the love of God. Their condition is better, a thousand times better, than if they had remained in Africa. They would there have sunk lower and lower, without any knowledge of a Saviour, for there can be little doubt that had not their bondage and slavery awakened the sympathies of mankind in their behalf, there would not have been such mighty efforts to evangelize Africa and other portions of the world. They were in darkness—gross darkness; but who will not say that "the people who sat in darkness have seen a great light," and that the state of the slaves is *now* better than it was before their bondage? I feel a deep interest in this matter. I am emphatically a negro preacher. I watch over them, attend their revivals, lead their classes, and labor among them from year to year; and have a heart as full of sympathy and love for them as any man's.

What is the duty of the Methodist Episcopal Church on the subject of slavery? There is danger of her stepping out of the track of duty, and engaging herself in political relations, and thus becoming a politico-ecclesiastical establishment. The Christian Advocate and Journal has correctly told us that we have no right to make laws. The very day you begin to make laws, you err, and the laymen will then have a right to representation; and have it they must, and have it they shall, if it can possibly be secured to them. Your government can be defended only on the ground that you make no laws. What, then, are you to do? Just tell the people what are the plain laws of God's word. Do that, and the people will not find fault with you; partisans may, but the intelligent of other denominations, and the whole body of your own Church, will not complain of you for that. The ministers are set apart to explain religion, to enforce God's laws, and teach the doctrines of the Bible, and should let all political subjects alone. I have now had the right to vote for more than twenty years, but I have never yet exercised it. It is no part of my business to meddle with politics. I do not, however, consider my omission to vote as an example for imitation. But, in regard to the principle that governs me, I shall never reconcile it to myself to interfere with politics farther than as a private citizen. I have a terrible warfare against this thing. I do n't believe in this doctrine of Methodist ministers' having to do with politics. The genius of our government is against it. I think that we should confine ourselves to our proper ministerial duties.

I suppose we ministers can never interfere with any legislation on political matters. And our laymen can come—[Some remarks were here lost by the reporter.] The genius of our Church government requires that we confine ourselves exclusively to spiritual matters. "My kingdom," says the Saviour, "is not of this world"—it is spiritual. Any interference by this General Conference, directly or indirectly, as an ecclesiastical council, with any political questions or relations whatever, is inappropriate to our duties, and extremely dangerous in its results. We are destined to become a great people. No human causes, that are likely to be brought to bear, can prevent our becoming the most numerous and popular branch of the American Church. God grant that when we come to be this great people, the glory may not have departed from us! But when this state of things shall come, what will be the condition of the country and the Church, if our ministers should not confine themselves, as ministers, exclusively to their appropriate spiritual duties, and leave the political questions and relations of the country to be managed by the laymen of the Church and other citizens? Why, sir, it is perfectly manifest, that if in that day it shall be found that the same men, *whether laymen or preachers*, who are making rules for the government of the Church, are also at the same time members of the different State Legislatures, or of the General Government, they will be making laws for the government of the State. With the reins of civil government in one hand, and the reins of ecclesiastical government in the other, what will be more easy than to unite both reins in one hand? or, in other words, unite Church and State? This, sir, is the unhappy result to be deprecated. It is this that makes any action of this body upon a subject purely political a just cause of suspicion by any discriminating mind. Do not, then, complain of the South, when she admonishes you to let the subject of slavery alone, because more appropriate to the civil legislature. The Scriptures furnish you with no example of ecclesiastical legislation on the subject of slavery, although it existed, in the days of Christ and the apostles, in a far more objectionable form than in the present day. The duty of the Church is plain. If you would bring around that state of things in the South, in which a different social condition will be as practicable as it is at all times confessedly desirable, let the General Conference, let all the ministers in the Church, confine themselves to their appropriate calling—*let them preach the grace of Christ*—and they will accomplish their object.

John A. Collins, an eloquent and gifted member of the Baltimore Conference, replied to Dr. Smith. He said:

I take the management of this case not without diffidence. To appear in defense of one of the oldest Annual Conferences in the Methodist Episcopal Church; one that has always stood by the Discipline of the Church, "in weal and woe;" that has done the utmost in her power to maintain the purity of our institutions entirely untarnished, might be considered a matter of some surprise to any man.

I am fortified, however, in the conviction that the Baltimore Conference, in this matter, as in all others of her official action, is not only pure, but above suspicion; and she has her best defense when her own acts speak in their own proper language. I am aware that the delicacy of the subject has invested it with considerable interest. Slavery and abolitionism have agitated the civil and ecclesiastical tribunals of our land, and for a long time convulsed the country; and, of course, every thing that has reference to slavery, or is connected with it, is a matter of peculiar interest. It is supposed, and I believe it to be the fact, that this appeal will bring up the connection of Methodism and Methodist preachers with slavery more distinctly and clearly than any other question ever brought before this Conference; and I am fully aware that we shall need all the prudence, and caution, and care, and freedom from excitement, that we can possibly bring to the management of this case; and I pray God to grant us wisdom, and prudence, and discretion, that we may fall upon the best means to promote the glory of God and the welfare of his Church.

I certainly was delighted to hear many of the expressions that fell from my friend from Virginia. I must congratulate him upon his conversion, for until yesterday morning I knew not that he, or those that think with him, were to be regarded as conservative—on this question. I am delighted to hear that they are so. I listened with pleasure to the warm and ardent manner in which he admitted the doctrines of the Discipline, in regard to the great evil of slavery. I was particularly delighted at it, as well as with his declaration, that he never had heard in the South that slavery was to be regarded as a social good, and the confirmatory response of the Southern delegations. I was gratified with all that was said, but could not help thinking, for the life of me, of a certain resolution passed at the Georgia Annual Conference, that "slavery is not a moral evil!" Not a moral evil! I should like to know what kind of an evil the prosecutor considers slavery. On the floor of the General Conference of 1836 and 1840, slavery was defended by a member of his own delegation, as in accordance with the word of God. I was pleased at the remarks of Brother Smith yesterday morning. I have seen a pamphlet, written by Mr. Sims, a Methodist preacher,* in which a very different view is presented to that which I was glad to hear advanced by Dr. Smith; and though he says that every man with sense enough to go to mill, would refuse to acknowledge such a sentiment, yet I know one of the most eminent of our clergy who has done so, and who had more than sense enough "to go to mill."

Still I am gratified at the change of sentiment, and at the change of *tone* still more so. There is, nevertheless, a drawback to all this; for my worthy friend, in carrying out some of his abstractions, which are always doubtful in character and dangerous in issue, has involved himself in an apparent contradiction. He believes slavery to be an evil in fact, and a *great* evil; he says that the Southerners are groaning under it, and that it is their affliction and sorrow; and yet contends that circumstances can make that thing good which in its commencement was evil. He deprecates the African slave-trade as abominable, and the means

---

* This is an error: the pamphlet referred to, though often attributed to Prof. E. D. Sims, who is a Methodist preacher, was written by *A.* D. Sims, Esq., a lawyer in Darlington, S. C.

employed to secure slaves as vile and treacherous; but that circumstances have taken away all that was offensive in its character, until slavery, as existing now, is RIGHT. If so, I contend, upon his own showing, it cannot be a great evil.

There is also another drawback. With all his strong expressions with respect to the *great* evil of slavery, before he got through with the "abstraction," he placed human beings on the same ground as the lands of New England and Pennsylvania, as goods and chattels. These things detract from the warm and strong declarations of my friend on this subject. Still I will give him credit for being a conservative as far as he goes.

I shall not follow the prosecutor in all his remarks, for though I listened with much interest to his able and powerful speech—a speech that did credit to his head and heart—there was a great deal that had nothing whatever to do with the question; and if our case had had the small-pox, two-thirds of his remarks would never have caught it. They had no relation to the case at all, and do not operate except to break down the fair issue which we wish to make before this Conference. I shall try to meet the case on its merits, and place the question on its true basis.

The prosecutor first complained of our journal, and strove hard to make the impression—and may have succeeded, to some extent—that there was informality in that journal. There is none whatever, not a particle of it, and he failed so clearly to make it out, that he dropped it suddenly. There was no real trial here, and there is every thing in the journal that ought to be recorded in its pages. Let us look at it fairly. On the calling of the name of Mr. Harding at the Conference in 1844, his Presiding Elder stated that by marriage he had become connected with slavery. Mr. Harding assented to the statement made by the Presiding Elder; whereupon the case was referred to a committee. They reported that the appellant be required to manumit his slaves at specified ages, and give a pledge to the Conference to that effect. He refused to abide by their decision, or to give the pledge required. He was "labored" with, (as our friends, the Quakers, say,) during the whole Conference. Finally, a committee was appointed to induce him to accede to the requisition of his brethren, and they reported that after all he had refused to comply.

Mr. Harding. Was that committee a committee to labor? They were appointed to inquire whether there was any legal difficulty in the case.

Mr. Slicer. The case is as the representative states it.

Mr. Collins. The great matter is this—Mr. Harding refused to abide by the decision of the Conference. He would not move a step on the issue. The question then became, whether the Baltimore Conference was to bow to Harding, or he to the Conference—whether we were to give up the ground always occupied by us on this delicate subject, or whether he should yield to us—whether he should be permitted to beard the Conference, or we should bring him up to the mark, and make the rule bear upon him. When we found that all attempts at reasoning with him were disregarded, and that all the means that brotherly affection could suggest and employ were ineffectual, we suspended him, as the only resource we had in the premises. All this is stated in the journal; clearly, fully, fairly, distinctly stated. What else do you want? What more was necessary? There were no witnesses examined on the occasion, for we wanted none. Brother Harding admitted the fact, which indeed was notorious. He admitted it by his non-denial of it before the committee, and by his response and pleadings in the premises; and all that we had to do was, to bring him to the bar of the Conference to answer for that which he acknowledged when the Presiding Elder made the statement of the fact. There was not a question raised for a moment as to whether he was innocent or guilty of what the Presiding Elder had charged him with. He *pleaded guilty to it.* There were no witnesses, and therefore the journal states all that it could state: the "questions" were never asked, the "answers to them" never received, and therefore no "entry" or record made of them on the journal.

The prosecution next relied upon the testimony of Brother Gere, whose recollections of the case were different from those of any other member of his delegation. If that brother were to state undeniably, positively, and distinctly, that he remembered the pledge in the words he states, then of course the negative testimony could not be sustained; for I am not of the opinion of the Irishman, who complained of being found guilty of the charge of theft, on the testimony of one witness, on the ground that he could bring a hundred persons who could testify that they never had seen him steal. If, therefore, Brother Gere does give positive and distinct testimony to the fact he states, I admit at once its weight and authority, and I now call upon him to answer me a question:

"Are your impressions distinct and positive that Harding said that he and his wife would consent that these persons should go to a free State?"

Dr. Smith. That is not the subject; but that Brother Harding pledged himself, for his wife and for himself, that he would send them to Africa if they wished, or that they might go to a free State.

Mr. Collins. Very well, I put it in that form.

Mr. Gere. I will state, as nearly as I can, what I said yesterday morning. I did not say that my recollection was *distinct*, but that the *impression* on my mind was as distinct and clear as if it had been told me yesterday morning. But I said that I might be mistaken, and I was aroused to this from what Brother Griffith said, otherwise I had no idea that any one would have doubted it. Brother Morgan referred to the case of Brother Hansberger, and said that he had pledged himself as I had said Brother Harding had done. I think that I may have identified them. I have been trying to conform to my brethren, but I still say that the impression remains, though I may have confounded the two cases.

Mr. Collins. I will show you now, in confirmation of Brother Morgan's account, that Brother Gere must be mistaken. If Brother Harding had ever given the pledge which he says he did—pledging himself and his wife—such was the disposition of the Baltimore Conference, that there would have been no such action as that which brings this business here. I know that he never did. But let that pass.

Mr. Harding. I did pledge myself as Brother Gere says.

Mr. Collins. Why, Mr. President, it is all we asked for. How could the case have got here if he had pledged himself to do the very thing we asked him to do? We would have given him the whole year. It is all *I* asked.

Mr. Harding. You never did ask it, sir. It never was asked.

Mr. Collins. Why, sir, we should then have acted very strangely, for that is all we asked in the resolution. Hear it:

"*Resolved*, That Brother Harding be required to execute, and cause to be recorded, a deed securing the manumission of the slaves hereinafter mentioned, etc., etc., and that Brother Harding be required to give to this Conference a pledge that the said manumission shall be effected during the ensuing Conference-year."

I shall proceed now to reply to the material parts of the argument for the prosecution in this matter.

First. That the laws of Maryland do not admit of manumission. Now, sir, this is not according to the fact in the case. The opinion of Judge Key has been read to the effect that slaves cannot be manumitted in Maryland; but the first law they read directly contradicts the opinion. The law of 1831 specifies the course that shall be taken with regard to manumitted slaves. It provides three modes of disposing of them. First, they may go to Africa; or second, to the non-slaveholding States; and thirdly, if they fail to do so, the sheriff is required, not to take them up and sell them again into slavery, but to convey them, against their will if need be, beyond the bounds of the State. The slave once free in Maryland is forever free. The question does not lie on that ground. By the Laws of Virginia, if a manumitted slave remains one year in the State after his manumission, he can be reënslaved; but in Maryland, when once free, he can never be reënslaved. That is the law referred to by the prosecution, and it contradicts Judge Key, and is directly against the ground taken. The law of 1832 simply concurs in this provision of the former law, and increases the fine upon the sheriff, if he refuses or fails to comply with the requisitions of the statute. But all its enactments clearly and distinctly recognize manumission. The law of 1843 is a strange and singular law. Its fundamental feature is against the law of God, for that makes man the head of his wife, and this law takes man from the position assigned to him by the Supreme Being. And I am satisfied that this law will work such evil that, as a matter of necessity, it will have to be repealed. I hope, therefore, that you will not judge us by this law. We cannot answer for the tergiversation of the Laws of Maryland, and cannot conform to all their changes. As they have gone so far as to pass a law deposing man from his rightful place in the domestic economy—a place assigned to him from the beginning of time by positive Divine injunction—they may pass a law requiring him to obey his wife. What may have been the intention of the Legislature in passing this law, I know not. They may have intended, in a sinister way, to nail slavery faster than ever, and to rivet its chains more firmly. They had attempted to pass a law which outraged public sentiment on this subject. It raised the indignation of the people to such a pitch, that they were compelled to retract it, after getting it into the Senate. Foiled in that, they may have intended to do that by stealth which they could not accomplish openly, and, binding the fetters still more strongly, render slavery more permanent, and manumission more difficult. But the eyes of the people of Maryland will be opened to the iniquity and oppression of this law also, and the Legislature will be driven to repeal it. Or the intention may have been benevolent, as the law heretofore provided that if a man married a wife with slaves, they became his property by such marriage, and could be seized by his creditors; hence this is entitled a law to regulate conjugal rights as they regard property. I say it may be benevolent in its design, and be intended to secure to the female protection, if so unfortunate as to be married to one whose extravagance or crime may reduce him to insolvency, and she be turned out to penury and want.

Nothing at all is said in this law about manumission. It repeals no law. There is no repealing clause in it; and it might be safely and well argued whether such a law were worth one cent. It does not destroy the power to manumit. In one of its sections it provides, that if the husband and wife unite, the slaves can be disposed of. Its only operation in this particular is to render manumission more difficult, by requiring the coöperation of the wife. Nor does it increase the difficulty much, if any. No pious and intelligent woman, (such as Mrs. Harding doubtless is,) who has a husband in whose judgment and discretion she confides, will jeopard his standing—especially if he be a Christian minister—for the consideration of a few slaves.

A member called Mr. C. to order, on the ground of making remarks prejudicial to the character of the ladies.

Dr. Smith hoped the speaker would not be interrupted, but allowed to go on without restraint, and say whatever he thought important to his case. Besides, he (Dr. S.) had the right of reply.

Mr. Collins. It is a fair argument. I do not impeach the ladies at all. I deny the allegation that I made any remark that could be construed into any such meaning. I say that the ladies love their husbands so tenderly, and with such affectionate devotion to their interests and happiness, that if the husband wished it, they would yield such a point at once, and not jeopardize his standing for the sake of a few negroes. What I meant

4

was, that the effort had not been made; that if half the pains were taken in order to obtain her consent, if such were necessary, to the manumission of these negroes, that were used in wooing the lady, the application would have been successful. I, therefore, always suspect the man to be a slaveholder at heart who rests his defense on such a plea. When God arrested man in Paradise, and questioned him concerning his transgression, he said, The woman had deceived him. I always thought that a dastardly act on the part of Adam. We are very easily tempted to do what we want to do, and then rest the blame on others; and my sex has kept up the dastardly conduct to the present time. We lay our wrongs and evils upon our wives, when they cannot be heard in self-vindication.

Sir, I would not set up such a defense as this. I would scorn to do it; and I know full well, I am perfectly convinced in my judgment, that if the appellant wanted to manumit these slaves, his wife would not stand in the way one moment. He need not to have brought that plea here. The difficulty is with Mr. Harding himself, who is at heart a slaveholder, and this plea is only put in for effect. In my judgment, if he had desired it, his wife would have consented to their manumission. After all that has been said about the Laws of the State of Maryland making it difficult to manumit slaves, it has been repeatedly done. Mr. Cornelius Howard, one of the most respectable citizens of that State, and brother of Colonel Howard, who led so gallantly the Maryland line at the battle of the Cowpens, and whose name stands out in proud distinction before his country, a citizen who understood law as well as any man, left his slaves free by will, and that deed is on record in the proper county court of Maryland. And how did he do it? Why, because he wanted to do it, and had, therefore, the power. The will is the great matter. The wish is "father to the thought." This man had slaves; he liberated every one of them, and had the deed of manumission recorded. And this during the last year, at the close of 1843; and this law, on which the prosecution lays so much stress as prohibiting such manumission, was passed in February, 1843. Brother Blake, one of the cases before the Annual Conference, against whom action was taken on precisely similar grounds as in this case, came up last Conference and told us he had manumitted his boy, and had the deed recorded in Baltimore County Court; and he did it last year. Now, with these facts on record, how shall it be plead here—how *can* it—that there is no power to manumit? There is such power. The facts that have transpired are an incontestable proof that the thing can be done; so that, as far as the law of Maryland is concerned, there is nothing that renders it impossible. The Baltimore Conference, then, in view of the law, acted rightly toward Mr. Harding. They did right; he could have manumitted these slaves, and they suspended him because he would not.

The second point urged by the prosecution is, that if the doctrine respecting the Laws of Maryland be doubtful, and if it be plead that Harding has the right of property in the slaves, yet the rule of Discipline is in his favor. He could not do it legally. Why not? The prosecution give me no answer to that question. So far as the Discipline of the Church is concerned, on this point we will take our stand. I say Mr. Harding did violate the Discipline. The rule does positively bear upon him, and the Baltimore Conference deserve thanks instead of the sneers that have been directed against them, that they have had the firmness, in the face of a slaveholding community, to enforce the Discipline. If we have not got the rule of Discipline on our side, we have a hard case to make out. But that we have it I will satisfy you. I wish the mind and the intelligence of the Conference to be directed to this point, that the Discipline of the M. E. Church contemplates the relation of its members with slavery in a threefold point of view. First, as it regards private members; secondly, as it respects local preachers;

and thirdly, as it concerns traveling preachers. It is essential to maintain this distinction in coming to an opinion on this case.

First. As to private members. The only rule for this class is found in the General Rules, and only prohibits the buying and selling of men, women, and children, with an intention to enslave them. A man, by this rule, may inherit slaves, or they may come to him by natural increase, and he may will them to his posterity, and there is nothing in this Discipline that can take hold of him, this being the only law that reaches private members. It is sufficiently latitudinarian.

Second. Official members. The rule on this point takes a stronger tie, and is different in that respect to the rule affecting private members:

"We declare that we are as much as ever convinced of the great evil of slavery; therefore no slaveholder shall be eligible to any official station in our Church hereafter, where the laws of the State in which he lives will admit of emancipation, and *permit the liberated slave to enjoy freedom.*"

Official members are required to emancipate. The private member is not. The official member must manumit, but still the rule comes down with comparatively less strictness, applying only in such States as will permit the slave to "enjoy his freedom."

Third. Traveling preachers. Here the Discipline is still more stringent:

"When any traveling preacher becomes an owner of a slave, or slaves, by any means, he shall forfeit his ministerial character in our Church, unless he execute, if it be practicable, a legal emancipation of such slaves, conformably to the laws of the State in which he lives."

Here nothing is said about the liberated slave being permitted to enjoy freedom. The simple act of manumission is treated of, and made compulsory on the traveling preacher. "If practicable," he is to manumit. There is no other condition; the exception is narrowed down, and then the law is binding, and compels him to manumit. And it is very right and proper, in the nature of the case, that the Discipline on this subject should be more strict upon the traveling preacher than upon the local preacher, for the same reason that it is drawn more tightly in the case of the local preacher than the private member. There is wisdom, great wisdom, in this regulation. Our private members are actual residents and citizens of given States. Necessity rules them, and therefore it might not do to make the law so tight in their case as in others. Our local ministers are residents of States; but, in the proper sense of the term, our traveling preachers are citizens of the world; not of Virginia, or Maryland, or South

Carolina; for the Bishop has power to take up a brother from South Carolina, and send him into Massachusetts. And this is especially the case in the territory embraced by the Baltimore Conference, which includes part of Pennsylvania. And because we are birds of passage, and can be removed at pleasure, by the authorities of the Church, out of the way of the local difficulties in the way of manumission, the law is, very properly, made more binding upon us. And remember, we have not brought a local preacher here, but a traveling preacher, and we try him under the rule that applies to traveling preachers.

The next point that the prosecution urges is, that their construction of the Discipline was confirmed by a resolution of the General Conference, in 1840. I deny it altogether in its application to a traveling preacher; and I could not help remarking, that though my friend brought forward the rule applying to traveling preachers, yet, after reading, he very quietly dismissed it, and kept the rule applying to a local preacher constantly before our eyes. I am not sure, sir, that he did not thereby mislead us a little. That I do not misstate him at all is plain, for he made a reference to the action of the last General Conference on a memorial from Westmoreland, respecting the ordination of some local preachers. What have we to do with that? Has it any thing to do in the premises? We have now to do with the Discipline that operates upon traveling preachers, and with that alone. The Baltimore Conference could not ordain those brethren, and they came up here to induce the General Conference to compel us to do it. There the action was upon the case of local preachers, and my friend brings up a stray resolution on their case! But let him show me where it says a word about traveling preachers. Their memorial was on their own behalf, as local preachers; and if they said one word about traveling preachers, they exceeded their power altogether.

The action of the General Conference on that application has no bearing whatever on the present case, unless they had said that the same rule was binding upon traveling preachers also, which they were careful not to do, so that the prosecution has altogether failed in making out their construction of the Discipline. He gave us, to be sure, a very strange definition of what was meant by legal emancipation; it deserved the credit of originality; it was this, that a slave must be permitted to enjoy his freedom. Now, legal emancipation simply means, emancipation according to law—the law of the State—whether the man shall be allowed to remain in the State or not. And you cannot show me any action of the General Conference by which a traveling preacher cannot effect a legal emancipation. How would this apply in Mr. Harding's case? Why, according to the law of Maryland, he must emancipate with the consent of his wife. Then he does it legally. The Discipline, sir, is against Mr. Harding, or it never was against any man in the world. It meets him right in the face, and he cannot get round it. The Baltimore Conference did right in suspending him; and though that Conference has been held up here to contempt and scorn, we are not ashamed of ourselves; for we have shown, with regard to the whole matter, that we have lain our interests upon the altar of principle and old Methodism, and from our present position we do not mean to be driven by Mr. Harding, or any other man.

The prosecutor has been pleased to refer to the conscience of the appellant in this matter. He had better let that alone for the present. This conscience is a strange affair. Where was his client's conscience when he entered into this business? Where his respect for the Discipline, to which he had solemnly vowed to submit himself? or for the oft-repeated wishes of the Baltimore Conference? He knew well that the step he was taking would meet with the disapprobation of almost every member on the floor of that Conference; and yet he had no smitings of conscience then! I have heard of a highwayman in Italy, who could rob a man and cut his throat without any compunction; but he happened to eat meat one day in Lent, and his conscience smote him tremendously. O yes; this conscience is at times a very facile thing! A man's interest will stretch his conscience tremendously. I won't press this point any farther.

The prosecutor rejoiced as one who had found great spoil; but really, I must dash his joy. I am for the Baltimore Conference against the whole world; and therefore, though my friend was very much pleased with what he supposed he had found, I must take some of his pleasure from him. He referred with an air of great triumph, and called the attention of Eastern and Northern men to some few words found in the report of this case. "The old ones having passed the age," etc., were to be retained. This is the clause my friend chuckled over so. He thought he had caught us tripping, and appealed to his Eastern brethren to see if we carried water on both shoulders. But, sir, we are straight; we stand erect and upright, unhurt and unharmed; and here let me say, that we are one kind of men—North, South, East and West, and Middle States—all stand on the same broad basis. He forgot to tell this General Conference that those very words were afterward stricken out. They never passed the Baltimore Conference. But suppose they had not been taken out of the report. My friend knows very well that it is the case almost everywhere, that when a slave arrives at a certain age, he cannot be manumitted without security be given by his owner that he shall not come upon the parish. This is the case in Maryland. In Virginia the law is still stronger. They cannot be got rid of, because they cannot take care of themselves. The prosecutor did not state this. If our journal had stated the case as he represented it, we would have been perfectly justified in the eye of the law. But we struck it out because we would not commit ourselves at all on the subject.

The fourth argument employed by the prosecutor was, that the spirit of the Discipline, as well as the letter, was in favor of Mr. Harding, and against the Baltimore Conference. It is a very hard matter to define what spirit is, and he did not favor us with any definition on the subject. He simply took it for granted that the Methodist Discipline was conservative. I hold that it is opposed to slavery, and that there is nothing in the Discipline of the Methodist Episcopal Church that sanctions slavery. What we mean by conservatism is this: A party in the South contend for slavery as proper and right, and essential even to the existence of the republic and social institutions, and that it ought never to be abolished. A party in the North say it is an evil and a sin, and ought to be abolished at once without regard to circumstances. Now between these two is conservatism. The views of the Discipline on the evil of slavery are absolute and positive. It pronounces it an evil, and a great evil. And in fact it asks the question, "What shall be done for the extirpation of the great evil of slavery?" and then specifies measures by which its purpose shall be effected. But it does not regard it as sin under all circumstances.

My friend referred very strangely and singularly to the happy interference of Northern abolitionism as destructive of colonization. I confess I do not understand him, sir. Hear him: "Slavery is an evil, a great evil"—it was severely felt as such. And yet he hails the action of abolitionists, because, in his judgment, it has resulted in riveting the chains of slavery—this admitted evil—more durably. How is this?

Dr. Smith interrupted for explanation. He insisted that Mr. C. was in error, and wished to correct him.

Mr. Collins. I do n't stand here as a gladiator, merely to gain a victory over Dr. Smith. If I am in error, put me right.

Dr. Smith. I stated awhile ago that I should be able to put the brother right in every thing; and if the brethren will let me take my notes, I will try and put him right in the premises.

Mr. Collins. I was going on to say, sir, that I do not come here to win any laurels from Dr. Smith, even if I had the power to do it. I came here in defense of the Baltimore Conference. If I have committed an error, it is unintentional; but I am satisfied I have committed no fundamental error this morning. All I want is to meet the question on Discipline, as set forth in the able argument of my friend, and all the desire I have on the subject is to put the matter in its right light, and then I am sure this appeal will be dismissed. I would just remark, in conclusion, here, that we were not ignorant of the Laws of Maryland. The note of Mr. Merrick, which was read here yesterday, was before us, but as a Conference we were acting on simple order. It was referred to a committee, and is therefore to be considered as having had our action upon it.

We come now, in the next place, to state the grounds on which we rest the defense of the Baltimore Conference in this matter.

First. Because the Discipline of our Church has been violated by Mr. Harding. We hold that he violated the Discipline in refusing to manumit his slaves, in a case where he could do it, and would not. This is one ground. I need here but refer to my former remarks to show that the law will admit of manumission. Such was the course pursued, that he seemed to court martyrdom, and in a rude manner denounced that venerable body as ultra abolitionists. I would not have brought in this irrelative matter had not such been brought in yesterday.

Secondly. Because Mr. Harding entered into this difficulty voluntarily. It was his own act, under circumstances of great and high aggravation. There are some cases in which *necessity* can be fairly plead, where the parties are residents in slaveholding States—in such instances the parties may claim something in mitigation. But for a man who was once free from slavery, and knowing all the consequences that would result from such action, *voluntarily* to involve himself in it, makes it a very different case. I hope the Conference will bear this distinctly in mind. He was no slaveholder when the Baltimore Conference received him on trial. They ordained him a deacon and elder; and well he knew that he could never have gone into orders had he been a slaveholder. And I hold it to be the highest breach of trust, for a minister of Jesus Christ, after being put in possession of all ministerial power, to forfeit his solemn oath of allegiance, and do an act which he well knows will be an insult to his brethren, and a contravention of the Discipline he has vowed to preserve. I say, sir, I hold it to be a high offense and breach of trust for a minister of Jesus Christ thus to act. Where was the compulsion? Why did he, comparatively a young man, thus violate the pledge solemnly given to his fathers in the gospel? Why run counter to the will of the whole Conference, and throw the apple of discord into that body, and seek to foment disunion among its members? There was no reason—no necessity for it. He might have been removed the next year to another station. It was, I repeat, a breach of trust of no ordinary character thus to fly in the face of the Church and his brethren. And this he did voluntarily and of his own accord. Sir, I hold that no Methodist preacher has a right to do just as he pleases. Even in the choice of a wife he is under obligations to make a prudent choice, and take counsel of his aged brethren. No, sir, not even in the delicate matter of marriage has a Methodist preacher a right to do as he pleases. The character and standing of the Conference are in some measure in his keeping, and he cannot at will shake off the obligation, and trifle with the trust that he himself has solicited, and which has been placed in his charge in perfect confidence and good faith.

Thirdly. Because he did it with his eyes open. He can plead no ignorance here. He knew the law of the State of Maryland, which he has pleaded in his defense here. And he also knew what ought to have been with him of preëminent importance, the law of the Baltimore Conference.

All this he knew, and that I may not appear to overstate my points, I beg permission to have read from our journal a case in point. It was that of Brother Hansberger. [Action of the Baltimore Conference in that case read, as recorded in the journals, by the Secretary. It was a similar case, in which the Conference had made a like requisition, and the member had submitted.]

Mr. Collins continued. The appellant had this case before his eyes when he entered upon the engagement and married these slaves. Such resolutions, passed by the Baltimore Conference, ought to have deterred him from taking this step. One of them goes to say, that if any brother do thus act in disregard of the wishes of the Conference in this matter, he shall be deemed guilty of contumacy. Yet, with this resolution before him, exposing himself to the charge of contumacy, he involved himself and the Conference in this difficulty.

Fourthly. Because, by becoming a slaveholder, he rendered himself unavailable to us as a traveling preacher.

The Baltimore Conference is composed of slaveholding and non-slaveholding territory, in nearly equal proportions. As a slaveholder, in the non-slaveholding portion of the Conference, they would not hear him preach. He would have to be confined entirely to the slaveholding section. And if this course were sanctioned, there would be increased difficulty entailed upon the appointing power of the Church in keeping one set of men perpetually in each section of the Conference. Nor is this all. It would have a direct tendency to locality, and would thus strike at the very root of our itinerant system; and no man has a right to involve himself so as to confine, necessarily, his labors to any one portion of the work, thus virtually giving up his relation as an itinerant minister, and rendering himself unavailable. We could then have nothing to do with him, but to get rid of him as easily as we could, and pray God to fill his place with some one who will not bring this discordance among us. I beg the Conference to look well to this single point connected with slavery. He would have been to us a semi-local preacher. Ought this to be sustained? Are there not tendencies enough already to locality in our system without increasing them? And ought such an obstruction as that in which Harding has involved himself to be forced upon a Conference which has always repudiated it? We want no such restraints; and because we do not, we have placed this brother in the situation he occupies.

Our fifth, and last reason, is this: Because of the position the Baltimore Conference has ever occupied on the subject of slavery. And I wish to define this position, that it may be clearly and correctly understood. The Baltimore Conference never has sanctioned the connection of any of its members with slavery. It has been tried by marriage contracts, but that plan failed. It has been tried also by other means, but they also failed; and never, remotely or directly, and in no sense, have they affected our integrity. The Baltimore Conference has maintained her independence at all times, and means to maintain it. And in taking this position she is fortified by the Discipline—call it conservative or what you will. She is on the old Methodist basis, where she was first put—on the ground on which she was first planted.

We had a definition yesterday of conservatism, and I thought it the strangest I ever heard in my life. If the prosecutor be a conservative, convinced of the great evil of slavery, why, I beg of him, will he force this thing upon us when we do not want it? We have taken no new ground on this subject. We are just where we always were—standing as a breakwater to pro-slavery in the South, and the waves of abolitionism from the North. I know that this has been sneered at, and much sarcasm has been spent upon it, but it is nevertheless true. We have not been propelled to our present position either by the North or the South. We are just where the venerable and venerated Asbury and our fathers were. Brother Smith has been largely professing conservatism! But what sort of conservatism is it? He admits that slavery is a great evil, and yet is favorable to perpetuating it, and forcing it upon a body that always repudiated it. 'T is a strange conservatism! We know it not. It never had an existence in the Baltimore Conference. We cannot comprehend it, and we would not if we could. I am not for any violent measure on the subject of slavery. I firmly believe that if this matter had been left alone and untouched, such is the influence of Methodism and other means, that, ere this day, the States of Maryland and Virginia would have made considerable advance in gradual emancipation. It is by the preaching of the gospel—the diffusion of the benevolent spirit of Christianity, that the rigors of slavery have been abated; and by the continuation of such means shall the broad, expansive principles of Christian liberty be promulgated until the spirit of freedom find a shrine in every cabin, and a home in every heart. I love the negro. My first recollections—those infantile associations that perish not amid the rougher conflicts of life—are of a negro who nursed me. I was raised among them, and I know how to love them. But let such love be shown, not by violent measures for their deliverance from bondage, but by carrying, in the true spirit of Methodist itinerancy and conservatism, the gospel to their cabins—by going to the poor African, and praying for him and with him—by visiting the poor and needy among them, the widow and the fatherless, the sick and in prison! Yes, sir, that is the man for me, who will thus "show me his faith by his works."

We had the vessel of colonization and gradual emancipation, fair and beautiful, and in fine trim, gliding swiftly and gracefully across the limpid waters, bounding from wave to wave before the propitious breeze. Joyously and gracefully she speeds along her trackless path; and the crested wave, kissing transiently her graceful bow, falls back into the tranquil sea—all, all is fair, and bright, and prosperous! But see! the heavens are darkening—the storm is howling—the sea heaves beneath the sudden tempest, and the waves thereof roar and toss themselves—the gale has struck her! What then? Shall we desert her? No, sir; the Baltimore Conference will not do so! They will not forsake the ship because the gale has struck her, and she bends beneath the storm! They will not rush below in terror and fright, or jump overboard with phrensied despair. Sir, they know us not who think we are the men to quail in the hour of danger. We will not strike our flag. We will not combine with the enemies of the African, either North or South. We will work the ship, hoping and believing that, by the blessing of God, we shall come off successfully at last! Abolitionism shall never make us pro-slavery. Why, sir, we saw the cloud to which my friend refers, in its deepening, spreading darkness—we heard the pealing thunder as it was borne up to us on the wings of the tempest-wind, and beheld the lurid glare of the lightning's flash; but we were not dismayed. The gallant ship—our good old Methodism—has outridden many a perilous storm, and will many another, and despite these passing dangers we mean to voyage in the old ship "o'er life's tempestuous ocean," and will never leave her nor forsake her, for ours is the right kind of conservatism. We acknowledge, as true conservatives, moral excellence and worth on both sides. Some of the best men and women we have known have been slaveholders, and we are well aware that some of these are slaveholders of necessity. It is a remarkable fact that the members of the Baltimore Conference, who have sustained this measure, were mostly raised in slaveholding States.

The speaker then paid a just tribute to certain members of the Baltimore Conference who had manumitted their slaves for Christianity's sake, and maintained that instead of being held up to reproach, that Conference was justly entitled to the thanks of Methodism in all its connections. He then proceeded to recapitulate the points which he had endeavored to establish. He thought he had proved that the journal of the Conference was correct—that the laws of the State of Maryland admit of manumission—that the Discipline of the Church did bear upon Mr. Harding's case—that that Discipline had been violated by him—that he was righteously liable to the consequences of that violation—that he had acted in the matter voluntarily and contumaciously, and that he had rendered himself unavailable, as a traveling preacher, to his brethren of the Baltimore Conference.

And now, having shown the reasons why the Baltimore Conference suspended Mr. Harding, he (Mr. C.) asked, Would the General Conference send him back again to them? He begged them to consider well, and with great calmness, before they did so. Did they wish to make another slaveholding Conference? Admit one slaveholder, and the Baltimore Conference has no longer the independent position they could now irreproachably assume! Once break down the barrier, and they must admit others! Would they thus humble their fathers in Christ, and thus trample on old Methodism? He trusted they would not, but would assist them still to occupy the ground they had, by much sacrifice, and with much difficulty, been able to take. If they did change their ground, it was hard to say where they would stop. Their young men would by marriage become slaveholders, and the principles which the Baltimore Conference so long had held would be sacrificed entirely. The question was a momentous one, not so much between Mr. Harding and the Baltimore Conference, but between the Baltimore Conference and all future candidates for the ministry in their Conference. He was aware that appeals would be made to their sympathies. In this the prosecution would have the advantage. But they must also remember that the appellant by his conduct had proved that he did not place much value upon his relation to his fathers and brethren, and therefore on that score he could claim really nothing.

He did not wish to wound the feelings of the Southern brethren. Among them were many venerable for their talents, and piety, and usefulness in the Church of God; but while he would not be the willing instrument of wounding their feelings, he was compelled to say what he had said, that he might put the act of the Conference he represented in its right and proper view before them. He prayed the blessing of God upon his Southern as well as his Northern brethren, and trusted they should live and labor on in love and friendship, and that time would mellow down all asperities on the painful subject which was agitating the Connection, so that they might dwell together as one family on earth, and then each, from North and South, and East and West, should enter triumphantly into the heaven they were seeking, where all minor distinctions would be swallowed up and lost in the beatific contemplation of Him who had washed them from sin in his own blood, and made them kings and priests unto God forever.

Mr. President, the ground of the Baltimore Conference is unquestionably the true one. She is truly conservative. She never has proclaimed—never will—anywhere, or at any time, or under any circumstances, that "slavery is a sin under all circumstances;" while at the same time she wishes to preserve the members of her body disconnected with slavery, that the influence of their example may tell silently and surely against its perpetuation. The head and front of our offending—that for which we are arraigned at the bar of this General Conference—is simply this: We wish to keep slavery from our traveling ministry. This is no new thing with us. The effort made now is to effect a change in the position of the Baltimore Annual Conference by making it a slaveholding body. This, I trust, will not be done. We cannot sacrifice our ground to accommodate Mr. Harding, or any other man who may choose to become a slaveholder. The issue of the case before us involves momentous consequences, affecting the whole Church; and in full confidence in the wisdom and integrity of the General Conference, we submit it to their decision.

The President said that any of the Baltimore

Conference delegation were now at liberty to speak on the subject, and

Mr. Slicer rose to address the Conference. He said he had been in doubt whether any other of the delegation besides the brother who had been specially intrusted with the case, ought to address them on this subject. He would, however, occupy their attention briefly. The memorial of certain local preachers had been frequently referred to. The brethren memorialized the several Conferences either to right them, or set them off. But the people were not willing to be set off, and when the General Conference sat in Philadelphia in 1832, the people south of the Rappahannock River memorialized the Conference not to let the Virginia people have them. And if the people there desired the ministration of the preachers of the Baltimore Conference, and not the Virginia Conference, was it not likely that the friends north of that river would have still stronger sentiments on the subject? Something had been said about "loaves and fishes." Now the people referred to were a clever, intelligent people, but their territory was by no means the most desirable portion under the care of the Baltimore Conference.

The reverend gentleman then gave a geographical description of the country, and said that the Baltimore Conference was in nowise disposed to part with them, unless they (the people) wished it.

5

They did not intend that any number of local preachers should separate them, but when a majority of the people wished it, it should be done. The people there were an admirable people, and a conservative people, too, having been supplied with antislavery preachers—so true was it that the people received their complexion from the ministry. At Whitemarsh, where the Roman Catholic priests own slaves almost without number, and sell them *ad libitum*, and pay the money into the "Lord's treasury," in that whole country slavery exists under the worst forms. The reverend gentleman gave a farther analysis of the country and the state of feeling in the various districts, illustrating his position, that the character of the people depended on the character of the ministry, and showed that the progress of emancipation had been from North to South.

He then proceeded to notice the position of the Baltimore Conference to the appellant before them. He (the appellant) was well aware that his becoming a slaveholder would be a disqualification for his usefulness among the people. He (Mr. Slicer) had known Mr. Harding from his youth up, had preached in his father's house, and was willing to make any sacrifice but of principle to meet his case, and to bring him into compliance with the wishes of the Conference. He must say, however, that all the labor and anxiety of a committee appointed for that purpose was met by the appellant, not only with no sympathy, but with utter contempt and disregard. If, however, he thought it more important to maintain his position than yield to the wishes of his brethren, the election was with him. The Conference could do without him quite as well as he could do without the Conference. If he were sent back twenty times, the Baltimore Conference would not change its ground; and he (Mr. S.) looked confidently, as he prayed earnestly, for the day when this dark spot should be wiped away from this free country.

Mr. Griffith had no intention to make a speech on the subject, but he wished to call the attention of the Conference to a few facts connected with the matter under their notice. It had been said that the Baltimore Conference occupied a territory nearly equally divided between slaveholding and non-slaveholding States, and embracing part of Virginia; yet the Baltimore Conference had always contrived to avoid any agitation of the question among the people of Virginia, and had never violated any of the laws of that State; and from this he thought a lesson might be learned. Yesterday, the brother, in advocating the cause of the appellant, had said, "only slavery where we must," as if he intended to make the impression that this young man was of necessity connected with slavery—tied hand and foot. Now this was far from being the fact—there was not a word of truth in it.' He could disentangle himself in an hour if he liked, the Laws of Maryland notwithstanding. In point of fact, the law against manumission is inoperative. It would be indeed strange if a freeman had not the right to make that disposal of his property which he might choose to make. Maryland never had said that a slave might be taken up and sold—she never had declared that slaves were property; and then in the same breath, that men should not do what they thought fit with their own property, and that she assumed the right to do that which she forbade the owner doing. No, sir, they know that a man has a right to set his slaves free—they know the illegality and imperfection of any act to the contrary—and yet they try to control it, and ward off the consequences of this kind of —— he hardly knew how to designate such kind of legislation.

One word farther. That young brother was perfectly at liberty to emancipate his slaves at any time he liked. No man in the State of Maryland doubted his right. Slaves were set free all over the State. And if the Virginia Conference had been as careful to preserve the integrity of her own original position as the Baltimore Conference, she would now have been as free from the great evil as the Baltimore Conference was. And why not? The Baltimore Conference keeps territory side by side with the Virginia Conference. Nothing but the Rappahannock River divides them. And the Baltimore Conference had occupied this territory with preachers free from slavery; and you will, on examining the statistics, find that we have had, at least, equal success with our Virginia brethren.

At the conclusion of Mr. Griffith's remarks, the President inquired whether the delegation of the Baltimore Conference had concluded, when Dr. Smith said he hoped not, for they had not yet attempted to show that the appellant was the owner of a single slave.

Mr. Collins. This is not the place. He has already acknowledged that he was so involved in slaveholding that he could not get rid of it.

Mr. Harding. I do not admit it—I deny it.

Mr. Collins. What did the Presiding Elder and the record on the journal say? Why, that Mr. Harding has "come into the possession of several slaves."

There were a variety of ways in which a man could become connected with slavery—one of which was by a marriage contract, of all other courses the most dishonorable and hateful. This shifting it upon the woman was adding meanness to injury, and was nothing but a mere special plea

—a disingenuous and disreputable quibble. He (the appellant) gets the benefit, and has the control of the property, and is therefore in fact a slaveholder. Let them not hang their defense on such a mere technicality.

Mr. Sargent. The whole action proceeded on the admitted fact that he was a slaveholder; and the fact was never denied, and this plea is entirely an after-thought.

Mr. Collins said that an honorable man would hate to get off by any such quibble. The man never denied that he was a slaveholder. And this was also in direct opposition to the plea set up yesterday, namely, that he offered to send these slaves to Liberia or any free State. If he had no slaves, either jointly or otherwise, why make that plea, and try to get off by saying that he had consented to remove them? And why pledge his consent if he had no ownership? Let them meet the case honestly and fairly. They were not arguing the matter before a set of quibbling lawyers. This was a mere *ruse*. But it would not do. The very law they had appealed to was against them. By Section 2, it made him joint owner with his wife to all intents and purposes, and the appellant knew it. Very sorry was he (Mr. C.) that the prosecutor should think it necessary to resort to such a quibble.

After Mr. Collins closed his speech, some conversation arose respecting the time at which the rejoinder should be heard, but the Conference adjourned without coming to any conclusion.

On the following day, Friday, May 10, by consent of the appellant's advocate, Mr. Collins again took the floor. He acknowledged the courtesy and Christian temper manifested by Dr. Smith. He wished to touch one or two points before he was ruled out by the discipline regulating the Conference. A rumor prevailed, he had learned, among the members of the Conference, that there were at present three or four slaveholders in the Baltimore Conference. He (Mr. C.) denied, distinctly and fully, that such was the case—they had not, nor would they have, a slaveholder among them. He then glanced at the various cases that had come before them, as an Annual Conference, and showed that in every case they had treated them exactly as they had dealt with Mr. Harding.

Messrs. Davis, Griffith, and Slicer emphatically denied the truth of such a rumor, and indorsed all Mr. C. had said upon the subject.

Mr. McMahon rose to order. He objected to this answering all the gossip they might hear out of door. If they were all to do so, he knew not where it might stop.

Bishop Waugh thought, as it was connected in some degree with the appeal before the Conference, in which the Conference had allowed some latitude to both sides, it was not necessary to interrupt the speaker. There was hardly any departure yet that could call for interference.

Mr. Collins resumed. He wished also to correct another wrong impression. It was partially believed that the Baltimore Conference, in suspending Mr. Harding, had acted in ignorance of the law of 1843. He begged to correct this misconception. They had before them the opinion of Justice Merrick with regard to this very law. But he would say boldly, that if the law had been tenfold what it is, if it had actually, outright and downright, without any possibility of avoiding it, taken these slaves from Harding's control, the Conference would still have acted just as they did; because they did not intend to change their ground, and could not pretend to alter their views with every shifting of the Legislature. Besides, the Legislature did not compel Mr. Harding to become a slaveholder.

Since the discussion, he had spoken with several preachers who were over here from the Baltimore Conference, and they all agreed that Mr. Harding never gave the pledge he said he did; so he (Mr. C.) thought that point was disposed of. As to the question of ownership, it was plainly laid down in the laws of the State that the husband had joint ownership. The law was designed simply to give the wife such control over her property that it should not be taken from her for any debts or contracts of her husband; and if the lady is a slaveholder, the husband is one too. The gentleman went through the different sections of the law with great ability, dissecting and analyzing them with much skill and minuteness, and then touched upon the Discipline of the Church, to show that it was more positive in requiring a traveling preacher to manumit his slaves than it was with local preachers and other officers of the Church. He then proceeded to show that public opinion at Baltimore, and throughout most of the territory under the charge of that Conference, was in their favor; and that there was no *practical* difficulty in the way of manumitting slaves in Maryland, for it was constantly done, and four-fifths of the colored people in Baltimore were free. And now, he inquired, were the Baltimore Conference to be made to lick the dust at the feet of the appellant, or were they to be supported in their action, as they ought to be? Would the General Conference say to the Baltimore Conference, after all her prayers, and efforts, and sacrifices, and reproach, that she was to take into her bosom a slaveholding minister? If so, the consequences would be calamitous in the extreme. The issue was fairly before them, and, whatever were the consequences, it must be fairly met.

He then made a most earnest and affectionate

appeal to his Southern brethren, calling upon them, by their avowal of the evil of slavery, not to force the "evil" upon a Conference that had hitherto kept clear of it; and addressing the other two sections of the Church, he implored them by their love of order, and their regard for discipline, to sustain the Baltimore Conference in this appeal.

Dr. Smith then rose to reply. He said, Sir, I wish most particularly to disclaim the obligations the speakers have felt themselves free to express for the indulgence extended them. It was no tax to my feelings to entertain the request to make an explanation this morning, and no risk to my cause to grant it. Although the "explanation" amounted to a second speech on the merits of the case, and occupied some two hours or more, yet I may safely commit the whole of it to our faithful reporter. If I understand myself, few things would have afforded me more pleasure than for the counsel, Mr. Collins, both on his own account and the reputation of his Conference, to have recovered his position before this body and the whole Church. No one, I am sure, will doubt his ability. He has exhausted his resources both of argument and eloquence. He has been indulged, both by myself and the Conference, in every advantage he asked. Still, sir, I feel satisfied, from the manifest weakness of his positions, that if he will suffer the reporter to do him justice, he will find reason to be ashamed of his cause. From various indications on this floor, there may be good reason to fear that the cause of the appellant finds but little sympathy with many. The American Methodist Church, however, may give a different verdict. The counsel may find as much cause ultimately to cower under this decision as he now finds to triumph under the strange sympathy which his offensive doctrines have met with in this body. Before I enter upon the true issues before the Conference, I must notice several points which the counsel and those who have come to his aid have dwelt upon as important to their cause. I shall treat them as preliminary to this discussion.

1. The speaker, Brother Collins, has complimented me—in very flattering terms to be sure—on what he considers my conversion from pro-slavery to antislavery principles. Sir, this was intended for effect. The impression may be made that I did not give my actual opinions on the subject of slavery. This is a short way of avoiding my argument. Why did not the speaker invalidate my position, by showing that slavery in its circumstances is necessarily sinful, and, therefore, the course of the Baltimore Annual Conference should be sustained? Why, sir? Because there was a much sounder discretion in declining to meet my arguments, and cover his retreat by the intimation that I did not myself believe the doc-

trines on which the vindication of Mr. Harding rests. But, sir, I cannot yield this advantage. My arguments, showing that slavery is not necessarily sinful, are unanswered—indeed, untouched. And until this be done, the action of the Baltimore Conference is wholly indefensible. *If moral turpitude, more or less,* does not necessarily attach to slavery, the decision of this court of ministers, depriving a member of their body of holy orders, simply because of his union by marriage with a lady who held property in slaves, is an outrage upon the feelings of the appellant, an indignity to a very large portion of the Church, and a reflection on the judgment of the Baltimore Conference. Sir, I should appreciate much more highly the position of the speaker had he met my argument fairly. But I am converted, it is said! When? Where? or at what altar? I honestly confess I know nothing about it. It is a change I never felt. I never, on any former occasion, attempted an extended expression of opinion before this body on the subject of slavery. On the subject of abolition I remember to have made a remark on the floor of the General Conference of 1832. I will quote it here: "Abolition is now in its egg state—now you can put your foot upon it, and crush it; but if, instead of this, you breathe upon it the warm breath of your approbation, it shall hatch a scorpion that shall sting you to the heart."

And now, sir, I ask whether my prediction is in a way to be verified or not? Twelve years only have passed away, and a purely abolition movement on the part of the Baltimore Annual Conference finds favor in this body. Yes, sir, such are the indications that it may be well if we be not on the eve of division. Your decision in this case may be the knell of our long-cherished union.

I affirmed, in my opening speech, that the South was not pro-slavery, but antislavery. The Georgia and South Carolina Conference delegation, with every other member from the South on this floor, united in a most hearty response to the appeal I made to them on this point. This, too, is seized upon, and these Conferences are also congratulated upon their conversion. This is based chiefly I suppose upon the resolutions adopted by these Conferences in 1831, declaring that slavery "is not a moral evil." But, sir, this argues no change. They still adhere to their position in the sense—and a good one, too—in which they used the phrase "moral evil." The popular sense of their resolutions, as understood everywhere, was simply this, *that slavery was not necessarily sinful.* They still believe so. Sir, no other meaning was ever attached to "moral evil," as a popular expression, until the editor of the Christian Advocate and Journal thought proper to call up a meaning unknown to the popular mind. To raise a platform on which the abolitionists of the North might stand, without identifying themselves with O. Scott, in his extreme measures of reforming the government of the Church, he called up the distinction between "moral evil" and sin. Thus he rallied the scattered forces of the North, dubbing Scott & Co. as "radico-abolitionists," and the Simon Pures as "abolitionists" merely. How far this consolidation of Northern forces was done with a view to consequences which now threaten the Church with division, I cannot say.

No, sir, we are not converted. We stand on the same ground we have occupied from the foundation of the Church—the grand conservative ground laid by our fathers in the Book of Discipline. Slavery, as it exists among us, is "a great evil;" and I will add, to none so great an "evil" as to the master. "It is not, however, necessarily a sin." I will add, it is only a sin to those individuals who abuse the institution. No, sir, we have not changed our ground. We have no hecatomb of slaughtered principles to offer upon the altar of abolition devotions. And if they *would* bind *our* principles, we would point them to the prophetic "he-goat" in Daniel's vision, as more symbolical of the desolating effect of their fanatical measures, and say to them, Take him for the sacrifice!

2. I made a strong point of the informality of

the Baltimore Conference journals, claiming on this ground that the case be at least returned for a new trial. The jealous concern of the counsel for the reputation of his Conference is peculiarly awaked at the indignity of such an imputation. Well, let us see. The Discipline of our Church requires that in the trial of a minister, "regular minutes of the trial shall be kept, including all the questions proposed to the witnesses, with their answers." According to the statement of the counsel, there was no witness in the case but Harding himself. Now, sir, according to the discussion the other day, and the argument of counsel, the merit of this case turns chiefly upon this point —Did Mr. Harding pledge himself and his wife, before the Conference, to send these slaves to Africa or to a free State, *if they would consent to go?* One of the delegation distinctly remembers that he did so pledge himself and his wife: the others do not remember to have heard the pledge. All, however, agree that the witness made many statements before the Conference; some of these you have heard plead against him by the counsel. Why, sir—seeing he was most unjustly made to witness against himself—why, I ask, do not the journals record his testimony, that he may now have the benefit of it? Are not the journals defective in this respect? And as a proof of the bearing of this fact upon the issue, I appeal to

Brother Tippett, a member of the delegation, had Harding been thus understood, if it is likely he would have been suspended. Brother Tippett, I see, is silent, sir. I understand his silence; he knows it to be so.

Mr. Tippett—from his seat—I deem it unnecessary to answer *now*, (the time for receiving testimony having passed.)

It is not important you should, sir. It might involve you in serious responsibilities. Your silence is sufficient. Now, sir, can any thing be more plain than this, that these journals are defective, and that in a point most material to the issue before us? Is it not the least we can do, in justice to the appellant, to send him back for a new trial? But, sir, the journals record material facts, which show the illegality and injustice of the whole proceeding so clearly, that he is entitled to be wholly released from the suspension. This I will show in the proper place.

3. The next point on which I should make some remarks is the reply of the General Conference of 1840 to the memorial from Westmoreland, Virginia. The origin of this memorial I have explained. I read the resolution adopted by the Conference. The counsel finds himself much embarrassed by this resolution, and contents himself with a flat denial that it admits of any application to the case of the appellant. He affirms

that it applied exclusively to local preachers. That it originated in the case of local preachers is admitted. But the report of the committee is an elaborate and most conclusive argument in support of a principle which applies to all preachers. The argument is not as to the meaning of Discipline in relation to *local* preachers merely, as he supposes. The report concludes with a resolution, which I have before read, and from which I will quote one clause: "The ownership of slave property in States or Territories where the laws do not admit of emancipation, and permit the liberated slave to enjoy freedom, constitutes no legal barrier to the election or ordination of ministers *to the various grades* of office known in the ministry of the Methodist Episcopal Church." "*Various grades of office.*" Can language be more explicit? On what authority, therefore, can it be pleaded that this applies to local preachers *only?* That constitutes but *one* of the grades of office. Sir, the assertion is a gross absurdity. I maintain, therefore, that the meaning of Discipline, by this decision of the General Conference of 1840, is settled in Mr. Harding's favor. Language cannot more clearly warrant a conclusion. And for this General Conference to sustain the Baltimore Conference in Harding's case, is to do it in the teeth of the Discipline as interpreted by themselves in 1840. It is to add to the afflictions of the outraged brethren of Westmoreland, who are the more grievously wronged in this, that to the present time, the Balimore Conference have continued to deny them their rights. Surely, sir, this Conference should be held to a rigid accountability for this act of injustice to the local brethren of Westmoreland, and of contumacy to the General Conference. But, instead of this, will you embolden them in a systematic course of wrong-doing, by refusing to sustain the appeal? I hope not.

In this connection I propose to notice several particulars of a kindred character, introduced by the counsel. It is affirmed that Mr. Harding's relation to slavery rendered him "unavailable" as a Methodist preacher. On this ground it is argued, that it was expedient to "*suspend him,*" because the Conference is authorized (and accustomed so to do) to locate men who are unavailable. That is, sir—to throw the language into a more logical form—because the Conference has an *authority*, which they are accustomed to exercise, to *locate* one who is unavailable as a traveling preacher, (*which,* be it observed, *leaves him in possession of his ministerial orders,*) therefore it was both legal and expedient to *suspend* the appellant, and thus *deprive* him of his ministerial orders! Fine logic this! But, sir, on what ground was Mr. Harding unavailable? Why, because a part of the Conference appointments are within a non-slaveholding

State. Well, sir, are all the members of this body considered "unavailable" whom it would not be prudent to send to any part of the work? How absurd! This Conference abounds with appointments to which the appellant could be sent with the greatest propriety. The plea is a mere pretext. The counsel affirmed that "slavery had ceased ere this in Maryland if it had been let alone." True, sir. Why, then, will not the Baltimore Conference let it alone? Do they let it alone by a systematic plan of proscription? No, sir, no.

I charged the Baltimore Conference with great and manifest inconsistency in suspending Mr. Harding, because he would not manumit the slaves of his wife, when at the same time they required him to retain a part of the servants in perpetual slavery. This, I said, was an abandonment of principle; and I now add that it shows that Mr. Harding was seized as a victim, whose sacrifice was the only way of reaching other and more influential members of the Conference. The counsel triumphed greatly in the assurance he gave you, that this feature of the report of the committee in Harding's case "was not adopted by Conference, but was struck out." But, sir, I cannot let the Conference escape in this way. I will hold them to their responsibility by the firm grasp of documentary truth. The vote of the Conference on the report of the committee in Harding's case, *did not strike out* the clause leaving him in possession of certain slaves, (specified by name,) but only struck out the clause assigning the reason for requiring him to keep them in slavery. Such is the fact, sir, according to the document, and the shame of the transaction will attach to the Baltimore Conference until they reform their ways. But the counsel is particularly liberal to us on this point, and equally fatal to his cause. He is free to tell us a part of his argument, what this reason was, namely, that the laws of the State did not admit of emancipation after a certain age. This he says to vindicate his Conference from the charge I urged, of inconsistency in holding the appellant to so pious an accountability to free himself, at the peril of his membership, from slavery, and at the same time require him to hold certain of them in perpetual bondage. Really, sir, it seems that the same evil genius which unquestionably presided over the deliberations of this body of grave divines, still holds uncontrolled dominion over the mind of the counsel. For, let me remind you, in a word, of the late law of Maryland, of 1843, which I read the other day. In this it is specifically provided that the old law, to which the counsel refers, be and is hereby rescinded, and hereafter all, without respect to age, shall be eligible to emancipation on the same conditions.

4. But, sir, the counsel sought to involve me in absurdity. I argued that slavery was not necessarily a sin, and that its circumstances are such that it is right to tolerate it, although it be connected with many evils. Now, if this position involves an absurdity, the converse of it, I suppose, must be true. That is, it is wrong to tolerate slavery (being connected with so many evils) because it is sinful under all circumstances. And whatever may be the speculative opinion of members of the Baltimore Conference on this point, I can see no reasonable ground on which they can stand respected in their own eyes for the decision in Harding's case but this, *that his relation to slavery was sinful.* Observe, sir, he was not located. This would have left him in possession of orders. He was not *reproved merely*. No, sir, he was *suspended* —that is, (in view of the declaration that he could not make the required pledge,) expelled the ministry—deposed from orders. And for what, sir? For no heterodoxy in doctrine, nor viciousness of life—that is, for no sin. Will they say this? Unless they do, *it follows that they looked upon his relation to slavery as constituting him a sinner*. And on what other hypothesis can we account for the paternity of a series of most offensive remarks which have grated so harshly upon our ears, especially from Messrs. Collins and Griffith? If Mr. Harding's connection with slavery (just such a connection as is

held by Southern men generally) be not in a high degree sinful, many remarks from these brethren are without any apology that I can conceive of. Why, sir, in the select phraseology of these speakers, slavery is always "a dark subject!" The appellant is charged with having involved himself in all the difficulties that embarrass and afflict him, "by marrying *the woman* he did"—and why? Because she had slaves. And, sir, for this crime he is *personally* charged on this floor by word, accompanied with a most emphatic gesticulation, with having violated his plighted faith to the Conference, and discarding "the godly admonitions of his brethren." Nay, he was asked where was his "conscience" when he formed this matrimonial connection? Yes, sir, so full of turpitude is the crime of marrying a lady with this property, that it must be hunted down, even at the expense of Mrs. Harding's feelings. It is affirmed, in allusion to her, that "no pious and intelligent woman" would jeopardize the standing (in the Baltimore Conference) "of a husband in whose judgment and discretion she confides, for the consideration of a few slaves." I really had thought that if the opinions of the speaker did not, that his gallantry, in view of these galleries, would save him from so far outraging the feelings of a lady. (*Mr. Collins explained, and disclaimed all intention to impugn the piety or intelligence of Mrs. Harding—he did not doubt either.*) I believe you, sir; and it was my purpose to offer, in your behalf, the best apology I could for the freedom of expression you employed in this delicate connection. Yes, sir, there is no doubt that it was the appellant who was to suffer by this reference to his lady. If the slaves were not manumitted, we were to understand it to be wholly his fault. This is the gist of the matter. But, sir, I am not right sure, after all, that he should be held to accountability in this way, for the disposition which his lady would make of property made hers—to be held in her own right —by a special law of the State. Indeed, I am not certain, if what I have learned of the counsel be true, but that his own success in wooing the consent of the ladies has long since satisfied him of the practical truth contained in the couplet:

> If she will, *she will,* you may depend on't;
> If she won't, *she won't,* so there's an end on't.

There is still another remark by which the speakers betray their affinities. More than one has invoked this body not to "drive them to take rank with a slaveholding Conference!" *Take rank with a slaveholding Conference!!* My dear sir, who are you, and what is your Conference, that you should deprecate a footing with your brethren of other Conferences? What elevation is this you have reached, that you must needs *stoop* to be on a footing with Virginia, and the Conferences south of you? You "take rank" with Virginia! Sir, I was not an indifferent observer of the kindred emotions which this pure abolition appeal awaked in certain quarters of this house. And however agreeable the response elicited by these remarks may be to the cherished affinities of the speakers, they may know that they aroused feelings of the deepest regret and mortification in other quarters. Sir, they cut harshly across the sensibilities of many a heart here, and must continue to jar in harsh discord amid the sweetest music of our long-cherished relations. It was not without cause, sir, that the counsel closed his remarks by asking forgiveness. True, we have much cause to complain. Yet I will venture to pledge him the forgiveness of every Southern man on this floor. I will cherish the hope that stress of circumstances, in defending a hopeless cause, has betrayed him to the use of so many offensive remarks. But you (addressing Mr. C.) must allow me to remind you, and those whose views you represent, that you are no "conservatives." You wisely choose a more expressive figure when you represent your body as the "breakwater" of the Conferences. And verily the "breakwater" ye are! for in your *branch* of the common stream it seems has accumulated the drift-wood and sawyers, so to speak, which have floated upon the bosom of Methodism, from the upper and nether sources of abolition, until the dam of error has stretched itself across your tide, and backed up your waters, until they have drowned, instead of fertilized, your lands.

5. I proceed to notice the remarks of Brother Slicer. As he did not design to enter into the merits of the subject, I felt indifferent. I was, however, soon roused by the announcement that he would disclose a transaction disreputable to the Virginia Conference. (He replied, Not so—I said discreditable.) Well, "discreditable." (No—I said a transaction not so creditable to Virginia.) Well, "not so creditable to Virginia," in the Westmoreland case. Sir, the announcement, I say, aroused me. I listened! heard the explosion—watched the slow progress of the spent ball—the sluggish missile fell far below its mark! He says he is not such a conservative as I am. Right glad am I of it. I may safely turn him over to our faithful reporter. He will do him justice, I have no doubt.

6. In concluding these preliminary remarks, I will notice one statement of Brother Griffith. He reminds us that a large part of the territory of the Baltimore Conference is in Virginia, west of the mountains. But few slaves, comparatively, are in this section of the State. This he attributes to the steady opposition of his Conference to slavery. This might be argued, sir, if they had found in

that section of the work a large slave population which had been gradually diminishing. But the reverse of this is precisely true. They found originally but few slaves, and the number of these has increased greatly since that time. If Brother Griffith had not been indebted to his imagination for this important fact, I might give him the credit of a good argument—bating always, however, his earnest deprecation of the dishonor which he supposes will attach to his being "driven to take rank" with brethren at least *his* equals!

Having disposed of these several points which appeared to me as preliminary merely, I now ask your indulgence, sir, for a short time, while I set before you the merits of this case as I find it in the journals of the Baltimore Conference.

To present it more clearly, I will read the record from the journal:

"Whereas, F. A. Harding, a member of the Baltimore Annual Conference, by his late marriage with Miss Swan, of St. Mary's county, Md., has come in possession of several slaves, viz., *one* named Harry, aged 52; *one* woman, named Maria, aged 56; one man, named John, aged 22; a girl, aged 13, named Hannah; and a child, named Margaret, aged 2 years; *and whereas, the Baltimore Conference, according to its well-known usage,* CANNOT, *and* WILL NOT, *tolerate slavery in any of its members;* therefore,

"*Resolved*, That Brother F. A. Harding is hereby required to execute, and cause to be recorded, a deed securing the manumission of the slaves hereinafter mentioned: the man named John, at the age of 28 years; the two female children, at the age of 23; the issue of the females, if any, to be free at the same time with their mothers. And that Brother Harding be farther required to give to this Conference, during its present session, *a* PLEDGE *that the said manumission shall be effected during the present Conference-year.*"

This is the report as adopted by the Conference. It should be noted that it does provide for the manumission of only a part of the slaves. The original report of the committee contained a clause assigning the *reason* simply for not requiring the manumission of all. This clause was struck out by a vote of the Conference.

The final decision in this case, after adopting the above report, was, on motion of Messrs. Collins and Emory, in the following language: "*Resolved*, That Brother Harding be suspended until the next Annual Conference, or until he assures the Episcopacy that he has taken the necessary steps to secure the freedom of his slaves."

The informality of this whole proceeding must be obvious to every one on the reading of the record. I will throw it into something like a legal form, such as it should have assumed before the Conference.

1. The indictment. F. A. Harding is charged with having violated the well-known usage and determined purpose of the Baltimore Annual Conference, not to tolerate slavery in any of its members.

2. *Specification.* He married Miss Swan, who was the owner of five slaves.

3. *The verdict.* That he execute, and cause to be recorded, a deed, securing the manumission of *three* out of *five* of the slaves, and that he give a pledge that this shall be effected during the present Conference-year.

4. *Penalty.* That he be suspended until the above conditions are submitted to—*that is, deposed from the order of the ministry.*

Now, sir, I deny the legality of the indictment—the justice of the verdict—and ask that the appellant be released from the operation of the penalty.

The indictment, I say, is illegal. He is charged with having violated the "well-known usage and determined purpose of the Baltimore Conference." Under what rule of our Discipline, sir, I would inquire, could an Annual Conference arraign and try a member for violating a usage or purpose of its body? The Discipline of the Church is the common charter under which any and every Methodist preacher holds his membership in an Annual Conference. It never before entered my mind, sir, that two opinions could exist among sane and sober-minded men on this point. The duties of an Annual Conference are so clearly defined in a series of plain questions at page 23 of the Discipline, and a few other separate rules in different parts of the book, that its powers cannot be a matter of doubt. They are executive only. The power to make "rules and regulations" for the government of the Church is ceded in the constitution of the Church to the General Conference only. This body has defined in the rules of Discipline the conditions of membership in an Annual Conference; and under this charter, and this alone, membership is held in these bodies. What rule of Methodist Discipline is he charged with violating? None, sir, none. The committee who brought in the indictment charges him in plain terms with having acted contrary to the "usage and determined purpose" of the Conference. For this, and this alone, he was tried—convicted upon his own testimony—condemned and dishonored! The indictment does not even specify the enactment of the Conference to which it makes direct reference. Did ever a more lawless procedure come to the knowledge of this body? The counsel, sir, seems to have entirely overlooked this fact, by which his cause is most fatally embarrassed—unless the paternity of abolition feeling pervading this body should shield it from the condemnation it deserves. He is bold to set forth in his argument, as the charge against Mr. Harding, "*that he knew, what ought to have been with him of preëminent importance,* THE LAW OF THE BALTIMORE CONFERENCE." What law, sir? The imperfect and informal indictment does not tell us. But the counsel is free to supply the deficiency. He tells us, a law to which the case of a Brother Hansberger gave rise; by which they *forbid any of their members to hold slaves under any circumstances,* and declared that any who might disregard the decision, "*should be deemed guilty of contumacy.*" Here, then, is the law of the Baltimore Conference under which he was informally indicted. Is this a legal indictment? This question involves another. Had this Conference a right to make a term of membership on the subject of slavery? Did Mr. Harding, or any other member, hold his membership under this legislation, or under the rules of Discipline? There surely can be no room for difference of opinion here. The Conference had no such legislative powers, and all attempts to suspend the membership of Mr. Harding upon conditions defined by their legislation, is wholly illegal. So confident am I of the correctness of this position, that at a proper time I may safely appeal to the bench of Bishops—some one or more of whom presided in this Conference—for the authority by which this was done. The matter involves higher responsibilities than that of the mere Conference. Why was it that an accredited member of this Conference was put upon his trial under an indictment framed upon the legislation of the Baltimore Conference? (Bishop Morris replied it was not so—he was tried for a breach of the Methodist Discipline.) Sir, you must stand corrected on this point. The document—the written indictment—is proof to the contrary. The argument of counsel on this floor makes him directly responsible for a breach of the "*law of the Baltimore Conference,*" on the ground that he was not ignorant of, but knew the law, its purpose, and design. The reply of the Bishop (for which I thank him) is a full concession that to try him for his membership, under any law of the Conference, was a wholly illegal proceeding. The indictment itself is the proof that he was so tried, and its illegality all must admit. Our Bishops are sent to preside in the Annual Conferences, for the specific purpose of preserving a unity in the administration by keeping them within the limits defined in the charter. I repeat, therefore, that at the proper time I may request the reason of this oversight. If, then, the indictment be illegal, the verdict and penalty which arose upon it are each illegal; the whole transaction is illegal, and a reproach to the Conference, and should be set aside as null and void.

The verdict, I say, is *unjust*, as well as illegal.

He was convicted, the Bishop tells us, and so the counsel argued also, for a breach of the Methodist Discipline. Allow, for the sake of argument, that this was so; it is still true that he was not indicted—he was not charged with this offense. And can it be just to indict a man for one offense, and try him for another? Or what amounts to the same, render a verdict against him for being guilty of another! And will this body sanction a proceeding so contrary to all the forms of law, and so utterly subversive of all the principles of justice? I trust not. I can hardly persuade myself that the most rabid and fanatical feeling on the subject of slavery which can be supposed to exist in any part of this house, could betray you into a decision so violative of all the principles of right reason. But it is assumed in the argument of the counsel that the legislation of the Baltimore Conference in the case is in conformity with the rules of Discipline on the subject of slavery. Allow this to be so, it does not help the cause of the Conference; for it would only be a conviction of a breach of Methodistic rules *by induction* merely. No one, I presume, should contend for the legality or justice of an act depriving him of his ministerial office, held under the rules of Discipline, when he was only convicted of a violation of these rules by *induction*. And, sir, we deny all right to an Annual Conference to pass resolutions interpreting the rules of the Discipline, and then trying their members under such resolutions, as the statutes of the Church. Such powers in an Annual Conference would entirely supersede the General Conference.

Again, we do not allow that the "law of the Baltimore Conference," in this case, is in accordance with the Discipline of the Church on the subject of slavery. We do not, therefore, allow that the appellant was *justly* convicted of a breach of Methodist rule by *induction* even. I need not go over the ground occupied on this point in my first speech. I will only meet the issues raised by the argument of counsel. First, he maintains, on behalf of the Conference, that the rule in relation to traveling preachers holding slaves requires an unconditional manumission, without regard to the fact whether or not the slave be permitted to enjoy his freedom under the laws of the State. He argues a distinction in the rules as to apply to members or to local preachers, and to traveling preachers. Sir, I propose to meet his argument fairly and squarely. He maintains that the rule, standing as the second answer to the questions on slavery, page 196, requires the traveling preacher to manumit his slaves, whether the laws permit them to enjoy freedom within the State or not. (If I do not state him correctly, let him put me right.) Now, sir, let it be regarded that the *first* answer in this section of Discipline, in which there is no ambiguity of language, settles the entire question of eligibility to office in the Church, so far as slavery is concerned—eligibility to any order in the ministry, to any office in the Church. The rule in regard to traveling preachers was passed in 1800. This, which covers the whole ground of eligibility, was adopted in 1816. It may, therefore, be taken as a fair exponent of the point in the former, which is supposed to be doubtful. Again, sir, the counsel overlooks the fact, in criticising this point, that the traveling preacher is only required to execute a "deed of emancipation" in this specified condition, "if it be practicable." Now surely, sir, it was not the design to require the *mere* execution of a deed! *This*, at all times, *is* practicable. The meaning of the rule is plainly this: it requires a traveling preacher to secure the *actual freedom* of his slaves, "conformably to the laws of the State in which he lives," "if it be practicable"—that is, if the laws will permit them to enjoy liberty.

But it is farther argued, that Harding's case is not covered by the rule of Discipline, because the laws of Maryland *do permit* the liberated slave to enjoy his freedom. I will not go over this point, which has been set before the Conference in the most satisfactory manner by reading the laws of the State, accompanied by the opinions of two gentlemen of great legal distinction in the State of Maryland, showing beyond doubt that this position of the counsel in the case is incorrect. Again, sir, if this were a doubtful point in itself, we have shown in opening this case, from the express statute of the State of Maryland, and the highest legal opinion upon it, Judge Key and the Hon. W. D. Merrick, both of Maryland, that Mr. Harding had no interest in the slaves of his wife, farther than what related to the proceeds of their labor. *He could not, without the consent of his wife*, execute a legal deed of emancipation, as he was required by the Conference to do. I do not know that a similar law exists in any State in this Union. So that if the laws of any State in the Confederacy cover the case of any member in the Church who has become possessed of slaves by marriage, the case of Mr. Harding is protected by the laws of the State in which he lives. Indeed, sir, it appeared to me that the counsel after all yielded this question—if my ear correctly caught his meaning. He argued vehemently against the laws of Maryland as most iniquitous in their tendency—such as no man ought to submit to. In this, sir, he yielded the point, and I claim the decision on behalf of the appellant. Surely this body will not give a decision in the teeth of State legislation, and also of an article of our religious faith, acknowledging the authority of the civil legislature, and an express statute in the Book of Discipline.

One other point, sir. Brother Collins allows what was implied by the silence of Brother Tippett, that if the appellant had been understood to "pledge himself and his wife, if the slaves should consent, to send them to Liberia, or to a free State, this case had never come here." The record itself, which has been read before this Conference, shows that he refused to give the required "pledge" *on the ground that he could not do it consistently with the laws of the State.* (I quote from memory, the journal not being before me.) This fully warrants the inference that he stood pledged to free his slaves on the terms provided by law—nay, the record committed him to do this. The law allows of emancipation, provided they will leave the State. The journal, therefore, is against the position of the counsel; for it is a fair inference from the record, that he was ready to free his slaves, with their consent to leave the State. This pledge necessarily involved the consent of his wife, who held the legal title. The recollection of Brother Gere is therefore correct, and that of the other members of the delegation is at fault. The counsel is still farther at fault. He affirmed, over and over again, that the argument urged by me, from the late law of Maryland, fixing the legal title to the slaves of Mrs. Harding, was an after-thought

—that he never heard of it before. This is particularly unfortunate, for he allows that the legal opinion of the Hon. W. D. Merrick was before the Conference; and in this he specifically alludes to the fact that the legal title to the slaves was in Mrs. Harding, and not in him. And yet, in the face of this clearly-implied pledge, and the proof of utter inability to effect the legal emancipation of the slaves without their consent, so rabid were they to effect an abolition purpose, that they expelled him the body.

Then, sir, I maintain the appellant violated no rule of Discipline. He only violated a law of the Baltimore Conference—a law which they had no right to make; and which, being made, is a plain and palpable contravention of the existing rule of Discipline on the subject. The indictment, then, is illegal; the verdict is equally unjust; and the penalty, by consequence, unwarranted and oppressive.

The 23d Article of our faith acknowledges the supreme authority of the State in all civil matters. The Conference act specifically subjects our rules on slavery to be controlled by State legislation. This, be it observed, is in special conformity with the article of religion just alluded to. It has been shown, from the statutes of Maryland, that the legal title to these slaves *was not* in Mr. Harding, but in his wife. It is farther shown, that if the title *was* in Harding, that he could not secure the freedom of the slaves without compelling them to go to Liberia, or to a free State. Now, if the decision of this Conference sustain the Baltimore Conference, you will require Harding to execute a legal deed, manumitting slave property which does not belong to him. You also require him to secure their freedom, contrary to the provisions of the laws of the State, (provided they *were* his,) which allows of their freedom only when they consent to leave the State. In all this will you not place yourselves in the most ridiculous attitude before the world? Will you not perpetrate a most wanton act of injustice toward the appellant? Will you not adopt a measure the most reckless of the claims of humanity that can be imagined? For, if Mr. Harding obeys your mandate, and manumits the slaves, without their consent to leave the State, *they will be forced*, under the operation of the civil authority, to dissolve the ties which now bind parents to children and other near relatives. In addition to this, you set up your authority in the premises as *supreme*, in plain and palpable violation of the 23d Article of religion, and the rule of Discipline in conformity thereto, which binds you, in the most solemn manner, to be subject to the civil legislature on the subject of slavery. Are you prepared for all this?

Again, Mr. Harding was tried according to the

indictment brought in by the committee, not for a breach of your Discipline, but for a violation of a law of the Baltimore Conference. If you sustain the Conference, you acknowledge the authority of an Annual Conference to legislate laws or conditions of membership in the body, in palpable violation of the constitution and Discipline of the Church, which assigns this authority to the General Conference alone. Are you prepared for this?

And still farther. The law of the Baltimore Conference, under which the appellant was bound, is not only unauthorized by the Discipline, but in flat violation of the compromise act of Discipline. If you sustain the Conference, you render null and void the plain construction of the Discipline under which hundreds of traveling and local ministers now hold office and orders in the Church. Are you prepared for all this? Surely you are not, unless you are prepared to dissolve the bonds which bind us together as a confederated body. I ask, then, that you sustain the appeal, and release Francis A. Harding from the act of the Baltimore Conference, by which he stands suspended from the ministry, which he has held with acceptability and usefulness for several years.

But if, after all, you should feel yourselves still in difficulty on any one point of argument or testimony out of which the foregoing conclusions are made to arise, then let it be remembered that the reading of the journal shows a manifest informality, while the face of the indictment itself is without all due form of law or usage, and well calculated to embarrass the decision. In view of this fact, the least the appellant has a right to expect is, that you should return him for a new trial. With these remarks, sir, I submit the case.

On the following day Dr. Smith asked permission to make some farther observations, of a personal character, in reference to Mr. Harding.

Considerable opposition was made to this, on the ground that both parties had been allowed a most extended and patient hearing, and that it was time the debate was closed.

The motion was put, and carried.

Dr. Smith said it would be remembered that a motion to locate Mr. Harding had been made at the Baltimore Conference; that either, on suggestion, it was withdrawn, or, being ruled out, the motion fell to the ground. He believed the reason of that movement was, that the only proper ground for location is unacceptability, which could not be alleged in this case. An impression, however, in consequence of that motion, having gone abroad prejudicial to the character of the appellant, either as to his prudence, or talent, or general acceptability, he (Dr. S.) begged the Conference to bear in mind that even were such impressions correct, the question before them was, the legality or the illegality of his suspension on the ground alleged in the record, and that alone was the question for their decision. At the same time he took that opportunity of saying, that the impression, however it might have been circulated, was altogether false.

Mr. Collins said that Dr. Smith had mistaken the reason of the withdrawal of the motion for location. The true reason was, that it was thought that rule was not the proper one to be applied to him, and the rule under which he had been tried was the proper one.

At the close of these observations the call for the vote became general, and Mr. Early moved that the decision of the Baltimore Conference be reversed. The same being seconded, was put, and a call made for the ayes and noes. The Secretary proceeded to read the names. Dr. Olin desired to be excused, on the ground that he had not heard the journals read, and had only heard a portion of the debates. Sometimes it was a pleasant thing to avoid a responsibility; but in this case he had no disposition to shrink from responsibility, and would much rather have voted, but he could not do it conscientiously.

The Conference excused him.

The Secretary announced the votes to be, noes 117, ayes 56; being a majority against the reversal of 61.

The President announced that this vote affirmed the decision of the Baltimore Conference. The decision of the chair was appealed against, but was sustained by a vote of 111 to 53.

Dr. Smith. I must and do ask the privilege of spreading my protest on the pages of the Conference journal, and I do so because, to my own personal knowledge, there are men on the floor of this house who voted against the resolution of Mr. Early because they deliberately and solemnly thought that the matter ought to go back to the Baltimore Conference. But by a majority we have been ruled out, and a fair decision of this Conference has not been given. And I wish my protest to go forth to the American Church, and American people, to serve as a beacon-light to warn the Church against the movements of a majority who can obliterate justice, and trample on the rights of a minority.

A long conversation arose as to whether the vote refusing to reverse the decision of the Baltimore Conference confirmed that decision. A multiplicity of motions and amendments were made, but eventually the discussion turned upon Dr. Smith's request to enter his protest. It was moved that he have liberty to enter the same, when Mr. Wiley said they had better wait and see what it was first, and then they could decide whether it should be entered upon the journal or not.

Dr. Smith said he trusted he knew too well what was due to himself as a gentleman, to those that acted with him, and to the Conference generally, to address them in any other than respectful terms; but if they thought the paper would be what they would like, they would find themselves mistaken. No! they would not like that paper, for it would contain truths that would burn in their cheeks. (Cries of "order," etc.) I am perfectly calm. I have got the floor, and you have got the votes; and you can, having the votes, put me down. Time was when such an excitement would have unarmed me, and thrown me off my defense; but no storm of excitement can now disarm me of my self-possession. You cannot drive me from my position; and you might as well attempt to chain the lightnings, or confine the winds in the caves of Eolus, as to put me down when I have a right to be heard. I shall prepare such a memorial as will fearlessly and thoughtfully express the sentiments of myself and those that think with me; and no consideration shall induce me to speak with timidity or fear at such a crisis.

Mr. Early said he hoped they would remember that large majorities were apt to be tyrannical—he trusted they would keep calm. He was quite so—as much as the affliction in which that vote had involved him, and those around him, would allow. After some farther conversation, the order of the day was resumed.

The intelligence of the action of the General Conference in the case of Mr. Harding was received throughout the South with feelings of sadness. It was regarded by the Church as an infringement upon the Constitution under which the two sections had lived and labored together so long in harmony.

The name of Dr. William A. Smith had been familiar to the Church for several years previous to 1844. His commanding talents, his sterling integrity, his fervent piety, his uncompromising devotion to principle, and his ardent love for Methodism, had earned for him a wide-spread reputation in the Church; but in his able defense of constitutional Church-government, as set forth in his speeches in the case of Mr. Harding, he attracted, as he had never before done, the attention of both the Church and the nation. In the gigantic strength of his mighty intellect he had scarcely a peer. Standing from this period in the front ranks of the American ministry, he seemed to live far in advance of all his contemporaries. In the family and social circle he possessed the simple-heartedness of a child—everywhere else a giant.

After a long and useful life, he entered into

rest. His last illness found him in the family of his friend, the Rev. John C. Granbery, D.D., in the city of Richmond, Virginia, where, on the first day of March, 1870, he breathed his last.

We copy the following tribute to his memory from the Minutes of the Virginia Conference:

The committee appointed to prepare a paper which shall express the sentiments of this Conference in regard to the death of Rev. Wm. A. Smith, D.D., report a sketch of his life, and the following resolutions in honor of his memory:

On the list of our dead for the year now closing, with grief and veneration we place the name of William Andrew Smith. We know that his work and fame are not the exclusive property of this Conference, but belong to the whole M. E. Church, South, of which he was so eminent a minister, if we should not rather say to American Methodism. It is also true that his name has appeared the three past years on the minutes not of the Virginia, but of the St. Louis Conference. Yet living, he was ours; and now that he is dead, we claim him, in a special sense. His large heart embraced the entire Church, his wise counsels guarded and fostered her general interests, his great abilities shed luster upon her name; and it is meet that Bishops and Conferences should do him honor,

Let the West cherish his memory on account of his two years of faithful pastoral labor in the city of St. Louis, and of that great and lasting work to which he devoted his extraordinary powers during the last year of his life—the establishment of Central University on a deep and broad foundation, not less by the awakening of a profounder interest on the subject of education, hallowed by religion, among the ministry and people, than by the collection of funds for an endowment. But in the bounds of our Conference he was born, brought up, converted; of this body he was a member more than forty years; of our history he is a large, essential, illustrious part; to us he gave his love and service from youth to old age, and we are glad to acknowledge the debt of gratitude and affection we owe him; among us he died, and in the beautiful cemetery of Hollywood in Richmond his dust reposes, awaiting the resurrection-morn. To some of us he was a brother dearly beloved, to more of us an honored father: if others loved him, we yet more.

Wm. A. Smith was born in Fredericksburg, Va., Nov. 29, 1802. His mother was a consistent member of the Methodist Church, and in death prayed that her son might live to preach the glorious gospel. His father was a man of honorable character and position. Both died when he was of a tender age. For a time the orphan boy had rough usage; but he was afterward adopted and brought up by Mr. Russell Hill, a friend of his father, and a worthy merchant of Petersburg. When seventeen years old, he was converted, and joined the M. E. Church. He had received a good English education, and had commenced the study of the classics; but feeling that he was called of God to the ministry, and not being able to attend college as he desired, he studied privately one year at the house of his uncle, Mr. Porter, in Orange county, and taught school two or three years in Madison. In 1824 he traveled the Gloucester Circuit under the Presiding Elder; in February, 1825, he was admitted on trial into the Virginia Conference. In 1833, while agent for Randolph Macon College, then in its infancy, he met with a fearful accident: the carriage which he was driving upset and fell on him, breaking his right thigh and dislocating his left hip, and badly laming him for life. He was a delegate to the General Conference of the M. E. Church every session from 1832 to 1844, and occupied a high position in that great council as an adviser and debater. In the memorable appeal case of Harding, and in the yet more important extrajudicial trial of Bishop Andrew, which led to the division of the Church, he won a reputation wide as the United States, and inferior to that of no minister of any denomination, for the highest deliberative and forensic eloquence.

He was a member of the Louisville Convention which organized the M. E. Church, South, and of all the General Conferences of this Church to the date of his death. He commanded universal respect and confidence among his brethren by the sincerity of his zeal, the wisdom of his counsels, and the power of his reasoning. His impress will long remain on the legislation and institutions of Southern Methodism. In 1846 he was called from the regular pastorate, by the urgency of the trustees of Randolph Macon College, sanctioned by the Virginia Conference, to the presidency of this institution. He was selected for that place because his courage, energy, and strength of intellect, seemed indispensable, not only to the prosperity, but even to the saving, of this noble institution. Twenty years of his life were consecrated to this cause—years of self-sacrifice, of unremitting toil, of courageous battling with difficulties and victory over them; of hope where others desponded, of faith where others doubted, of resolution where others wavered. He was diligent in his study, diligent in his lecture-room, diligent in travel through Virginia and North Carolina to collect money and to arouse interest in behalf of the College. The number of students steadily increased, the standard of scholarship was elevated, and through the joint efforts of Dr. Smith and the agents of the College, an endowment-fund of $100,-

000 was raised. Then came the terrible war which emptied those classic halls, and swept away the funds which had been gathered with so much toil. Yet not in vain had he labored. Scores of ministers, hundreds of pious young men, educated under his care, molded by his influence, are this day in their several spheres carrying on the same grand work to which he was devoted, and have learned, from his teachings and example, never to surrender, never to despair of Randolph Macon.

We have not spoken of Dr. Smith as a preacher and pastor. He soon rose to eminence in the ministry, and stood with the foremost in the pulpit and pastorate for faithfulness, ability, and success. He had a deep, distinct, happy, constant experience of the saving grace of God in Christ Jesus. His zeal for the cause of religion was pure, steady, consuming. He was fully consecrated to the work of the ministry. The doctrines and polity of our Church had no stronger, nobler expounder and champion than he. His sermons were "logic on fire"—grand and solid discussions of the leading truths of the gospel, animated with deep emotion. Thousands were converted under his ministry; many of them became preachers of the word, in our own and in other denominations; the Churches he served were ever edified and trained, not less by his pastoral fidelity than by his luminous discourses.

As a man, he was of marked character. Who, that ever saw him, could forget that bold, frank, noble face and forehead, which revealed at a glance the lofty attributes of his intellect, the loftier attributes of his heart? Cunning and deceit he knew not; to fear he was a stranger; his convictions he was ever ready to avow and maintain. Yet, with all his courage and indomitable energy of will, he had a tender, sympathetic heart, and much of a child-like spirit, simple, unselfish, trustful, easy to be entreated.

In the fall of 1866 he was transferred to the St. Louis Conference. In the summer of 1869 he visited Virginia to build up his shattered constitution. He suffered severely with chronic dysentery, complicated with other disorders, and grew worse each succeeding month, until he breathed his last March 1, 1870, in the city of Richmond. He retained the clearness of his faculties, and delighted to speak of the great themes of Christianity, especially that saying of John, "God is love." He told us that from the day he gave his heart to God in youth, that self-surrender had never been recalled, and his trust in Christ had never wavered. He compared his state of mind to a lake embosomed in a deep forest, whose peaceful surface the rough winds could not reach.

We offer for adoption by the Conference the following resolutions:

1. *Resolved,* That in the death of Rev. Wm. A. Smith, D.D., not only has the Church lost a bright and shining light, but this Conference is called to mourn the loss of an honored father, who for many years was to us a strong tower of defense and an able leader in every good enterprise.

2. *Resolved,* That we glorify God in the exalted character, the abundant labors, the enduring fruits of usefulness, and the happy death of Dr. Smith; and that we will cherish his memory, and teach our children to hold him in honor.

3. *Resolved,* That we convey to his widow and children the assurance of our deep sympathy in their bereavement, and of our prayers that the blessing of Providence and the comfort of the Holy Spirit may be richly vouchsafed to them in their hour of need.

4. *Resolved,* That Rev. J. E. Edwards and Asa Snyder be appointed a committee to procure a suitable monument and have it placed over the grave of Dr. Smith, and that they be authorized to receive contributions to defray the expenses of the same.

LEROY M. LEE,
J. C. GRANBERY,
D'ARCY PAUL.

CHAPTER II.

The influence of the action of the General Conference in the case of Francis A. Harding—Resolution of Drs. Capers and Olin—Speeches of Drs. Olin and Durbin—Committee of Pacification appointed—Dr. Durbin's resolution, proposing a day of fasting, humiliation, and prayer—The committee fail to agree on any plan of compromise—Resolution of Mr. Collins in reference to Bishop Andrew—Report of the Committee on Episcopacy—Bishop Andrew's statement—The report of the committee made the special order of the day for the 22d of May—Great interest felt—Alfred Griffith's speech—Benjamin M. Drake's motion to amend the preamble—Bishop Soule addresses the Conference—Speeches of Peter P. Sandford and Dr. William Winans—Speeches of Elias Bowen and Dr. Lovick Pierce—Speeches of Jerome C. Berryman, Seymour Coleman, Dr. Smith, and Thomas Stringfield—Sketch of Thomas Stringfield—Speech of Thomas Crowder—Sketch of Thomas Crowder—Speech of Dr. Nathan Bangs.

The influence of the action of the General Conference in the case of Francis A. Harding was felt throughout the Church. It was not difficult for any one of ordinary discernment to foresee that it must result in the alienation of one section from the other.

The South in this case had only demanded what was pledged by the constitutional enactments and provisions of the Church. With less than this, they could not and ought not to have been satisfied. But this now being denied them by a dominant majority, they could no longer feel secure in the rights and privileges which had been guaranteed them by the Discipline. The North at the same time, inflated with victory, were unwilling to yield any advantage they had achieved in a contest in which some of them had been struggling for the mastery for years. The General Conference, however, was not without conservative men who resided in the North, and who were anxious to avert the catastrophe which threatened not only the peace, but the continued unity, of the Church. Among these, Dr. Stephen Olin, of the New York Conference, and Dr. John P. Durbin, of the Philadelphia Conference, were prominent. Dr. Olin had spent several years of his ministry in the South Carolina Conference, and Dr. Durbin was born and reared in Kentucky; and they were fully aware that the recent action of the General Conference must imperil, if not destroy, Methodism in the South, unless some pacific measures should be adopted. In connection with Dr. William Capers, of the South Carolina Conference, Dr. Olin signed the following resolution, which was presented:

"In view of the distracting agitation which has so long prevailed on the subject of slavery and abolition, and especially the difficulties under which we labor in the present General Conference, on account of the relative position of our brethren North and South on this perplexing question; therefore,

"*Resolved*, That a committee of three from the North and three from the South be appointed to confer with the Bishops, and report within two days as to the possibility of adopting some plan, and what, for the permanent pacification of the Church."

A member moved as an amendment that three delegates from the Middle States be added to the committee.

Dr. Capers said: There are only two points named in the resolution—slavery and abolition. I presume there must have been such an interpretation put upon the resolution as the writer did not mean. I did not intend to say that this General Conference was made up of either proslavery men or abolitionists, and that there is a third party, who are neither. The question has only two sides—slaveholders and non-slaveholders. These two positions present, perhaps, in the different aspects; the general state of the Church. Two interests only are generally recognized; and in providing for the committee, I am far from intending to say that all the brethren in the non-slaveholding States are abolitionists, any more than that the others are all slaveholders. If in this view I am mistaken, I am unfortunate.

A motion to lay the amendment on the table was made, and Dr. Durbin, and almost at the same moment Dr. Olin also, rose. Dr. Durbin offered to give way, but the chair said that Dr. Olin could not speak to the original motion, and Dr. Durbin proceeded. He hoped the amendment would not prevail. He understood Dr. Capers to mean by the North, non-slaveholding States, (Dr. Capers assented,) so that the chair could appoint either from the North, East, or West.

The motion to lay the amendment on the table was carried.

Dr. Olin spoke to the original motion. He spoke under the most powerful emotion, and in a strain of tenderness that moved every member of the Conference. He said he felt, from his relation to the Conference as a member for the first time, it became him to explain why his name was attached to the resolution. It had been shown to him within five minutes, and he had asked upon it the advice of one whose opinion was entitled to great weight. He could not refuse to second it, believing it was offered in a spirit of conciliation. He had feared for these two or three days that, though possibly they might escape the disasters that threatened them, it was not probable. He had seen the cloud gathering, so dark that it seemed to him there was no hope left for them unless God should give them hope. It might be from his relation to both extremities, that, inferior as might be his means of forming conclusions on other topics, he had some advantages on this; and from an intimate acquaintance with the feelings of his brethren in the work, he saw little ground of encouragement to hope. It appears to me (he continued) that we stand committed on this question by our principles and views of policy, and neither of us dare move a step from our position. Let us keep away from the controversy until brethren from opposite sides have come together. I confess I turn away from it with sorrow, and a deep feeling of apprehension that the difficulties that are upon us now threaten to be unmanageable. I feel it in my heart, and never felt on any subject as I do on this. I may take it for granted that we speak as opponents here. I have had no part in this controversy. It has pleased God that I should be far away, or laid upon a bed of sickness. I have my opinions and attachments, but I am committed by no act of mine to either side; and I will take it on me to say freely that I do not see how Northern men can yield their ground, or Southern men give up theirs. I do indeed believe, that if our affairs remain in their present position, and this General Conference do not speak out clearly and distinctly on the subject, however unpalatable it may be, we cannot go home under this distracting question without a certainty of breaking up our Conferences. I have been to eight or ten of the Northern Conferences, and spoken freely with men of every class, and firmly believe that, with the fewest exceptions, they are influenced by the most ardent and the strongest desire to maintain the Discipline of our Church. Will the Southern men believe me in this—when I say I am sincere, and well informed on this subject? The men who stand here as abolitionists are as ardently attached to Methodist Episcopacy as you all. I believe it in my heart. Your Northern brethren, who seem to you to be arrayed in a hostile attitude, have suffered a great deal before they have taken their position, and they come up here distressed beyond measure, and disposed, if they believed they could, without destruction and ruin to the Church, to make concession. It may be that both parties will consent to come together and talk over the matter fairly, and unbosom themselves, and speak all that is in their hearts; and as lovers of Christ keep out passion and prejudice, and with much prayer call down the Holy Spirit upon their deliberations, and feeling the dire necessity that oppresses both parties, they will at least endeavor to adopt some plan of pacification, that if they may go away it may not be without hope of meeting again as brethren. I look to this measure with desire rather than with hope. With regard to our Southern brethren—and I hold that on this question, at least, I may speak with some confidence—if they concede what the Northern brethren wish—if they concede that holding slaves is incompatible with holding their ministry—they may as well go to the Rocky Mountains as to their own sunny plains. The people would not bear it. They feel shut up to their principles on this point. They love the cause, and would serve God in their work. I believe there is not a man among them that would not make every sacrifice, and even die, if thereby he could heal the division. But if our difficulties are unmanageable, let our spirit be right. If we must part, let us meet and pour out our tears together; and let us not give up until we have tried. I came into this Conference yesterday morning to offer another resolution. It was that we should suspend, now that the Sabbath had intervened, and shed its calmness and quiet over our agitated spirits, that we should suspend our duties for one day, and devote it to fasting and prayer that God may help us, so that, if we have not union, we may have peace. This resolution partakes of the same spirit. I cannot speak on this subject without deep emotion. If we push our principles so far as to break up the Connection, this may be the last time we meet. I fear it! I fear it! I see no way of escape. If we find any, it will be in mutual moderation, in calling for help from the God of our fathers, and in looking upon each other as we were wont to do. These are the general objects I had in view in seconding the resolution, as they are of him who moved it.

The reverend gentleman sat down amid the most deep and hallowed excitement, and the responsive prayers of the whole Conference.

At the close of Dr. Olin's speech, Dr. Durbin addressed the Conference. He had but a word to say. He could never forget the scene before him that morning. Dr. Olin had said that he scarcely indulged the hope, though he felt a strong desire, that the measure proposed would be successful. For himself, he thought he could discern light, notwithstanding the darkness that hung around the question; and he felt not only a *desire*, but a strong *hope*, that they should yet be delivered from the dangers which impended over their heads. Yes, he clung to the hope of the continued unity of the Church. Abraham, in great difficulties, believed in hope against hope, and yet most gloriously realized his hope, and became the father of many nations. He said he saw ground for this hope in the tenderness of spirit which had been manifested so generally since the introduction of the resolution; and he felt now, as he had felt since his arrival in the city, the most confident assurance that brethren of all parties would sacrifice every thing but their ulterior principles, for the continued unity of the Church. Dr. Olin had told them very justly, that if they said slavery, *under all circumstances*, is incompatible with the functions of the gospel ministry, they put their brethren in the South in a position which must destroy all hopes of usefulness on their part in the Church. Sir, (continued Dr. D.,) we have not said this; we cannot say it; the committee will not say it. I do not believe our gallant vessel is yet to be unloosed from her moorings. She was exposed to a dangerous rock in the South, and an equally dangerous one in the North. There is an open sea between them. The brethren of the North will not drive us upon the rock in the South, if the brethren in the South will not drive us upon the rock in the North. If the committee address themselves to the difficulties in the spirit which now pervades the Conference, we shall yet see brighter and better days. The two days, during which the committee will have this subject under consideration, will be an era in the history of Methodism, and I think that one of them at least should be observed as a day of fasting and prayer. The Wesleyan Conference in England, after the death of Mr. Wesley, was on the brink, apparently, of dissolution, and yet the wise counsel of a few brethren, and the compromising spirit of the general body, devised a plan of permanent pacification. I would say, then, let every heart and tongue be quiet during these momentous two days. It is almost in my heart to say, Cursed be he that shall speak a word to inflame or exasperate any one, while this subject is in the hands of the committee.

In the discussion of this resolution, in addition to the gentlemen already named, Mr. Drake, of the Mississippi, Mr. Crandall, of the New England, Mr. Early and Dr. Smith, of the Virginia, and Mr. Dow, of the New York Conference, took part. On motion of Mr. Collins, the resolution was unanimously adopted, after changing the verbiage, substituting the words "a committee of six," for "a committee of three from the South and three from the North." Dr. Capers, of South Carolina, Dr. Winans, of Mississippi, and Mr. Early, of Virginia, represented the South in the committee; while the North was represented by Dr. Olin, of New York, Mr. Crandall, of New England, and Mr. Hamline, of Ohio.

On the same day Dr. Durbin offered the following resolution, which was adopted:

"*Resolved,* That to-morrow be observed by this Conference as a day of fasting and humiliation before God, and prayer for his blessing upon the committee of six, in conjunction with the Bishops, on the present difficulties; and that the hour from twelve to one o'clock be devoted to religious services in the Conference."

In the discussion of the resolution offered by Drs. Capers and Olin, the possibility of the division of the Church was referred to by speakers on both sides of the line. It was very evident, even to a casual observer, that the continued unity of the Church was scarcely to be hoped for.

On the 15th of May, "a few minutes before twelve o'clock, Bishop Soule was invited into the chair by Bishop Andrew, to conduct the prayer-meeting which the Conference" had appointed the day "before under the resolution offered by Dr. Durbin." "Bishop Soule gave out two hymns, and at his request, Brothers Richey and Early, and Brothers Crandall and Winans, led the devotions of the Conference. After these exercises, Bishop Hedding was called into the chair, gave out another hymn, and invited Brothers Capers and Fillmore to lead in prayer."

The committee of six were expected to report on the 16th of May. Instead of presenting their report, Bishop Soule asked, in their behalf, for longer time for consideration. Unable to agree on any plan of compromise, by which the two sections could be reconciled, on the 18th they communicated this intelligence to the Conference.

All efforts at compromise thus far had failed. Neither the resolution offered by Drs. Capers and Olin, asking for the committee of six, nor yet the one offered by Dr. Durbin, had effected any settlement of the points in controversy.

When Dr. Smith said, "The South does not desire disunion—come when it may, it shall be forced upon us," he expressed the sentiment of not only the delegates in the General Conference from the Southern States, but also of the entire laity whom they represented. The South did not desire division—yet to avert it seemed impossible. Nor do we think that the North wished the division of the Church, abstractly considered; but, feeling an opposition to slavery, they resolved to carry their point, though in violation of a solemn compact which had been entered into, and under which the Church had flourished, even if in so doing they would drive the last vestige of Methodism from the South.

Frequent efforts have been made to impress the public mind with the conviction that the connection with slavery, by marriage, of the Rev. James O. Andrew, D.D., one of the Bishops of the Methodist Episcopal Church, had led to the division of the Church, and no pains have been spared to devolve on this distinguished minister of the gospel the responsibility of the separation.

It will be seen, however, that up to this period the name of Bishop Andrew, as connected with slavery, had not been referred to in the official proceedings of the General Conference. The subject had been brought before the Conference in the shape of memorials and petitions, and in the appeal of Mr. Harding. The excitement, too, was already intense. The clouds of disunion were rolling up from the horizon of the Church in every direction, previous to the arrest of the official character of Bishop Andrew. Unwilling as the Southern delegates were to entertain the idea of the division of the Church, they were, nevertheless, forced to apprehend such a result.

Bishop Andrew, however, had become connected with slavery several years previous to this General Conference, without his consent. A lady of Augusta, Georgia, had bequeathed to him a mulatto girl, in trust until she should be nineteen years of age; the will provided that he should then send her to Liberia, if she was willing to go. If, however, she would not consent, then he should retain her and make her as free as the laws of Georgia would admit. When the time arrived, she refused to go to Liberia, and was consequently *legally* the slave of Bishop Andrew. She continued to reside in her own house, on a lot owned by the Bishop—he deriving no pecuniary benefit from her services—and having the privilege of going to Liberia at any time. She, however, steadily refused to leave the State of Georgia, and as the laws of that State would not permit her emancipation, nor admit to record any deed of emancipation, Bishop Andrew was legally her master.

Bishop Andrew had also inherited, by the death of his former wife, a colored boy, whom he could not liberate in the State of Georgia, but whom he proposed to set free as soon as he was prepared to earn his own living, provided he would leave the State.

He had also married a lady in January, 1844, who held certain slaves, inherited from her former husband, and belonging solely to her. Unwilling to become their owner, and the law not permitting their emancipation, he secured them to his wife by a deed of trust.

It will be seen by the above statements, that Bishop Andrew's connection with slavery was accidental, and not in violation of any law of the Church.

The compromise-law, adopted by the General Conference of 1816, that "no slaveholder shall be eligible to any official station in our Church hereafter, where the laws of the State in which he lives will admit of emancipation, and permit the liberated slave to enjoy freedom," was still in full force. This law evidently conveys the meaning not only that where the laws of the State "will admit of emancipation, and permit the liberated slave to enjoy freedom," no slaveholder shall be eligible to any official station in the Church until he manumits his slaves, but also that in those States where the laws will not "admit of emancipation, and permit the liberated slave to enjoy freedom," the owning of slaves should constitute no barrier to *any office.*

In the State of Kentucky, and in other States where the laws admitted of emancipation, and permitted the liberated slave to enjoy freedom, preachers were not elected to orders; while in Tennessee, and the Southern States, it was very common for our preachers to own slaves.

As late as the autumn of 1844, after the action of the General Conference in the cases of Harding and Bishop Andrew, Bishop Janes, who presided over the Kentucky Conference, refused to ordain preachers elected to orders who were slaveholders, but at the same time, in reply to an inquiry made by the Rev. J. B. McFerrin, of the Tennessee Conference, who was present, declared his willingness to ordain any preachers in Tennessee who might be elected to orders, without any reference whatever to their connection with slavery. Bishop Andrew resided in the State of Georgia, and although a slaveholder, was not involved in slavery in any offensive sense. Moreover, the laws of that State would not admit of emancipation, nor could any slave emancipated in Georgia enjoy freedom. And hence, in the eye of the law, he was as fully protected as any other minister in the Church.

The spirit of fanaticism was rife. The doctrines of a "higher law" were threatening to overflow the mound of recognized authority. Emboldened by their success in the case of Mr. Harding, on the 20th day of May, Mr. Collins offered the following preamble and resolution:

"Whereas, it is currently reported, and generally understood, that one of the Bishops of the M. E. Church has become connected with slavery; and, whereas, it is due to the General Conference to have a proper understanding of the matter; therefore,

"*Resolved,* That the Committee on the Episcopacy be instructed to ascertain the facts in the case, and report the result of their investigation to this body to-morrow morning."

On the 21st of the month the committee presented the following report:

The Committee on Episcopacy, to whom was referred a resolution, submitted yesterday, instructing them to inquire whether any one of the superintendents is connected with slavery, presented their report on the subject.

The committee had ascertained, previous to the reference of the resolution, that Bishop Andrew was connected with slavery, and had obtained an interview with him on the subject; and having requested him to state the whole facts in the premises, they presented a written communication from him in relation to this matter, and asked leave to offer it as his statement and explanation of the case:

"To the Committee on Episcopacy:

"Dear Brethren:—In reply to your inquiry, I submit the following statement of all the facts bearing on my connection with slavery. Several years since an old lady, of Augusta, Georgia, bequeathed to me a mulatto girl, in trust that I should take care of her until she should be nineteen years of age; that *with her consent* I should then send her to Liberia; and that in case of her refusal, I should keep her, and make her as free as the laws of the State of Georgia would permit. When the time arrived, she refused to go to Liberia, and of her own choice remains *legally* my slave, although I derive no pecuniary advantage from her, she continuing to live in her own house on my lot, and has been and still is at perfect liberty to go to a free State at her pleasure; but the laws of the State will not permit her emancipation, nor admit such deed of emancipation to record, and she refuses to leave the State. In her case, therefore, I have been made a slaveholder legally, but not with my own consent.

"2d. About five years since. the mother of my former wife left to her daughter, *not to me*, a negro boy; and as my wife died without a will more than two years since, by the laws of the State he becomes legally my property. In this case, as in the former, emancipation is impracticable in the State; but he shall be at liberty to leave the State whenever I shall be satisfied that he is prepared to provide for himself, or I can have sufficient security that he will be protected and provided for in the place to which he may go.

"3d. In the month of January last I married my present wife, she being at the time possessed of slaves, inherited from her former husband's estate, and belonging to *her*. Shortly after my marriage, being unwilling to become their owner, regarding them as strictly hers, and the law not permitting their emancipation, I secured them to her by a deed of trust.

"It will be obvious to you, from the above statement of facts, that I have neither bought nor sold a slave; that in the only circumstances in which I am legally a slaveholder, emancipation is impracticable. As to the servants owned by my wife, I have no legal responsibility in the premises, nor could my wife emancipate them did she desire to do so. I have thus plainly stated all the facts in the case, and submit the statement for the consideration of the General Conference.

"Yours respectfully,
(Signed) "JAMES O. ANDREW."

All which is respectfully submitted.
(Signed) ROBERT PAINE,
Chairman of Committee on Episcopacy.

Upon the presentation of the report of the committee, accompanied by the statement of Bishop Andrew, Mr. Collins moved that the report be laid on the table, to be taken up to-morrow as the special order of the day. His reason for so moving was that a meeting of the Northern delegates was to be held at four o'clock this afternoon. He wished any of the Southern brethren to attend who might choose to do so.

The 22d of May, the time fixed upon for the commencement of the prosecution of Bishop Andrew, on motion, the case was proceeded with.

Mr. Griffith, of the Baltimore Conference, rose and said, I beg leave to present a resolution and suitable preamble in reference to the subject now pending before the Conference, and made the order of the day.

The Secretary then read the following preamble and resolution:

"Whereas, the Rev. James O. Andrew, one of the Bishops of the Methodist Episcopal Church, has become a slaveholder; and, whereas, it has been, from the origin of said Church, a settled policy and the invariable usage to elect no person to the office of Bishop who was embarrassed with this 'great evil,' as under such circumstances it would be impossible for a Bishop to exercise the functions and perform the duties assigned to a general superintendent with acceptance in that large portion of his charge in which slavery does not exist; and, whereas, Bishop Andrew was himself nominated by our brethren of the slaveholding States, and elected by the General Conference of 1832, as a candidate who, though living in the midst of a slaveholding population, was nevertheless free from all personal connection with slavery; and, whereas, this is, of all periods in our history as a Church, the one least favorable to such an innovation upon the practice and usage of Methodism as confiding a part of the itinerant general superintendency to a slaveholder; therefore,

"*Resolved*, That the Rev. James O. Andrew be, and he is hereby affectionately requested to resign his office as one of the Bishops of the Methodist Episcopal Church. ALFRED GRIFFITH,
JOHN DAVIS."

If the trial of Francis A. Harding awakened a

general interest throughout the Church and the nation, that interest was greatly augmented in the case before us. The Conference was held in the Green Street Methodist Episcopal Church, the galleries of which were crowded to overflowing, while the intelligence of the arrest of the official character of Bishop Andrew sent a thrill of sadness to every Southern heart.

As has been already stated, Bishop Andrew had violated no law of the Church. He had exercised the functions of a Bishop in the Methodist Episcopal Church since 1832, at which time he was elevated to the Episcopal office. For the office which had been confided to his trust, he was eminently fitted. His executive abilities were of a high order, his pulpit qualifications commanding, and as a platform speaker he had scarcely a peer among his brethren. His moral and religious character, too, was above reproach. For twelve years he had presided over Conferences in the North as well as in the South, with the greatest acceptability. But he was connected with slavery, it matters not how, and the fell spirit of religious frenzy must strike him down.

The resolution requesting Bishop Andrew to resign his office, having been offered by Mr. Griffith, he addressed the Conference in its support at considerable length. He took the position that "a Bishop is only an officer of the General Conference, created for specific purposes, and for no other than the purposes specified;" that originally it was not "intended to constitute the Bishop an officer for life under all circumstances, but they reserved to themselves, as Annual Conferences, power even to change every feature of the system of government—to change every thing pertaining to the character of the Church, save the doctrines." These views had been held for more than twenty years by Mr. Griffith, and in the radical war against the powers of the Episcopacy, as exercised according to the Discipline in the appointment of Presiding Elders, had been freely expressed by him. They had never, however, been avowed in any previous General Conference.

At the close of the speech of Mr. Griffith, Dr. Longstreet proposed an amendment to the preamble and resolution, to which Mr. Griffith objected. Mr. Drake, of Mississippi, then suggested that the preamble be altered so as to read, "Whereas, Bishop Andrew has become connected with slavery as stated in his communication," to which no objection being offered, the chair announced it incorporated with the preamble and resolution.

Bishop Soule then addressed the Conference, and said, I rise, sir, seeing no other speaker on the floor, and I assure you and the Conference, strange as it may seem, with as perfect calmness of spirit as I ever remember to have possessed at any period of my life. I cannot, and I need not, conceal from you, sir, or from this General Conference, that, since the commencement of this session, I have been the subject of deep mental distress and agony. But in this respect the season of my bitterness has passed away. Conscious that I have pursued, with close thought and prayer, such a course as was within my power to harmonize the brethren, and to strengthen, if possible, the peace and unity of this body and of the whole Church, I have calmly submitted the whole matter to the overruling and superintending providence of Almighty God. I stand connected with this subject individually, and in connection with my colleagues, in a peculiar point of view, but I have at this period no personal interest whatever in the matter. I am, I assure you, willing, entirely willing, so far as I am myself concerned, to be immolated; but I can be immolated only on one altar, and that is the altar of the UNION of the Methodist Episcopal Church. You cannot, all the powers of earth cannot, immolate me upon a Northern altar, or a Southern altar. Here I take my stand, my position. But I did not rise, with the indulgence of this body, this morning, even to touch the merits of the question now before this body. It would ill become me in the relation I sustain to this body and to the Methodist Episcopal Church to do it. But I have risen to suggest to the Conference some considerations which I hope may have their influence upon the mode of conducting this weighty concern. I speak to men of God—to men of experience—to men who have analyzed the elements of human nature, and of ecclesiastical and civil polity—to men of thought, who have been accustomed to trace causes and their effects through all the diversified forms of human society. I speak to Christian men and Christian ministers—I speak to young men, who have not had the same time as the aged, nor the same opportunities from experience and observation, to grasp fully these great and interesting subjects. I trust I shall hear on the floor of this Conference the voice of age and of experience; and I beseech you, brethren, by the deepest interests that can affect our beloved Zion—I beseech you by a voice from the tomb of a Wesley and a beloved Asbury, and from the sleeping-places of our venerated fathers, to let your spirits on this occasion be perfectly calm and self-possessed, and perfectly deliberate. I advise, in the place in which I stand, that the younger men hear the voice of age. I beg you, brethren, to remember that you stand at this moment before several tribunals. You are before (I speak to the General Conference) a tribunal in the galleries; and whatever view you may take of this subject, if they cannot judge of the merits of the case before you, such are their enlightened ideas of what belongs to the spirit of Christianity, and the office of Christian ministers, that they will sit in judgment on you. I would also observe here that, as a great branch of the Protestant Christian community, our position in regard to this subject is unique and distinguished from all other branches of that community. So far as I know, there is not a single sister (Protestant) Church in these United States, or in the world, having any legislation on the subject of slavery. I say, in this we are unique, we are alone. We therefore stand in our action on this subject before the tribunal of all the Christian Churches of our own land, and our actions will certainly be judged of by that tribunal. We act here also in the capacity of a General Conference, and every thing we do here is to go out before the whole body of ministers and people whom we here represent—it is to go out in the face of the whole Church, and they will judge with respect to our action in the premises. We are, too, before the tribunal of public opinion, and statesmen, civilians, and jurists, have an interest in this matter, and they will judge us on other grounds, and in reference to our standards, and rules of action, and not as we shall be judged by the great mass. They will judge by the rules of the "book," according as our action is founded on facts, and is in accordance with the rules of that book which contains the constitution and laws of the Church. This consideration will certainly occupy your minds on this question. I have only to add, and with this remark I shall take my seat, waiting results not without solicitude and anxiety, not without the deepest concern for the perpetual union, and undivided interests of this great body; but calm, and perfectly undisturbed, waiting the issue, and committing all to God. A word about decorum, and the mode of conducting your debates. I myself love to hear hard arguments, but I love to hear them in soft words; and I believe that any man who has carefully weighed this matter will concede that arguments are proportionably stronger as they are conveyed in soft words. The effect of argument in debate certainly does not depend on the loudness with which we speak. It is not necessary to raise your voices so that you may be heard in the remotest parts of this house, and even in the street. Let me admonish brethren who may take part in this discussion, that it is far from being important to their case that they should use great strength of voice, and where this is done an almost universal opinion is awakened that there is undue excitement of passion in the case. Avoid all reflection on each other. Meet brethren's arguments if you can. Confute those arguments if you can, but do it in a Christian spirit, and with a calm and undisturbed mind. Then whatever shall be the report concerning the General Conference, it shall at least be said that we have conducted ourselves with that calmness, and with that Christian and ministerial sobriety, which becomes so grave an assembly, and so grave a question. I thank the Conference for their indulgence while I have spoken.

The Conference was then addressed by Mr. Sandford, of the New York Conference, who supported the resolution exclusively on the ground of expediency, and basing that expediency on the convulsions that would follow, and the loss of very large numbers of their members if they failed to remove Bishop Andrew.

Mr. Sandford was followed by Dr. Winans, of the Mississippi Conference, who made the first speech on the Southern side. "Dr. Winans was an impetuous speaker, after the Greek model, very plain in attire and appearance, wearing no cravat, making no flourishes. But if any adversary supposed that this unpretending exterior indicated a mind of ordinary caliber, he very soon changed his opinion. Massive strength, put in motion by a glowing spirit, furnished a mighty momentum which struck like the swell of the sea when stormy winds rule the waters." He said:

I appreciate the remarks of our venerable superintendent, especially in regard to the manner in which this discussion should be conducted. There is one point, however, on which I must put in a disclaimer against the inference which the Bishop's remarks would warrant. I cannot speak on any subject without speaking loud; and I beg to advertise this Conference, and the spectators, that in speaking loud I give no indication of exasperated feeling. It is the misfortune of my constitution, and depends on no particular excitement on the question, and I approach this subject with as much calmness as I do any other. It may be, sir, that it is the calmness of despair, yet result it from what it may, I *am* calm, and perfectly so. That the Conference has a right, an abstract right, with or without cause, to request any member of that body to retire from the Episcopacy, I am not prepared to deny. I will readily admit, Mr. President, that if you, or any one of your venerable body, should be subject to that fearful misfortune, alienation of mind, it would be proper to obtain your consent to retire from your very important station, if indeed you might be competent to give your consent in such a case. I do not, then, dispute the abstract right of this Conference to memorialize Bishop Andrew on the subject of his retiring from the office he sustains; nor do I conceive it to be out of the limits of that proper right for each member to assign the reasons for adopting a course so unusual. Conceding this right, I claim, on the other hand, a full and perfect right for every member to assign the reasons why he should not join in this request. It is farther the privilege of every member closely to scrutinize, and rigidly to criticise, the reasons assigned for this remarkable act, by those who move it. It will be my purpose to use hard arguments, but not hard terms, though I confess I find it difficult to avoid them. If, however, I do use hard terms, they shall not proceed from hard feelings.

I do not know, sir, whether I am to consider it at all necessary to notice the arguments that have been already presented in support of the request which is attempted to be made to the Bishop. But I shall call your attention, and the attention of the Conference, to the arguments in the preamble of the resolution inviting the Bishop to retire. I say, then, that the first statement, the very first statement or proposition in the preamble is not true. I do not mean to say that those who placed it there intended to state an untruth. I believe they thought it was true when they made the statement; but according to my views of the matter, it is not true that the settled and invariable usage of the M. E. Church has been not to elect a person having slaves to the office of a Bishop. The mere fact that a thing has not been done, does not constitute usage. I admit that it is a fact that no slaveholder has been elected, and it would be true to affirm that it has been the invariable custom of the M. E. Church to choose for Bishops those who were not slaveholders. It may be, sir, that slaveholders have never possessed an individual among them suitable for the office; or sectional matters may have influenced the vote. How are we to arrive at the fact that the mere election of a man not a slaveholder proves the settled usage of not electing slaveholders? The term is improperly employed, and I could prove beyond question that this has not been the usage of the Church. I could take you back to the General Conference at Philadelphia, and show that it was in the purpose of the Western and Middle men to choose for the office of Bishop a slaveholder, and in all probability he would have been elected to the office, had there not been management and interference on the part of the Baltimore Conference to defeat the design. The usage of the Church is not against the election of a slaveholder to the office of Bishop. I will correct myself—I should say, such a Bishop would have been elected, had it not been for the management and trickery, not of the Baltimore Conference, but of certain members of that Conference.

The next point is more palpably untrue than that I have just dismissed. It is not true in point of fact, though it has the show of truth. It goes on the principle that Bishop Andrew was elected to the office on Southern nomination. That some Southern brethren were concerned in his nomination is true, and we do not deny it. But that the Southern party, the great Southern sectional division of the M. E. Church, elected him, is not true, and it is well known not to be the fact. There was a report prevailing that some Southern brethren were drawn into a conspiracy by which the rights of the South would have been invaded. Brother Pickering nominated a man to the office who was known to be a slaveholder, and who would have been elected had not Bishop Andrew—

Mr. Pickering. I would correct the brother. I never nominated any such man.

Dr. Winans. I am glad to be corrected, sir; but there are on the floor of this house those who are enlisted in the enterprise of degrading Bishop Andrew from his office who did propose such a measure. When we stated on this question, that we were prepared to vote for a slaveholder for the office of Bishop, we were met by the introduction of James O. Andrew; and but for this, a slaveholder would, in all probability, have been elected in 1832, and selected by Northern and Western men. I do not believe that I shall be contradicted on this subject, and in contradiction to the statement in the preamble of this resolution I may say, that we only just missed the election of a slaveholding Bishop.

Well, now, sir, what are the facts of the case? Let us look them in the face. Suppose it had been inconsistent with the genius of Methodism—though it is not, and you know it is not, you dare not assert it, for the Discipline stares you in the face if you do—but suppose it was contrary to the Discipline to elect a man to this office who held slaves; suppose all this, what are the facts of the case? Why, that Bishop Andrew had no part in constituting himself a slaveholder, inasmuch as he gave no consent thereto, and had no opportunity of expressing his dissent. This, I presume, will not be denied, inasmuch as the Bishop's statement, having been incorporated in the preamble, was presumed to be true. Well, then, what does he say in the first instance? Why, that without his consent, and indeed against it—for he labored to free the girl who was left to him, but was overruled by the strange fact that the girl, at years of discretion and intelligence, preferred to be a slave, and refused to be set free. This would appear strange to the North, but we in the South know all about it. Well, by the girl's own free and unrestrained determination to continue his slave, he was prevented from emancipating her, and her will bound him up to the destiny of being a slaveholder, in spite of all his desire to the contrary. The other case is of a similar character: the providential devolvement upon him of a slave whom he now declares free to go when and wherever he will, provided there be assurance that he will be provided for, or will be able to provide for himself. Bishop Andrew did not wish to be a slaveholder, but became one in spite of his efforts to the contrary.

Well, he was a slaveholder in 1840, exposed to the malediction of the North, and just as unfit for the general superintendency of the Union in December, 1843, as in January, 1844, for he was then a slaveholder. And what harm was there in marrying a woman who had been pronounced by one of the most venerated of our ministers to be as fit a lady for a Bishop's wife as he ever saw? What evil had he done by becoming a slaveholder farther by that marriage, when he was already a slaveholder beyond control? What had he done, by that marriage, to prejudice his case? Just nothing at all, for he was already a slaveholder by immutable necessity. In forming a matrimonial alliance, in seeking one who was to become the mother of his children and the companion of his declining years, he had married a pious and estimable lady, and that is the whole matter; and yet he is advised to leave the superintendency on this ground. It seems to me that this is the only ground maintained by the advocates of the resolution.

What has he done by executing the deed of

trust? What did he do to alter the position of the slaves? Did he bring upon them any consequences prejudicial to them? Or did he incur any obligation to deprive that lady of her property because she had given him her hand? Why, the position will be this, that James O. Andrew must cease to be a Bishop because he has married a lady; for he has done these negroes no harm by his momentary possession of them. Was it his duty to marry this lady in order that he might set these slaves free? If not, did such duty arise out of the fact that he had married the lady? The proposition condemns itself, inasmuch as a change of relation has taken place by marrying that lady, and he is now no longer a slaveholder except against his consent. By the providence of God at first, and by the unsolicited operations of fellow-beings, he is constituted a slaveholder, from which relation the laws of Georgia will not permit him to disengage himself. Being in this situation, and being exposed to the resentment of the North, he marries an interesting woman, and places her property back in her hands, under the precise circumstances in which it was before the marriage. And in spite of all this, this General Conference gravely meditates the act of removing him from that office he has filled with such entire satisfaction to the Church.

But, sir, the main point relied upon in this matter, is the expediency of the course contemplated. Expediency! Or, in other words, such a state of things has been gotten up in the North and in the West as renders it necessary for Bishop Andrew to retire from the office of the superintendency, if we would preserve the union of the Church. Sir, I will meet this by another argument on expediency. By the vote contemplated by this body, and solicited by this resolution, you will render it expedient—nay, more, you render it indispensable—nay, more, you render it *uncontrollably necessary*, that as large a portion of the Church—and, permit me to add, a portion always conformed in their views and practices to the Discipline of the Church—I say that by this vote you render it indispensably, ay, uncontrollably, necessary that that portion of the Church should —I dread to pronounce the word, but you understand me. Yes, sir, you create an uncontrollable necessity that there should be a disconnection of that large portion of the Church from your body. It is not because there are prejudices waked up by unceasing agitation year after year, in opposition to the spirit and language of the Discipline, but it arises out of the established laws of society —from a state of things that is under the control of political and civil government, which no minister of the gospel can control or influence in the smallest degree. If you pass this action in the mildest form in which you can approach the Bishop, you will throw every minister in the South *hors de combat;* you will cut us off from all connection with masters and servants, and will leave us no option—God is my witness that I speak with all sincerity of purpose toward you—but to be disconnected with your body. If such necessity exists on your part to drive this man from his office, we reässert that this must be the result of your action in this matter. We have no will, no choice in this thing. It comes upon us as destiny; it comes with overwhelming force, and all we can do is to submit to it. Let us, then, pass before you, and then give such weight as you think fitting to the argument for expediency embraced in the preamble to this resolution, and let that determine your vote in this matter. There may come a time when your hearts will bleed at the recollection of having cut off from your body—for we will never go voluntarily—as firm and good friends, and as honest in our attachment to Discipline, as any other portion of the Church. Yes, the time may come in your after-lives when you will lament an act that has been done so hurriedly. I say hurriedly, because it has been scarcely three weeks under consideration—hurriedly, because you have had no intercourse with your societies on the subject—hurriedly, because the question has not even been mooted in those regions where you apprehend your difficulty—and hurriedly, because you are cutting off thirteen hundred preachers and four hundred and fifty thousand members, against whom lies no allegation of having departed from the principles and laws of your Book of Discipline. Sir, I protest against the vote that is sought on this question; and I conjure you by the love of God, by your regard for the Discipline of the Church, and by the interests of the South, to pause ere you take this step. I throw out of the consideration the interests of the masters of slaves, those hated, and abhorred, and despised beings—I leave out of the question the spiritual welfare of thousands of those poor oppressed people for whose interests and welfare you profess so much solicitation—the bleeding slave himself, cut off, by your action, from our approach, ministry, and counsels—I leave these things out of the question, and conjure you to let the union of our beloved Church plead effectually to prevent you from giving the vote which is sought by this resolution. Already, (and perhaps this may be the last time I shall have the opportunity to speak on the floor of this General Conference,) I say, already the evil effects of the abolition excitement are becoming apparent, for to that is to be traced the dire necessity you plead in the case. It has hedged in the poor negro, and shut him up from access to his minister, and it has shut the mouth of the minister, and will you throw the blackness and darkness of death over him by your vote? Will you drive us from the Connection, or will you hold back your hands and prevent the pernicious effects of such action as is at present sought at your hands? I leave the matter with you, and youı conscience, and your God.

Bishop Wightman, in his Life of Bishop Capers, in reference to Dr. Winans's speech, says it was delivered with "true Demosthenean force. The irrepressible emotion, the 'erect countenance,' the flashing eye, and ringing voice, the unfaltering prediction of consequences that were to follow, and resound through all Methodist history, made the speech memorable."

Mr. Bowen, of the Oneida Conference, spoke in favor of the resolution, but in his speech no new argument was presented, advocating simply the plea of expediency.

At the close of Mr. Bowen's speech, Dr. Lovick Pierce, of Georgia, addressed the Conference. In his speech he said:

Can anybody, therefore, expect that this man, blameless before heaven and before this congregation of ministers, even if he were asked to do this thing by two-thirds of this Conference, could do it, would do it, dare do it, with the effects that would grow out of the movement written, with the finger of God, upon his heart? Is it the doctrine of expediency, sir? I believe that this is the only plea that can be put in that has one single vestige either of truth, justice, or propriety; and allow me to say, that unless I am greatly mistaken, the adoption of the resolution now before the General Conference, on the ground of expediency, is an act done by Methodist ministers by which, in the very nature of the case, they invert the established order of the New Testament. In the difficulties which arose in the Church in the days of the great apostle to the Gentiles, he said, in reference to this point, "All things are lawful for me, but all things are not expedient." Shall we ask Bishop Andrew to pay this tribute to expediency? Why, if it were lawful to demand it, and the yielding of it would produce such disastrous results as must be produced, it would be inexpedient for this body of God-fearing ministers to make any such demand. To the law and to the testimony I feel myself bound closely to adhere. I would not say any thing that has been said by any predecessor in this case; yet I beg leave to add, in farther confirmation of the remarks made by my worthy Brother Winans, that of all notions that were ever defended before a body of Christian ministers, the notion of asking an act of this sort on the ground of expediency, when it is as inexpedient for one portion of a united body of Christians to this as it is expedient for the other that it should be done, is, to me, the most fearful mockery of all sound logic. Do that which is inexpedient for us, because for you it is expedient! Never, while the heavens are above the earth, let that be recorded on the journals of the General Conference of the Methodist Episcopal Church! What is the evidence that it is expedient that this thing should be done in any portions of these growing States? The opinion and testimony of the brethren? Take our brethren on their own ground in other portions of the United States equally linked together by that golden chain which, if it be possible to avert it, I pray God may never be broken. Do you ask us how this matter is to be met? It is to be met by the conservative principle and the compromise laws of this Book of Discipline. Show your people that Bishop Andrew has violated any one of the established rules and regulations of the Church, and that he refuses to conform himself to those established laws and usages, and you put yourselves in the right, and us in the wrong.

My beloved brethren, there is but one man older than myself in the land that I live in who is now in the ministry, and he is at present an inefficient man. I am the oldest efficient minister belonging to the Georgia Conference. I never wedded my heart to my family with less desires that this wedlock should be ruptured, than I did to the Church which found me a sinner, and I hope, through God's grace, will land me in heaven. And since the day that I made myself acquainted with the Methodist Church—and will the recording angel write it this moment in the book of eternity?—I affirm, that, so far as religion has been concerned in the South, no question has ever done so much harm to saving godliness as the intermeddling of the Methodist Church with the question of slavery; and could the cap of hell be lifted today, I fear that the groans of many damned would be heard coming up, and dating the ground of their fall from the merciless act of the Church against a free constitution and the laws of the land. The Methodist Church may have had much to do with slavery in the concrete, as it is called, but has no more business with slavery in the abstract than with the tariff; and, what is a great misfortune, you may put what construction you please on your actions and doings in this case, but you have "passed the Rubicon." In the year 1836 I desired that a protest should be entered on the journal of the Conference against what was then believed to be the doctrine, that any man who, by any circumstance, was connected with domestic slavery, should be deemed as living under an act of outlawry with this Church.

Finally, I say, pass this resolution, and the whole of the Southern States are hurled into confusion at once; and the brother that would lie down to be trampled upon by such an act of this body, would be regarded as unworthy the office he held, and unworthy to preach the gospel of Jesus. I am against the resolution, and am glad to make it known that I am against it on principles pure as those that kindle the glory of high heaven—not because I am a pro-slavery man, but because God did not call me to legislate on these matters.

Jerome C. Berryman, of the Missouri Conference, next spoke in opposition to the resolution. He was followed by Seymour Coleman, of the Troy Conference, who was in favor of the resolution. Give them a slaveholding Bishop, he said, and you blow up the fortress from its foundations. He had expected a most peaceful Conference, supposing, as he did, that the firebrands had left their ranks last year, and he thought that now they should have peace in their borders. The Southern brethren knew little of the labors of the Northern men to secure their comfort and safety. Give them a slaveholding Bishop, and they make the whole of the North a magazine of gunpowder, and the Bishop a firebrand in the midst. The position Bishop Andrew sustained in the Church had made this matter to cause more trouble than any thing he had ever known to take place in the Church. The step was wonderfully unfortunate.

To the brief speech of Mr. Coleman, Dr. Smith, of Virginia, made the following reply: He wished to correct the brother in his statement of a fact, and one on which the whole merit of his argument was based. It was that he, in deep sympathy with the South, had successfully warred against abolitionism. They had not so understood it, and if he would make his point good by argument he would have accomplished a great thing. They had viewed it differently, and believed it to be different. The arguments of the abolitionists had been as harmless as the lispings of helpless infancy in their influence on the South. They gained some bad eminence, and were the means of doing harm to the poor blacks. That the North opposed the abolitionists out of sympathy for the South, would demand proof. In 1836 the Northern brethren complained that it was among them that abolitionism was doing all the mischief; that there its desolating footsteps were to be marked and mourned over, and groaned under, as a burden intolerable to be borne. And such was the truth of the case. In 1836 we were asked to leave this matter alone, and were told that the Northern brethren had more at stake than we had. And they succeeded in shutting the mouths of some of the brethren, but not with my consent. They now would have it understood that it was for the South they then labored.

Messrs. Thomas Stringfield, of the Holston Conference, Thomas Crowder, of Virginia, John Spencer, of Pittsburgh, and Dr. Nathan Bangs, of New York, were the next speakers—the two former in opposition to the resolution, and the two latter in favor of it. Messrs. Stringfield and Crowder, in their remarks, were courteous, dignified, convincing. The argument, based upon *expediency*, that had been urged by Northern men, was triumphantly met by Mr. Stringfield. It is *inexpedient*, said he, that Bishop Andrew should resign. If the Bishop be shuffled out of office, some one must be elected to fill his place; and such a one, whoever he may be, will meet with as little favor in the South as Bishop Andrew would, with all his disabilities, in the North. Who, sir, will elbow Bishop Andrew out of the pulpit, and fill his place in our Southern congregations? Will any one do so that lifts his hand in favor of this resolution? It is not likely, sir, that another Southern man will be elected; and, sir, a *line* is to be drawn by this vote. It will be a *test* vote—a *party* vote; and, sir, I know not what sort of heart a man must have that could go to the South, as Bishop Andrew's successor, under these circumstances. I am sure he would be unfit for a Bishop.

I know this is a delicate subject—and some may think it should not be mentioned here—but it will be thought of by the people, and, in spite of us, it will have its bearings. There are two sides to this question. Inexpediency is set over against inexpediency—one evil against another evil; and as a *lesser evil* is a *relative good,* it is to my mind clearly *inexpedient* for Bishop Andrew to resign.

Thomas Stringfield was a Kentuckian by birth, his parents having removed to that State previous to 1796, in which year he was born. Blessed with religious instruction from early childhood, at eight years of age he openly professed faith in Christ. In 1806 his parents removed to Alabama, where he resided until at the age of sixteen years, when, in obedience to his country's call, he entered the American army under General Jackson. In the army he was no less distinguished for his faithful adherence to the religion he professed, than for his intrepid courage in the field of battle. During his connection with the army, while on guard, he received a shot, from an Indian's gun, in the forehead, which left a scar for life.

At the Tennessee Conference in 1816, he offered himself as an itinerant, and was accepted. From the time he entered the ranks as an itinerant preacher until God called him home, he performed the duties of an evangelist with commendable zeal.

A careful examination of the appointments filled

by Mr. Stringfield, and an acquaintance with the territory which they embraced, impresses us at once, not only with the vastness of his labors, but with the privations he endured, and the sacrifices he made for the cause of Christ.

At the General Conference of 1836 he was elected to the editorship of the South-western Christian Advocate, located in Nashville, Tennessee, in which position he remained until 1840.

Retiring from the duties of an editor, he travels for five years as Agent for the American Bible Society, and then returns to the pastoral work, where, with unabated zeal, he prosecutes his high and holy calling. At one time we find him the valiant leader of the hosts on an extensive and laborious District, and then we see him performing the duties of an evangelist in a more circumscribed sphere; and anon as Agent for Strawberry Plains College.

The immense labors he had performed through a period of thirty-seven years, told fearfully upon his constitution, and in 1853 he was placed on the superannuated roll. Rallying again, in 1854 he travels the Dandridge Circuit, and in 1855 is appointed to Loudon Station. Unable longer to go in and out before his brethren in the active duties of an itinerant preacher, he returns to the superannuated list, where he remains until called from labor to reward. At half-past two o'clock, on the 12th of June, 1858, he sweetly fell asleep in Jesus.

Mr. Crowder said: Our Discipline demands of a minister of Jesus Christ the same purity of heart and rectitude of life which are inculcated in the Bible; and if these remain as fair as those of any other elder in the Methodist Episcopal Church, then he has violated no rule of our Discipline—because he could not have a fair moral and ministerial character if he were a transgressor of either the precepts of religion or the rules of Discipline. On what, then, I ask again, does this expediency stand as its foundation? Its foundation, sir, is a combination of circumstances; and this combination of circumstances has been brought about *chiefly* by a spirit which I may call "Legion." But where did this spirit start up? In the South? No, sir; the South has not been troubled at all. Its course has been quiet, obedient, and kind, leaving myself out of the question. The South, sir, has never made your table groan with petitions and memorials for changes in our Discipline. The South has never made any aggressive complaints against the North. Sir, this spirit came up in the North and East; I mean the spirit of "abolition." This spirit has put the causes in operation which have brought about the combination of circumstances that is the basis of this expediency. Now, sir, I ask these fathers and these brethren if this basis of expediency is not too dark in origin, and ruinous in results, on which to depose our beloved Bishop Andrew? Can you do this, brethren?

. . . . . It is well known how seriously the abolition movement affected the South, bringing about strife and division between them and the North. Now, sir, let it go abroad that this General Conference requested Bishop Andrew to resign on the ground of an expediency so doubtful as this, because he may not be cordially received in some portions of the North, and the division of our Church may follow—a civil division of this great confederacy may follow that, and then hearts will be torn apart, master and slave arrayed against each other, brother in the Church against brother, and the North against the South—and when thus arrayed, with the fiercest passions and energies of our natures brought into action against each other, civil war and far-reaching desolation must be the final results. My dear brethren, are you prepared for this? No, I am sure you are not. Then refuse to pass the resolution now pending before the Conference, and permit our beloved Bishop still to go on his way of usefulness, and I am persuaded that the fears which many brethren honestly entertain will never be realized. Brethren, we have, as instruments in the hands of God, been doing a great work in the North and South; let us still work together for the honor of our common Saviour and the salvation of the souls of the people, white and colored—let us bring the hearts of the community generally under the influence of religion, and the work of emancipation will come on as a natural result.

It is with pleasure that we contemplate the character of such a man as Thomas Crowder. He was born in Wake county, North Carolina, September 22, 1797. His parents were members of the Methodist Episcopal Church, were deeply pious, and endeavored to bring up their children "in the nurture and admonition of the Lord."

It had been the intention of Mr. Crowder to prepare for the bar. No profession opened up before a young man of promise at that period a more attractive field than that of the law, and none more readily invited to fortune or to fame. To prepare for this profession, he had labored of nights during his minority, and to attain this object he was prosecuting his collegiate course. But God had destined him for a higher and nobler work.

He entered the Virginia Conference in 1821, and soon took high rank among his brethren, and filled many of the most important appointments in that Conference.

The reply of Mr. Spencer was unworthy the

occasion and the Conference of which he was a representative. He said:

Well, sir, it is alleged that our present action is a novel procedure. Admitted; but whose fault is it? We never, till now, had occasion to complain of any of our Superintendents. We now have, and therefore our proceedings must be new. This is plain. The inquiry is raised, By what rule can we touch Bishop Andrew? What specific rule has he violated? We ought to remember that the mere silence of the Discipline in regard to a particular case is no evidence that action in that case would be contrary to our rules. An illustration will place this in its true light. Suppose that instead of marrying a respectable lady owning slaves, Bishop Andrew had married a colored woman. Would Southern or Northern brethren say, either that he had broken an express rule of Discipline, or that he would nevertheless be well qualified for a Bishop in our Church? Neither the one nor the other. They doubtless would depose him at once, though there is no rule to be found declaring, in so many words, that no white man shall marry a colored woman on pain of degradation. It is thought by some that before the case can be reached a new rule must be made; and if so, it would be an *ex post facto* law. So says some driveler in the Tribune Extra found yesterday in the Conference-room. He was ashamed to give his name, and well he might, as he knew he was meddling with other people's business, and at the same time dealing in slanderous allegations. Let us look at this. An *ex post facto* law is always retrospective. But if we made a rule to rid ourselves of our present difficulty, it would not be to punish a past offense, but to remove from our ecclesiastical car a present incumbrance, and one that must be removed or crush us into ruin.

. . . .

We hear much concerning the Constitution. The word constitutional is repeated again and again. Here I am at a loss. I cannot tell what brethren mean. I suppose the Constitution of our Church to be embodied in our Articles of Religion, our Restrictive Rules, and our General Rules. But where is it said, in these, that a slaveholding Bishop must remain in office despite of the General Conference? or that no rule can be made to touch such a case? Nowhere. Then is it not plain that these are high-sounding words used without meaning? But, sir, much is said of expediency. Well, let us look at *expediency*. It is alleged that it would be a dreadful thing to pass the resolution before us, as a matter of expediency. This is a grave subject. But is not expediency at the foundation of many grave and important subjects? Mr. President, how did you and your colleagues get into the Episcopal office? Expediency put you there, expediency keeps you there, and when expediency requires it, you shall be removed from your seats—yes, every one of you. Expediency is the foundation of our Episcopacy. Nay more, it is the very basis of Methodism. We are conjured by a brother, in a solemn manner, to refrain, lest we ruin souls. He doubts not that, if we could open the doors of perdition, and look down into the world of woe, we should find that souls were lost by being driven from the Methodist Church through her action against slavery in the days of our fathers! I meet this by remarking, some think in that event we would be likely to hear wailings arising from those doomed to hell by reason of our connivance at slavery.

. . . .

Fearful things are said about division. Our feelings have been roused up. We have wept and prayed. The clouds have gathered in the distance. We have seen the lightning. We have heard the muttering thunders. Our destruction is threatened. But if it comes, how can we help it? We have made no change, and we ask none. Who has brought this evil upon us? If we are ruined, on whose head will rest the blood of a murdered Church? The Lord have mercy on us! We now come to this point: Shall we stand by our principles? Will we maintain true Methodism? Or shall we suffer the most daring innovation upon our usages? Must our foundations be uprooted, and our fair edifice be tumbled into destruction, by retaining a slaveholder in the Episcopacy?

The speech of Dr. Bangs was moderate in temper. He congratulated the Conference on the kind and Christian spirit they had hitherto maintained, which he hoped would be preserved through the whole of this important debate. He would make a few remarks on what fell from Dr. Winans. That gentleman had said that the preamble contained in the proposition was not true, because it affirmed that the having a slaveholding Bishop was contrary to usage. Must they adopt a practice to make it contrary to usage? When a practice has always been adopted, it certainly is according to usage. Now (said Dr. Bangs) I think that any thing that has not been introduced into the practice of the Church is contrary to the usage of the Church. This appears to me to be self-evident. But the brother affirmed, if I understood him right, that Northern men were ready to vote for a slaveholding Bishop, and consequently it had like to have become the usage of the Church to have such in the Episcopacy. Now, I never understood from any Northern man that he was willing to vote for a slaveholding Bishop. It was farther affirmed that it was only defeated by trick and management. I do not know any thing about such a trick. I never was in a caucus at all about the nomination of a Bishop. But I have heard from the mover of this resolution, that in 1832, the Baltimore delegation sent a committee to wait on a slaveholder from the South, and ask him if he was willing to emancipate his slaves, if they would nominate him for the office of Bishop. He very courteously, and in a Christian spirit, took time to deliberate, and eventually told them he could not do it, and that was the reason why they declined to nominate him. Did that look like nominating a slaveholder to the Episcopacy? And they nominated James O. Andrew because he was not a slaveholder; but at that time he was not generally known to the General Conference, and I am given to understand that only about a dozen votes were given him from the South, or slaveholding States. At any rate, he had not a majority of the Southern States, and he could not have been elected without the votes of the Northern Conferences. So much, then, as to the allegation that the appointment of a slaveholder to the office of Bishop was not contrary to the usage of the Church and to its principles. We have been uniform on that subject. Now, sir, I wish to correct an error the brother from Virginia made yesterday. He said that this originated in abolitionism. This is a mistake. It is the old Methodistic antislavery feeling, and I would make no allusion either to abolitionists or slaveholders. I love them both, God knows I do. Now, with respect to the propriety of the resolution before the Conference. I think there are many things that would disqualify a man for holding the office of Bishop that do not amount to immorality. Suppose Bishop Hedding should come out and declare that it was a sin to hold slaves under any circumstances. This would identify him with the ultra party, and I would vote for his retiring, because it would disqualify him for his work as Superintendent over the whole Church. I will suppose another case. Let one of our Bishops be unmarried, and go into the work, and marry a free colored woman, would it not, in the sense of the whole community, disqualify him for his office? And yet it would not be an act of immorality. And it is on this principle that I say Bishop Andrew has disqualified himself by connecting himself with slavery, because he cannot acceptably exercise his duties as a general officer of the Church.

Now the doctrine of expediency has been referred to. Let me give you one item of expediency that the Apostle Paul practiced: "If meat make my brother to offend, I will eat no flesh while the world standeth, lest I make my brother to offend;" and if Bishop Andrew had practiced that kind of expediency we should not have had the present difficulty. But his connection with slavery was "against his will!" I will acknowledge that, in the first case, he had no agency; but will any one avow that he was not a free agent when he connected himself with this lady? No one will avow that. He therefore acted imprudently. As was shown by the brother who opened this case, there is a marked difference between an Elder, a Deacon, and a Bishop. The office and work of a Bishop are of a general character, not confined to any particular place; and when he disqualifies himself from exercising his office for the good of the whole Church, he disqualifies himself from holding that office. With regard to our Southern brethren, I hold them to be entitled to all the offices of the ministry, and never will I perform any act that will go to deprive them of their rights, and never will I perform an act that will go to abridge the privileges of the abolitionists. I never did believe, nor do I now believe, that holding slaves under all circumstances is a sin. Others believe that, and sincerely, and every one knows how we boldly contended against such a conclusion in the New York Conference. We acted then in the integrity of our hearts, and as we believed would be for the good of the Church, and the preservation of its union. I wish, sir, to concentrate all my remarks on this one point, that any thing that would disqualify a man for the office of Bishop is fit ground for the action of this General Conference; and I say, to declare that every man who holds a slave sins in so doing, would be a disqualification; and so also, that to enter upon the possession of slaves under the peculiar circumstances would unfit a man for the high office of a General Superintendent of the Methodist Episcopal Church. We do not touch the moral character of Bishop Andrew at all. We do not wish to do it. We say that he has acted imprudently, and that we think it necessary in view thereof that he should resign his office as a Bishop. But while we thus press this matter, we no less fervently pray that the great Head of the Church may overrule all our deliberations and decisions for the promotion of his glory and the good of a lost world.

At the close of the speech delivered by Dr. Bangs, explanations of a personal character, in reference to the proposed nomination of Dr. Capers for the Episcopal office in 1832, were made, in which Drs. Capers, Durbin, and Winans, and Messrs. Finley and Davis took part.

CHAPTER III.

Resolution of James B. Finley—Speech of Dr. Olin—Speech of Benjamin M. Drake—Speech of George F. Pierce—Speech of Jesse T. Peck—Speech of Bishop Andrew—Bishop Soule addresses the Conference—Speech of Dr. Capers—Address from the Bishops—The adoption of Mr. Finley's Resolution.

In the previous chapter we have seen the official character of Bishop Andrew arrested by the General Conference, and have noticed the efforts made to remove him from the Episcopal office, on the mere plea of *expediency*.

The resolution offered by Mr. Collins, instructing the Committee on Episcopacy to inquire into the facts of Bishop Andrew's connection with slavery, and report to the Conference, was submitted on the 20th of May. On the 21st the committee presented their report, and, immediately upon its reading, Mr. Collins "moved that the report be laid on the table, to be taken up to-morrow as the special order of the day." On the following day, the 22d of the month, Mr. Griffith offered a resolution "*affectionately*" requesting Bishop Andrew to resign the Episcopal office.

On the preamble and resolution of Mr. Griffith, speeches were delivered by several of the most eminent men in the North; to which, however, Southern delegates replied in no unmistakable terms. The speeches of Drs. Winans and Pierce, to say nothing of those delivered by Stringfield and Crowder, had, for a time, arrested the tide that threatened to sweep every thing before it, and impressed upon the minds of the General Conference the conviction that even fanaticism could invent no plausible excuse for the adoption of the preamble and resolution offered by Mr. Griffith.

Dr. Bangs was one of the most popular and influential men in the body from the North, and his speech, the last delivered on the resolution, failed to make any impression in its favor.

Under these circumstances it was the policy of the Northern members to apparently change their base of operations. They abandoned the preamble and resolution that had been discussed for nearly two days, and substituted it by the following, offered by James B. Finley, from Ohio:

"Whereas, the Discipline of our Church forbids the doing any thing calculated to destroy our itinerant general superintendency; and, whereas, Bishop Andrew has become connected with slavery by marriage and otherwise, and this act having drawn after it circumstances which, in the estimation of the General Conference, will greatly embarrass the exercise of his office as an itinerant general superintendent, if not in some places entirely prevent it; therefore,

"*Resolved*, That it is the sense of this General Conference that he desist from the exercise of this office so long as this impediment remains.

(Signed) J. B. Finley,
J. M. Trimble."

While the phraseology of the original preamble and resolution and that of the substitute materially differ, yet in their legitimate result they were the same. Neither of them charged the Bishop with the violation of any law of the Church, yet each proposed his virtual deposition from the Episcopal office.

Mr. Finley accompanied his resolution with a few general remarks, after which Dr. Olin said:

I give to the substitute offered by the venerable brother from Ohio a decided preference over the original resolution. I feel strong objections to that resolution, and no less to the preamble. I am not prepared to say that the Discipline of the Methodist Episcopal Church contains, or is meant to contain, any provision against the election of a slaveholding Bishop, nor do I believe that any such inference is fairly deducible from it. I must hesitate, therefore, to avow such a doctrine. I may not affirm directly, or by any implication, that the Discipline is averse to the election of a slaveholder to that office. Now, it seems to me that this idea is conveyed when it is said that such an election, or that the holding of slaves by a Bishop, is contrary to the "settled policy and usage" of the Church. Since the organization of the federal government on its present basis, the office of President has been occupied during thirty-five years by citizens of Virginia, and forty-three by slaveholders, while that high honor has been enjoyed only twelve years by Northern statesmen. Would it be a proper use of language to say that it is the "settled policy and usage" of our country, that the office of President should be, for the most part, confined to Southern men? "Usage" carries, to some extent, at least, the idea of common law and acknowledged right or privilege. In this sense it is obviously inapplicable to the case in hand. We have hitherto had no slaveholder for Bishop, not that we have a law against it, but because the non-slaveholding candidates have always received a majority of the votes. The majority will always be able to judge of what the interests or sentiments of the whole Church from time to time may demand, and such a declaration as that in the preamble is uncalled for, as well as not strictly true. The facts alleged as the ground of the resolution, if true, are at least disputable, as we have the best possible proof in the discussions and explanations to which we have just listened. They are not matters of record, or history, or general notoriety, and they are not adapted to be the basis of our solemn decision in a case of such grave importance.

I do not like the issue to which that resolution sought to lead us. I do not wish, by any act or vote of mine, to say or insinuate that Bishop Andrew is not a most desirable man for the Episcopacy. Undoubtedly, under the pressure of our difficulties, had he voluntarily come forward and done what the Conference, by that resolution, ask him to do, it might have been the best way to relieve us from the embarrassment. At least some may think so. But I doubt the propriety of asking him to do, under the constraining influence of our vote, what, if done at all, ought to be done voluntarily; for it might thus be understood that even if he were free from this embarrassment, we still should not prefer to have him for a Bishop.

I look upon this question after all, not as a legal, but as a great practical question; and my views are quite disembarrassed from constitutional scruples or difficulties. We came to this General Conference from the North, South, East, and West, with the best dispositions in all parties to harmonize as well as we might, and to make the least of our differences. There were few symptoms of discontent or disaffection, and it was generally thought that we should now make a satisfactory settlement of our difficulties, and go home more harmonious than ever in feeling and action. I had good reason for coming to this conclusion. I knew, or thought I knew, the feelings of my brethren in the North and East, and I had enjoyed a pretty free correspondence and intercourse with brethren of the South; and I am sure we all came up to this Conference with the best purposes and the best hopes. I was ill, and did not reach the Conference at the commencement, and it was not until I had taken my seat on this floor, and heard of the difficulties which surrounded us, that my mind was robbed of these hopes. I was stunned and overwhelmed with the tidings, and in ten minutes made up my mind that our embarrassments were stupendous, if not insuperable. I have since made diligent inquiries from brethren as to the actual condition and sentiments of the Northern Churches, and what would be the results there, if things remain as they are. I have, for the most part, refrained from going to the men who have taken part in the controversies that have agitated us hitherto, because I thought their testimony, in a case of this sort, might not perhaps be so much relied upon; but I have addressed my inquiries to men whom I know to be opponents of the abolition movement; and they concur in believing that this is precisely the state of things in which they most fear to return home to their flocks—and they declare, with one consent, that the difficulty is unmanageable and overwhelming. I hope it will turn out in the end that their fears outrun the reality. But, I confess, I know not where to look for testimony in this matter, but to the accredited, and venerable, and discreet representatives of the various Conferences; and I repeat, that, forming my conclusions on this ground, our most prudent men do regard our present condition as pregnant with danger, and as threatening manifold disasters and disaffections throughout the Methodist Episcopal Church; and, after making what allowance we can for any local or partial view, I am still compelled to regard the evil as a great and portentous one. It addresses itself to us as the only tribunal having the legitimate authority to act in the premises.

The calamity has come without warning. The intelligence has fallen down upon us like a thunder-bolt from a serene sky; but we must grapple with the difficulties. It is for this General Conference alone to dispose of them in some way. It must be remembered, however, that this Conference is limited in its action by constitutional restrictions, which it may not transcend for the removal of the most ruinous evil. I can conceive of questions coming up here, so beset with legal and constitutional embarrassments, that this General Conference could only weep over them, and give such counsel as it might judge proper. If there ever was a question beset with great practical difficulties, surely it is that under which we now groan; it is so hedged about and filled with evils, which this Conference cannot hope to prevent or cure. Yet our powers are so great as to allow us to make some provision against them, and to some extent, at least, meet the wants of the Church in this great emergency. We may do much, and we may make many arrangements in regard to the Episcopacy; but our powers are still limited and restricted in two things. We cannot do away with the Episcopacy; we cannot infringe upon its character as a general superintendency. Within these limits, it seems to me, that we have large powers—plenary powers for carrying out through the Episcopacy the general purposes of the Conference and the Church. We may almost do what we will, avoiding to come in conflict with the General Rules, and the rights of individuals. Unquestionably the Conference cannot touch the ministerial rights of any one of its members or officers. I believe we are all prepared to recognize the right of Southern brethren to hold slaves under the provisions of the Discipline. We shall acknowledge and guarantee the entire of the privileges and immunities of all parties in the Church. I here declare, that if a remedy should be proposed that would trench on the constitutional claims of Southern ministers, I would not, to save the Church from any possible calamity, violate this great charter of our rights. I am glad of the opportunity of saying that no man, who is a Methodist, and deserves a place among us, can call in question here any rights secured by our charter. I do not say that he may not be a very honest, or a very pious man, who doubts the compatibility of slaveholding, on the conditions of the Discipline, with the ministerial office; but in this he is not a Methodist. He may be a very *good man*, but a very *bad Methodist;* and if such a man doubts if the Church will reform, or is too impatient of delay, let him, as I would in his place, do as our friends in New England did last year, go to some other Church, or set up one for himself.

Not only is holding slaves, on the conditions and under the restrictions of the Discipline, no disqualification for the ministerial office; but I will go a little farther, and say that slaveholding is not constitutionally a forfeiture of a man's right, if he may be said to have one, to the office of a Bishop. The Church, spread out through all the land, will always determine for itself what are disqualifications and what are not, and it has a perfect right to determine whether slaveholding, or abolitionism, or any other fact, shall be taken into consideration in its elections.

These are my principles. I have never doubted with regard to them. I will add, that I can never give a vote which does violence to my sentiments in regard to the religious aspect of the subject. I here declare that, if I ever saw the graces of the Christian ministry displayed, or its virtues developed, it has been among slaveholders. I wish here to divest myself of what, to some, may seem an advantage that does not belong to me. I will not conceal—I avow that I was a slaveholder, and a minister at the South, and I never dreamed that my right to the ministry was questionable, or that in the sight of God I was less fitted to preach the gospel on that account. And if the state of my health had not driven me away from that region, I should probably have been a slaveholder to this day. In this day of reform, and manifold suggestions, I go farther, and say, that if by a vote of this General Conference, you might call in question the right of our Southern brethren to the ministry, and make their claim to the sacred office dependent on their giving immediate freedom to their slaves, I do not think that that would be a blessing to the slaves, or to the Church. I do not believe the slave fares worse for having a Christian master, and I think the preachers may have more of public confidence on our present plan. I know these opinions may, by some, be regarded as unsound, and I make them not because they have any special value or novelty, but because I profess to speak my sentiments freely.

With regard to the particular case before us, I feel constrained to make one or two remarks. If ever there was a man worthy to fill the Episcopal office by his disinterestedness, his love of the Church, his ardent, melting sympathy for all the interests of humanity, but, above all, for his uncompromising and unreserved advocacy of the interest of the slave—if these are qualifications for the office of a Bishop, then James O. Andrew is preëminently fitted to hold that office. I know him well. He was the friend of my youth, and although by his experience and his position fitted to be a father, yet he made me a brother, and no man has more fully shared my sympathies, or more intimately known my heart, for these twenty years. His house has been my home; on his bed have I lain in sickness, and he, with his sainted wife now in heaven, has been my comforter and nurse. No question under heaven could have presented itself so painfully oppressive to my feelings as the one now before us. If I had a hundred votes, and Bishop Andrew were not pressed by the difficulties which now rest upon him, without any wrong intention on his part I am sure, he is the man to whom I would give them all. I know no man who has been so bold an advocate for the interests of the slaves; and when I have been constrained to refrain from saying what perhaps I should have said, I have heard him at camp-meetings, and on other public occasions, call fearlessly on masters to see to the spiritual and temporal interests of their slaves, as a high Christian duty. Excepting one honored brother, whose name will hereafter be recorded as one of the greatest benefactors of the African race, I know of no man who has done so much for the slave as Bishop Andrew. I know, sir, I am not speaking to the question, but I am stating facts—facts which I am sure will lead brethren to act with caution and tenderness in this business.

It will be readily inferred, from what I have said, that if we cannot act without calling in question the rights of the Southern brethren, we had better, in my opinion, not act all, for I believe it would be better to submit to the greatest calamities than infringe upon our own constitution. Yet it seems to me that we are not shut up to such a disastrous course, and that we may so dispose of this case as to escape both these difficulties. We cannot punish. I would not vote for any resolution that would even censure; and yet, with the powers that confessedly belong to the General Conference, I trust some measure may be adopted that may greatly palliate and diminish, if it cannot wholly avert, the dangers that threaten us. The substitute now proposed I regard as such a measure. In it this General Conference expresses its wish and will that, under existing circumstances—meaning, by that word, not merely the fact that Bishop Andrew has become a slaveholder, but the state of the Church, the sentiments that prevail—the excitement, and the deep feeling of the people on the subject—feeling, it may be, which disqualifies them for calm, dispassionate views in the premises—that, under these circumstances, it is the wish and will of the brethren of this Conference that Bishop Andrew, against whom we bring no charge, on whose fair character we fix no reproach, should, for the present, refrain from the exercise of his Episcopal functions. This resolution proposes no punishment. It does not censure. It expresses no opinion of the Bishop's conduct. It only seeks to avert disastrous results by the exercise of the conservative, of the self-preserving, powers of this Conference.

If the brethren who occupy the extreme positions in this question seek rather to allay than excite the fever of feeling, we will yet hope—even allow me to *believe*—that these difficulties may be removed. I had even thought, if we could so manage this question as to avoid casting any reflections upon the South; if we could hold Bishop Andrew without an impeachment; if we are careful to save that point as far as possible, I have confidence that, whenever he believes he can do it without compromising a principle which I know, in the present situation, he feels himself called upon to represent and maintain—if we could save that point, and hold up a shield over the interests dearer to him and others than his own life even—I do not allow myself to despair that, as soon as circumstances will allow, and difficulties, now insuperable, shall be removed, he will be ready to make great sacrifices for the general good of the Church. I have no right to say so. I only give it as my conviction, that if he can possibly relieve us of our embarrassment he will. My confidence in the man is such, that I have no hesitation in asserting this. I look at this proposition not as a punishment of any grade or sort. It is as if you were to say to Dr. Peck, your editor, who, for some cause, might have become unpopular, "You are our agent. Circumstances, at present, are unfavorable to your exercising your functions; and in the exertion of our just discretion in the case, and because your want of favor with the public interferes with the success of that department over which you are placed, we withdraw you, for the present, from this particular field of duty. *We* do not censure you, and we cordially retain you in the ranks of our ministry." I am not learned in constitutional law. It is, perhaps, for want of larger experience that this is the only view I am able to take of this subject; at which, however, I think I have arrived by a course, I will not say of sound argument, but by natural and easy approaches. With my constitutional views, I am allowed to inquire in this case which course will do the least harm? And I believe that which is proposed by this substitute to be a constitutional measure, dishonorable to none, unjust to none. As such I should wish it to go forth, with the solemn declaration of this General Conference that we do not design it as a punishment, or a censure; that it is, in our apprehension, only a prudential and expedient measure, calculated to avert the great evils that threaten us.

I know the difficulties of the South. I know the excitement that is likely to prevail among the people there. Yet, allowing our worst fears all to be realized, the South will have this advantage over us—the Southern Conferences are likely, in any event, to harmonize among themselves—they will form a compact body. In our Northern Conferences this will be impossible in the present state of things. They cannot bring their whole people to act together on one common ground; stations and circuits will be so weakened and broken as in many instances to be unable to sustain their ministry. I speak on this point in accordance with the conviction of my own judgment, after having traveled three thousand miles through the New England and New York Conferences, that if some action is not had on this subject calculated to hold out hope—to impart a measure of satisfaction to the people—there will be distractions and divisions ruinous to souls, and fatal to the permanent interests of the Church.

I feel, sir, that if this great difficulty shall result in separation from our Southern brethren, we lose not our right hand merely, but our very heart's blood. Over such an event I should not cease to pour out my prayers and tears as over a grievous and unmitigated calamity. It was in that part of our Zion that God, for Christ's sake, converted my soul. There I first entered on the Christian ministry. From thence come the beloved, honored brethren who now surround me, with whom and among whom I have labored, and suffered, and rejoiced, and seen the doings of the right hand of the Son of God. If the day shall come when we must be separated by lines of demarkation, I shall yet think often of those beyond with the kindest, warmest feelings of an honest Christian heart. But, sir, I will yet trust that we may put far off this evil day. If we can pass such a measure as will shield our principles from all infringement—

if we can send forth such a measure as will neither injure nor justly offend the South—as shall neither censure nor dishonor Bishop Andrew, and yet shall meet the pressing wants of the Church; and, above all, if Almighty God shall be pleased to help by pouring out his Spirit upon us, we may yet avoid the rock on which we now seem but too likely to split.

I will add one word in reference to what has been so often repeated about the abolition excitement in New England and the North. I have never thought it a good thing to introduce agitation into the Church. I have thought it better, so far as practicable, to keep clear from all controversies, and, for myself, have felt bound to do so. I have been kept from taking any part in the great abolition controversy by the arrangements of Providence; but I must declare that the interests, the purposes, the measures, which seem at this time to unite the North in sympathy, have not originated with abolitionists, usually so called. The concern felt on the subject now before us is much more general. The New York Conference, of which I was made a member when abroad, and without my knowledge, was never an abolition Conference. Some of my friends, members of that Conference, and themselves decided abolitionists, have complained to me of the action of that body in suspending some young preachers for their activity in the abolition cause, as flagrantly tyrannical and unjust. The Troy Conference is not an abolition Conference, and never was. These, and other Northern Conferences, have firmly opposed the abolition movement. They have been as a wall of brass to turn back the strong tide, and protect the Southern rights and interests.

Ministers and laymen, in some portions of our work, have agitated this question in their Conferences and Churches, but generally Northern Methodists have been opposed to such action. They commonly regard slavery a great evil, though not necessarily a sin; but it would be a great mistake to conclude that the antislavery sentiments of Methodists have been wholly, or mostly, the fruits of Church-action or agitation. Brethren fall into a great error in imagining that all the abolition influences abroad in the Northern Churches originated in them. On the contrary, our common newspapers, the contests and canvassings connected with our elections, our periodical literature, are rife with abolitionism on other and broader grounds. It is, perhaps, to be regretted that this embarrassing subject is so much discussed at the North; but it is certainly true that Methodists here derive their sentiments chiefly from such sources as I have intimated—from their reading, and from intercourse with their fellow-citizens. They are abolitionists naturally and inevitably, because they breathe the atmosphere of this country—because the sea is open to free adventure, and their freighted ships bring home periodicals and books from all the countries of Europe, tinged, or, if any prefer, infected with these views. The difficulties of this question, then, do not arise chiefly from its relation to abolitionism in the Church, but from the general tone of feeling among the people of the non-slaveholding States. I trust, sir, that in pronouncing our sentiments on the subject under consideration, we shall not regard ourselves as acting for distinct and antagonist interests—that we shall not inquire whether we may inflict an injury upon one portion of the Church regarded by itself, and no doubt justly, as ever mindful of its constitutional obligations, to save another portion from evils engendered in the hot-beds of abolitionism—a part of the Church ever ready to trample down constitutional barriers, and remove old landmarks and securities.

That is not the true issue; for in four-fifths of the antislavery Conferences, to say nothing of the rest, there have been no agitations, no seeds of abolition sown, but the people have formed their opinions as citizens of the country; and notwithstanding these convictions on the subject, they have as tender a regard for the interests of the Church as any of their brethren. As a member of the New York Conference, I do most earnestly protest against any declaration which shall go forth before the world, affirming or intimating that the New York Conference, as such, has at all meddled in this matter, except to prevent apprehended evil, and to perform what it regarded as a pressing, though painful, duty to the whole Church. I will only say farther, that in our action in the case of a venerable and beloved Bishop, we have trouble and sorrow enough heaped upon us—Pelion on Ossa—afflictions on affliction. Let not, then, this drop of bitterness be wrung into the cup which we are compelled to drink. Let it not be said that we are groaning under the pressure of difficulties arising from an agitation which we have got up and cannot now allay. Let it not be said that we are now suffering the consequences of our unconstitutional meddling with the subject of slavery—that the seed sown by us has sprung up, and we are now reaping the harvest. As a delegate from the New York Conference, I sympathize with its honor; and I declare, before heaven and earth, that it is no fault of that body of ministers that we are now pressed down with such a burden of difficulties. Sir, there are men in this Conference who have suffered much in vindicating what they regarded the rights of the South. My venerable friend on the right has, on this account, received great and unmerited obloquy. Another excellent minister on my left, and many more not now in my eye, have been reproached as pro-slavery men and men-stealers for the part they thought it their duty to take against the ultra views and measures that threatened to prevail a few years ago. They have deserved well—I think they have merited the thanks—of Southern brethren for their earnest efforts to shield them and their rights against encroachments on the constitution of the Church. Sir, I have done. I do not pretend to have succeeded in making a constitutional argument. My object was to do my duty in stating, as well as I was able, the just and proper grounds of the proposed resolution.

In this remarkable speech, Dr. Olin conceded every thing demanded by the South, with the exception that violent hands should not be laid on Bishop Andrew. He admitted "that the Discipline of the Methodist Episcopal Church contains" no "provision against the election of a slaveholding Bishop;" "that Bishop Andrew was a most desirable man for the Episcopacy;" "that the General Conference was limited in its action by constitutional restrictions which it may not transcend;" "that if a remedy should be proposed that would trench on the constitutional claims of Southern ministers," he "would not, to save the Church from any possible calamity, violate this great charter of our rights." He farther says, "Not only is holding slaves, on the conditions and under the restrictions of the Discipline, no disqualification for the ministerial office," and adds, "but I will go a little farther, and say that slaveholding is not constitutionally a forfeiture of a man's right, if he may be said to have one, to the office of a Bishop." His speech abounds in expressions and sentiments similar to these.

With the expression of these views, however, Dr. Olin avowed his purpose to support the resolution of Mr. Finley, and offers as his reason for so doing that, "in it this General Conference expresses its wish and will that under existing circumstances—meaning by that word, not merely the fact that Bishop Andrew has become a slaveholder, but the state of the Church, the sentiments that prevail, the excitement and the deep feeling on the subject—feeling, it may be, which disqualifies them for calm, dispassionate views in the premises—that under these circumstances it is the wish and will of the brethren of this Conference that Bishop Andrew, against whom we bring no charge, on whose fair character we fix no reproach, should, for the present, refrain from the exercise of his Episcopal functions."

We are unable to reconcile the two opposite positions taken by Dr. Olin in this speech, unless it be that he entertained the belief that the division of the Church was an absolute necessity for the success of Methodism in the North as well as the South.

Dr. Olin was followed by Benjamin M. Drake, from Mississippi.

He thought that in no vital principle did the substitute differ from the original resolution, though in the preamble he thought it preferable. But he could not see the difference between the Bishop's resigning his office, and refraining from the exercise of its functions, especially as his circumstances are such as he has no control over, and therefore the request contemplated would be equivalent to a request to resign, to all intents and purposes.

To say that we can deprive a Bishop of his office, and yet not censure him—to say that we can depose, and yet leave his Episcopal robe unstained—is, to my mind, absurd in the extreme. Sir, we cannot pass this resolution without hanging up Bishop Andrew before the whole Church as having committed a sin either against Methodism or against Christ! And against which has he sinned? Now, according to the exposition of the last speaker, he has not sinned against Methodism, and I have yet to hear that he has sinned against Christianity; so that, according to their own showing, they cannot punish him without committing an extrajudicial act. Nor can this course be pursued, and the union of the Church be preserved.

Bishop Andrew must be continued in the Episcopal office, or you certainly divide the Church.

Henry Slicer, of the Baltimore, Phineas Crandall, of the New England, and William D. Cass, of the New Hampshire Conference, were the next speakers, all of them supporting the substitute.

The speech of Mr. Cass was distinguished for nothing, except its extreme ultraism and bitterness.

On Friday morning, May the 24th, Bishop Waugh was in the chair, and the religious services were conducted by Samuel Dunwody, of South Carolina. The preliminary business being finished, the order of the day (Finley's substitute) was resumed. Mr. Cass had not finished his speech the day previous, when the hour of adjournment arrived, and his right to the floor was consequently recognized by the chair. He, however, waived his privilege, remarking that "he had been interrupted in his speech the day before, and his rights had been trampled upon, and he had no farther speech to make."

George F. Pierce, of Georgia, followed Mr. Cass. Mr. Pierce was a young man, being only thirty-three years of age. This was the second General Conference of which he had been a member. Before Mr. Pierce was born his father was a Methodist preacher. Brought up in the lap of Methodism, in the sixteenth year of his age he was soundly converted to God. He loved its doctrines and was devoted to its usages. Divinely called to the work of the Christian ministry, before he was twenty years old he entered the itinerant ranks, and pledged to the prosecution of his high and holy calling his youth, his manhood, and his declining years. His first field of labor was the Alcovie Circuit, with Jeremiah Freeman in charge. His second appointment was to the city of Augusta, as the colleague of James O. Andrew.* Having in the early part of his ministry been associated with Mr. Andrew, he had formed an attachment for him that had increased with each successive year. His popularity in the Georgia Conference had placed him in the front ranks of his delegation, while his brilliant talents, his burning eloquence, his spotless character, his uncompromising devotion to the Church, and his fervent zeal, which knew no bounds save his wasting strength, rendered him a universal favorite in the South. As a preacher, if he had a peer, he had no superior, in the Church. His appearance on the floor of the General Conference, in opposition to the substitute of Mr. Finley, was expected. He said:

I speak from convictions of duty, and not because I expect to change the opinion of any man

* It was during this year that Mr. Andrew was elected to the Episcopal office.

before us; nor would I presume, as some have done, that there will be in the course of my remarks the evolutions of any new light. I do not, sir, feel a great deal of solicitude about the issue of the case, and my solicitude is diminished, because I regard the great question of unity as settled by the previous action of the Conference in another case; but I desire to animadvert very briefly on one or two points, as connected with the manner in which the question has been considered.

The brethren who have spoken on the other side of the question, many of them, have adopted a trick of oratory—a sort of legerdemain in debate, which is this: they state abstract propositions of right, which no man will pretend to deny, and then deduce elaborate argumentations, and make them to bear on conclusions with which these conclusions have no more to do than the law of the tides has with the polar star. But the design is very obvious. The idea is more readily adopted —the conviction more readily embraced—because it falls in with preconceived opinions and long-established prejudices. There is no logical connection between the premises and the arguments which have been advanced here. Things are put in apposition which have no relation to each other. Sir, there has been, in every speech which has been made on the other side of the question, a false issue attempted. Whatever may be affirmed of expediency, and the disqualification of Bishop Andrew for the office of General Superintendent, in view of circumstances over which it is declared brethren have no control, it is not to be forgotten or disguised that this is not an abstract, but a practical question, that it involves the constitutional rights and equality of privileges belonging to Southern ministers. It is a practical question, too, which cannot be set off from its connection with the past, and its bearings on the future. It is part and parcel of a system, slowly developed, it may be, yet obvious in its designs and unwearied in its operation, to deprive Southern ministers of their rights, and to disfranchise the whole Southern Church. You cannot take the question out of its relations. It cannot be made to stand as brethren have tried to make it stand, isolated and alone. If there had been no memorials on your table, praying for the establishment of a law of proscription—if there had not been declared, over and over again, a settled purpose, if not in unequivocal terms, yet in unequivocal acts, to work out the destruction of this evil, and free the Episcopacy and the Church itself from this evil, the question before us would be different in its aspects, and the action of the South in regard to it might be modified accordingly. I beg this Conference to consider this question in the light of its connection with the previous action in the case of the appeal from the Baltimore Conference. Sir, the preposterous doctrine was asserted in that Conference, that its purposes and usages are paramount to the law of the land, and the doctrine of that Conference has been affirmed here. Sir, the action of this Conference on the subject has brought the whole Methodist Episcopal Church into a position of antagonism to the laws of the land. I consider such action not only an outrage on the common justice of the case, but decidedly revolutionary in its movements, and destined to affect, unless repealed, the character of the Conference and all the ramifications of the Church. What is the position? The ground was taken there and here—the Church, the Bible, the Discipline, and the laws of the land to the contrary notwithstanding—that we have a right to make a man's membership depend upon the condition of his doing a thing which, as a citizen of the State, he has no power or right to do. The act which is proposed in the resolution is part and parcel with the same affair. When Bishop Andrew has been invited to resign or desist from the exercise of his official functions, or is impeached, or deposed, it ought to be, and can be, considered as neither more nor less than collateral in its designs and effects with the action of the Conference in the case to which I have referred. This is a practical question, make what disclaimers you please, or any amount of them. The common sense of the country will consider it as an infraction of the constitutional, or, if you please, the disciplinary rights of the Southern brethren, however it may be considered by those in the so-styled more favored and less-incumbered portions of the Union.

The argument for expediency I am compelled to believe has not half the force assigned to it. I think I speak advisedly when I say, that whatever effect the passing of Bishop Andrew's character without censure, or laying the whole business on the table, might have with the New England Conferences, I am not prepared to believe that any considerable damage would be done in the middle Conferences. I do not believe the people of New York would decline to receive Bishop Andrew for their Bishop. I do not believe that he would be objected to either in New Jersey, Pennsylvania, or Maryland, or in any of the Conferences of the Western States. The difficulties are with the New Englanders. They are making all this difficulty, and may be described, in the language of Paul, as "intermeddlers with other men's matters." I will allow, as it has been affirmed, again and again, that there may be secession, Societies broken up, Conferences split, and immense damage of this sort be done within the New England Conferences; but what then? I speak soberly, advisedly, when I say, I prefer that all New England should secede, or be set off, and have her share of the Church property. I infinitely prefer that they should go rather than that this General Conference should proceed to make this ruthless invasion upon the Connectional union, and the integrity of the Church. Let New England go, with all my heart. She has been for the last twenty years a thorn in the flesh—a messenger of Satan to buffet us! let her go, and joy go with her, for peace will stay behind. The Southern Church has nothing to fear, and she has nothing to ask on this subject. As far as we are concerned, sir, the greatest blessing that could befall us would be a division of this union. There, sir, at the South, we dwell in peace, and the good Shepherd watches the flock and guards us from all harm. There are no jarring strings, no discordant sounds, no incarnate emissaries of the evil one going about seeking whom they may devour, but there we "lie down in green pastures, beside the still waters." If we had not the spirit of the Master, if we were selfish enough to enjoy the bounty of our heritage, we would court division, pray for it, demand it.

But, sir, I will present one view of this question that has not been touched upon. Set off the South, and what is the consequence? Do you get rid of embarrassment, discord, division, strife?

No, sir; you multiply divisions. There will be secessions in the Northern Conferences, even if Bishop Andrew is deposed or resigns. Prominent men will abandon your Church. I venture to predict that when the day of division comes—and come I believe it will, from the present aspect of the case—that in ten years from this day, and perhaps less, there will not be one shred of the distinctive peculiarities of Methodism left within the Conferences that depart from us. The venerable man who now presides over the Northern Conferences may live out his time as a Bishop, but he will never have a successor. Episcopacy will be given up, Presiding-eldership will be given up, the itinerancy will come to an end, and Congregationalism will be the order of the day. The people will choose their own pastors, and preachers will be standing about the ecclesiastical market-places, and when men shall ask, "Why stand ye here all the day idle?" the answer will be, "Because no man hath hired us." We have unity and peace, and seek it because of its effects on the Connection, and I believe, to-day, that if the New England Conferences were to secede, the rest of us would have peace. There would be religion enough left among us to live together as a band of Christian brothers.

Sir, I object to the substitute for another reason. I would have preferred the original resolution. The substitute presents a most anomalous view of the whole subject. Suppose that view is adopted; what is it? What do you do with the Bishop? You cannot put him on a circuit or station: he is a Bishop in duress—a Bishop in prison-bounds—an anomaly—a fifth wheel in the machine of Methodism—doomed to live on the Book Concern, while no provision is made for his rendering the Church any service—if this resolution is adopted.

I promise not to detain you long, for others are wishing to speak; but I felt that I could not go home satisfied unless I took this occasion to make a few remarks. If I did not know there were others better qualified to defend this subject, I would trespass on the patience of the Conference by the hour. I tell you that unless Bishop Andrew is passed free of censure of any kind, the days of Methodist unity are numbered. What do brethren mean when they come and eulogize him as they have done? It has been avowed that he is a blameless man, pure and spotless—that he has high executive talents—that he is one of the most efficient administrators of law—that he is as well qualified for this as any of the worthy men who occupy the Episcopal bench. Yet in the face of this, is the Conference to come out and say, that on the question of expediency he shall resign, refrain from the exercise of his office, or be deposed? What mean these eulogies? Are brethren in earnest? Is the Conference heaping garlands on the victim they destine for slaughter? Has it come to this, that a large body of sober and reverend men, in the face of their own acknowledgment of blamelessness, are going to inflict one of the severest penalties on an innocent, unoffending man? Why will you blight with a breath the bliss of this worthy man? Will you offer him up to appease that foul spirit of the pit which has sent its pestilential breath to blast and destroy the Church? You have unchained the lion, and now that he is raging and roaring for his prey, you select a venerable Bishop—one of the ablest and best of the whole college—to immolate *him* on the altar of this Juggernaut of perdition! Think you we will sit here and see this go on without lifting a voice or making a protest against it? Are we to see this noble man sacrificed for the sake of New England? God forbid it! God forbid, I say, and speak it from the depths of my heart.

Brethren may say what they please, disclaim what they please, eulogize as they will, they cannot make any thing of this but the deprivation of a constitutional right. In the case of the appeal from the Baltimore Conference many voted, not because they believed the Conference had done right, but for extraneous reasons; but in this question the vote goes out upon its naked merits, irrespective of any disclaimer or acknowledgments that may be made in reference to the Bishop's rights, character, or capacity. But to come to the point—Has he a right to hold slaves under the Discipline of the Church? If he has, I adjure you not to lay violent hands upon him. If he has, I ask brethren to pause and say, if in the prospect of facing a scrutinizing world, they can go out with the stinging recollection in their hearts that they have sacrificed a man worthy to preside over them, to the restless demands of an arrogant and insatiable spirit of abolition? I do hope brethren will pause before they drive us to the fearful catastrophe now earnestly to be deprecated, but inevitable if they proceed.

Dr. Longstreet, of Mississippi, followed Mr. Pierce on the same side, with a speech remarkable for its force and clearness.

Jesse T. Peck, of the Troy Conference, spoke in reply to Mr. Pierce:

The only occasion upon which I have thought it consistent for me to appear in this discussion, is in reply to the distinguished member from the Georgia Conference, Rev. G. F. Pierce. The near agreement in our ages is my apology. The reverend gentleman commenced his remarks by stating that this controversy, as it appeared to him, had been conducted upon the part of the North by attempted feats of legerdemain. I understood him to say that we had done this by stating self-evident propositions, and then forthwith deducing conclusions from them that had no more connection with them than the law of the tides had with the polar star. If he had taken the trouble to point out a few instances of this kind of defect, I could have given it the attention due to reasoning; but as he was not pleased to do so, and as he is an educated man, he will doubtless be satisfied by my giving him credit for a piece of *beautiful declamation.* He says we have made *a false issue* in this discussion. And what is it? Why, that we have discussed it as an individual matter, confined in its application to Bishop Andrew himself; whereas it was in truth a great practical question, bearing upon the whole South. We admit it, Mr. President; it is a great practical question, bearing not upon the South merely, but upon the *whole Church.* We utterly disclaim the limitation of the question to any man. We take up the issue exactly as he has laid it down. It is upon the assertion and action of a great principle of immense *practical bearing* that we predicate our arguments. It is, verily, the brother may be well assured, a matter of great *practical importance* to us, and to the Church, whether we have a slaveholding Bishop or not. Here, then, I have no contention with him.

But, Mr. President, the brother alarmed me! He made a declaration which was to me utterly surprising! He says the great question of unity is decided! (Mr. P. explained. "Prospectively decided!") *Prospectively* decided? to be sure! Did any one suppose it had been decided *retrospectively?* Division, then, in his mind is really inevitable! Surely, sir, *I* had not thought so. And I am happy to say I know many brethren, North and South, much more distinguished for age and experience than either of us, who do not think so. The *division* of our excellent Church decided! The unity of our common Methodism destroyed! May Heaven forbid it! I do not believe it, sir. The strong bonds that hold us together, I trust, are not sundered! But, he says, the Baltimore appeal case virtually decided it. I do not so understand it. There were, it is true, several points of analogy between the case of Mr. Harding and that of Bishop Andrew. But the action contemplated in the case of the Bishop is widely different from that had in the case of Mr. Harding. In that case we did nothing more than to *affirm* the decision of the Baltimore Conference; and in that act say, that we would not allow slavery to be crowded on her, after she had *nobly declared she would not have it.* The appellant stood suspended from his ministerial functions. But was any such thing intended in the case of Bishop Andrew? Did the resolution affirm any such thing? Certainly not. It merely proposed that he should *desist* from the exercise of the Episcopal office until he should free himself from the embarrassment of slavery. The cases then were widely different. Brethren were undoubtedly premature in asserting that the decision of the Conference in the Baltimore appeal case had prospectively determined the division of the Church! Indeed, the gentleman himself seemed to have doubts about it, when he came to consider a little; for after he had progressed in his argument so far as to consider the influence of the proposed action in the case of the Bishop, he declared, "Pass that resolution, and the great question of Methodistic unity is decided forever." Indeed! Then it *remains to be decided,* the Baltimore appeal case to the contrary notwithstanding! I thank the brother for that. My judgment in the case cannot be altogether groundless, since it derives support from his own declarations. Be assured, sir, I greatly rejoice in this.

But the respected brother from Georgia insists that *the ultimate design* is the disfranchisement of all Southern ministers! *The ultimate design!* Really, sir, this is extraordinary sagacity! If he had been content to show us what was the legitimate *result* of our action, we must have corrected him, or submitted. But since he has thought proper to declare our *design*, we must demur. We have serious doubts as to the competency of any man to tell our designs, unléss we avow them. Disfranchise all Southern preachers! I disclaim it, sir. In the name of the Troy Conference, which I have the honor in part to represent, and in the name of the whole North, I disclaim it. I appeal to you, brethren, every man of you, to know whether you have ever known of any such idea at the North. I am fully sustained; no such thought can be in existence. But the argument by which my respected friend sustained this extraordinary proposition was not fully developed. If he will have the goodness to give his attention to see whether I do it correctly, I will state it for him. The North are not willing that a slaveholder should be a Bishop; *ergo*, they are determined that no slaveholder shall be a minister! If the brethren of the South have any argument to support this doctrine of universal proscription, this certainly must be it. But is it legitimate? Is there any connection between the antecedent and the consequent—the premises and the conclusion? I cannot see it. The Discipline prescribes the circumstances under which a traveling preacher may hold slaves. But does it say any thing of circumstances under which *a Bishop* may hold slaves? Certainly not; for the condition of a Bishop is widely different from that of any ordinary traveling preacher. He is really and truly the pastor of the whole Church, and slavery will not allow him to be so.

Brethren talk of the infringement of their constitutional rights. But what do they mean by it? That *any man* has a constitutional right to be a Bishop! Such a right as he had to graduation from a probationer to Elder's orders! Has any man living such a constitutional right to be elected to the Episcopal office, or remain in it after he is elected? I never heard of such a thing. Sir, there is no constitution in the case. Neither the Discipline nor the General Conference has ever said what special qualifications would, or would not, be required in a Bishop. It is true, sir, that the Discipline nowhere says that a slaveholder *shall not be a Bishop*, and I should be sorry if it did. It has nowhere said that a *rum-drinker* shall not be a Bishop; and yet, surely, no man would say that this was any the less an utter disqualification for the office, because it was not so declared in the Discipline. (I beg, Mr. President, you will not understand me to compare slavery with rum-drinking. I mean no such thing. I introduce it only for purposes of illustration.) No, sir, there are no *constitutional rights* invaded. As to whether a man will do for a Bishop, or not, the

General Conference is the sole judge, either as to his election, or retention; and their judgment will have its true expression in the ballot-box. A constitutional right to be a Bishop! You might as well talk of a constitutional right to be an Editor, or a Book Agent, or any other General Conference officer.

But the brother from Georgia says this measure will not save us from secessions. We shall have secessions in New England! We shall have them everywhere! What can be done to satisfy New England? Sir, as the name of *New England* struck my ear, I felt a thrill of the most intense interest. But, the reverend gentleman proceeded, "they are busy-bodies in other men's matters! A thorn in the flesh! A messenger of Satan to buffet us!" And, alluding (as I understood him to do) to a certain movement in New England, and certain principles upon which that movement was based, he called it "the foul spirit of the pit! The Juggernaut of perdition!" etc. Upon this language, Mr. President, I may not remark! I must, of necessity, leave it without animadversion! But with the utmost respect, this dear brother will excuse me for saying I much prefer the terms used by some of his highly-respected associates. I like the chaste and beautiful language of the sweet-spirited and eloquent Mr. Crowder, and the dignified and forcible style of the reverend gentleman who last preceded me. I must say, Mr. President, I deprecate the use of such language in a controversy of such solemn importance —a controversy invested with more elements of moral grandeur than any which has engaged the attention of the American people for half a century! I hope the brother will not use it again, and certainly not on the floor of this General Conference. But my friend from the Georgia Conference says, "Let New England go! I wish in my heart she would secede! And joy go with her, for I am sure she will leave peace behind her!" Let New England go? I cannot forget this exclamation. It vibrates in my soul in tones of grating discord. Why, sir, what is New England that we should part with her with so little reluctance? New England! The land of the Pilgrims—the land of many of our venerated fathers in Israel—the land of Broadhead, of Merritt, of the revered man [pointing to George Pickering] who sits by my side, and a host of worthies whom we have delighted to honor as the bulwarks of Methodism in its early days of primitive purity and peril. Let New England go? No, sir, we cannot part so easily with the pioneer land of the devoted and sainted Jesse Lee!

But, Mr. President, our brethren of the South utterly mistake the truth in this matter! Why, sir, they can't get half way to New England in this war! They must wade through numbers and forces of which they never dreamed! They must encounter us in the center, whose opposition to slavery is uncompromising. And Baltimore (honor to her self-sacrificing devotion to the cause of humanity!) will be a formidable obstacle in the way of their advance. But if they ever should subdue us, and reach the land of the Pilgrims, rest assured, sir, they would find there a wall of brass which would remain forever impregnable to the assaults of the slave-power! We are happy that New England is with us to a man in this fearful conflict—that the united West, and North, and East, form an insuperable barrier to the advance of slavery! O sir, I fear me much our brethren at the South are deceiving themselves in this matter. This has never been a question of *principle* between us and New England. We have always been agreed in fundamental antislavery sentiments, and I am the more careful to allude to this, because, so far as I remember, it is a distinction that has not been made in this discussion. It has been purely a question of *measures* between us. In this, it is true, we have differed, but in opposition of principle to slavery, North, East, and West, we always have been, and I trust shall ever remain, inseparably united. We resist *as one man* the advancement of slavery, which, not content to be confined within its own geographical limits, threatens to roll its dark waves over the North. *It claims the right to give us a slaveholding pastor! a slaveholding Bishop!* Do not then be surprised that we are so perfectly united in asking to be set back exactly where we were a few months ago. O, sir, that our brethren could roll the wheels of time back to where they were last November, when we had, comparatively, no difficulties to encounter! But this they cannot do. What less, however, can they expect us to ask, than that they should do what is equivalent to it—give us our Bishop without the slaves?

My brother, sir, judges about as poorly of the principles and condition of the North as I should of the South; for I have never been to the South. I am sorry I have not. I should like to strike the hands of these dear, very dear brethren, whom I have learned to love upon this Conference floor, as I never should have supposed possible, at their own dear homes. I should like to go there, sir, if I might, my antislavery principles to the contrary notwithstanding! [Cries of several voices, "Come on—come on—we shall be glad to see you."] Let New England go! No, sir, never. And here I beg to say, that our Southern brethren can't induce us to use such language in reference to them. They can't provoke us to it, sir. Let the South go! No, sir, we love them too well. We love them for their goodness, and respect them for their talents. We love them for their stern, unbending regard to principle and adherence to Discipline. We love them for their conservatism, ultra sometimes though it may be, we love them for it. Let the South go! No, sir, we cannot part with our brethren, whom we love so well. True, we cannot compromise principle, to save *them*—nor to save the East. But we need not. They are too magnanimous to demand it. We shall live and die with them—*we will not let them go* unless they tear themselves from our arms bedewed with the tears of affection. *Never! no, never!*

On the next day, May 25, Mr. Peck, resuming the discussion, said:

Mr. President: It would have been agreeable to me if I might have concluded my remarks yesterday, without interruption; but the arrival of the hour for adjournment compelled me to leave the argument in an unfinished state. Much as I regretted this, however, I should have preferred, if my friends would have allowed me to do it, to have left it there. To this, it is due to myself to state, I could not get their consent. In obedience, therefore, to a judgment to which I always feel bound to defer, I resume the floor to-day.

"Ten years from now, and our glorious General Superintendency, and our time-honored itinerancy will have expired!" So says the prophecy of yesterday! *Only ten years* will suffice to pull down this beautiful edifice, and annihilate the very materials of which it is constructed! The strong confidence it has inspired in its votaries—the ardent attachment of those whom it has saved—the profound admiration which its almost supernatural wisdom and adaptation have gathered around it, from all classes of people—all these *cannot save it.* It is doomed, and fall it must! Only ten years, and the last flickerings of this once brilliant and glorious light will have died away in the socket! But, Mr. President, as I am but a child in these matters, and so have seen but little of the secret workings of small, but mighty agencies, upon the basis of this noble fabric, I am curious to inquire into the cause of this prophetic fate. What is it that is to work such devastation and ruin to the fair heritage of God? Let this *reason* stand out in bold relief, stripped of all its drapery, where we can see it just as it is. This is certainly no time for rhetorical ornament. At a time when interests so vast and solemn are pending upon the action of a single principle, let that principle be exhibited naked and unadorned, that we may not mistake it. What, then, is the *cause* that is destined to effect the overthrow of institutions venerable with age, and potent for the amelioration of the condition of man? Why, sir, if I have not mistaken it, it is simply this: *This General Conference is likely to say that a slaveholder cannot be a Bishop.*

Look at it, undisguised, and alone, as it is. Examine it carefully, in all its dimensions and bearings, and see if you can discover any adequacy in the cause to produce the predicted effect. Can it be that the Almighty arm will be withdrawn from beneath us for this? That we shall be abandoned to destruction for the want of a union between slavery and the Episcopate? What element of our purity and primitive simplicity will it destroy? What adaptation of our noble system will it annihilate, to have no slaveholding Bishop? Will God, indeed, be angry with us, and leave us to ourselves *for this?* Is this the foundation-stone of our spiritual edifice, that it must inevitably crumble to ruins when it is removed? If God should forsake us, we *are* ruined—irrecoverably ruined! But, sir, *I cannot believe he will.* He has not in former times, and we have been without a slaveholding Bishop for sixty years! The grand itinerant plan of publishing salvation to the perishing world has gone on gloriously, dispensing its invaluable blessings to almost every land, notwithstanding. Now, I know, sir, if I were reasoning of *a man,* and were to say, He *has* not forsaken us, therefore he *will* not, that I should be justly chargeable with the legerdemain in debate which my friend from the South so gracefully ascribed to us yesterday. But, sir, when I say it of the unchangeable God, *he did not,* therefore, in the same circumstances, *he will not,* I feel myself fully sustained. No, Mr. President, I cannot adopt this dismal prophecy. It has too much of the air of romance about it. If nothing more is justly laid to our charge than the simple refusal to depart from our former state in this matter, I verily believe the everlasting arms will be underneath us still. The wheels of the itinerancy will continue to roll on, and the ages of the future will yet exhibit the now undeveloped power of this wonderful plan.

I will now, sir, ask attention to what appears to me to be a very singular, and yet very frequent, exclamation from Southern brethren, and I do it not in the spirit of casuistry. They, almost to a man, call upon us *to pause!* "Pause!" say they, "we beseech you; pause before you advance another step!" Indeed, sir; this is a very extraordinary prayer under the circumstances. My neighbor moves his fence, and barn, and house on my farm! and when I begin to insist upon his taking them off, he cries out, *Pause!* "Pause, sir, I beseech you! Your measures will be productive of immense injury to yourself and me!" What, sir, should I say to him in this case? Why, sir, can any one doubt that I should instantly reply, This is the wrong time to call for a pause? The time to pause was when you began to make your arrangements to move your buildings on my land! *Then,* if some kind friend had called out to *you,* in the language you address to *me,* it would have been exceedingly relevant. But now, from the nature of the case, *there can be no pause,* until you retrace your steps, and relieve my premises of your effects. Need I make the application of this homely illustration? I am sure I need not. It is obvious and necessary. But I shall not fail to look well to the only hinge upon which this argument turns. The great question is, Who has been the aggressor in this case? (I use the term in no bad sense.) Upon whom rests the responsibility of the present fearful issue? Does it rest upon us of the North? Does it rest upon this General Conference? I verily believe it does not, sir. When, or where, may I be allowed to ask, have we infringed the rights of our brethren at the South? It is true, we have laid our petitions at your feet. But in this have we done any thing more than to exercise the natural rights of freemen? The citizens of this free republic must be allowed to petition, and we must receive their petitions respectfully expressed, and give them the consideration which their nature and importance demand. Petitions have been presented to you, sir; petitions, to be sure, which, from the state of the public mind in which they originated, have required careful analysis; but many of which have deserved a most patient hearing. But, sir, what have we done? What single decision of this body, since this excitement commenced, has not been adapted with singular care to the interests of the South? Nay, sir, we have cautiously guarded the South, in every official act that looked toward this exciting subject. We are aware that it is a perfect system of sensitiveness—a complete bundle of nerves! And we have always acted with this fact fully in view. Indeed, sir, I am honestly in doubt—and I know my brethren of the South will allow me to express it—whether we have not more reason to ask the pardon of the East than of the South in this matter. This I will not, however, attempt to decide, because it is unnecessary. But, sir, the question returns, Whence is the origin of our present difficulty? Does it come from the North? Certainly not. Have we originated this innovation? I need not answer. I ask, then, most respectfully, When was the proper time to pause? This question brings us no relief. *It is too late,* and I will not repeat it. But surely the call *to pause* will be suspended by our brethren of the South, until they have put themselves right in regard to the question at issue. If it be inquired where *the blame* is located, since we will not allow it to rest upon the North, I answer *I locate it nowhere.* Indeed, I will not talk of *blame.* It can do no good. The question is one of *remedy.* We cannot fear that we shall be blamed for *press-*

ing the question of *remedy*. It ought not to be asked of us, that we should be satisfied to have the Bishop of the whole territory trammeled by peculiar and local institutions. It is not *necessary* for the good of that part of the work where slavery exists, and it *must*, from the very nature of the case, be ruinous to that large part of it where it does not exist.

But, Mr. President, I am exceedingly thankful that there is *one* common ground to the South and North. Not, perhaps, to the whole South, but to many of its most distinguished men—I refer to the magnanimous concessions which have been freely made upon the *election* of a slaveholding Bishop. It has been conceded, with a frankness and Christian candor which deserve, and shall receive, our highest praise—not, indeed, that no slaveholder should be eligible to the Episcopal office—for our Southern brethren talk with precision on this difficult question—but that it was inexpedient to attempt an election on any such ground. In the very style of considerate Northern men, it has been urged in the South that the Bishop is the officer of the whole Church, and it is not advisable to trammel him with a local difficulty. It must not be a question of North and South, but simply who is the best man for the office. Where is the man of God upon whom it will be safe to devolve such a fearful responsibility? This is noble. But will our Southern brethren abide by this principle? I am aware that I have no right to charge the necessary correlate of an acknowledged sentiment upon an opponent, unless he avow it. But it is my right to show what is implied in that sentiment, and what results necessarily follow it. And I will ask brethren, What objection have we to the *election* of a slaveholding Bishop? None, surely, but what is based upon the idea of *having* one. Why do we of the North object to *electing* a man in such circumstances to the Episcopacy? For no other reason in the world than that we have no use for him when he is elected. He cannot be a true Methodist itinerating Superintendent. No, sir, it is not to *electing*, but to *having* one, that insuperable objections arise in the minds of Northern men. Need I apply these remarks? Can brethren fail to see that nothing more is needed to relieve us from our present difficulties than the legitimate action of the principle universally claimed by the North, and so extensively conceded by the South? No, sir, let it be distinctly borne in mind that the vote upon the present resolution must depend upon precisely the same principles as the vote for an election. We grant, it is a much more *delicate* matter; so much so, indeed, as to almost appall the stoutest heart; but *the principle is the same, and the action must be the same.*

But, Mr. President, there is, I must say, one attitude taken by my brethren from the South to which I find it difficult to reconcile my feelings. It is, I confess, a matter of extreme delicacy for me to allude to it; and yet I know I shall have the indulgence of Southern brethren. If I had ever had any doubts in regard to Southern magnanimity, they would have been removed by what has taken place on the floor of this Conference during this discussion. They do not condemn a man for speaking his sentiments out fully. No, sir. I doubt not, that, if I were to appeal to my reverend friend on my right, (Dr. Smith, of Virginia,) to whose eloquent remarks we have so frequently listened with the most intense interest, he would say, "It is *cowardly* and *mean* for a man to shrink from an honest and frank avowal of his opinions and feelings upon a question of such magnitude as this for fear of difference with those who had other opinions and other feelings." I will therefore mention that subject, with which my mind has been burdened and afflicted for several days. Connected with the arguments of our Southern brethren, there is constantly held up before us the *idea* (I will not call it a menace) of *a division* of the Church, if we persist in our course! Do not brethren know that, by this course, they throw a fearful difficulty in the way of a free and safe discussion of this subject? an impediment almost sufficient to drive us from the discussion altogether? I know our dear brethren cannot fail, upon the mere mention of this matter, *to think* of the results which *may* follow to the interests of their flocks and charges in the South. I know very well that they do not feel themselves at the disposal of good men and Methodists in this thing —that it is in the power of wicked men to break up their missions and destroy their usefulness— and they are not at liberty to be *reckless* of results. But can they not waive their *discussion*, at least for the present? It is enough, sir, to chill the blood of any man to look these difficulties in the face as they are presented by Southern brethren. It is *almost* enough (but I thank God not quite enough) to make us forego a great principle to relieve ourselves from the responsibility of deciding the case. I will therefore ask it as a favor to Methodism, that this great and intimidating question of DIVISION may be allowed to sleep a few days, till we can talk over the great principle at issue. I dread, I confess to you, sir, to approach the question with such a fearful contingency suspended, *in terrorem*, over my head. Division of the Methodist Episcopal Church! It frightens me to think of it. I am compelled, however reluctantly, to admit in my own mind, that there is fearful truth in the hazard to our nation, to which brethren refer, in such a result. Divide the Church just as we are rallying our energies to prosecute with united power our missionary labors! just as we are about to combine our strength for the purpose of efficient action in the great cause of Christian education! Divide the Church at a time when most of all the great principle of Methodistic unity is indispensable to form an insuperable barrier to the advance of Roman Catholicism, which threatens to throw its withering blight over all that is fair and lovely in this glorious republic, and menaces the very frame-work of our political freedom! O no, sir; it is *here* that I would call upon brethren to pause. Again, I entreat, hush this frightful dream to sleep, that we may calmly study, undisturbed, the merits of the question between us.

I must, Mr. President, notice one thing more in the remarks of my honored friend from Georgia, and then I must leave him; for then I think he will admit that I have given him at least a respectful degree of attention. He anxiously inquires what we are to do with Bishop Andrew, if he should resign his Episcopal office. He would be a *fifth wheel* in Methodism, an anomaly, and an inoperative member! This, Mr. President, is really strange. An Elder in the Church of God—a man of unbounded popularity—a man of ardent piety and gushing sympathies—with the whole South before him, in every part of which he would be hailed with acclamations of joy—and where more work will crowd upon him than any two men can have strength to perform—*nothing to do!* A fifth wheel in the ministry! it must be impossible, sir, for a man to be serious, in such an attempt to *create* a difficulty. But, sir, we have been asked, what do we mean by our eulogies of Bishop Andrew! The tributes paid to his character have been described in the beautiful rhetoric of my friend from Georgia, as garlands decking a victim for the sacrifice. Really, sir, this is very extraordinary language. Is it strange, that as we feel ourselves compelled to lay our hands upon his official relation, we should think it proper to disclaim any attack upon his Christian and ministerial character? Is it not due to him, and due to us, to disavow any want of respect or affection for the man? Indeed, sir, our brethren have mistaken the bearing of our allusions to Bishop Andrew's worth altogether. This is one of the most trying aspects of the case. 'T is for this very reason that we deserve the respect and sympathy of both friends and foes. How, I ask, could we more clearly exhibit our regard for a great principle than to refuse to allow even the exalted virtues and worthy character of Bishop Andrew to divert our attention from it? Sir, this is what in every thing else the world calls moral heroism, and we deserve respect, and not reproaches for it. It is the worth of the man, as well as the exalted character of his office, that overwhelms us with grief, at every step of our progress. It is a mournful task, and if at any time during this discussion there has been manifested, anywhere, a disposition to levity, I regret it, sir; it pains me beyond measure to see it, when our business is characterized by the deep-toned sorrow of funeral solemnities!

I cannot here avoid an allusion to a remark of yesterday, from the Rev. Mr. Longstreet, though I adhere to my purpose not to reply to his speech. He found the community of New York charged with sympathy for Bishop Andrew. It is undoubtedly true, sir, and I should be grieved if it were otherwise. The generous sympathies of noble hearts in our crowded gallery, and rear, and throughout this community, find a most sincere and hearty response upon this Conference-floor. I would not for the world dry up this crystal fountain or divert it from its legitimate channels. The reverend gentleman is correct in regard to the facts, but he has misinterpreted them. He has imagined that these genuine pulsations of nature rise up in rebellion to *us*, and yield to the demands for a slaveholding Bishop. No, sir, he is greatly mistaken. I beg to assure him that a greater error could scarcely have been committed. These are the sympathies upon which we cast ourselves for support, in this trying crisis. It is this that secures to us, as well as to our afflicted Bishop, the prayers and the tears of the noblest men and women of which human nature can boast.

Perhaps I ought to apologize, sir, for the warmth and emotion with which I defended New England yesterday. It was the land of my sire. There repose the ashes of my fathers back to the earliest generations of this land. It is the birthplace of at least two of our venerable Bishops, who, thanks to Providence, are with us to-day—of our honored Olin, and venerated Bangs. It was the land of the sainted Fisk. And never, while our moral heavens are radiant with the glories of this luminary of the Church, shall the fair fame of the land that gave *him* birth be aspersed. *Peace to his ashes, and honor to his memory!* He was a good and a great man—one of New England's proudest sons. Let me here only say, sir, that from this same land are rising up now a host of strong men, who already stand forth as champions in the fearful conflict with sin. How can I speak otherwise than *warmly* when reproach has been heaped upon a land that has furnished so many of the brightest luminaries of the Church?

Sir, I have done. I thank you, and I thank the Conference, for the indulgence I have received. Sure I am that I have not deserved it, and I feel my obligations of gratitude the more. I embarked in this noble "ship" when I was but a boy, and I cannot be persuaded to leave her. I like her form, her structure, and her machinery well. I like her passengers, her officers, and her crew. I like the sea on which she sails, and the port to which she is bound. True, she is exposed to storms, and may sometimes stagger beneath the beating tempest, and reel amid the engulfing floods. And at such a time be not surprised if the signals of distress be heard—the life-boat launched, and numbers, forsaking her in fright, commit themselves to the merciless waves. Other craft, of sprightly form and splendid sails, may heave alongside, and invite us aboard. But, sir, do not be in haste to go. Look well to her ballast and build, for I fear she is too crank and loose to survive the perils of this frightful sea. No, sir, let us stay on board the "old ship." Sunshine or storm, darkness or light, I see her riding safely on the waves—triumphing over every danger—and gallantly bearing her precious burden toward the haven of rest. In every gale that shall strike her, as she is proudly careering amid the raging elements, my voice shall be heard above the noise of wind and wave, in the words of the dying Lawrence, "DON'T GIVE UP THE SHIP!"

Mr. Pierce rose to explain, and said he should be very glad to reply at length; but as he spoke by courtesy and not by right, he would confine himself to explanation. He observed he was exceedingly startled at the proposition of Brother Peck, that a Bishop had no constitutional right to be a Bishop. He had always understood that when a man is legitimately appointed to office, he has a constitutional right to that office for the whole term—that he cannot be ejected unless he has been in fault. As to the perhaps unfortunate expression which he yesterday made use of toward New England, some apology might be due; but, on the whole, he would not regret it, as it had afforded his honored brother such a theater for displaying his peculiar talents. He intended to say that for New England to secede, or to be set off with a *pro rata* division of the property, would be a light evil compared with the immolation of Bishop Andrew on the altar of a *pseudo* expediency. He meant that the loss of New England was as the dust of the balance compared with such a gross, palpable, unjust, outrageous violation of law. He intended to convey the idea that the great Head of the Church did not require the sacrifice of an innocent and unoffending man for the sake of maintaining peace and order in the Church. The Church required no such sacrifice for her unity or her character. As to the unkind epithets to which the brother had referred, he wished to be understood, not as having applied them to New

England, but to abolition and its misguided abettors. If all New England was engaged in this unhallowed war on the South and on Southern institutions, then he meant New England; if not, he would be understood otherwise. He intended no disrespect or injustice to New England. He would cheerfully acknowledge, because he honestly believed, in accordance with the views so eloquently expressed by the brother who had preceded him, that there were many noble sons from New England. As the last speaker had referred to Bishop Soule, he (Mr. Pierce) hoped he should be permitted to say that, from his father's representations, he had learned to admire him before he saw him, and acquaintance had ripened admiration into reverence. There was an honored representative of the New York Conference, (Dr. Olin,) who favored the Conference with his opinions a few days ago, whom he had loved from his early boyhood, and never more than now; and he took this occasion to assure him, that whatever might be his vote on this trying question, he would still remain enshrined in the fervid affections of a heart too warm to speak prudently on an occasion like this.

And, sir, I recognize you (addressing Mr. Peck) as a man with a soul in your body, warm, generous, glowing. I admire your spirit—your genius. The beauty of the bud gives promise of a luscious blossom—the early beams foretell a glorious noon.

And now, sir, though my speech shocked your nerves so badly, I trust my explanation will not ruffle a hair upon the crown of your head. [A burst of laughter, Mr. Peck being very bald.]

The discussion was continued until the 30th of May, during which time, in addition to the speeches already referred tc, Messrs. Hamline, of Ohio, Comfort, of Oneida, Collins, of Baltimore, Finley, of Ohio, Cartwright, of Illinois, and Dr. Durbin, of Philadelphia, addressed the Conference in favor of the substitute, and Messrs. Green, of Tennessee, Smith, of Virginia, Stamper, of Illinois, Sehon, of Ohio, Dunwody and Dr. Capers, of South Carolina, against it.

The speeches delivered on this occasion have seldom been equaled, and never surpassed, in the Senate-chamber of the United States.

A leading journal published in New York said: "It is but simple justice to say that the Conference was worthy of eminent distinction on the score of talent. Its members were all clergymen, and therefore public speakers by profession, and many of them were gifted with the highest order of eloquence. Perhaps no body of men in the country ever contained in a higher degree those peculiar talents which give strength and force to oral discussion."

However pleasant it might be to record the

speeches delivered on the occasion, to do so would swell this volume far beyond our design.

During the discussion, on the 28th day of May, and immediately following the speech of Mr. Collins, Bishop Andrew addressed the Conference. He said:

Mr. President:—I have been on trial now for a week, and feel desirous that it should come to a close. For a week I have been compelled to listen to discussions of which I have been the subject, and I must have been more than man, or less than man, not to have felt. Sir, I have felt, and felt deeply. I am not offended with any man. The *most* of those who have spoken against me, have treated me respectfully, and have been as mild as I had any right to expect. I cherish no unkind feelings toward any. I do not quarrel with my abolition brethren, though I believe their opinions to be erroneous and mischievous. Yet, so long as they conduct themselves courteously toward me, I have no quarrel with them. It is due that some remarks should be made by me, before the Conference come to a conclusion upon the question, which I hope will be speedily done, for I think a week is long enough for a man to be shot at, and it is time the discussion should terminate.

As there has been frequent reference to the circumstances of my election to the Episcopal office, it is perhaps proper that I give a brief history of that matter. A friend of mine, (Brother Hodges,) now with God, asked me to permit myself to be put in nomination for that office. I objected—the office had no charms for me. I was with a Conference that I loved, and that loved me. What was I to gain to be separated from a happy home —from a wife and children whom I loved more than I did my own life? But my friend urged me; he said my election would, he believed, tend to promote the peace of the Church, and that he believed it would be especially important to the prosperity of Methodism at the South. Finally I consented, with the hope of failure; but I was nominated and elected. I was never asked if I was a slaveholder—no man asked me what were my principles on the subject—no one dared to ask of me a pledge in this matter, or it would have been met as it deserved. Only one man, Brother Winans, spoke to me on the subject: he said he could not vote for me because he believed I was nominated under the impression that I was not a slaveholder. I told him I had not sought the nomination, nor did I desire the office, and that my opinions on the propriety of making non-slaveholding a test of qualification for the office of Bishop were entirely in unison with his own. Sir, I do not believe in this matter of secret will as a rule of action, either in the revelations of the

Bible, or in the prescriptions of the Book of Discipline. I believe in the revealed will of God, and in the written law of the Church as contained in the Book of Discipline. I took office upon the broad platform of that book, and I believe my case is covered by it. It was known that I was to reside at the South; I was elected in view of that very thing, as it was judged important to the best interests of the Church that one of the Bishops should reside in that section of the work, and it was judged I could be more useful there than elsewhere. Well, what was I to do then? I was located in a country where free persons could not be obtained for hire, and I could not do the work of the family—my wife could not do it—what was I to do? I was compelled to hire slaves, and pay their masters for their hire; but I had to change them every year—they were bad servants, for they had no interest in me or mine—and I believe it would have been less sin before God to have bought a servant who would have taken an interest in me and I in him; but I did not do so. At length, however, I came into the possession of slaves; and I am a slaveholder, (as I have already explained to the Conference,) and I cannot help myself. It is known that I have waded through deep sorrows at the South during the last four years; I have buried the wife of my youth and the mother of my children, who left me with a family of motherless children, who needed a friend and a mother. I sought another; (and with this the Conference has nothing to do;) I found one who, I believed, would make me a good wife, and a good mother for my children. I had known her long—my children knew and loved her. I sought to make my home a happy one, and I have done so. Sir, I have no apology to make. It has been said I did this thing voluntarily, and with my eyes open. I did so deliberately and in the fear of God—and God has blessed our union. I might have avoided this difficulty by resorting to a trick—by making over these slaves to my wife before marriage, or by doing as a friend who has taken ground in favor of the resolution before you suggested: "Why," said he, "did you not let your wife make over these negroes to her children, securing to herself an annuity from them?" Sir, my conscience would not allow me to do this thing. If I had done so, and those negroes had passed into the hands of those who would have treated them unkindly, I should have been unhappy. Strange as it may seem to brethren, I am a slaveholder for conscience' sake. I have no doubt that my wife would, without a moment's hesitation, consent to the manumission of those slaves, if I thought proper to do it. I know she would unhesitatingly consent to any arrangement I might deem it proper to make on the subject. But how am I to free them? Some of them are old, too old to work to support themselves, and are only an expense to me; and some of them are little children; where shall I send these? and who will provide for them? But, perhaps, I shall be permitted to keep these; but, then, if the others go, how shall I provide for these helpless ones? and as to the others, to what free State shall I send them? and what would be their condition? Besides, many of them would not go—they love their mistress, and could not be induced, under any circumstances, to leave her. Sir, an aged and respectable minister said to me, several years ago, when I had stated just such a case to him, and asked him what he would do, "I would set them free," said he, "I'd wash my hands of them, and if they went to the devil, I'd be clear of them." Sir, into such views of religion or philanthropy my soul cannot enter. I believe the providence of God has thrown these creatures into my hands, and holds me responsible for their proper treatment. I have secured them to my wife by deed of trust since our marriage. The arrangement was only in accordance with an understanding existing previous to marriage. These servants were hers—she had inherited them from her former husband's estate—they had been her only source of support during her widowhood, and would still be her only dependence if it should please God to remove me from her. I have nothing to leave her. I have given my life to the Church from the days of my youth, (and I am now fifty,) and although, as I have previously remarked, she would consent to any arrangement I might make, yet I cannot consent to take advantage of her affection for me to induce her to do what would injure her without at all benefiting the slaves.

Sir, I did not, for a moment, believe that this body of grave and reverend ministers would make this a subject of serious discussion. I thought it likely that there might be some warm ultra brethren here who would take some exception to my course, and on that account I did not make the deed of trust before marriage, lest some should suppose I designed to dodge the responsibility of the case. Those who know me must know that I could not be governed by the mere matter of dollars and cents. What can I do? I have no confession to make—I intend to make none. I stand upon the broad ground of the Discipline on which I took office, and if I have done wrong, put me out. The editor of the Christian Advocate has prejudged this case. He makes me the scapegoat of all the difficulties which abolition excitement has gotten up at the North. I am the only one to blame, in his opinion, should mischief grow out of this case. But I repeat, if I have sinned against the Discipline, I refuse not to die. I have spent my life for the benefit of the slaves. When I was but a boy, I taught a Sunday-school for slaves, in which I taught a number of them to read; and from that period till this day I have devoted my energies to the promotion of their happiness and salvation; with all my influence in private, in public, with my tongue, with my pen, I have assiduously endeavored to promote their present and eternal happiness. And am I to be sacrificed by those who have done little or nothing for them? It is said I have rendered myself unacceptable to our people. I doubt this. I have just returned from Philadelphia, where they knew me to be a slaveholder; yet they flocked to hear me, and the presence of God was with us; we had a good, warm, old-fashioned meeting. I may be unacceptable in New York, yet from the experience I have had, I doubt even that. To whom am I unacceptable? Not to the people of the South—neither masters nor slaves. Has my connection with slaves rendered me less acceptable to the colored people of the South—the very people for whom all this professed sympathy is felt? Does the fact that I am a slaveholder make me less acceptable among them? Let those who have labored long among them answer the question. Sir, I venture to say that in Carolina or Georgia I could to-day get more votes for the office of Bishop from the colored people, than any supporter of this resolution, let him avow himself an emancipator as openly as he pleases. To the colored people of the South there, and to their owners—to the entire membership of the slaveholding Conferences—I would not be unacceptable; but, perhaps, they are no part of "our people;" in short, sir, I believe that I should not be unacceptable to one-half of the Connection; but on this question I have nothing to say. Should the Conference think proper to pass me, there is plenty of ground where I can labor acceptably and usefully. The slaveholding Conferences will present a field sufficiently large for me, should I live to the age of Methuselah; and the Bishops, in arranging the work, will certainly have discretion enough not to send me where I would not be received; nor would I obtrude myself upon any Conference, or lay my hands upon the head of any brother, who would feel himself contaminated by the touch. However, on this subject I have nothing to say. The Conference can take its course; but I protest against the proposed action as a violation of the laws of the Discipline, and an invasion of the rights secured to me by that Book. Yet let the Conference take the steps they contemplate; I enter no plea for mercy—I make no appeal for sympathy; indeed, I love those who sympathize with me, but I do not want it now. I wish you to act coolly and deliberately, and in the fear of God; but I would rather that the Conference would change the issue, and make the resolution to depose the Bishop, and take the question at once, for I am tired of it. The country is becoming agitated upon the subject, and I hope the Conference will act forthwith on the resolution.

On the 29th of May, Bishop Soule addressed the Conference in a very impressive manner, urging upon the body the importance of calmness. He said:

I do not know but this may be a favorable moment for me to offer to the Conference the few remarks I desire to make before final action shall be had on the subject which is now pending before the Conference. I have had no solicitude with regard to the period of time when I should offer these remarks, only that it might be a time of calmness and reflection. I will indulge the hope that this is such a time, and therefore avail myself of the opportunity. I rise, sir, at this moment, as I once said before, with all the calmness which the occasion, I think, requires. But this is not the calm that precedes the tempest and the storm; it is not the calmness of indifference; it cannot be. It is, sir, the calmness of conviction. It is the calmness of principle. If indeed I could be persuaded that my very respectable brother from the Pittsburgh Conference was entirely correct in his opinion, that all the light which could be furnished on this subject had been furnished, I should not rise here. There is a possibility that the brother may be mistaken. I cannot say that I should have forborne to rise, though I had been convinced of the correctness of the judgment of the respected brother from New England, that though we should sit here till January next, no brother would be changed in his vote on this question. I say, I do not know that I should have forborne my observations, though I might have been convinced of the correctness of this opinion; but if no more *light* could be produced, any thing that I could say would be unavailing.

There are periods, sir, in the history of the life of every man who sustains any important station in society, who holds any important relations to it, when his individual character cannot, must not, be neutralized by the laws of association. Under this view, in what I shall say to this Conference, I involve no man in responsibility. My venerable colleagues are in no way concerned in what I shall say to this Conference; so that however I may be involved, they are not involved. The South, on my right, is not involved. The North, on my left, is not involved. I stand in this regard alone. I hope not, indeed, alone in the sentiments that I shall express to the Conference. Brethren have manifested a solicitude to bring this question to an issue—to close the debate and come to the vote. I ask brethren if it is not possible, nowithstanding the time which has been employed in this discussion, notwithstanding the enlarged views which brethren have expressed on the question before them—I ask if it is not possible that action on the resolution may not yet be premature? Society, sir, whether civil or religious, has much more to fear from the passions of its members, than it has to fear from calm investigation and sober inquiry. I am not afraid to meet the calmness of deliberation anywhere. I am not afraid to meet it here; I am not afraid to meet it in the Annual Conference; I am not afraid to meet it before the great religious community of which we are members and ministers. I am not; but I fear the rage of the passions of men. I fear excitements—ardent excitements, prematurely produced in society; and I apprehend that if we trace the history of associations, whether civil or ecclesiastical, we shall find that these premature excitements, waking up the rage of passion, have produced greater calamities than ever were produced by the calmness of deliberation and the sobriety of inquiry, however extensive those investigations may have been. The sound of the trumpet of alarm may go forth from within these consecrated walls—the sound may spread itself on the wings of the wind, or of the whirlwind, over the length and breadth of these lands; but, sir, when this sound shall have died away, when the elements which may have been awakened to boisterous and tumultuous action, shall subside into the calmness of inquiry and reason, a voice may return to this hall, wafted on a counter-breeze; and though the voice be not heard in the thunder, the earthquake, or the storm, it may pierce through the veil of our speculations, and of our theories, and the first sound will be heard in the inquiry, "*What is the cause?*" Well, sir, it will be the province of reason and sobriety to answer. Here it is, sir, spread out before me, spread out before you, in a plain, unsophisticated statement of facts by Bishop Andrew. I have not heard a brother from the North—I have not heard a brother from the South—(and I have listened to hear)—allege that there were any other facts, that there were any other circumstances, having any bearing whatever on the merits of the case now before you. I take it for granted, then, that we have the entire facts of the case before us; and these facts are the cause of whatever alarm, whatever excitement, may have spread through our beloved Zion, and over this continent.

Now, sir, I will beg the indulgence of the Conference while I read an extract from the address of your general superintendents at your last session. You will indulge me in this.

"The experience of more than half a century, since the organization of our ecclesiastical body, will afford us many important lights and landmarks, pointing out what is the safest and most prudent policy to be pursued in our onward course as regards African slavery in these States, and especially in our own religious community. This very interesting period of our history is distinguished by several characteristic features, having a special claim to our consideration at the present time, particularly in view of the unusual excitement which now prevails on the subject, not only in the different Christian Churches, but also in the civil body. And, first, our general rule on slavery, which forms a part of the constitution of the Church, has stood from the beginning unchanged, as testamentary of our sentiments on the principle of slavery and the slave-trade. And in this we differ in no respect from the sentiments of our venerable founder, or from those of the wisest and most distinguished statesmen and civilians of our own and other enlightened and Christian countries. Secondly, in all the enactments of the Church relating to slavery, a due and respectful regard has been had to the laws of the States, never requiring emancipation in contravention of the civil authority, or where the laws of the States would not allow the liberated slave to enjoy freedom. Thirdly, the simply holding or owning slaves, without regard to circumstances, has at no period of the existence of the Church subjected the master to excommunication. Fourthly, rules have been made, from time to time, regulating the sale, and purchase, and holding of slaves, with reference to the different laws of the States where slavery is tolerated; which, upon the experience of the great difficulties of administering them, and the unhappy consequences both to masters and servants, have been as often changed and repealed.

"These important facts, which form prominent parts of our past history as a Church, may very properly lead us to inquire for that course of action in future which may be best calculated to preserve the peace and unity of the whole body, promote the greatest happiness of the slave population, and advance generally, in the slaveholding community of our country, the humane and hallowing influence of our holy religion. We cannot withhold from you, at this eventful period, the solemn conviction of our minds, that no new ecclesiastical legislation on the subject of slavery at this time will have a tendency to accomplish these most desirable objects. And we are fully persuaded that, as a body of Christian ministers, we shall accomplish the greatest good by directing our individual and united efforts, in the spirit of the first teachers of Christianity, to bring both master and servant under the sanctifying influence of the principles of that gospel which teaches the duties of every relation, and enforces the faithful discharge of them by the strongest conceivable motives. Do we aim at the amelioration of the condition of the slave? How can we so effectually accomplish this, in our calling as ministers of the gospel of Christ, as by employing our whole influence to bring both him and his master to a saving knowledge of the grace of God, and to a practical observance of those relative duties so clearly prescribed in the writings of the inspired apostles? Permit us to add, that although we enter not into the political contentions of the day, neither interfere with civil legislation nor with the administration of the laws, we cannot but feel a deep interest in whatever affects the peace, prosperity, and happiness of our beloved country. The union of these States, the perpetuity of the bonds of our national confederation, the reciprocal confidence of the different members of the great civil compact; in a word, the *well-being* of the community of which we are members, should never cease to lie near our hearts, and for which we should offer up our sincere and most ardent prayers to the Almighty Ruler of the universe.

"But can we, as ministers of the gospel, and servants of a Master 'whose kingdom is not of this world,' promote these important objects in any way so truly and permanently as by pursuing the course just pointed out? Can we, at this eventful crisis, render a better service to our country than by laying aside all interference with relations authorized and established by the civil laws, and applying ourselves wholly and faithfully to what specially appertains to our 'high and holy calling;' to teach and enforce the moral obligations of the gospel, in application to all the duties growing out of the different relations in society? By a diligent devotion to this evangelical employment, with an humble and steadfast reliance upon the aid of divine influence, the number of 'believing masters' and servants may be constantly increased, the kindest sentiments and affections cultivated, domestic burdens lightened, mutual confidence cherished, and the peace and happiness of society be promoted. While, on the other hand, if past history affords us any correct rules of judgment, there is much cause to fear that the influence of our sacred office, if employed in interference with the relation itself, and consequently with the civil institutions of the country, will rather tend to prevent, than to accomplish, these desirable ends."

Sir, I have read this extract that the members of this General Conference who were not present at the last session, and this listening assembly, who may not have heard it before, may understand distinctly the ground on which I, with my colleagues, stand in regard to these questions. I desire that this document may stand recorded, with my name to it, till I sleep in the dust of the earth. (Amen.) I desire to leave it as a legacy to my children and my children's children; and, if I might be permitted to say so, I would leave it as a legacy to the Church when I am no more. I want no man to write my epitaph. I will write it myself. I want no man to write and publish my Life. I will do that myself as far as I think it may be necessary for the interests of posterity, or for the benefit of the Church of God. I regret, in reading the Life of my venerable colleague, who has gone from earth to heaven since your last session, that this document, as it stood connected with his name, has not appeared in that memoir. I thank the author of "The History of the Methodist Episcopal Church"—I mean Dr. Bangs—for having presented this document in that History. I met it in Europe, and I am glad it is there. I never wished my name detached from it; no, never, *never*. When this was written, your superintendents believed that they were acting in perfect accordance with the Pastoral Address of the General Conference at its session in Cincinnati. We think so now. Well, sir, I have only one farther remark to make before I proceed to the chief object for which I address the Conference this morning.

It is this: I desire that no undue influence may be produced from the peculiar relation in which I stand to the Church. Sympathy may exert too great an influence when it is brought to bear on great principles. The only subject which has awakened my sympathies during this whole discussion, is the condition of my suffering brethren of the colored race, and this never fails to do it. No matter where I meet the man of color, whether in the South, or in the North with the amount of liberty he enjoys, the sympathies of my nature are all awakened for him. Could I restore bleeding Africa to freedom, to independence, to the rights—to *all* the rights—of man, I would most gladly do it. But this I cannot do—you cannot do. And if I cannot burst the bonds of the colored man, I will not strengthen them. If I cannot extend to him all the good I would, I will never shut him out from the benefits which I have it in my power to bestow. But, sir, I cannot withhold this sentiment from the Conference, that with the mental and physical labors of this relation I could never have been sustained—I could never have supported myself—I could never have ministered to the Church unless I had been settled down on some principles equally as changeless as the throne of God, in my estimation—never, never. It is a constant recurrence to these great principles that has sustained me in the discharge of what I conceive to be my duties—duties which grow out of my relation to the Church, and not simply to this Conference. These principles have sustained me in the city, and in the desert waste; they have sustained me in the North, and they have sustained me in the South; they have sustained me in the quarters of the black man, and in the huts of the red man. Shake me from these principles, and I am done—I have done, I say. But what is this? Why, sir, is the Methodist Episcopal Church dependent upon me? Far from it; her interest hangs not upon my shoulders at all. She can do a great deal better without me than I can without her; much better. Well, sir, laying aside this point—endeavoring to disengage myself as far as possible, consider me as expressing my own opinions, without reference to my colleagues. I wish to say, explicitly, that if the superintendents are only to be regarded as the officers of the General Conference of the Methodist Episcopal Church, and consequently, as officers of the Methodist Episcopal Church, liable to be deposed at will by a simple majority of this body, without a form of trial, no obligation existing growing out of the constitution and laws of the Church, even to assign cause wherefore—I say, if this doctrine be a correct one, every thing I have to say hereafter is powerless, and falls to the ground. But brethren will permit me to say, strange as it may seem, although I have had the honor and the privilege to be a member of the General Conference of the Methodist Episcopal Church ever since its present organization, though I was honored with a seat in the convention of ministers which organized it, in this respect I have heard for the first time, either on the floor of this Conference, in an Annual Conference, or through the whole of the private membership of the Church, this doctrine advanced; this is the first time I ever heard it. Of course it struck me as a novelty. I am not going to enter the arena of controversy with this Conference. I desire that my position may be defined. I desire to understand my landmarks as a Bishop of the Methodist Episcopal Church—not the Bishop of the General Conference, not the Bishop of any Annual Conference. I thought that the constitution of the Church—I thought that its laws and regulations—I thought that the many solemn vows of ordination, the parchment which I hold under the signatures of the departed dead—I thought that these had defined my landmarks—I thought that these had prescribed my duties—I thought that these had marked out my course. In my operations I have acted under the conviction that these were my directions and landmarks, and it affords me great consolation this day to stand, at least in the judgment of this body, to which I hold myself responsible, and before which I will always be ready to appear to answer to any charge they shall prefer against me—I say it affords me some gratification to have stood acquitted for twenty years in the discharge of the high trust committed to my hands; and I here desire to offer my grateful acknowledgments to the Episcopal Committee for the report they have brought to this body, and to the Conference for their cordial acceptance of that report. I say I do it with sentiments of sincerity; and it is the more cordial to me in view of what may yet be to come. In this regard, although I have trembled beneath the weight of responsibility, and shrunk before the consciousness of my inability, and especially as I have felt my physical infirmities coming upon me, and knowing that I must be in the neighborhood of mental infirmity, I stand this day acquitted in my own conscience—(O that I may be acquitted at the bar of my eternal Judge!)—that I have, to the best of my ability, with sincerity of heart, and with the ardent desire to promote the great interests of the Church, and the cause of God, in the discharge of the duties which you have intrusted to me—I have never, in the discharge of this trust—God is my witness—I have never given an appointment to any preacher with a desire or design to afflict him. Indeed, if I could do it, I should abhor myself. Now, sir, whether this Conference is to sustain the position on which I have acted, or not, they are very soon to settle in the vote which is before them; I mean, they are to settle this question, whether it is the right of this body, and whether they have the power to depose a Bishop of the Methodist Episcopal Church; whether they have a right to depose my colleague —to depose me, without a form of trial; see ye to that. Without specification of wrong, and by almost universal acclamation over this whole house, that Bishop Andrew has been unblamable in his Christian character; without blame in his ministerial vocation; that he has discharged the duties of his sacred office to the Church of God with integrity, with usefulness, and with almost universal acceptability, and in good faith; with this declaration before the community, before the world, will this Conference occupy this position, that they have power, authority, to depose Bishop Andrew, without a form of trial, without charge, and without being once called on to answer for himself in the premises—what he did say was voluntary.

Well, brethren, I had conceived, I had understood, from the beginning, that special provision was provided for the trial of a Bishop. The constitution has provided that no preacher, no person, was to be deprived of the right of trial, according to the forms of Discipline, and of the right of appeal; but, sir, if I understand the doctrine advanced and vindicated, it is that you may depose a Bishop without the form of trial; you may depose him without any obligation to show cause, and therefore he is the only minister in your Church who has no appeal. It seems to me that the Church has made special provision for the trial of the Bishop, for the special reason that the Bishop has no appeal. Well, now, sir, I only make these observations, as I said, to the ear of reason. You will remember that this whole thing is going out before the world, as well as the Church. I wish to know my landmarks, to find out where I stand; for indeed I do not hesitate to say to you, that if my standing, and the relation in which I have been placed to the Methodist Episcopal Church, under my solemn vows of ordination—if my relation is to stand on the voice of a simple majority of this body, without a form of trial, and without an obligation even to show me cause why I am deposed, I have some doubt whether there is the man on this floor that would be willing to stand in my place. Now, brethren will at once perceive the peculiar situation in which I am placed. Here are my brethren from the Ohio and other Conferences. We have been together in great harmony and peace. There has been great union of spirit everywhere; but I said at the beginning, there were periods in the history of every man occupying any important relation or station in society, when his individual character and influence could not be neutralized by the laws of association. You must unmoor me from my anchorage on the basis of this book; you must unsettle me from my principles—my settled and fixed principles. From these I cannot be shaken by any influences on my right hand or on my left hand; neither the zeal of youth nor the experience of hoary age shall move me from my principles. Convince me that I am wrong, and I yield. And here it may be necessary that I should make an observation in regard to what I have said before: it seems to have been misunderstood. I said, You may immolate me, but you cannot immolate me on a Southern altar; you cannot immolate me on a Northern altar; I can only be immolated on the altar of the union of the Methodist Episcopal Church. What do I mean by this? I mean—call it a compact—call it compromise, constitutional Discipline, what you will—I mean on the doctrines and provisions of this book, and I consider this as the bond of union of the M. E. Church. Here, then, I plant my feet, and here I stand. Let brethren, sir, not misunderstand me in another point; a point in which they may misunderstand me, in which I have been misunderstood; and you join me on this point. I hold that the General Conference of the Methodist Episcopal Church has an indisputable right—constitutional, sacred—to arraign at her tribunal every Bishop; to try us there; to find us guilty of any offense with which we are charged on evidence, and to excommunicate—expel us. I am always ready to appear before that body in this regard. I recognize fully their right. But not for myself—not for these men on my right hand, and on my left hand; but for your sakes, and for the Church of God, of which you are members and ministers, let me ask you, let me entreat you, not to rush upon the resolution which is now before you. Posterity, sir, will review your actions—history will record them; and whatever we may do here will be spread out before the face of the world; the eyes of men will be fixed upon it. In this view I was not surprised at all to hear brethren say, "Pause, brethren, I beseech you, pause," and I was not surprised to see men of mind and of thought approach the thing with fear and trembling. But brethren apprehend that there are great difficulties involved in this subject; they apprehend that fearful consequences are to take place, on whichever side of the question they shall move. Pass it, and the South suppose themselves involved in irretrievable ruin. Refuse to pass it, and the North consider the consequences perilous to them. Permit me to say, sir, that I have had some acquaintance, personal acquaintance, both with the North and the South; I think I have been able to cast an impartial eye over these great departments of the Church. I may err in judgment, but I apprehend that the difficulties may not be as insurmountable as brethren have apprehended them to be. I know that some of my brethren of the North are involved in such a manner that I cannot apprehend—I perceive no way in which they can compromise this question. Why? For the obvious reason that it involves a principle. I will compromise with no man when a principle is involved in the compromise. What is that principle? The men that avow it are as honest as any men on this floor. I know them; in the men there is no guile. What is the principle? It was advanced by my worthy Brother Cass the other day. Can he compromise the principle? You must convince him of the error of his principle before he will compromise it. What is it? It is that slavery, under all circumstances, is a sin against God.

Mr. Cass interposed. May I correct the Bishop? I believe I did not say so; I said it was a moral evil.

Bishop Soule proceeded. Well, I am glad to be corrected. That is not Brother Cass's principle. A moral evil—a moral evil, and not a sin, under all circumstances. It affords me a great deal of pleasure to hear my worthy brother's statement, for it greatly increases my hope that we shall have a compromise.

Now, sir, notwithstanding brethren have thought,

and with perfect sincerity, that they were ready to act on the resolution; although undoubtedly a large majority of this body have been prepared for it for some time, I cannot but believe that it might be premature in the Conference taking action on it even now. I will offer one or two reasons why I think the Conference is not prepared for action on the resolution. We have been informed here, from documents—to a great extent petitions and memorials—on the subject of slavery in its various aspects and interests. These documents, these petitions and memorials, have been received with the respect due to the right of petition. They have been committed to a large and judicious committee to examine and report. That committee has not reported to this body; it will report; I need not say to you that it will report. The respect due to some thousand petitioners to this body will lay them under solemn obligation to report; and is it not possible that this report—on the subject immediately connected with the resolution before you—may afford you some light? You will have in the report of that committee several important items of information clearly developed before you. You will know the number of the petitioners, of the memorialists, in each of the Annual Conferences. You will know the relative proportion of these petitioners to the whole number of the Methodist Church within these

Conferences. You will know the aggregate number of all these memorialists and petitioners, and you will consequently know the relative number in regard to the whole community of the M. E. Church. It will not be disputed, I think, on the floor of this General Conference, that the subjects, so far as they have been presented when the memorials were up, that the subjects on which you are memorialized in these documents are not local. They are not subjects appertaining specially and exclusively to the memorialists. So far as I heard, every subject was of a general character, in which every member of the Methodist Episcopal Church, East, West, North, and South, has an equal interest and concern. The report of your committee may throw much light on this great subject. But this is not all. I beg to suggest to the brethren that the views of the great body of the Methodist Church, and the great body of her ministers, are not, and cannot be represented here, in regard to the special point before you; and if this be a subject in which all the ministers of the M. E. Church, and all the members of the M. E. Church, have an equal interest and concern, is it safe for this body to proceed to such an important action in regard to the whole interests of the Church, without having a more full development of the subject, both from ministers and Church, than the memorials as yet presented afford? I ask it. Now will the delegation from New York tell us what are the views of the great body of the Methodists within the New York Conference on this subject? We have been sitting here, Mr. President, on this case almost from the time we commenced it. It has been, however, before this community. It has been out before the whole Church, and from the views the brethren have taken, I have been almost surprised that we have not had memorials from the city where we sit; I have been almost surprised that we have not had memorials from the people in Philadelphia, from the people in Baltimore, and from the people in Boston. We have had no memorials. There has been no expression on their part, as I have heard; and yet, in the midst of this enlightened body of Methodists, are we prepared thus to say what is the view of the people around us on this question? and, under such circumstances, do you hesitate to stay the question in the resolution before you? I beg the brethren to go a little farther on this subject. I will go with my brethren to Ohio. Now I do not know—I am a resident in Ohio, I have some acquaintance in Ohio; both with preachers and with our very excellent and worthy membership in Ohio, my brethren from them, these delegates, have more, and, doubtless, can say more—I should not dare, on the floor of this Conference, to say that the act would meet the approbation of the great body of preachers and members in Ohio; I dare not say it. It is sufficient for me, however, in the present position I occupy, to say that the Church has not known the subject, and has expressed no opinion on the subject whatsoever. I settle it down, then, as the basis on which I shall proceed, that we have not, and cannot have, the views of our ministers and people generally on this subject, so fully expressed to us as to others.

The adoption of that resolution deposes Bishop Andrew without form or trial; such is my deliberate opinion. I do not believe it is safe for our community; I do not believe it is safe for you; and I am out of this question. What shall be done? The question, I know, wakes up the attention of every brother. Can it be possible that the Methodist Episcopal Church is in such a state of excitement—in such a state, I had almost said, of revolution—as to be unprepared to send out the plain, simple facts in the case to the Churches, to the Annual Conferences, everywhere through our community, and waive all action on this subject till another General Conference?

I said, almost at the commencement of these remarks, sir, that I was not afraid of the *deliberation* of men, of our Annual Conferences, of the General Conferences—I am afraid of the passions of men, and I could present before you some considerations to illustrate the views that I have given you; and if I give you these views in error of judgment, be assured that they are not views which originate on the spur of the moment; they are the result of sober and deliberate investigation. Can it be possible that the simple circumstance of Bishop Andrew's holding an office as a Bishop of the Methodist Episcopal Church four years longer, with this statement of facts in the case—simple facts in the case—spread out before the enlightened body of this great Methodist community—is there to be an earthquake? I am not prepared to believe it; I soberly am not prepared to believe it. Well, sir, this is the view that I take of the subject. Permit me to make one other suggestion. The providence of God directs the whirlwind and the storm; clouds and darkness indeed may be round about us, but righteousness and justice are the habitation of his throne. Let us be careful that we never suffer a human arm to impede the operations of Providence. My beloved colleague, Bishop Andrew, and myself, and all my colleagues, may have passed away from these scenes of trouble and the passions which now agitate the Church of God—may go to sleep, in God's providence, long before four years go by.

How easy it is for God to direct the elements of society! Don't be surprised, then, brethren, when I say to you, Pause. Brethren may possibly have a little more light; there may be some ray from heaven or earth yet to shine upon this subject. Now it is the solemn conviction of my mind that the safest course you can pursue in the premises is to pass this subject without any implication of Bishop Andrew's character at all, and to send out officially the plain and simple facts in the case to all your societies—to all your Conferences. Let it be read everywhere, and then we may have a farther expression of opinion, without any kind of agitation. I am about to take my leave of you, brethren. You must know—you cannot but know, that with the principles I have stated to you—with the avowal of my sentiments in regard to this subject—it will not be Bishop Andrew alone that your word will affect! No, sir, I implicate neither my colleagues on my right hand nor on my left; but I say the decision of the question cannot affect Bishop Andrew alone. I wish it to be distinctly understood, it *cannot affect him alone.* I mean specially in this point—I say that the resolution on which we are just about to act goes to sustain the doctrine that the General Conference have power and right to depose one of the Bishops of the Methodist Episcopal Church without the form of trial—that you are under no obligation from the constitution or laws of the Church to *show cause* even. Now every man must see, and every man must know, that Bishop Andrew cannot be involved alone in the vote. It is the principle which is involved. It goes to say that when this Conference shall vote on the subject—a simple majority of this Conference—without form of trial, can depose a Bishop of the Methodist Episcopal Church. Do you understand it so? If I am mistaken, I shall stand corrected—and I need not say to this Conference that such a decision will involve others beside. It involves the office; it involves the charge; it involves the relation itself.

And now, in taking leave, I offer devout prayer to Almighty God that you may be directed wisely in the decision you are about to make. I have given to you what, in my sober and deliberate judgment, is the best and safest course which you can pursue—safest for all concerned. I want that opinion to have no more influence upon you than it justly deserves in the Conferences—all the Conferences. I thank the Conference for the attention they have been pleased to give me. I thank the audience for their attention. I very well know—I am not at all unapprised that the position I occupy—in which I stand on the principles of that resolution—on the principles involved in it—may seal my fate. I say I am not at all unapprised of that. Let me go; but I pray you hold to principles—to principles; and with these remarks, I submit the whole to your and God's direction. (Amen!)

Dr. Capers was the last speaker on the Southern side who addressed the Conference.

"The first point Dr. Capers made was in respect to the unity of the Church. His argument was in substance this: Bishop Andrew is under arrest as a slaveholder, because thereby he has made it impossible for himself to exercise in the non-slaveholding States his Episcopal functions. Very well. You maintain that a General Conference is the supreme power in the Church, to which the Bishops are subordinate and responsible. How absurd is the clamor against a slaveholding Bishop, as a contamination upon a part of the Church, when the General Conference itself includes slaveholders, who thus, by the very unity of the Church, connect these immaculate Conferences inextricably with 'the great evil.' 'Yes, sir,' he said, 'they and I are brethren, whether they will or no. The same holy hands have been laid upon their heads and upon my head. The same vows which they have taken, I have taken. At the same altar where they minister, do I minister; and with the same words mutually on our tongues. We are the same ministry, of the same Church; not *like*, but *identical.* Are they Elders? So am I. Spell the word. There is not a letter in it which they dare deny me. Take their measure. I am just as high as they are, and they are as low as I am. We are not one ministry for the North, and another ministry for the South; but one, and one only, for the whole Church.'

"It could not have made his argument more conclusive or irresistible, had he added, that by virtue of this same unity and connectionalism of the Church, he, a slaveholder, had himself been called on by Northern as well as Southern votes to represent the entire American Methodist Church, a few years previously, before the British Wesleyan Conference. Had the lapse of these few years altered the immutable law of Christian morals, and made that to be wrong to-day which was perfectly right then?

"After a brief examination of the new doctrine which had been improvised to cover the approaching action, that, namely, which held Bishops to be merely officers of the General Conference, liable to be set aside as class-leaders, at the mere pleasure of a majority, and showing what a solemn farce the consecration service would become on such a supposition, Dr. Capers went on to exhibit the *unconstitutionality* of the contemplated proceeding. He maintained that whatever else the Constitution of the Church might be, it must first be Christian, and secondly, Protestant, and thirdly, consistent with the great object for which the Methodist Church was raised up, to spread scriptural holiness over these lands. In elaborating this last point, he showed how the proceedings against the Bishop must impede the course of the ministry in many of the States, and debar access altogether to large portions of the colored population. He was now approaching a point of view where, from the very office he had held under the General Conference for the last four years—that of Missionary Secretary for the South—he was entitled to speak with the highest authority. If any man in America could be supposed to be well informed on this subject, Dr. Capers was that man. And what was his testimony? 'Never, never,' said he, 'have I suffered, as in view of the evil which this measure threatens against the South. The agitation has begun there; and I tell you that though our hearts were to be torn from our bodies, it could avail nothing when once you have awakened the feeling that we cannot be trusted among the slaves. *Once you have done this, you have effectually destroyed us.* I could wish to die sooner than live to see such a day. As sure as you live, there are tens of thousands, nay, hundreds of thousands, whose destiny may be periled by your decision on this case. When we tell you that we preach to a hundred thousand slaves in our missionary field, we only announce the beginning of our work—the beginning openings of the door of access to the most numerous masses of slaves in the South. When we add that there are two hundred thousand now within our reach who have no gospel unless we give it them, it is still but the same announcement of the beginnings of the opening of that wide and effectual door, which was so long closed, and so lately has begun to be opened, for the preaching of the gospel by our ministry, to a numerous and destitute portion of the people. O close not this door! Shut us not out from this great work, to which we have been so signally called of God.'

"In this strain he went on to the conclusion of his speech. Had it been within the possibility of human agency to close or bridge the gulf of separation which yawned between the Northern and Southern sections of the Church, this fervid, telling, and powerful appeal to the Christian principles and emotions of the majority, must have done it. Were they not the very men by eminence, who were clamoring about the civil and social condition of the negro population of the Southern States? But were they not, also, the very preachers whose business it was to ask the question, 'What shall it profit a man if he shall gain the whole world, and lose his own soul?' Was it possible that these men cared nothing for the souls of the negroes? Swallowed up, as some of them no doubt were, in the abstractions of a fanaticism which was blind to all spiritual and eternal interests, and hardened as some of them possibly were by the hypocritical cant of abolitionism, there was yet enough of sound Christianity among the majority of that General Conference to *feel* the force of those considerations—irresistible to a good man—which in so touching a style this speech had set before them. Why, then, did they carry out the measure objected to on such weighty considerations? The answer is, that all considerate men among them saw that the time had come for a separation. They meant to meet the emergency with a steady determination to do justice to the claims of that portion of the Church represented by the minority. Subsequent acts show that they are entitled to the justification found alone in such a determination.

"Dr. Few, of Georgia, whose want of health had deprived the South of his important services as a delegate, upon reading Dr. Capers's speech, made the following remark: 'I would be willing to risk the whole cause upon that speech alone, with every sound-minded, unprejudiced man, although he should be required to read all that was said on the opposite side.'"

The able speech of Dr. Capers was delivered on the 30th of May, immediately after which Dr. Peck suggested the propriety of bringing the debate to a close. Bishop Andrew also asked that the question might be taken. The motion for the

---

* Wightman's Life of Capers, pp. 403–408.

previous question having failed, Bishop Hedding then requested that the Conference might not sit this afternoon, in order that the superintendents might have an opportunity to consult together with a view to fixing upon a compromise; and he requested the Conference to revive the committee of Northern and Southern brethren, discharged some days since, that they might meet the Bishops in council on this important question.

Dr. Durbin hailed the proposition with delight, but he suggested that it would be better in the circumstances not to revive the committee. Let the Bishops meet together—Bishop Andrew as well as the rest—and let them invite any brethren to meet with them whom they pleased. He would give them plenipotentiary powers in the case. This suggestion was agreed to.

Dr. Olin then moved that the case of Bishop Andrew be deferred till to-morrow morning.

On the 31st of May, the following address of the Bishops was read by Bishop Waugh:

To the General Conference of the M. E. Church:

Rev. and Dear Brethren:—The undersigned respectfully and affectionately offer to your calm consideration the result of their consultation this afternoon in regard to the unpleasant and very delicate question which has been so long and so earnestly debated before your body. They have, with the liveliest interest, watched the progress of the discussion, and have awaited its termination with the deepest solicitude. As they have poured over this subject with anxious thought, by day and by night, they have been more and more impressed with the difficulties connected therewith, and the disastrous results which, in their apprehension, are the almost inevitable consequences of present action on the question now pending before you. To the undersigned it is fully apparent that a decision thereon, whether affirmatively or negatively, will most extensively disturb the peace and harmony of that widely extended brotherhood which has so effectively operated for good in the United States of America and elsewhere during the last sixty years, in the development of a system of active energy, of which union has always been a main element. They have, with deep emotion, inquired, Can any thing be done to avoid an evil so much deprecated by every friend of our common Methodism? Long and anxiously have they waited for a satisfactory answer to this inquiry, but they have paused in vain. At this painful crisis they have unanimously concurred in the propriety of recommending the postponement of farther action in the case of Bishop Andrew until the ensuing General Conference. It does not enter into the design of the undersigned to argue the propriety of their recommendation, otherwise strong and valid reasons might be adduced in its support. They cannot but think that if the embarrassment of Bishop Andrew should not cease before that time, the next General Conference, representing the pastors, ministers, and people of the several Annual Conferences, after all the facts in the case shall have passed in review before them, will be better qualified than the present General Conference can be to adjudicate the care wisely and discreetly. Until the cessation of the embarrassment, or the expiration of the interval between the present and the ensuing General Conference, the undersigned believe that such a division of the work of the general superintendency might be made, without any infraction of a constitutional principle, as would fully employ Bishop Andrew in those sections of the Church in which his presence and services would be welcome and cordial. If the course pursued on this occasion by the undersigned be deemed a novel one, they persuade themselves that their justification, in the view of all candid and peace-loving persons, will be found in their strong desire to prevent disunion, and to promote harmony in the Church.

Very respectfully and affectionately submitted,

JOSHUA SOULE,
ELIJAH HEDDING,
B. WAUGH,
T. A. MORRIS.

This address was followed by remarks from several members, among whom was Dr. Bangs, who proposed that it be referred "to a committee of nine," which was finally agreed to.

On the 1st of June, Bishop Hedding expressed a wish to withdraw his name from the communication presented by the Bishops on the previous day, offering the following reasons for this desire: That he signed the address "as a peace measure," and that "he believed it would be generally acceptable to the Conference," but that "in both these expectations he was disappointed." Bishops Waugh and Morris wished their names to remain, the former until "he saw other reasons than had yet appeared" for an abandonment of the position he had taken, and the latter "as a testimony that he had done what he could to preserve the unity of the body."

Bishop Soule said he "put his signature to the document with the same views and under the same convictions as his worthy colleagues did, and neither his views nor his convictions were changed in any way. And he wished that document to go forth through a thousand channels to the world. It is already before the American people, and he might not, and would not, withdraw it."

On motion of Dr. Bangs, the communication was laid on the table by a vote of 95 to 83.

After this vote, Dr. Bangs said it was well

known that he had used every effort in his power to have this matter brought to a compromise, and he had indulged a hope that this would be the result. It was with that view that he labored to have this document referred to a committee. But from what had been told him by members from the North and South, not a vestige of this hope remained, and he would now urge immediate action upon the substitute, if it was before the house. He believed wisdom, and prudence, and Christianity, and brotherly love, dictated that course, and that farther discussion would not change one mind.

Dr. Winans said the last speaker had referred to the South, and his remarks in their connection went to say that the South were opposed to the proposition from the superintendents. He begged to say that the Southern delegates were of one mind to entertain the proposition of the superintendents.

Dr. Bangs explained that he did not mean to say that the South objected to the proposal of the Bishops, but that the Conference could not come to any general compromise on the subject. He should not, himself, move the previous question.

Mr. Collins opposed the motion for taking up the order of the day. He had not given up all hopes of peace; and if they would wait a few minutes and listen to a proposal from Dr. Durbin, he thought a compromise might yet be effected. They were bound to make a settlement of the question, he knew, but in their proposed action the Bishops were against them; and if they would withdraw their names from the communication they had made, and allow Dr. Durbin to use it as his own, he (Mr. Collins) believed a plan of pacification might still be concocted. The proposition was, as a last effort to bring peace and save the Church from division, to add to the suggestion of the Episcopacy some resolutions expressive of the regret of that General Conference that Bishop Andrew had become connected with slavery, and request him to rid himself of the embarrassment as soon as possible; and, in addition, a resolution to take off the journals all that related to the colored testimony question. He thought such a measure would answer their purpose, and heal the wound of the Church.

Mr. Blake was pursuing his labors as a minister among the colored people, and little thought that the question of slavery would be brought up. He had no anticipation of a storm, but he found that the foundations of the great deep were broken up, and the ark of their Church was floating on the waves. But he thanked God that in the distance he saw a blessed Ararat. He went on describing the various forms under which slavery had been discussed in the present Conference, alluded to the definitions of the Episcopal office during the debate, and thought that Dr. Durbin's substitute would not reconcile the difficulties.

Mr. Longstreet said, as long as there was any hope of reconciliation, he would desire that this question be postponed. As yet, the South had not made one proposition to adjust the matter amicably. He trusted, therefore, that the door would not be closed. Time was a matter of very little consequence compared with the importance of the questions at issue. He wished to wait, and see what time would bring forth.

Dr. Paine said he was a man of peace. He deeply regretted to hear unkind words from both sides. He never dealt in wholesale denunciation. The South felt calm as they could feel when the importance of the question was considered. He considered the substitute to be mandatory. It acted as a mandamus; it had been so described. This placed the South in an awkward position. He hoped some ground would be proposed by the North that both could occupy. If there was no such common ground, the South was prepared for the result.

Mr. Porter recalled the attention of the Conference to the discussion of the last fortnight as evidence of the peace-loving character of the Northern members. They wanted to be one body. He did not believe they could live as one body with any thing less than the substitute. He asked what was the prospect of peace—Bishop Andrew had declared that he could not recede from his position, and the South had taken the same ground. It was no use to discuss the question farther, therefore, but they had better come up square to the question, and decide the point at once, that the people might be satisfied.

Mr. Mitchell proposed an amendment, to be appended to the resolution, to the effect that the Bishop should so resign until a majority of the Annual Conferences desired him to resume his office. Mr. M. did not think it necessary to enter into a discussion whether the resolution respecting Bishop Andrew was advisory or mandatory. He wished the substitute to come before the Conference this morning.

On motion, the order of the day was taken up.

Bishop Soule said he had good reason to believe that brethren had entertained erroneous views with respect to the position he occupied at the time he addressed the Conference on this subject; and he now wished to correct those views, that there might be a proper understanding in the matter before they had action on the substitute. It must have occurred to the brethren that his remarks at that time were entirely irrelevant, except on the understanding that the resolution was mandatory. He looked upon it as suspending Bishop

Andrew. There was a great difference between suspension and advice. If this action was not intended to be judicial, he should withdraw many of his remarks. If it was a mandatory act, it was judicial. One member said it was merely a request to Bishop Andrew to resign; but several had declared it to be judicial, and were not contradicted. Again: the argument was, that slavery could not exist in the Episcopacy of the Methodist Church. One brother had said, that if the resolution passed, Bishop Andrew was still a Bishop of the Methodist Episcopal Church. If this was the case, his remarks, he must repeat, were irrelevant. He considered the proceeding as a judicial one, suspending Brother Andrew from his duties as Bishop of the Methodist Episcopal Church.

Mr. J. T. Peck moved the previous (that is, the main) question, which was carried. The resolution was then read, and the ayes and noes were taken; Bishop Soule observing, that definite action must necessarily be hereafter taken to decide whether the resolution was mandatory or advisory. The votes were given amid the most profound stillness.

The resolution (Mr. Finley's substitute) read as follows:

"Whereas, the Discipline of our Church forbids the doing any thing calculated to destroy our itinerant general superintendency; and, whereas, Bishop Andrew has become connected with slavery, by marriage and otherwise, and this act having drawn after it circumstances which, in the estimation of the General Conference, will greatly embarrass the exercise of his office as an itinerant general superintendent, if not, in some places, entirely prevent it; therefore,

"*Resolved,* That it is the sense of this General Conference that he desist from the exercise of this office so long as this impediment remains."

The yeas and nays being called by delegations, were as follows:

YEAS.

New York Conference: Nathan Bangs, Stephen Olin, Phineas Rice, George Peck, John B. Stratten, Peter P. Sandford, Fitch Reed, Samuel D. Ferguson, Stephen Martindale, Marvin Richardson. *Troy:* Truman Seymour, John M. Wever, James Covel, jr., Tobias Spicer, Seymour Coleman, James B. Houghtaling, Jesse T. Peck. *Providence:* J. Lovejoy, F. Upham, S. Benton, Paul Townsend. *New Hampshire:* Elihu Scott, J. Perkins, Samuel Kelly, S. Chamberlain, John G. Dow, J. Spaulding, C. D. Cahoon, William D. Cass. *New England:* J. Porter, D. S. King, P. Crandall, C. Adams, G. Pickering. *Pittsburgh:* William Hunter, H. J. Clark, J. Spencer, S. Elliott, R. Boyd, S. Wakefield, J. Drummond. *Maine:* M. Hill, E. Robinson, D. B. Randall, C. W. Morse, J. Hobart, Heman Nickerson, G. Webber. *Black River:* A. D. Peck, A. Adams, G. Baker, W. W. Ninde. *Erie:* J. J. Steadman, John Bain, G. W. Clark, J. Robinson, T. Goodwin. *Oneida:* J. M. Snyder, S. Comfort, N. Rounds, D. A. Shepherd, H. F. Row, E. Bowen, D. Holmes, jr. *Michigan:* E. Crane, A. Billings, J. A. Baughman. *Rock River:* B. Weed, H. W. Reed, J. T. Mitchell. *Genesee:* G. Fillmore, S. Luckey, A. Steele, F. G. Hibbard, S. Seager, A. Abell, W. Hosmer, J. B. Alverson. *North Ohio:* E. Thompson, J. H. Power, A. Poe, E. Yocum, W. Runnells. *Illinois:* P. Akers, P. Cartwright. *Ohio:* C. Elliott, William H. Raper, J. M. Trimble, J. B. Finley, L. L. Hamline, Z. Connell, J. Ferree. *Indiana*: M. Simpson, A. Wiley, E. R. Ames, J. Miller, C. W. Ruter, A. Wood, A. Eddy, J. Havens. *Texas:* J. Clark. *Baltimore:* J. A. Collins, A. Griffith, J. Bear, N. J. B. Morgan, J. Davis. *Philadelphia:* J. P. Durbin, L. Scott. *New Jersey:* I. Winner, J. S. Porter, J. K. Shaw. 111.

NAYS.

New York Conference: C. W. Carpenter. *Michigan:* G. Smith. *Rock River:* J. Sinclair. *Illinois:* J. Stamper, J. Van Cleve, N. G. Berryman. *Kentucky:* H. B. Bascom, W. Gunn, H. H. Kavanaugh,

E. Stevenson, B. T. Crouch, G. W. Brush. *Ohio:* E. W. Sehon. *Holston:* E. F. Sevier, S. Patton, T. Stringfield. *Tennessee:* R. Paine, J. B. McFerrin, A. L. P. Green, T. Maddin. *Missouri:* W. W. Redman, W. Patton, J. C. Berryman, J. M. Jameson. *North Carolina:* J. Jameson, Peter Doub, H. G. Leigh. *Memphis:* G. W. D. Harris, S. S. Moody, William McMahon, T. Joyner. *Arkansas:* J. C. Parker, W. P. Ratcliffe, A. Hunter. *Virginia:* J. Early, T. Crowder, W. A. Smith, L. M. Lee. *Mississippi:* William Winans, B. M. Drake, J. Lane, G. M. Rogers. *Texas:* L. Fowler. *Alabama:* J. Boring, J. Hamilton, William Murrah, G. Garrett. *Georgia:* G. F. Pierce, W. J. Parks, L. Pierce, J. W. Glenn, J. E. Evans, A. B. Longstreet. *South Carolina:* William Capers, W. M. Wightman, C. Betts, S. Dunwody, H. A. C. Walker. *Baltimore:* H. Slicer, J. A. Gere, T. B. Sargent, C. B. Tippett, G. Hildt. *Philadelphia:* T. J. Thompson, H. White, W. Cooper, I. T. Cooper. *New Jersey:* Thomas Neal, Thomas Sovereign. 69.

So the resolution was adopted by a vote of 111 against 69.

CHAPTER IV.

The effect of the action of the General Conference on the Church in the South—Notice given by Dr. Pierce that the Southern Delegates would enter their Protest—Resolutions offered by Henry Slicer—Resolutions offered by Dr. Capers—Referred to a Committee—Declaration of the Southern Members—Dr. Elliott proposes its reference—Speech of Peter P. Sandford—Reply of Dr. Longstreet—Dr. Olin's Remarks—Declaration referred—Resolution of Instruction to the Committee—Protest of the Minority—Communication from Bishops Soule, Hedding, Waugh, and Morris—Reply of the Conference—Report of the Committee of Nine—The Report discussed—Its adoption—The Adjournment of the General Conference.

THE adoption of the substitute offered by Mr. Finley, virtually deposing Bishop Andrew from the Episcopal office, was not unexpected to the Southern delegates. Indeed, from the moment when his official character was arrested, they apprehended such a result. Knowing the effect that these extrajudicial proceedings would have in the South, they deemed it their duty to the Church, to the welfare and advancement of which they had consecrated their energies and their lives;

to the African race residing in the South, so many thousands of whom had been brought to Christ through the instrumentality of Methodism; and to the people among whom they lived and labored, to manifest their disapproval in language entirely free from ambiguity.

A quiet submission to the action of the General Conference, would not only be the price of their influence as ministers of the gospel of Christ among the people they served, but would result in the exile of Methodism from the Southern States. Standing upon the New Testament basis, they had preached to the master and the slave, teaching humanity to the former, and obedience to the latter, and had succeeded in winning both to Christ. The smiles of Heaven were resting on their labors, and the approval of the Almighty was seen and felt in the happy conversion of thousands.

Immediately after the vote of the Conference on the substitute, Dr. Lovick Pierce arose and said:

It would be within the recollection of the members and spectators who had listened to this discussion with so much interest, that, in the event of the Conference deciding upon the passage of this resolution, the Southern delegation had declared that they would enter their solemn protest against it, without a dissenting voice or faltering step. They should, at the earliest possible moment, do so, and it should be a manly, ministerial, and proper protest against this action of the Conference, as an extrajudicial act, that their sentiments on the subject might go down to posterity.

He contended that, however conscientiously—and he gave them full credit for that—they had acted, still they had acted contrary to the rule of compromise. The constitutionality, or otherwise, of their proceeding would probably be tried before other tribunals. It had never entered into his heart in any thing to depart from the spirit and intention of the Discipline of the Church, and those who were his brethren in the South were of the same mind. He believed that, when the public mind had been sounded, and the deep tones of public opinion came pealing up from all quarters of the Connection, there would be a verdict in favor of the South.

On the 3d of June, Mr. Slicer, of Baltimore, offered the following resolutions:

"*Resolved*, That it is the sense of this General Conference that the vote of Saturday last, in the case of Bishop Andrew, be understood as advisory only, and not in the light of a judicial mandate.

"*Resolved*, 2dly, That the final disposition of

Bishop Andrew's case be postponed until the General Conference of 1848, in conformity with the suggestion of the Bishops, in their address to the Conference on Friday, 31st May.

"H. SLICER,
"T. B. SARGENT."

These resolutions were laid on the table by a vote of 75 to 68—the South voting unanimously against laying on the table.

On the same day Dr. Capers offered the following resolution:

"*Be it resolved by the delegates of all the Annual Conferences in General Conference assembled,* That we recommend to the Annual Conferences to suspend the constitutional restrictions which limit the powers of the General Conference so far, and so far only, as to allow of the following alterations in the government of the Church, viz.:

"1. That the Methodist Episcopal Church, in these United States and Territories, and the Republic of Texas, shall constitute two General Conferences, to meet quadrennially, the one at some place *south*, and the other *north* of the line which now divides between the States commonly designated as free States and those in which slavery exists.

"2. That each of the two General Conferences thus constituted shall have full powers, under the limitations and restrictions which are now of force and binding on the General Conference, to make rules and regulations for the Church, within their territorial limits, respectively, and to elect Bishops for the same.

"3. That the two General Conferences aforesaid shall severally have jurisdiction as follows: The Southern General Conference shall comprehend the States of Virginia, Kentucky, and Missouri, and the States and Territories lying southerly thereto, and also the Republic of Texas, to be known and designated by the title of the 'Southern General Conference of the Methodist Episcopal Church of the United States.' And the Northern General Conference to comprehend all those States lying north of the States of Virginia, Kentucky, and Missouri, as above, to be known and designated by the title of the 'Northern General Conference of the Methodist Episcopal Church in the United States.'

"4. *And be it farther resolved,* That as soon as three-fourths of all the members of all the Annual Conferences shall have voted on these resolutions, and shall approve the same, the said Southern and Northern General Conferences shall be deemed as having been constituted by such approval; and it shall be competent for the Southern Annual Conferences to elect delegates to said Southern General Conference, to meet in the city of Nashville, Tennessee, on the first of May, 1848, or sooner, if a majority of two-thirds of the members of the Annual Conferences composing that General Conference shall desire the same.

"5. *And be it farther resolved, as aforesaid,* That the Book Concerns at New York and Cincinnati shall be held and conducted as the property and for the benefit of all the Annual Conferences as heretofore: the Editors and Agents to be elected once in four years at the time of the session of the Northern General Conference, and the votes of the Southern General Conference to be cast by delegates of that Conference attending the Northern for that purpose.

"6. *And be it farther resolved,* That our Church organization for foreign missions shall be maintained and conducted jointly between the two General Conferences as one Church, in such manner as shall be agreed upon from time to time between the two great branches of the Church as represented in the said two Conferences."

Dr. Bangs moved that the resolutions be referred to a select committee, consisting of Messrs. Capers, Winans, Crowder, Porter, Fillmore, Akers, Hamline, Davis, and Sandford. On the 5th of June, Dr. Capers announced "that they could not agree on a report which they judged would be acceptable to the Conference."

In the afternoon session of the same day, Dr.

Longstreet presented the following "Declaration of the Southern members:"

"The delegates of the Conferences in the slave-holding States take leave to *declare* to the General Conference of the Methodist Episcopal Church, that the continued agitation on the subject of slavery and abolition in a portion of the Church—the frequent action on that subject in the General Conference—and especially the extrajudicial proceedings against Bishop Andrew, which resulted, on Saturday last, in the virtual suspension of him from his office as superintendent—must produce a state of things in the South which renders a continuance of the jurisdiction of that General Conference over these Conferences inconsistent with the success of the ministry in the slaveholding States."

Virginia Conference.—John Early, W. A. Smith, Thomas Crowder, Leroy M. Lee.

Kentucky.—H. B. Bascom, William Gunn, H. H. Kavanaugh, Edward Stevenson, B. T. Crouch, G. W. Brush.

Missouri.—W. W. Redman, William Patton, J. C. Berryman, J. M. Jameson.

Holston.—E. F. Sevier, S. Patton, Thomas Stringfield.

Georgia.—G. F. Pierce, William J. Parks, L. Pierce, J. W. Glenn, J. E. Evans, A. B. Longstreet.

North Carolina.—James Jameson, Peter Doub, B. T. Blake.

Illinois.—J. Stamper.

Memphis.—G. W. D. Harris, Wm. McMahon, Thomas Joyner, S. S. Moody.

Arkansas.—John C. Parker, William P. Ratcliffe, Andrew Hunter.

Mississippi.—William Winans, B. M. Drake, John Lane, G. M. Rogers.

Texas.—Littleton Fowler.

Alabama.—Jesse Boring, Jefferson Hamilton, W. Murrah, G. Garrett.

Tennessee.—Robert Paine, John B. McFerrin, A. L. P. Green, T. Maddin.

South Carolina.—W. Capers, William M. Wightman, Charles Betts, S. Dunwody, H. A. C. Walker.

Dr. Elliott proposed the reference of the paper to a committee of nine.

Mr. Sandford said he had some objections to that motion in the present form of the communication just read. It alleged what he presumed the General Conference would not admit, that there had been extrajudicial proceedings against Bishop Andrew. For one he denied that that was the fact, and he supposed a majority of the Conference would coincide in that view of the matter, and he did not see how they could allow a paper to come under their action which alleged that which they did not believe to be true. He was aware that during the discussion speakers on the other side had said this was the case, but it was expressly disavowed on the floor of that Conference; and he knew that the member who had presented the document now before them had said, just before the vote was taken, that unless he heard some expression to the contrary, he should take the meaning attached to it by the friend of the mover as its proper meaning. He (Mr. S.) heard no response in contradiction to the construction thus put upon the resolution. How then could it come to pass that men who heard this avowal could now come forward and say that this Conference had been guilty of an extrajudicial act? To him the course taken appeared as a direct insult to that body, and such as they should not yield to. Let those who had presented this paper make a communication according to existing and acknowledged facts, but not asserting what the General Conference denied to be true. If they thought the proposed course necessary, let them say so without adding insult thereto, and the Conference would hear them, but he could not consent to having such a paper as the present one referred to a committee.

Mr. Longstreet said he believed this was the third speech they had had from that brother on the subject of the sentence, or advice, or counsel, or whatever name they choose to give the action on Saturday against the Bishop, and he had hoped that in some one of those speeches he would have told them how he did understand that action. He (Mr. L.) had striven to get at it in vain. When he rose some days ago to address the Conference, he remarked that there was some ambiguity in the form of the resolution, but that the plain import of its language was, when taken in connection with the facts, *mandatory*—imperative was his word—and that he should thus understand it unless he was corrected by somebody. Nobody did correct him, nor did he hear, until Dr. Durbin got up, from the lips of any one that he had misinterpreted the resolution. After that explanation he (Mr. L.) said then, unless he was corrected he should understand it as so explained, and nobody objected, so he was at liberty to understand it either way! He could not have conceived that that Conference could have taken a position so strictly ambiguous. When an explanatory resolution on the subject was introduced the other day, Mr. Sandford rose and said, that he thought it very plain, but he never told us how he viewed it. The vote of this Conference against the South was then both mandatory and advisory. Will any one dispute that? [No answer.] Well, now, it is not disputed! Will that brother tell us how he understood it? Then it appears to me we are thrown back upon its plain legitimate terms, which, in connection with the facts, make it mandatory upon the Bishop. Why? Because you substituted it for the request, and changed the terms to "it is the sense of this Conference," etc. What was the use of the substitute unless it was the design of this Conference, which he could not believe, to have two or three positions on which each man could take his stand to explain his views? Then, he should maintain, it was a sentence; and did their saying so insult the Conference? Now, a judicial sentence is one in which the tribunal having cognizance of the case pronounces its judgment after due forms of law, on the finding of a court or jury, after hearing all the circumstances of the case. But had there been one single sentence in this whole proceeding which partakes of a judicial proceeding? Certainly not. Then the resolution was the sense of the house expressed extrajudicially.

Nothing (said Mr. L.) could have been farther from our intention than to offer an insult to this body. We have now the calmness of despair. This has been thrown out as an olive branch of peace. It is hoped that we can now meet on some common ground, for the thing is done, and the mischief is accomplished, and now we are in a situation to come together, and viewing the wreck, see what we can save from it. We express our opinion that it is no longer desirable that this Conference should have jurisdiction. This continual harassing us on a subject from which we cannot escape, only brings us to quarrel with each other. Now the question is, whether we cannot meet with something that will harmonize us all. Let me relieve the persons who present that paper from any intention to insult or cast firebrands into this Conference. The word objected to is so commonly used with reference to the recent action of this Conference, that it has become a household word with us, and I regret that the brother should so generally take these verbal exceptions, and should exhibit this morbid sensibility about mere words. I regret that he has not more charity than to suppose that the fifty-two should design to insult the one hundred and twenty-eight.

Mr. Sandford explained, that he did not attribute design in the matter.

Mr. Longstreet. Then it is an insult, which the fifty-two had not capacity to discover.

At the request of the President, Mr. Longstreet farther defined and illustrated what he conceived to be meant by a judicial act. A man must be brought to the judgment of a court of some kind, according to the forms of law necessary to bring him within the range of the judge's power, when by due form he is put upon his trial, and the jury or court, having heard him, sentence is passed upon him, and such sentence I take to be a judicial sentence. But if brought up without any precept having been directed to him setting forth the accusation; and if, without examination of witnesses, he is made to testify against himself, and out of that testimony are extracted the charges against him, the prosecutors being the parties against whom the alleged offense has been committed, the prosecutors trying him, and pronouncing sentence without forms of law, and without examining witnesses, then it is truly and properly an extrajudicial act.

Dr. Olin said he would not have supported the substitute if he had regarded its operations as judicial or punitive. He considered that Bishop Andrew was not punished, was not tried; that the Conference did not depose him, nor in the legal meaning or consequences of the terms employed in that resolution did he consider that the Bishop was in any way disqualified from performing the functions of his office. His acts now would not be invalid, though constitutionally he would be liable to appear before the next General Conference and answer for his conduct. He would embody his sentiments in the form of resolutions, which, however, he would not press upon the Conference.

"*Resolved*, That this Conference does not consider its action in the case of Bishop Andrew as either judicial or punitive, but as a prudential regulation for the security and welfare of the Church.

"*Resolved,* That having made a solemn declaration of what, in their judgment, the safety and peace of the Church require, it is not necessary or proper to express any opinion as to what amount of respect may justly belong to their action in the premises."

The Declaration was then referred to a committee of nine, consisting of Messrs. Paine, Fillmore, Akers, Bangs, Crowder, Sargent, Winans, Hamline, and Porter.

The following resolution of instruction to the committee was adopted:

"*Resolved,* That the committee appointed to take into consideration the communication of the delegates from the Southern Conferences be instructed, provided they cannot in their judgment devise a plan for an amicable adjustment of the difficulties now existing in the Church, on the subject of slavery, to devise, if possible, a constitutional plan for a mutual and friendly division of the Church.

"J. B. McFerrin,
"Tobias Spicer."

It was apprehended by some of the Southern delegates that the question of jurisdictional division might be embarrassed by constitutional scruples, and hence it was moved by Mr. Crowder, of Virginia, to amend the instruction by striking out the word "constitutional." This, however, was defeated, the Conference determining on a constitutional division if any. The committee were to provide "a constitutional plan for a mutual and friendly division of the Church," provided they cannot, in their judgment, devise a plan for an amicable adjustment of existing difficulties.

On the 6th of June, Dr. Henry B. Bascom, of Kentucky, read the following Protest of the Minority in the case of Bishop Andrew:

In behalf of thirteen Annual Conferences of the Methodist Episcopal Church, and portions of the ministry and membership of several other Conferences, embracing nearly five thousand ministers, traveling and local, and a membership of nearly five hundred thousand, constitutionally represented in this General Conference, we the undersigned, a minority of the delegates of the several Annual Conferences in General Conference assembled, after mature reflection, impelled by convictions we cannot resist, and in conformity with the rights and usages of minorities, in the instance of deliberative assemblies and judicial tribunals, in similar circumstances of division and disagreement, *Do most solemnly, and in due form, protest* against the recent act of a majority of this General Conference, in an attempt, as understood by the minority, to degrade and punish the Rev.

James O. Andrew, one of the Bishops of the Methodist Episcopal Church, by declaring it to be the sense or judgment of the General Conference that he desist from the exercise of his Episcopal functions, without the exhibition of any alleged offense against the laws or discipline of the Church, without form of trial, or legal conviction of any kind, and in the absence of any charge of want of qualification or faithfulness in the performance of the duties pertaining to his office.

We protest against the act of the majority in the case of Bishop Andrew, as extrajudicial to all intents and purposes, being both without law and contrary to law. We *protest* against the act because we recognize in this General Conference no right, power, or authority, ministerial, judicial, or administrative, to suspend or depose a Bishop of the Methodist Episcopal Church, or otherwise subject him to any official disability whatever, without the formal presentation of a charge or charges, alleging that the Bishop to be dealt with has been guilty of the violation of some law, or at least some disciplinary obligation of the Church, and also upon conviction of such charge after due form of trial. *We protest* against the act in question as a violation of the fundamental law, usually known as the compromise law of the Church, on the subject of slavery—the only law which can be brought to bear upon the case of Bishop Andrew, and the assertion and maintenance of which, until it is constitutionally revoked, is guarantied by the honor and good faith of this body, as the representative assembly of the thirty-three Annual Conferences known as contracting parties in the premises.

And we protest against the act farther, as an attempt to establish a dangerous precedent, subversive of the union and stability of the Methodist Episcopal Church, and especially as placing in jeopardy the General Superintendency of the Church, by subjecting any Bishop of the Church at any time to the will and caprice of a majority of the General Conference, not only without law, but in defiance of the restraints and provisions of law. The undersigned, a minority of the General Conference, in *protesting,* as they do, against the late act of the majority, in the virtual suspension of Bishop Andrew, regard it as due to themselves and those they represent, as well as to the character and interests of the Church at large, to declare, by solemn and formal avowal, that after a careful examination of the entire subject, in all its relations and bearings, they protest as above, for the reasons and upon the grounds following, viz., 1st. The proceeding against Bishop Andrew in this General Conference has been upon the assumption that he is connected with slavery—that he is the legal holder and owner of slave property. On the subject of slavery in the Methodist Episcopal Church, both as it regards the ministry and membership, we have special law, upon which the adjudication of all questions of slavery must, by intention of law, proceed. The case of Bishop Andrew, therefore, presents a simple question of law and fact, and the undersigned cannot consent that the force of circumstances and other merely extrinsic considerations shall be allowed to lead to any issue, except that indicated by the law and the facts in the case. In the late act of the majority, law, express law, is appealed from, and expediency in view of circumstances—relative propriety—assumed necessity, is substituted in its place as a rule of judgment. It is assumed, and the assumption acted upon, that expediency may have jurisdiction even in the presence of law—the law, too, being special, and covering the case, in terms. In the absence of law, it might be competent for the General Conference to act upon other grounds; this is not disputed, nor yet that it would have been competent for the Conference to proceed upon the forms of law; but that the terms and conditions of a special enactment, having all the force of a common public charter, can be rightfully waived in practice, at the promptings of a fugitive unsettled expediency, is a position the undersigned regard not merely as erroneous, but as fraught with danger to the best interests of the Church.

The law of the Church on slavery has always existed since 1785, but especially since 1804, and in view of the adjustment of the whole subject, in 1816, as a *virtual, though informal, contract of mutual concession and forbearance,* between the North and the South, then, as now, known and existing as distinct parties, in relation to the vexed questions of slavery and abolition. Those Conferences found in States where slavery prevailed constituting the Southern party, and those in the non-slaveholding States the Northern, exceptions to the rule being found in both. The rights of the legal owners of slaves, in all the slaveholding States, are guarantied by the Constitution of the United States, and by the local Constitutions of the States respectively, as the supreme law of the land, to which every minister and member of the Methodist Episcopal Church within the limits of the United States' government professes subjection, and pledges himself to submit, as an article of Christian faith, in the common creed of the Church. Domestic slavery, therefore, wherever it exists in this country, is a civil regulation, existing under the highest sanctions of constitutional and municipal law known to the tribunals of the country, and it has always been assumed at the South, and relied upon as correct, that the North or non-slaveholding States had no right, civil or moral, to interfere with relations and interests thus secured to the people of the South by all the graver forms of law and social order, and that it cannot be done without an abuse of the constitutional rights of citizenship. The people of the North, however, have claimed to think differently, and have uniformly acted toward the South in accordance with such opposition of opinion. Precisely in accordance, too, with this state of things, as it regards the general population of the North and South, respectively, the Methodist Episcopal Church has been divided in opinion and feeling on the subject of slavery and abolition since its organization in 1784: two separate and distinct parties have always existed. The Southern Conferences, in agreeing to the main principles of the compromise law in 1804 and 1816, conceded by express stipulation their right to resist Northern interference in any form, upon the condition, pledged by the North, that while the *whole Church*, by common consent, united in proper effort for the mitigation and final removal of the evil of slavery, the North was not to interfere, by excluding from membership or ministerial office in the Church, persons owning and holding slaves in States where emancipation is not practicable, and where the liberated slave is not permitted to enjoy freedom. Such was the compact of 1804 and 1816, finally agreed to by the parties after a long and fearful struggle, and such is the compact now—the proof being derived from history and the testimony of living witnesses. And is it possible to suppose that the original purpose and intended application of the law was not designed to embrace every member, minister, order, and office of the Methodist Episcopal Church? Is the idea of excepted cases allowable by fair construction of the law? Do not the reasons and intendment of the law place it beyond doubt, that every conceivable case of alleged misconduct that can arise, connected with slavery or abolition, is to be subjected by consent and contract of parties to the jurisdiction of this great conservative arrangement?

Is there any thing in the law or its reasons creating an exception in the instance of Bishops? Would the South have entered into the arrangement, or in any form consented to the law, had it been intimated by the North that Bishops must be an exception to the rule? Are the virtuous dead of the North to be slandered by the supposition that they intended to except Bishops, and thus accomplished their purposes, in negotiating with the South, by a resort to deceptive and dishonorable means? If Bishops are not named, no more are Presiding Elders, Agents, Editors—or, indeed, any other officers of the Church, who are nevertheless included, although the same rule of construction would except them also. The enactment was for an entire people, East, West, North, and South. It was for the Church, and every member of it—for the common weal of the body—and is, therefore, universal and unrestricted in its application; and no possible case can be settled upon any other principles, without a direct violation of this law both in fact and form. The law being what we have assumed, any violation of it, whatever may be its form or mode, is as certainly a breach of good faith as an infringement of law. It must be seen, from the manner in which the compromise was effected, in the shape of a law, agreed to by equal contracting parties, "the several Annual Conferences," after long and formal negotiation, that it was not a mere legislative enactment, a simple decree of a General Conference, but partakes of the nature of a grave compact, and is invested with all the sacredness and sanctions of a solemn treaty, binding respectively the well-known parties to its terms and stipulations. If this be so—and with the evidence accessible who can doubt it?—if this be so, will it prove a light matter for this General Conference to violate or disregard the obligation of this *legal compromise*, in the shape of public recognized law? Allow that the present parties in this controversy cannot be brought to view the subject of the law in question in the same light, can such a matter end in a mere difference of opinion, as it respects the immediate parties? The law exists in the Discipline of the Church. The law is known, and its reasons are known, as equally binding upon both parties, and what is the likelihood of the imputation of bad faith under the circumstances? What the hazard that such imputation, as the decision of public opinion, it may be from a thousand tribunals; will be brought to bear, with all the light and force of conviction, upon any act of this body, in violation of the plain provisions of long-established law, originating in treaty, and based upon the principles of *conventional compromise?*

In proportion to our love of truth, of law, and order, are we not called upon to pause and weigh well the hazard, before, as a General Conference, we incur it beyond change or remedy? The undersigned have long looked to the great *conservative law* of the Discipline, on the subject of slavery and abolition, as the only charter of *connectional union* between the North and the South; and whenever this bond of connection is rendered null and void, no matter in what form, or by what means, they are compelled to regard the Church, to every practical purpose, as already divided, without the intervention of any other agency. By how far, therefore, they look upon the union of the Methodist Episcopal Church as essential to its prosperity, and the glory and success of American Methodism, by so far they are bound to *protest* against the late act of the General Conference, in the irregular suspension of Bishop Andrew, as not only without law, but in direct contravention of legal stipulations known to be essential to the unity of the Church. And they are thus explicit in a statement of facts, that the responsibility of division may attach where, in justice, it belongs. The minority, making this protest, are perfectly satisfied with the law of the Church affecting slavery and abolition. They ask no change. They need—they seek no indulgence in behalf of the South. Had Bishop Andrew been suspended according to law, after due form of trial, they would have submitted without remonstrance, as the friends of law and order.

They except and protest, farther, against the lawless procedure, as they think, in the case of Bishop Andrew, because apart from the injustice done him and the South by the act, other and graver difficulties, necessarily incidental to this movement, come in for a share of attention. The whole subject is, in the very nature of things, resolved into a single original question: Will the General Conference adhere to, and in good faith assert and maintain, the compromise law of the Church on the vexed question dividing us, or will it be found expedient generally, as in the case of Bishop Andrew, to lay it aside and tread it under foot? No question on the subject of slavery and abolition can be settled until the General Conference shall settle *this* beyond the possibility of evasion. In the present crisis, it is the opinion of the undersigned that every Bishop of the Methodist Episcopal Church, and every member of this General Conference, is especially called upon, by all the responsibilities of truth and honor, to declare himself upon the subject; and they deem it proper respectfully and urgently to make such call a part of this protest. When so much depends upon it, can the General Conference, as the organ of the supreme authority of the Church, remain silent without incurring the charge of trifling both with its interests and reputation? Law always pledges the public faith of the body ostensibly governed by it to the faithful assertion and performance of its stipulations; and the compromise law of the Discipline, partaking, as it does, of the nature of the law of treaty, and embracing, as has been seen, all possible cases, pledges the good faith of every minister and member of the Methodist Episcopal Church against saying or doing any thing tending to annul the force or thwart the purposes of its enactment. The only allowable remedy of those who object to the law is to seek a constitutional change of the law, and in failure, to submit, or else retire from the Church. All attempts to resist, evade, or defeat the objects and intended application of the law, until duly revoked, must be regarded as unjust and revolutionary, because an invasion of well-defined conventional right. And the undersigned except to the course of the majority, in the informal prosecution of Bishop Andrew and the anomalous *quasi* suspension it inflicts, as not only giving to the compromise a construction rendering it entirely ineffective, but as being directly subversive of the great bond of union which has held the North and South together for the last forty years. Turning to the confederating Annual Conferences of 1804, and the vexed and protracted negotiations which preceded the General Conference of that year, and finally resulted in the existing law of the Discipline, regulating the whole subject, and glancing at nearly half a million of Methodists, now in the South, who have come into the Church with all their hopes and fears, interests and associations, their property, character, and influence, reposing in safety upon the publicly-pledged faith of the Methodist Episcopal Church, only to be told that this is all a dream, that a part of what was pledged was never intended to be allowed, and that the whole is at all times subject to the discretion of a dominant majority, claiming, in matter of right, to be without and above law, competent not merely to make all rules and regulations for the proper government of the Church, but to govern the Church without rule or regulation, and punish and degrade without even the alleged infringement of law, or the form of trial, if it be thought expedient, presents a state of things filling the undersigned with alarm and dismay. Such views and facts, without adducing others, will perhaps be sufficient to show the first and principal ground occupied by the minority in the protest. They cannot resist the conviction that the majority have failed to redeem the pledge of public law given to the Church and the world by the Methodist Episcopal Church.

2d. The undersigned are aware that it is affirmed by some of the majority, but meanwhile denied by others, and thus a mooted, unsettled question among themselves, that the resolution censuring and virtually suspending Bishop Andrew, as understood by the minority, is mere matter of advice or recommendation; but, so far from advising or recommending any thing, the language of the resolution, by fair and necessary construction, is imperative and mandatory in form, and, unqualified by any thing in the resolution itself, or in the preamble explaining it, conveys the idea plainly and most explicitly, that it is the judgment and will of the Conference that Bishop Andrew shall cease to exercise the office of Bishop until he shall cease to be the owner of slaves. "*Resolved,* That it is the sense of this Conference that he desist." That is, having rendered himself unacceptable to the majority, it is their judgment that he retire from the bench of Bishops, and their field of action.

No idea of request, advice, or recommendation is conveyed by the language of the preamble or resolution; and the recent avowal of an intention to advise is, in the judgment of the undersigned, disowned by the very terms in which, it is said, the *advice* was given. The whole argument of the majority, during a debate of twelve days, turned upon the right of the Conference to displace Bishop Andrew without resort to formal trial. No one questioned the legal right of the Conference to advise; and if this only was intended, why the protracted debate upon the subject? But farther, a resolution, respectfully and affectionately requesting the Bishop to resign, had been laid aside, to entertain the substitute under notice; a motion, too, to declare the resolution advisory, was promptly rejected by the majority; and in view of all these facts, and the *entire* proceedings of the majority in the case, the undersigned have been compelled to consider the resolution as a mandatory judgment, to the effect that Bishop Andrew desist from the exercise of his Episcopal functions. If the majority have been misunderstood, the language of their own resolution, and the position they occupied in debate, have led to the misconception; and truth and honor, not less than a most unfortunate use of language, require that they explain themselves.

3d. We except to the act of the majority, because it is assumed that conscience and principle are involved, and require the act complained of, as expedient and necessary under the circumstances. Bishop A. being protected by the law of the Church having cognizance of all offenses connected with slavery, such connection in his case, in the judgment of all jurisprudence, can only be wrong in the proportion that the law is bad and defective. It is not conceived by the minority, how conscience and principle can be brought to bear upon Bishop A., and not upon the *law*, and the *Church* having such law. They are obliged to believe that the law and the source from which it emanates must become the object of exception and censure before Bishop A., who has not offended against either, unless the Church is against the law, can be subjected to trial, at the bar of the conscience and principles of men who profess subjection and approval, in the instance both of the law and the Church.

The undersigned can never consent, while we have a plain law, obviously covering an assumed offense, that the offense shall be taken, under plea of principle, out of the hands of the law, and be resubjected to the conflicting opinions and passions which originally led to a resort to law, as the only safe standard of judgment. They do not understand how conscience and principle can attach grave blame tc action not disapproved by the law —express law, too, made and provided in the case —without extending condemnation to the law itself, and the body from which it proceeds. The Church can hardly be supposed to have settled policy and invariable custom, in contravention of law; the avowal of such custom and policy, therefore, excluding from the Episcopacy any and every man, in any way connected with slavery, is mere *assumption.* No contract, agreement, decree, or purpose of this kind, is on record, or ever existed. No such exaction, in terms or by implication, was ever made by the North or conceded by the South. No conventional understanding ever existed to this effect, so far as the South is concerned, or has been informed. That it has long, perhaps always, been the purpose of the North not to elect a slaveholder to the office of Bishop, is admitted. But as no law gave countenance to any thing of the kind, the South regarded it as a mere matter of social injustice, and was not disposed to complain. The North has always found its security in numbers, and the untrammeled right of suffrage, and to this the South has not objected. The assumption, however, is entirely different, and is not admitted by the South, but is plainly negatived by the law and language of the Discipline, as explained by authority of the General Conference.

No such concession, beyond peaceable submission to the right of suffrage, exercised by the majority, will ever be submitted to by the South, as it would amount to denial of equal abstract right, and a disfranchisement of the Southern ministry, and could not be submitted to without injury and degradation. If, then, the North is not satisfied with the negative right conceded to the South by law in this matter, the minority would be glad to know what *principle* or *policy* is likely to introduce beyond the existing provisions of law. As the contingency which has occasioned the difficulty in the case of Bishop Andrew, and to which every Southern minister is liable at any time, does not and cannot fall under *condemnation* of existing law, and he cannot be punished, nor yet subjected to any official disability, without an abuse of both right and power, on the part of this General Conference, the minority are compelled to think that the majority ought to be satisfied with the consciousness and declaration, that they are in no way responsible for the contingency, and thus, at least, allow Bishop Andrew the benefit of their own legislation, until they see proper to change it. This attempt by the majority to protect a lawless prosecution from merited rebuke, by an appeal to conscience and principle, condemning Bishop Andrew, while the law and the Church, shielding him from the assault, are not objected to, is looked upon by the minority as a species of moral, we will not say legal casuistry, utterly subversive of all the principles of order and good government.

4th. The act of the majority was ostensibly resorted to because, as alleged, the Church in the Middle and Northern Conferences will not submit to any, the slightest, connection with slavery. But if connection with slavery is ruinous to the Church in the North, that ruin is already wrought. Who does not know that the very Discipline, laws, and legislation of the Church necessarily connect us all with slavery? All our provisional legislation on the subject has proceeded on the assumption that slavery is an element of society—a principle of action—a household reality in the Methodist Episcopal Church in the United States. It is part and parcel of the economy of American Methodism, in every subjective sense. It has given birth to law and right, conventional arrangements, numerous missions, and official trusts. Every Bishop, every minister, every member of the Church, is of necessity connected with slavery. Each is brother and co-member, both with slave and master, by the very laws and organization of the Church.

If, then, connection with slavery is so disastrous, the only remedy is to purify the Church by reörganization, or get out of it as soon as possible. And would not this aversion to slavery—would not conscience and principle, so much pleaded in this controversy—appear much more consistent in every view of the subject, in striking at the root of the evil, in the organic structure of the Church, than in seeking its personification in Bishop Andrew, protected although he be by the law, and proceeding to punish him, by way of calling off attention from the known toleration of the same thing, in other aspects and relations?

Impelled by conscience and principle to the illegal arrest of a Bishop, because he has incidentally, by bequest, inheritance, and marriage, come into possession of slave property, in no instance intending to possess himself of such property, how long will conscience and principle leave other ministers, or even lay members, undisturbed, who may happen to be in the same category with Bishop Andrew? Will assurances be given that the lawlessness of expediency, controlled, as in such case it must be, by prejudice and passion, will extend no farther—that there shall be no farther curtailment of right as it regards the Southern ministry? Yet what is the security of the South in the case? Is the public faith of this body, as instanced in the recent violations of the compromise-law, to be relied upon as the guarantee for the redemption of the pledge? What would such pledge or assurance be but to remind the South that any departure at all from the great conservative pledge of law, to which we appeal, was much more effectually guarded against originally, than it is possible to guard against any subsequent infringement, and to make the South feel farther that disappointment in the first instance must compel distrust with regard to the future? The Church having specific law on the subject, all questions involving slavery must inevitably, by intention of law, come within the purview of such special provision, and cannot be judged of by any other law or standard, without a most daring departure from all the rules and sobrieties of judicial procedure, and the undersigned accordingly except to the action of the majority in relation to Bishop Andrew, as not only without sanction of law, but in conflict with rights created by law.

5th. As the Methodist Episcopal Church is now organized, and according to its organization since 1784, the Episcopacy is a coördinate branch, the executive department proper of the government. A Bishop of the Methodist Episcopal Church is not a mere creature—is in no prominent sense an officer—of the General Conference. The General Conference, as such, cannot constitute a Bishop. It is true the Annual Conferences select the Bishops of the Church by the suffrage of their delegates, in General Conference assembled; but the General Conference, in its capacity of a representative body, or any other in which it exists, does not possess the power of ordination, without which a Bishop cannot be constituted.

The Bishops are, beyond a doubt, an integral constituent part of the General Conference, made such by law and the constitution; and because elected by the General Conference, it does not follow that they are subject to the will of that body, except in conformity with legal right and the provisions of law, in the premises. In this sense, and so viewed, they are subject to the General Conference, and this is sufficient limitation of their power, unless the government itself is to be considered irregular and unbalanced in the coördinate relations of its parts. In a sense by no means unimportant, the General Conference is as much the creature of the Episcopacy, as the Bishops are the creatures of the General Conference. Constitutionally, the Bishops alone have the right to fix the time of holding the Annual Conferences; and should they refuse or neglect to do so, no Annual Conference could meet according to law, and, by consequence, no delegates could be chosen, and no General Conference could be chosen, or even exist. And because this is so, what would be thought of the impertinent pretension, should the Episcopacy claim that the General Conference is the mere creature of their will? As *executive officers* as well as *pastoral overseers*, the Bishops belong to the Church as such, and not to the General Conference as one of its counsels or organs of action merely.

The General Conference is in no sense the Church, not even representatively. It is merely the representative organ of the Church, with limited powers to do its business, in the discharge of a delegated trust.

Because Bishops are in part constituted by the General Conference, the power of removal does not follow. Episcopacy even in the Methodist Church is not a mere appointment to labor. It is an official consecrated station under the protection of law, and can only be dangerous as the law is bad or the Church corrupt. The power to appoint does not necessarily involve the power to remove; and when the appointing power is derivative, as in the case of the General Conference, the power of removal does not accrue at all, unless by consent of the coördinate branches of the government, expressed by law, made and provided in the case. When the Legislature of a State—to appeal to analogy for illustration—appoints a judge, or senator in Congress, does the judge or senator thereby become the officer or creature of the Legislature? or is he the officer or senatorial representative of the State of which the Legislature is the mere organ? And does the power of removal follow that appointment? The answer is negative in both cases, and applies equally to the Bishops of the Methodist Episcopal Church, who, instead of being the officers and creatures of the General Conference, are *de facto* the officers and servants of the Church, chosen by the General Conference, as its organ of action, and no right of removal accrues, except as they fail to accomplish the *aims* of the Church in their appointment, and then only in accordance with the provisions of law. But when a Bishop is suspended, or informed that it is the wish or will of the General Conference that he cease to perform the functions of Bishop, for doing what the law of the same body allows him to do, and of course without incurring the hazard of punishment, or even blame, then the whole procedure becomes an outrage upon justice, as well as law.

The assumption of power by the General Conference beyond the warrant of law, to which we object, and against which we protest, will lead, if carried into practice, to a direct violation of one of the restrictive rules of the constitution. Suppose it had been the "sense" of this General Conference, when the late communication from the Bishops was respectfully submitted to the Conference, that such communication was an interference with their rights and duties—an attempt to tamper with the purity and independence, and therefore an outrage upon the claims and dignity, of the Conference not to be borne with. And, proceeding a step farther, suppose it had been the "sense" of the Conference that they *all* desist from performing the functions of Bishops until the "impediment" of such offense had been removed—assume this, (and, so far as mere law is concerned, no law being violated in either case, it was just as likely as the movement against Bishop Andrew,) and had it taken place, what had become of the general superintendency? If a Bishop of the Methodist Episcopal Church may, without law, and at the instance of mere party expediency, be suspended from the exercise of the appropriate functions of his office, for one act, he may for another. Admit this doctrine, and by what tenure do the Bishops hold office? One thing is certain, whatever other tenure there may be, they do not hold office *according to law.*

The provisions of law and the faithful performance of duty, upon this theory of official tenure, afford no security. Admit this claim of absolutism, as regards right and power on the part of the General Conference, and the Bishops of the Methodist Episcopal Church are slaves, and the men constituting this body their masters and holders. They are in office only at the discretion of a majority of the General Conference, without the restraints or protection of law. Both the law and themselves are liable and likely at any time to be overborne and trampled upon together, as exemplified in the case of Bishop Andrew. If the doctrine against which we protest be admitted, the Episcopal office is, at best, but a quadrennial term of service, and the undersigned are compelled to think that the man who would *remain* a Bishop, or allow himself to be *made one*, under such circumstances, "desires a good work," and is prepared for *self-sacrifice*, quite beyond the comprehension of ordinary piety.

As it regards Bishop Andrew, if it shall be made to appear that the action in his case was intended only to *advise* and *request* him to desist from his office, it does not in any way affect the real or relative character of the movement. When a body, claiming the right to compel, asks the resignation of an officer, the request is, to all official and moral purposes, *compulsory*, as it loads the officer with disability, and gives notice of assumed unworthiness, if not criminality. The request has all the force of a mandate, inasmuch as the officer is, by such request, compelled either to resign or remain in office contrary to the known will of the majority. A simple request, therefore, under the circumstances supposed, carries with it all the force of a decree, and is so understood, it is believed, by all the world.

To request Bishop Andrew to resign, therefore, in view of all the facts and relations of the case, was, in the judgment of the minority, to punish and degrade him; and they maintain that the whole movement was without authority of law, is hence of necessity null and void, and, therefore, not binding upon Bishop Andrew, or the minority protesting against it.

6th. We protest against the act of the majority, instructing Bishop Andrew to desist from the exercise of his office, not merely on account of the injustice and evil connecting with the act itself, but because the act must be understood as the exponent of principles and purposes, as it regards the union of the North and South in the Methodist Episcopal Church, well-nigh destroying all hope of its perpetuity. The true position of the parties in relation to a long-existing conventional arrangement, on the subject of slavery and abolition, has been fully under notice; and when men of years and wisdom, experience and learning—men of no common weight of character, and with a well-earned aristocracy of Church influence thrown about them—assume and declare, in action as well as debate, that what a plain law of the Church—the only law applicable in the case—sustained and enforced, too, by an explanatory decree of this body, at a previous session—*decides* shall *not* be a disqualification for office of any grade in the ministry—when such men, the law and decision of the General Conference notwithstanding, are heard declaring that what law provides for and protects nevertheless *always has been*, and *always shall be*, a disqualification, what farther evidence is wanting to show that the *compromise basis of unoin.*

from which the South has never swerved, has been abandoned both by the Northern and Middle Conferences, with a few exceptions in the latter, and that principles and purposes are entertained by the majority, driving the South to extreme action, in defense both of their rights and reputation? And how far the long train of eventful sequences, attendant upon the threatened result of division, may be traceable to the Northern and Middle Conferences, by the issue thus provoked, is a question to be settled not by us, but by our contemporaries and posterity.

It is matter of history, with regard to the past, and will not be questioned, that now, as formerly, the South is upon the basis of the Discipline, on the subject of slavery. The minority believe it equally certain that this is not true with regard to the North proper especially. In view, then, of the unity of the Methodist Episcopal Church, which party has been, in equity, entitled to the sympathy and protection of the Middle or *umpire* Conferences? those who, through good and evil report, have kept good faith and adhered to law, or those whose opinions and purposes have led them to seek a state of things in advance of law, and thus dishonor its forms and sanctions?

7th. In proportion as the minority appreciate and cling to the unity of the Methodist Episcopal Church, they are bound farther to except to the position of the majority in this controversy. Allow that Bishop Andrew, without, however, any infringement of law, is, on account of his connection with slavery, unacceptable in the Northern Conferences. It is equally known to the majority that any Bishop of the Church, either violating, or submitting to a violation, of the compromise-charter of union between the North and the South, without proper and public remonstrance, cannot be acceptable at the South, and need not appear there. By pressing the issue in question, therefore, the majority virtually dissolve the government of the Methodist Episcopal Church, because in every constitutional aspect it is sundered by so crippling a coördinate branch of it as to destroy the itinerant general superintendency altogether. Whenever it is clearly ascertained that the compromise-law of the Church, regulating slavery and abolition, is abandoned, every Bishop, each of the venerable and excellent men who now adorn the Church and its councils, *ceases* to be a general superintendent. The law of union, the principle of gravitation, binding us together, is dissolved, and the general superintendency of the Methodist Episcopal Church is no more!

8th. The South have not been led thus to protest merely because of the treatment received by Bishop Andrew, or the kindred action of this body in other matters. The abandonment of the compromise—the official refusal by the majority, as we have understood them, to abide the arbitrament of law, is their principal ground of complaint and remonstrance. If the minority have not entirely misunderstood the majority, the abolition and anti-slavery principles of the North will no longer allow them to submit to the law of the Discipline on the general subject of slavery and abolition; and if this be so, if the compromise-law be either repealed or allowed to remain a dead letter, *the South cannot submit, and the absolute necessity of division is already dated.* And should the exigent circumstances in which the minority find themselves placed, by the facts and developments alluded to in this remonstrance, render it finally necessary that the Southern Conferences should have a *separate, independent* existence, it is hoped that the character and services of the minority, together with the numbers and claims of the ministry and membership of the portion of the Church represented by them, not less than similar reasons and considerations on the part of the Northern and Middle Conferences, will suggest the high moral fitness of meeting this great emergency with strong and steady purpose to do justice to all concerned. And it is believed that, approaching the subject in this way, it will be found practicable to devise and adopt such measures and arrangements, present and prospective, as will secure an amicable division of the Church upon the broad principles of right and equity, and destined to result in the common good of the great body of ministers and members found on either side *the line of separation.*

Signed by the following delegates, viz.:

Kentucky Conference.—H. B. Bascom, William Gunn, H. H. Kavanaugh, Edward Stevenson, B. T. Crouch, G. W. Brush.

Missouri.—W. W. Redman, William Patton, J. C. Berryman, J. M. Jameson.

Holston.—E. F. Sevier, S. Patton, Thomas Stringfield.

Tennessee.—Robert Paine, John B. McFerrin, A. L. P. Green, T. Maddin.

North Carolina.—B. T. Blake, James Jameson, Peter Doub.

Ohio.—E. W. Sehon.

Memphis.—G. W. D. Harris, S. S. Moody, W. McMahon, Thomas Joyner.

Arkansas.—John C. Parker, William P. Ratcliffe, Andrew Hunter.

Virginia. — John Early, T. Crowder, W. A. Smith, Leroy M. Lee.

Mississippi.—William Winans, B. M. Drake, John Lane, G. M. Rogers.

Philadelphia.—I. T. Cooper, W. Cooper, T. I. Thompson, Henry White.

Texas.—Littleton Fowler.

Illinois.—N. G. Berryman, J. Stamper.

Alabama.—Jesse Boring, Jefferson Hamilton, W. Murrah, G. Garrett.

Georgia.—G. F. Pierce, William J. Parks, L. Pierce, J. W. Glenn, J. E. Evans, A. B. Longstreet.

South Carolina.—W. Capers, William M. Wightman, Charles Betts, S. Dunwody, H. A. C. Walker.

New Jersey.—T. Sovereign, T. Neal.

New York, June 6, 1844.

Mr. Simpson offered a resolution to the following effect: That while they could not admit the statements put forth in the Protest, yet, as a matter of courtesy, they would allow it to be placed on the journal; and that a committee, consisting of Messrs. Durbin, Olin, and Hamline, be appointed to make a true statement of the case, to be entered on the journal.

Dr. Winans objected to the word "courtesy." The minority asked no courtesy at the hands of the majority. They demanded it as a right. The chair decided that the first part of the resolution was not in order, as a minority had a right to have their Protest entered on the journal. In this decision two of his colleagues concurred, and one dissented.

Several members here rose to points of order.

Mr. Simpson withdrew the first part of his resolution, and the remainder was then adopted.

On motion, the special committee of nine were allowed to retire.

The Committee appointed by the General Conference to reply to the Protest of the Minority, performed their work and presented their report on the 10th of June.

At the close of the General Conference, before leaving New York, Dr. Bascom, by whom the Protest was written, gave notice, through the papers of the Church, of his intention to review at his convenience the Reply of Drs. Durbin, Peck, and Elliott, to the Protest of the Minority of the General Conference. This review, under the title of "Methodism and Slavery," made its appearance just previous to the Louisville Convention, and met with a wide circulation. An edition of six thousand copies was sold in a few days. "This powerful production made a strong impression favorable to the cause of the Church, South, which was strongly seconded by the clear and able Report of the Committee of the Louisville Convention on a Southern Organization, drawn up by the same hand.

"Dr. Bascom's Review was replied to by Dr. Peck, one of the Committee who replied to the Protest, and Editor of the Methodist Quarterly Review. This attempt to answer the clear reasoning of Dr. Bascom's work, was a remarkable failure. The work of Dr. Peck abounds in special pleading—imputes to the South doctrines never entertained by it or Dr. Bascom, and advocates at length opinions never broached until the General Conference of 1844, as the orthodox doctrines of Methodism."

"The action of the Conference had involved the Bishops in a perplexing difficulty. The Conference had declared it the *sense* of the body that Bishop Andrew should cease to exercise the functions of his office; but the resolution was so conveniently ambiguous, that while on the one hand Mr. Hamline had pronounced it 'a *mandamus* measure, whose passage would ABSOLUTELY *suspend the exercise of the superintendent's functions, until he complied with the prescribed condition*—the power to do which was the same with that required to *suspend* or *depose* a Bishop'—on the other hand, Dr. Durbin said that the resolution 'only proposed to express the sense of this Conference in regard to the matter which it cannot, in duty and conscience, pass by without a suitable expression; and having made the solemn expression, it leaves Bishop Andrew to act as *his* sense of duty shall dictate.' He even said, that if any man should charge him, in voting for the resolution, (the *mandamus* measure of *absolute* suspension of Mr. Hamline,) with voting to *depose* Bishop Andrew, he would consider it a personal insult. Now, it became the duty of the Bishops to make out and publish their plan of Episcopal visitation for the succeeding four years, at the close of the General Conference; and if the construction of the Hamline section was correct, Bishop Andrew was 'absolutely suspended,' and of course could not be taken into the plan of Episcopal labor; but if the Durbin section of the party was right, then the General Conference having expressed its *sense* of the matter, left Bishop Andrew perfectly free to be governed by *his* sense of duty, and of course there was nothing to prevent his being rendered available in the Episcopacy. In this state of conflicting opinions among the Northern leaders, the Bishops found it necessary to apply again to the oracle for a less equivocal response; for act as they might, they must come into conflict with one or other division of the majority. They therefore addressed to the General Conference the following inquiries:

"'To the General Conference:

"'Reverend and Dear Brethren:—As the case of Bishop Andrew unavoidably involves the future *action* of the superintendents, which in their judgment, in the present position of the Bishop, they have no discretion to decide upon, they respectfully request of the General Conference *official* instruction, in answer to the following questions:

"'*First.* Shall Bishop Andrew's name remain as it now stands in the Minutes, Hymn-book, and Discipline, or shall it be struck off these official records?

"'*Second.* How shall the Bishop obtain his support? as provided for in the form of Discipline, or in some other way?

"'*Third.* What work, if any, may the Bishop perform? and how shall he be appointed to the work?

"'JOSHUA SOULE,
"'ELIJAH HEDDING,
"'BEVERLY WAUGH,
"'THOS. A. MORRIS.'

"To these inquiries the Conference returned the following answer:

"'*Resolved,* 1st. As the sense of this Conference, That Bishop Andrew's name stand in the Minutes, Hymn-book, and Discipline, as formerly.

"'*Resolved,* 2d. That the rule in reference to the support of a Bishop and his family, applies to Bishop Andrew.

"'*Resolved,* 3d. That whether in any, and in what work, Bishop Andrew be employed, is to be determined by his own decision and action, in relation to the previous action of this Conference in his case.'

"The first of these resolutions was adopted by

a vote of 155 to 17, none voting against it but ultra northerners or abolitionists.

"The second resolution was adopted by a vote of 152 to 14.

"On the third, the grand mystifying resolution, which placed the matter just where it was before, the vote stood as follows:

"YEAS.—Nathan Bangs, Phineas Rice, George Peck, John B. Stratten, Peter P. Sandford, Fitch Reed, Samuel D. Ferguson, Stephen Martindale, Marvin Richardson, J. Lovejoy, F. Upham, S. Benton, Paul Townsend, J. Porter, D. S. King, P. Crandall, C. Adams, G. Pickering, M. Hill, E. Robinson, D. B. Randall, C. W. Morse, J. Hobart, Heman Nickerson, G. Webber, Elihu Scott, S. Chamberlain, Samuel Kelley, J. Perkins, J. Spaulding, C. D. Cahoon, William D. Cass, Truman Seymour, James Covel, Tobias Spicer, Seymour Coleman, James B. Houghtaling, Jesse T. Peck, A. D. Peck, A. Adams, G. Baker, W. W. Ninde, J. M. Snyder, S. Comfort, N. Rounds, D. A. Shepherd, H. F. Row, E. Bowen, D. Holmes, G. Fillmore, S. Luckey, A. Steele, F. G. Hibbard, A. Abell, W. Hosmer, J. B. Alverson, J. S. Steadman, John Bain, G. W. Clarke, J. Robinson, T. Goodwin, William Hunter, H. J. Clark, J. Spencer, S. Elliott, S. Wakefield, J. Drummond, C. Elliott, William H. Raper, J. M. Trimble, J. B. Finley, L. L. Hamline, Z. Connell, J. H. Power,

A. Poe, E. Yocum, W. Runnells, E. Crane, A. Billings, J. A. Baughman, M. Simpson, A. Wiley, E. R. Ames, J. Miller, C. W. Ruter, A. Wood, A. Eddy, J. Havens, B. Weed, H. W. Reed, J. T. Mitchell, P. Akers, P. Cartwright, A. Griffith, J. Bear, N. J. B. Morgan, J. A. Collins, J. Davis, J. P. Durbin, L. Scott, I. Winner, J. S. Porter, J. K. Shaw—103.

"NAYS.—C. W. Carpenter, John G. Dow, R. Boyd, G. Smith, J. Stamper, J. Van Cleve, N. G. Berryman, W. W. Redman, J. C. Berryman, J. M. Jameson, H. B. Bascom, W. Gunn, H. H. Kavanaugh, E. Stevenson, B. T. Crouch, G. W. Brush, E. F. Sevier, S. Patton, T. Stringfield, R. Paine, J. B. McFerrin, A. L. P. Green, T. Maddin, G. W. D. Harris, S. S. Moody, William McMahon, T. Joyner, J. C. Parker, W. P. Ratcliffe, A. Hunter, L. Fowler, William Winans, B. M. Drake, J. Lane, G. M. Rogers, William Murrah, J. Boring, G. Garrett, J. Hamilton, G. F. Pierce, L. Pierce, W. J. Parks, J. W. Glenn, J. E. Evans, A. B. Longstreet, William Capers, W. M. Wightman, C. Betts, S. Dunwody, H. A. C. Walker, Peter Doub, B. T. Blake, J. Early, L. M. Lee, W. A. Smith, T. Crowder, H. Slicer, C. B. Tippett, T. B. Sargent, J. A. Gere, G. Hildt, T. J. Thompson, H. White, I. T. Cooper, W. Cooper, T. Neal, T. Sovereign --67.

"This resolution allowed one party at the North

still to regard the action of the General Conference as *mandatory*, and the other to consider it merely *advisory*. And up to the present time not the smallest advance has been made toward any settled or agreed understanding on the part of the majority, as to the true nature and intention of the action against Bishop Andrew."

On the 7th of June, Dr. Paine, chairman of the select committee of nine, reported the following Plan of Separation:

"The select committee of nine to consider and report on the Declaration of the delegates from the Conferences of the slaveholding States, beg leave to submit the following report:

"Whereas, a declaration has been presented to this General Conference, with the signatures of *fifty-one* delegates of the body, from thirteen Annual Conferences in the slaveholding States, representing that, for various reasons enumerated, the objects and purposes of the Christian ministry and Church organization cannot be successfully accomplished by them under the jurisdiction of this General Conference as now constituted; and

"Whereas, in the event of a separation, a contingency to which the Declaration asks attention as not improbable, we esteem it the duty of this General Conference to meet the emergency with

Christian kindness and the strictest equity; therefore,

"*Resolved*, by the delegates of the several Annual Conferences in General Conference assembled,

"1st. That, should the delegates from the Conferences in the slaveholding States find it necessary to unite in a distinct ecclesiastical Connection, the following rule shall be observed with regard to the Northern boundary of such Connection: All the Societies, Stations, and Conferences adhering to the Church in the South, by a vote of a majority of the members of said Societies, Stations, and Conferences, shall remain under the unmolested pastoral care of the Southern Church; and the ministers of the Methodist Episcopal Church shall in nowise attempt to organize Churches or Societies within the limits of the Church, South, nor shall they attempt to exercise any pastoral oversight therein; it being understood that the ministry of the South reciprocally observe the same rule in relation to Stations, Societies, and Conferences adhering, by vote of a majority, to the Methodist Episcopal Church; provided also that this rule shall apply only to Societies, Stations, and Conferences bordering on the line of division, and not to interior charges, which shall in all cases be left to the care of that Church within whose territory they are situated.

"2d. That ministers, local and traveling, of every grade and office in the Methodist Episcopal Church, may, as they prefer, remain in that Church, or, without blame, attach themselves to the Church, South.

"3d. *Resolved, by the delegates of all the Annual Conferences in General Conference assembled,* That we recommend to all the Annual Conferences, at their first approaching sessions, to authorize a change of the sixth restrictive article, so that the first clause shall read thus: 'They shall not appropriate the produce of the Book Concern, nor of the Chartered Fund, to any purpose other than for the benefit of the traveling, supernumerary, superannuated, and worn-out preachers, their wives, widows and children, and to such other purposes as may be determined upon by the votes of two-thirds of the members of the General Conference.'

"4th. That whenever the Annual Conferences, by a vote of three-fourths of all their members voting on the third resolution, shall have concurred in the recommendation to alter the sixth restrictive article, the Agents at New York and Cincinnati shall, and they are hereby authorized and directed to deliver over to any authorized agent or appointee of the Church, South, should one be authorized, all notes and book accounts against the ministers, Church-members, or citizens within its boundaries, with authority to collect the same for the sole use of the Southern Church, and that said agents also convey to the aforesaid agent or appointee of the South, all the real estate, and assign to him all the property, including presses, stock, and all right and interest connected with the printing establishments at Charleston, Richmond, and Nashville, which now belong to the Methodist Episcopal Church.

"5th. That when the Annual Conferences shall have approved the aforesaid change in the sixth restrictive article, there shall be transferred to the above agent of the Southern Church so much of the capital and produce of the Methodist Book Concern as will, with the notes, book accounts, presses, etc., mentioned in the last resolution, bear the same proportion to the whole property of said Concern that the traveling preachers in the Southern Church shall bear to all the traveling ministers of the Methodist Episcopal Church; the division to be made on the basis of the number of traveling preachers in the forthcoming Minutes.

"6th. That the above transfer shall be in the form of annual payments of $2,500 per annum, and specifically in stock of the Book Concern, and in Southern notes and accounts due the establishment, and accruing after the first transfer mentioned above; and until all the payments are made, the Southern Church shall share in all the net profits of the Book Concern, in the proportion that the amount due them, or in arrears, bears to all the property of the Concern.

"7th. That —— be and they are hereby appointed commissioners to act in concert with the same number of commissioners appointed by the Southern Organization, (should one be formed,) to estimate the amount which will fall due to the South by the preceding rule, and to have full powers to carry into effect the whole arrangements proposed with regard to the division of property, should the separation take place. And if by any means a vacancy occurs in this Board of Commissioners, the Book Committee at New York shall fill said vacancy.

"8th. That whenever any agents of the Southern Church are clothed with legal authority or corporate power to act in the premises, the agents at New York are hereby authorized and directed to act in concert with said Southern agents, so as to give the provisions of these resolutions a legally binding force.

"9th. That all the property of the Methodist Episcopal Church in meeting-houses, parsonages, colleges, schools, Conference-funds, cemeteries, and of every kind within the limits of the Southern Organization, shall be forever free from any claim set up on the part of the Methodist Episcopal Church, so far as this resolution can be of force in the premises.

"10th. That the Church so formed in the South shall have a common property in all the copy-rights in possession of the Book Concern at New York and Cincinnati, at the time of the settlement by the commissioners.

"*Resolved*, That the Bishops be respectfully requested to lay that part of this report requiring the action of the Annual Conferences before them as soon as possible, beginning with the New York Conference. ROBERT PAINE, *Chairman*.

"New York, June 7, 1844."

Dr. Elliott moved the adoption of the report. He said: He had had the opportunity of examining it, and had done so narrowly. He believed it would insure the purposes designed, and would be for the best interests of the Church. It was his firm opinion that this was a proper course for them to pursue, in conformity with the Scriptures, and the best analogies they could collect from the ancient Churches, as well as from the best-organized modern Churches. All history did not furnish an example of so large a body of Christians remaining in such close and unbroken connection as the Methodist Episcopal Church. It was now found necessary to separate this large body, for it was becoming unwieldy. He referred to the Churches at Antioch, at Alexandria, at Jerusalem, which, though they continued as one, were at least as distinct as the Methodist Episcopal Church would be if the suggested separation took place. The Church of England was one under the Bishops of Canterbury and York, connected and yet distinct. In his own mind it had been for years perfectly clear that to this conclusion they must eventually come. Were the question that now unhappily agitated the body dead and buried, there would be good reason for passing the resolutions contained in that report. As to their representation in that General Conference, one out of twenty was but a meager representation, and to go on as they had done, it would soon be one out of thirty. And the body was now too large to do business advantageously. The measure contemplated was not schism, but separation for their mutual convenience and prosperity.

Dr. Paine said the committee wished a verbal alteration made. In the fifth resolution "preachers" were spoken of in the Southern Church, and "ministers" in the Northern. Nothing was said there of the Chartered Fund—the committee had prepared the following additional resolution to meet the omission:

"12. *Resolved,* That the Book Agents at New York be directed to make such compensation to the Conferences South for their dividend from the Chartered Fund as the commissioners to be provided for shall agree upon."

Speeches were made in opposition to the report by Messrs. Griffith, Cartwright, and Sandford, and in its favor by Drs. Bangs, Paine, and Luckey, and Messrs. Fillmore, Finley, Hamline, Collins, and Porter.

During the pending of the discussion, Dr. Paine moved to insert the word "Conferences," instead of "delegates," in the first resolution, which was agreed to. In the afternoon session of the same day, the report was taken up and each resolution voted on separately. The first resolution was adopted by a vote of 142 to 22; and after the change suggested by Dr. Paine, inserting Conferences instead of delegates to decide on the necessity of a separation, the vote was again taken, and stood ayes 135, noes 15. The second resolution was adopted by 135 in the affirmative to 7 in the negative; the third resolution by 147 to 10; the fifth resolution by 153 ayes to 13 noes; and the remainder with the preamble, without a division.

Dr. Bangs then moved that the blank in the seventh resolution be filled, and Dr. Bangs, Dr. Peck, and James B. Finley were appointed as commissioners on the part of the General Conference. The report was then adopted as a whole.

On the 10th of June the Conference adjourned *sine die.* It was the last General Conference in which the Representatives of the two sections ever met. The separation was final.

CHAPTER V.

The Meeting of the Southern Delegates in New York—Plan of action recommended to the Annual Conferences—Their Address to the members of the Church in the Slaveholding States and Territories—Excitement throughout the Church—Resolutions adopted in Virginia, in Alabama, in North Carolina, in South Carolina, in Georgia, in Louisiana, in Tennessee, in Kentucky—Dr. Elliott advocates Division—The action of the several Annual Conferences—Bishop Andrew's position—Letter from Bishop Soule to Bishop Andrew—Letter from Bishop Soule in reply to Dr. Bond—Communication from the College of Bishops.

WHEN the General Conference of 1844 adjourned, there was probably not a member of the body who entertained any hope of the continued unity of the Church, under one jurisdiction. As we have already seen, impressed with the belief, that the interests of Methodism in the South would demand a separate organization, provision was made not only for the formation of "a distinct ecclesiastical Connection" of the Conferences in the slaveholding States, under the jurisdiction of a Southern General Conference, but also defining the *status* of societies, stations, and Conferences on the border, both North and South. In order to preserve the unity of the Church on the border, it had been agreed that "all the societies, stations, and Conferences, adhering to the Church, South, by a majority of the members of said societies, stations, and Conferences, shall remain under the unmolested pastoral care of the Southern Church; and the ministers of the M. E. Church shall, in nowise, attempt to organize Churches or societies within the limits of the Church, South." This rule was to be reciprocal.

Provision was also made for an equitable division of the Book Concerns in New York and Cincinnati, and the Chartered Fund, and at the same time securing to the Southern Church "all the property of the Methodist Episcopal Church in meeting-houses, parsonages, colleges, schools, Conference funds, cemeteries, and of every kind within the limits of the Southern organization," making these "forever free from any claim set up on the part of the Methodist Episcopal Church, so far as this resolution can be of force in the premises." We cannot but admire the sense of justice, as well as the spirit which prompted it, by which the majority were influenced in the adoption of the Plan of Separation, by which the rights of the South were secured. It was worthy such a body of Christian ministers.

It is true that the obligation to carry out these resolutions depended upon the necessity of the organization of the Conferences in the slaveholding States into a separate ecclesiastical jurisdiction. This necessity, however, was left to be determined by the judgment of the Annual Conferences in the Southern and South-western States. They alone were to be the umpires in deciding this question. As the best method of ascertaining the sense of the several Annual Conferences, before leaving New York, the Southern delegates held a meeting for consultation, at which they adopted the following plan of action, to be recommended to the Conferences they represented:

"With a view to promote uniformity of action in the premises, we beg leave to submit to your consideration the expediency of concurring in the following plan of procuring the judgment of the Church within the slaveholding States, as to the propriety of organizing a Southern division of the Methodist Episcopal Church in the United States, and of effecting such an organization should it be deemed necessary:

"1. There shall be a Convention held in Louisville, Kentucky, to commence the 1st May, 1845, composed of delegates from the several Annual Conferences within the slaveholding States, appointed in the ratio of one for every eleven members.

"2. These delegates shall be appointed at the ensuing session of the several Annual Conferences enumerated, each Conference providing for the expenses of its own delegates.

"3. These several Annual Conferences shall instruct their delegates to the proposed Convention on the points on which action is contemplated —conforming their instructions, as far as possible, to the opinions and wishes of the membership within their several Conference bounds.

"W. WINANS, Ch'n.

"New York, June 11, 1844."

They also sent abroad the following Address:

"To the Ministers and Members of the Methodist Episcopal Church in the Slaveholding States and Territories:

"The undersigned, delegates in the late General Conference of the Methodist Episcopal Church, from *thirteen* Annual Conferences in slaveholding States and Territories, would most respectfully represent—that the various action of the *majority* of the General Conference, at its recent session, on the subject of *slavery and abolition,* has been such as to render it necessary, in the judgment of those addressing you, to call attention to the *proscription and disability* under which the Southern portion of the Church must of necessity labor in view of the action alluded to, unless some measures are adopted to free the minority of the South from the oppressive jurisdiction of the majority in the North, in this respect.

"The proceedings of the majority, in several cases, involving the question of slavery, have been such as indicate most conclusively that the legislative, judicial, and administrative action of the General Conference, as now organized, will always be extremely hurtful, if not finally ruinous, to the interests of the Southern portion of the Church; and must necessarily produce a state of conviction and feeling in the slaveholding States, entirely inconsistent with either the peace or prosperity of the Church.

"The opinions and purposes of the Church in the North on the subject of slavery, are in direct conflict with those of the South; and unless the South will submit to the dictation and interference of the North, greatly beyond what the existing law of the Church on slavery and abolition authorizes, there is no hope of any thing like union or harmony. The debate and action of the General Conference in the case of the Rev. Mr. Harding, of the Baltimore Conference; the debate and action in the case of Bishop Andrew; and the opinions and purposes avowed and indicated in a *manifesto* of the majority, in reply to a *protest* from the minority against the proceedings complained of, together with hundreds of petitions from the East, North, and West, demanding that slavery, in all its possible forms, be separated from the Church; these, and similar demonstrations, have convinced the undersigned that they cannot remain silent or inactive without hazard and injustice to the different portions of the Church they represent.

"They have, therefore, thought proper to invoke the attention of the Church in the South to a state of things they are compelled to regard as worthy the immediate notice and action of the Church throughout all the slaveholding States and Territories. The subject of slavery and abolition, notwithstanding the plain law of the Discipline on the subject, was agitated and debated in the late General Conference for *five successive weeks;* and even at the very close of the session, the aspect of things was less satisfactory and more threatening to the South than at any former period; and under such circumstances of mutual distrust and disagreement, the General Conference adjourned.

"Some time before the adjournment, however, upon a *declaration* made by the Southern delegations, setting forth the impossibility of enduring such a state of things much longer, the General Conference, by a very large and decided majority, agreed to a *plan of formal and pacific separation,* by which the Southern Conferences are to have a distinct and independent organization of their own, in no way subject to Northern jurisdiction. It affords us pleasure to state that there were those found among the majority who met this proposition with every manifestation of justice and liberality. And should a similar spirit be exhibited by the Annual Conferences in the North, when submitted to them, as provided for in the plan itself, there will remain no legal impediment to its peaceful consummation.

"This plan is approved by the undersigned as the best, and, indeed, all that can be done at present, in remedy of the great evil under which we labor. Provision is made for a peaceable and constitutional division of Church-property of every kind. The plan does not decide that division shall take place; but simply, and it is thought securely, provides that it may, if it be found necessary. Of this necessity you are to be the judges, after a careful survey and comparison of all the reasons for and against it.

"As the undersigned have had opportunity and advantages which those at a distance could not possess, to form a correct judgment in the premises, and it may be expected of them that they express their views fully on the subject, they do not hesitate to say that they regard a separation at no distant day as inevitable; and farther, that the plan of separation agreed upon is as eligible as the Southern Conferences have any right to expect at any time. We most respectfully, therefore, and with no common solicitude, beseech our brethren of the ministry and membership in the slaveholding States, to examine this matter carefully, and weighing it well in all its bearings, try to reach the conclusion most proper under the circumstances. Shall that which, in all moral likelihood, must take place soon, be attempted now, or are there reasons why it should be postponed?

"We deprecate all excitement; we ask you to be calm and collected, and to approach and dispose of the subject with all the candor and forbearance the occasion demands. The separation proposed is *not* schism, it is *not* secession. It is a State or family, separating into two different States or families, by mutual consent. As the 'Methodist Episcopal Church' will be found North of the dividing line, so the 'Methodist Episcopal Church' will be found South of the same line.

"The undersigned have clung to the cherished unity of the Church with a firmness of purpose and force of feeling which nothing but invincible necessity could subdue.) If, however, nominal unity must coëxist with unceasing strife and alienated feeling, what is likely to be gained by its perpetuation? Every minister and member of the Church in slaveholding States must perceive at once that the constant, not to say interminable, agitation of the slavery and abolition question in the councils of the Church, and elsewhere, must terminate in incalculable injury to all the Southern Conferences. Our access to slave and master is, to a great extent, cut off. The legislation of the Church in conflict with that of the State—Church-policy attempting to control public opinion and social order—must generate an amount of hostility to the Church, impossible to be overcome, and slowly but certainly to diminish both the means and the hope of usefulness and extension on the part of the Church.

"Disposed, however, to defer to the judgment of the Church, we leave this subject with you. Our first and most direct object has been to bring it fully before you, and, giving you an opportunity to judge and determine for yourselves, await your decision. The minority from the South, in the late General Conference, were most anxious to adjourn the decision in the case of Bishop Andrew, with all its attendant results, to the Annual Conferences and to the Church at large, to consider and decide upon during the next four years—as no charge was presented against the Bishop, and especially as this measure was urgently recommended by the whole bench of Bishops, although Bishop Hedding subsequently withdrew his name. The proposition, however, to refer the whole subject to the Church, was promptly rejected by the majority, and immediate action demanded and had. But as all the facts connected with the equivocal suspension of Bishop Andrew will come before you in other forms, it is unnecessary to detail them in this brief address, the main object of which is to place before you, in a summary way, the principal facts and reasons connected with the proposed separation of the Southern Conferences into a distinct organization.

"Adopted at a meeting of the Southern delegations, held in New York, at the close of the General Conference, June 11th, 1844, and ordered to be published.

" Signed on behalf of the Kentucky, Missouri, Holston, Tennessee, North Carolina, Memphis, Arkansas, Virginia, Mississippi, Texas, Alabama, Georgia, and South Carolina Annual Conferences.

"*Kentucky Conference.*—H. B. Bascom, William Gunn, H. H. Kavanaugh, Edward Stevenson, B. T. Crouch, G. W. Brush.

"*Missouri.*—W. W. Redman, William Patton, J. C. Berryman, J. M. Jameson.

"*Holston.*—E. F. Sevier, S. Patton, Thomas Stringfield.

"*Tennessee.*—Robert Paine, John B. McFerrin, A. L. P. Green, T. Maddin.

"*North Carolina.*—B. T. Blake, James Jameson, Peter Doub.

"*Memphis.*—G. W. D. Harris, S. S. Moody, W. McMahon, Thomas Joyner.

"*Arkansas.*—John C. Parker, William P. Ratcliffe, Andrew Hunter.

"*Virginia.*—John Early, T. Crowder, W. A. Smith, Leroy M. Lee.

"*Mississippi.*—William Winans, B. M. Drake, John Lane, G. M. Rogers.

"*Texas.*—Littleton Fowler.

"*Alabama.*—Jesse Boring, Jefferson Hamilton, W. Murrah, G. Garrett.

"*Georgia.*—G. F. Pierce, William J. Parks, L. Pierce, J. W. Glenn, J. E. Evans, A. B. Longstreet.

"*South Carolina.*—W. Capers, William M. Wightman, Charles Betts, S. Dunwody, H. A. C. Walker."

It must not be understood that during the pending of the action in the case of Bishop Andrew, the Church in the South was indifferent. The assertion so frequently made, that the popular mind of the South was inflamed by the delegates on their return from the General Conference, and that but for their appeals to passions easily aroused, there would have been no dissatisfaction among the people, is not sustained by the facts in the case.

Previous to the adjournment of the General

Conference, and before the action in the case of Bishop Andrew was known, primary meetings were held in different portions of the South, expressing the greatest dissatisfaction at the arrest of his official character.

On the Chesterfield Circuit, in the Virginia Conference, a meeting was held at Damascus Church, on the 8th of June, where several resolutions were adopted condemnatory of the course of the General Conference; among them the following:—

"*Resolved,* That while we deeply and sincerely sympathize in the wounded feelings of our much-loved Bishop Andrew, we solemnly contemn the principles, and hold in sovereign contempt *the men who can, reckless of consequences, urge such principles* against the spirit and letter of our excellent Book of Discipline, in the attempt to degrade from his office the man who, in spite of men and devils, has filled to the full the high prerogatives of the Episcopal chair, and whom every Southern Methodist delights to respect, honor, and obey."

In Russell county, Alabama, on the same day, the following resolutions were adopted at a meeting not assembled for religious purposes:

"*Resolved,* That this meeting has witnessed, with intense interest and painful anxiety, the agitation of the slave question in the General Conference of the Methodist Episcopal Church, now convened in the city of New York. They have seen that a topic, which hitherto has excited the bad passions of man only in the orgies of fanaticism, or in the strife of factions in their unprincipled struggle for political power, has been transferred to the foot of that throne which ought to be sacred to charity, peace, and good-will among brethren of the same faith. They have beheld, with unutterable indignation, the humiliating fact of a Bishop of the State of Georgia, eminent for his piety, learning, ability, and Christian virtues, put, in effect, upon his trial as a culprit, for the alleged sin of marrying a lady possessed of slaves, by which it is insultingly affirmed, that a slaveholder is an unfit teacher of the word of God, and must submit, if tolerated as a member of the Church of Christ, to a subordinate station in the ministry—a discrimination which finds no warrant in the sacred oracles of God, and which involves both insult and outrage to the people of an entire section of this Union.

"*Be it farther resolved,* That if Bishop Andrew should be deposed from his Episcopal functions, we earnestly invoke the clergy of the Methodist Episcopal Church, at the South, to take immediate measures for their secession from a Conference which has placed so gross a stigma not only on themselves, but on their respective flocks—an insult which can admit of but one remedy, in the application of which they may be assured of the warm sympathy and unalterable support of the religious congregations of the whole Southern States of every sect and denomination."*

As the intelligence of the degradation of Bishop Andrew flashed over the country, the Church and people everywhere throughout the South were aroused. At Wilmington, North Carolina, on the 10th of June, the following resolutions were adopted:

"Whereas, the General Conference of the Methodist Episcopal Church now in session, has taken action in sundry matters deeply interesting and vitally important to the Southern portion of the Church; first, in the affirmation of the decision of the Baltimore Conference in the case of the Rev. Francis A. Harding; secondly, in requesting that Bishop Andrew desist from the exercise of his office because of his connection with slavery, which request can only be regarded as a virtual deposition from office; and, thirdly, in the rescission of the resolution of the General Conference of 1840 respecting the testimony of colored persons in Church-trials; and, whereas, these various steps have been taken against the remonstrances, protests, and declarations of the Southern delegations, and with full assurances of the ruinous ef-

* Western Christian Advocate, August 9, 1844.

fects which such proceedings must have upon the peace and unity of the Church; therefore,

"1. *Resolved,* That we have viewed, with deep regret and pain, the introduction into the highest judicatory of the Church, of questions wholly civil and political, and with which ecclesiastical assemblies have no right to interfere.

"2. *Resolved,* That the course pursued by the majority in the present General Conference, has evinced a fixed determination to drive the minority into a secession from the body ecclesiastic.

"3. *Resolved,* That we highly approve the dignified, manly, and Christian firmness exhibited by the delegates from the Southern and South-western Conferences, in the trying position in which they have been placed.

"4. *Resolved,* That we entertain the highest esteem and veneration for our beloved and faithful Bishop, the Rev. James O. Andrew—that we deeply sympathize in the affliction to which his feelings have been subjected, by the reckless and tyrannical conduct of a majority of the General Conference—and that we highly approve his dignified and Christian bearing throughout the whole transaction.

"5. *Resolved,* That we regard the action of the majority of the General Conference in the case of the Rev. Bishop Andrew, as a gross and flagrant violation of the constitution and Discipline of the

Methodist Episcopal Church, and as such *null and void*, and that it is the sense and desire of this meeting that Bishop Andrew continue the exercise of his Episcopal office.

"6. *Resolved,* That in view of the late action of the General Conference, the present union of the Methodist Episcopal Church ought to be *immediately dissolved*, and we look with confidence and hope to the Southern and South-western Conferences to form a Southern organization as soon as possible.

"7. *Resolved,* That we recommend to our brethren, the male members of our Churches, throughout the South and South-west, to hold meetings, and express their views on this action of the General Conference as early as possible."*

At Norfolk and Fincastle, Virginia, at Beaufort, Concord, Newbern, and Wadesboro, North Carolina, at Charlotte and Marion, South Carolina, at Milledgeville, Columbus, Newnan, La Grange, Perry, Savannah, and Augusta, Georgia, at Tuskaloosa and Greensboro, Alabama, at New Orleans, Louisiana, and at Nashville, Tennessee, as well as in Kentucky and other States, meetings were held and resolutions adopted expressive of sympathy with Bishop Andrew, and the deepest dissatisfaction with the action of the General Conference, jus-

* Western Christian Advocate, August 9, 1844.

tifying the delegates from the South for their manly and dignified course, demanding immediate separation from the North, and declaring that the continuance any longer in ecclesiastical connection with the M. E. Church would imperil the existence of Methodism in the South.

Long before the meeting of the Annual Conferences, it became apparent that the necessity for a separation from the M. E. Church was as important as Methodism was dear to the ministry and membership of the Church in the slaveholding States.

It was not only obvious to the Church in the South that separation was inevitable, but leading men in the North foresaw this result. In the Western Christian Advocate of August 16, 1844, the Editor, the Rev. Charles Elliott, D.D., said: "Calculating, then, from present appearances, we see no other prospect than that the South will form an independent Methodist Episcopal Church."

Indeed, Dr. Elliott, whatever may have been his subsequent views, at this date became a champion for the division of the Church. In the same editorial from which the above extract is taken he says:

"We may be wrong in our view; but we confess we can see no injury that will accrue to religion from this new organization, or rather modification or adjustment of the old one. At an early age, Christianity was resolved into many distinct connectional organizations, called Churches, such as the Churches of Antioch, Jerusalem, Alexandria, Rome. Even in the Established Church of England, there is the Church of Ireland, and England, and that of England is divided into two archiepiscopal dioceses, possessing peculiar independent powers. Even Methodism has given examples of similar character. There is the British Conference, the Irish Conference, the Canadian Conference, all acting independently—all coöperating—all in friendly relations. Our Church is actually become unwieldy in consequence of its great size, and the vast extent of territory over which it is spread, with people entertaining different views on topics calculated to create different action. Nor can we see any more evil that can arise from dividing the Church into two great independent ecclesiastical confederations, than (comparing small with greater) in dividing classes, Circuits, Stations, Districts, Conferences, etc. We know that another division or separation may follow in time. But this is no more to be deplored than that the two Circuits made out of the old one must again be divided, and then there will be three or four in the place of one, because the number of souls added to the Church is so great that these divisions are necessary. Nor can we see wherein missionary operations will be less, but greater. Besides, our General Conference, under the present organization, will soon be so large as to become an unwieldy body; and if the ratio of representation be diminished, then representation itself must be almost done away by reducing it.

"We may be almost alone in our views. We barely expressed the sentiment at General Conference, not having the fortitude, or rather the gift, of arguing our views in such an assembly. We do not utter those things now to enter into controversy with any person on this topic. Still it may not be amiss to look over, after awhile, the *history* of the Church in reference to such organizations. Indeed, we are persuaded that distinct organizations *must* exist in the *nature of things* in the Methodist Episcopal Church in the United States; and that *necessity* and *Scripture principles* will inevitably enforce them. We believe that the *unity*, *purity*, *power*, and *extending influence* of Methodism may be promoted by these means. Such thesis we are prepared to maintain; but we wish not to take the least advantage of our position as editor to support them."

At a later period, it is true Dr. Elliott avowed a different doctrine, and used the influence of his official position to defeat the Plan of Separation. The Christian Advocate and Journal, the central organ of the Church, had for its editor Dr. Thomas

E. Bond, a writer of distinguished ability. This paper had an extensive circulation throughout the South, and its columns were replete with editorials denouncing the Plan of Separation as unconstitutional, and avowing that no necessity existed for a separate ecclesiastical organization. Other papers in the North, published in the interest of the Methodist Episcopal Church, followed in the wake of Dr. Bond. (Whether those Church organs hoped to prevent the division of the Church, as provided for in the Plan of Separation, or whether their object was to arrest the heavy tide of opposition, which in the North had set in immediately after the General Conference, to the legislation of that body in the cases of Mr. Harding and Bishop Andrew, and which threatened to overthrow the Church in the Northern States, we may not decide.) If the South was agitated, the North was by no means quiet. Dissatisfaction as widespread as the Methodist Episcopal Church in America existed, and if the Church in the North had at that time been consulted there is scarcely a doubt that the action of the General Conference would have been reversed, and the connectional unity of the Church preserved.

The necessity of a separation, however, was not left to Northern Church-journalists, but to "the Annual Conferences in the slaveholding States." They, and not the North—either individually, in their press, or in ecclesiastical assemblies—were to be the umpires in the settlement of this important question, in which the existence of Methodism in the South was involved.

The reference of this question to the Annual Conferences was eminently proper. The resolutions adopted in some of the primary meetings were severely worded, although an apology may be found in the revolutionary measures against which they protested.

Several months were to elapse before the Annual Conferences would convene, and during that period the people would have time for calm deliberation, and the preachers, mingling freely in their intercourse with the laity, would become thoroughly familiar with their sentiments and purposes.

The Kentucky Conference was the first to assemble. On the 11th of September it convened in Bowling-green, Kentucky. A committee was appointed to take into consideration the state of the Church, and, after mature deliberation, reported that the division of the Methodist Episcopal Church was unavoidable, unless the North should make reparation for past injury, and give assurance against future aggressions on the rights of Southern preachers and members.

The report of the committee was adopted by the Conference with only one dissenting voice.

The action of the Kentucky Conference found an echo in the heart of the entire Church throughout the South. The Annual Conferences in the slaveholding States met in quick succession, and passed resolutions similar to those adopted by the Kentucky Conference. The Missouri, Holston, Tennessee, Memphis, Mississippi, Arkansas, Virginia, North Carolina, South Carolina, Indian Mission, Georgia, Florida, Texas, and Alabama Conferences, as with one voice, declared that Methodism in the South could no longer accomplish its work of doing good, if the unity of the Methodist Episcopal Church should be preserved. They demanded a separation, as the only means of preventing the wreck of every hope they had cherished "of spreading scriptural holiness over these lands."*

The continual agitation of the question of slavery had previously done much to weaken the bonds of union between the two sections, and if peace could be restored at all, and become permanent, it could only be procured by the division provided for in the Plan of Separation.

The position of Bishop Andrew in the meantime was anomalous. Notwithstanding the action of the General Conference, requesting him to de-

---

*For the action of the several Annual Conferences, see Appendix B.

sist from the exercise of Episcopal functions, it was resolved that his name should still "stand in the Minutes, Hymn-book, and Discipline," as a Bishop in the Church; "that the rule in relation to the support of a Bishop and his family applied to" him, and "that whether any and in what work" he should "be employed," should "be determined by his own decision and action in relation to the previous action of this Conference in his case."

The plan of Episcopal visitation for the next four years was made out and published without assigning Bishop Andrew to any work.

"The fact was this, the board of Bishops agreed that Bishop Andrew should be taken into the plan of Episcopal visitation, provided he should apply for work, and to meet that contingency they prepared a second plan of visitation including Bishop Andrew, which plan was to be published in place of the first, in case he made such application. This *reserved plan* was committed to the hands of Bishop Soule, to be published if Bishop Andrew should make application, in writing, for Episcopal work. But of all this arrangement Bishop Andrew had no notice whatever, except in vague rumor. In this condition matters remained for some months. For a time the general current of opinion among the Bishop's friends seemed to be against his performing any Episcopal labor;

for it was more than intimated that if he did so, he would be impeached for a violation of the expressed will or 'sense' of the General Conference. When, however, it appeared to be settled that the Bishop would not take work, there were not wanting among those who favored his suspension, men who urged the propriety, and even duty, of his performing Episcopal labor. The measure was urged in one or more of the Northern Church papers, and in a more private way it was said that as the Bishop was supported by the Church, he had no right to withhold his labors, and it was strongly suggested that such neglect of official duty might very properly constitute just ground of impeachment.

"At this crisis, Bishop Andrew received a letter from Bishop Soule, inviting him into the field. This was the first authentic information Bishop Andrew received of the arrangement entered into by the Bishops at the close of the General Conference."

The letter from Bishop Soule is as follows:

"To the Rev. James O. Andrew, D.D., Bishop of the Methodist Episcopal Church:

"LEBANON, OHIO, Sept. 26, 1844.

"MY DEAR BISHOP:—Since the close of the recent eventful session of the General Conference, I have been watching, with deep solicitude, the 'signs of the times,' and tracing causes, as far as I was able, to their ultimate issues. Some *general* results growing out of the action of the Conference, it required no prophetic vision to foresee. To prevent the measures which, in my judgment, would lead to these results with demonstrative certainty, I labored day and night with prayers and tears, till the deed was done—the eventful resolution passed. From that perilous hour my hands hung down, discouragement filled my heart, and the last hope of the *unity* of our beloved Zion well-nigh fled from *earth* to *heaven*. My last effort to avert the threatening storm appears in the joint recommendation of all the Bishops to suspend all action in the case until the ensuing General Conference. At the presentation of this document some brethren perceived that instead of *light*, the darkness around them was increased tenfold. *Others will judge*, have judged already. And those who come after us will examine the history of our acts. The document was *respectfully* laid upon the table, probably under the influence of deep regret that 'our Bishops should enter the arena of controversy in the General Conference.' *But it cannot—does not sleep there.* I have heard many excellent ministers, and distinguished laymen in our own Communion, not in the slave States, refer to it as a measure of sound Christian policy, and with deep regret that the Conference had not adopted it. Many of our Northern brethren seem now deeply to deplore the division of the Church O that there had been *forethought* as well as *afterthought!* I have seen various plans of compromise for the adjustment of our difficulties and preservation of the unity of the Church. The most prominent plan provides that a fundamental article in the treaty shall be, That no abolitionist or slaveholder shall be eligible to the office of a Bishop in the Methodist Episcopal Church. Alas for us! Where are our men of wisdom, of experience? Where are our fathers and brethren who have analyzed the elements of civil or ecclesiastical compacts? who have studied man in his social relations? Who are the 'high contracting parties,' and will they create a *caste* in the constitutional eldership in the Church of Christ? Will this tend to harmonize and consolidate the body? Brethren North and South *will know* that the *cause* must be removed, that the *effect* may cease. That the *fountain* must be dried up before the *stream* will cease to flow. But I must pause on this subject. The time has not fully arrived for me to define my position in regard to the causes and remedies of the evils which now agitate and distract our once united and peaceful body. Still I trust I have given such proofs, at different times, and under different circumstances, as not to render my position *doubtful* in the judgment of sober, discriminating men, either North or South. The General Conference spoke in the language of wisdom and sound Christian policy when, in the pastoral address of 1836, it solemnly and affectionately *advised* the ministers and members of the Church to abstain from all agitation of the exciting subject of slavery and its abolition. Nor was the adoption of the Report of the committee on the memorial of our brethren from a portion of Virginia, within the bounds of the Baltimore Conference, less distinguished by the same characteristics of our holy Christianity, and the sound policy of our Discipline in providing for the case.

"It has often been asked through the public journals, and otherwise, 'why Bishop Andrew was not assigned his regular portion of the Episcopal work for the four ensuing years, on the plan of visitation formed by the Bishops and published in the official papers?' It devolves on the majority of my colleagues in the Episcopacy, (if indeed we have an Episcopacy,) rather than on me, to answer this question. Our difference of opinion in the premises, I have no doubt, was in Christian honesty and sincerity. Dismissing all farther reference to the *painful* past till I see you in the South, let me now most cordially invite you to meet me at the Virginia Conference at Lynchburg, November 13th, 1844, should it please a gracious Providence to enable me to be there. And I earnestly desire that you would, if practicable, make your arrangements to be with me at all the Southern Conferences in my division of the work for the present year, where I am sure your services will not be 'unacceptable.' I am the more solicitous that you should be at Lynchburg from the fact that my present state of health creates a doubt whether I shall be able to reach it. I am now laboring, and have been for nearly three weeks, under the most severe attack of asthma which I have had for six or seven years—some nights unable to lie down for a moment. Great prostration of the vital functions, and indeed of the whole physical system, is the consequence. But no effort of mine shall be wanting to meet my work; and the inducements to effort are greatly increased by the present position of the Church, and the hope of relief from my present affliction by the influence of a milder and more congenial climate. I cannot conclude without an expression of sincere sympathy for you, and the sharer of your joys and sorrows, in the deep afflictions through which you have been called to pass. May the grace of our Lord Jesus Christ sustain you both!

"Yours with sentiments of affection and esteem,

"Joshua Soule."

"This invitation of Bishop Soule called down on him severe censure from the North. Dr. Elliott, Dr. Bond, Dr. Bangs, and others, denounced the measure as not only unauthorized, but high-handed, and in contravention of the decision of the General Conference and the Board of Bishops. That it contravened no action of the General Conference is very clear, from the fact, that whether the Bishop should labor or not was to depend on his own decision. That decision was now had, and as the General Conference had prescribed no particular mode in which it should be obtained or given, there could have been no infraction of the law or expressed will of that body in the proceeding.

"As regards the Board of Bishops, the *spirit* of their decision was, that if Bishop Andrew should signify a willingness to take work on the Episcopal plan, it should be given him; and the *letter* of that decision was, that he should have work assigned him when he should make *written* application for it. That the spirit of the decision was fully met when he accepted Bishop Soule's invitation to aid him in his circuit of Conferences, can hardly be doubted; and as that acceptance was a written one, and as the Bishops had not prohibited the making of an inquiry or the giving of an invitation, which might call forth an expression of willingness to labor, or an application for work, both the spirit and the letter of the decision appear to have been sufficiently fulfilled."

Bishop Soule explains and defends his own course in this matter, in the following letter, which was published in the Southern Christian Advocate, dated

"AUGUSTA, GA., January 4, 1845.

"DEAR BROTHER:—In the editorial of the Christian Advocate and Journal of the 18th ultimo, I find the following assertion with special reference to myself: 'He, therefore, claims for the Episcopacy—nay, for any one of the Bishops—a right to decide on the legality of any act of the General Conference, and to veto it, if, in his judgment, it is not in accordance with the Discipline of the Church. Thus a new issue is added to the one which has agitated the Church so fearfully, and one on which it is impossible to come to a compromise, without changing the cardinal principles of our ecclesiastical economy.' This is a plain and positive assertion of Dr. Bond, relative to what I claim as the *right* of Bishops or *any one of them.* The Doctor must permit me, as plainly and positively, to assert the *direct converse* of his position, and thus change the 'new issue' from the Northern and Southern departments of the Church, to *him* and *myself*, with the hope that he may enjoy the happiness of still believing that 'there will be no division,' and yet shout 'glory to God' over propositions for compromise, without 'changing the cardinal principles of our ecclesiastical economy.' And I assure the Doctor, and all concerned, that I will heartily join with him in the shout, when a plan of compromise shall be proposed which does not invade chartered rights and privileges of any 'grade' of our ministry or membership. But that the Doctor should attempt to make me the author of a 'new issue' in this controversy, and that issue of such a nature as to preclude all compromise without a change of the fundamental principles of our Church polity, and thus transfer the responsibility of the results of the controversy from the parties concerned to me, I cannot but regard as at variance with those principles which I have been taught to believe should govern the actions of Christian ministers toward each other. The Doctor must not, he *cannot*, make me the 'scapegoat,' to bear away this responsibility from those to whom it justly belongs.

"I assert, without fear of contradiction, that I never have claimed, either for myself, or any one of the Bishops, or all of them conjointly, the 'right' which Dr. Bond charges on me as claiming. And now I cannot but sincerely and ardently desire that this 'new issue' being thus fairly made, so far as I am concerned, exclusively between the Doctor and myself, it may not be made a matter of exciting agitation in the Church, in addition to all which has 'so fearfully' agitated her before, at least till the point is settled between us, on which the 'new issue' is now made.

"It is very possible that in writing my letter of invitation to Bishop Andrew to meet me at the Virginia Conference, and accompany me to the others in my Southern tour, with a view to his affording me aid in the superintendency, I may have traveled out of the record of the *official* instructions of the General Conference for the government of the '*action*' of the Superintendents in the Bishop's case, *according to Dr. Bond's 'sense' of those instructions.* But *according to my best judgment* of those instructions, given to the Bishops, *not to Dr. Bond,* I have done nothing but what is fully provided for, and covered by the record. And I trust I may presume, without ostentation, that I have as good a 'right' to judge of the meaning and import of *such* instructions as my good friend of the Christian Advocate and Journal; especially as I am amenable, not to him, but to the General Conference. And I confess I should hesitate to charge Dr. Bond before the Church and the community, with 'claiming a right to veto the acts of the General Conference,' or of disregarding official instructions relating to his office, because in my judgment he had not kept within the official record. But it may be the

Doctor thinks that *his office* requires him to keep us all right.

"I might have thought that the Doctor's office required him to take a more decided and active position in sustaining and carrying out the plan adopted by the General Conference for the amicable separation of the Church, and equitable division of the funds; and to have guarded his columns against the hostile attacks which were made both upon the Conference and the measure. But doubtless he acted in strict conformity to his sense of the duties of his office, in regard both to the Conference and their action in the premises. It certainly could not have been the sense of the General Conference, that any of their editors should pursue a course which was either designed or calculated to defeat their own official acts; especially one which was adopted with so great unanimity, and truly Christian sympathy and kindness, as the one here alluded to. But it does not belong to my office to accuse Dr. Bond before the Church or the public, however I might differ from him in judgment with regard to his course. He and myself are both strictly 'amenable' to a constitutional tribunal; and with all deference to the Doctor's age, and talents, and office, and high respectability, both in the civil and religious community, I must be permitted to question his 'right' to prejudge me, either by virtue of his office, or otherwise, and that too before I can be heard in my own defense. If the Doctor thinks, *under all these circumstances*, that such a course is calculated to effect the unity and peace of the Church, an object which he so ardently desires, and at the first dawning prospect of which he shouts 'glory to God,' I can only say that in this, as well as in regard to the *high probability* of the division of the Church, on which we have freely expressed our opinions before, we differ widely in judgment, and future events will show which of us is in error.

"Very respectfully, JOSHUA SOULE."

After Bishop Andrew had been laboring with Bishop Soule for some months, in attending the Southern Conferences, four of the Bishops made the following publication, which, as it properly belongs to this history, is here inserted:

"DEAR BRETHREN:—The time has arrived, when, in the judgment of the undersigned, it is proper they should respond to calls which have been made, both privately and publicly, for authentic information in regard to the action of a majority of the Superintendents, by which the name of Bishop Andrew was omitted from the Plan of Episcopal Visitation, which was arranged at the close of the late General Conference, and published in the Christian Advocate and other official journals of the Church. The statements which follow, will, it is believed, place that action and the grounds thereof in a view intelligible to all; and beyond this, they have neither desire nor intention to go in this communication.

"On the first day of June last the following preamble and resolution were adopted by the General Conference of the Methodist Episcopal Church:

"'Whereas, the Discipline of our Church forbids the doing any thing calculated to destroy our itinerant general superintendency, and whereas Bishop Andrew has become connected with slavery by marriage and otherwise, and this act having drawn after it circumstances which, in the estimation of the General Conference, greatly embarrass the exercise of his office as an itinerant general superintendent, if not in some places entirely prevent it; therefore,

"'*Resolved*, That it is the sense of the General Conference, that he desist from the exercise of his office so long as this impediment remains.'"

On the 6th of June the following note was presented to the General Conference:

"Reverend and Dear Brethren:—As the case of Bishop Andrew unavoidably involves the future *action* of the Superintendents, which in their judgment, in the present position of the Bishop, they have no discretion to decide upon, they respectfully request of this General Conference *official* instruction, in answer to the following questions:

"1. Shall Bishop Andrew's name remain as it now stands in the Minutes, Hymn-book, and Discipline, or shall it be struck off these official records?

"2. How shall the Bishop obtain his support? as provided for in the form of Discipline, or in some other way?

"3. What work, if any, may the Bishop perform? and how shall he be appointed to his work?

"Joshua Soule,
"Elijah Hedding,
"Beverly Waugh,
"Thos. A. Morris."

To which the General Conference responded:

"1. *Resolved,* As the sense of this Conference, That Bishop Andrew's name stand in the Minutes, Hymn-book, and Discipline, as formerly.

"2. That the rule in reference to the support of a Bishop and his family, applies to Bishop Andrew.

"3. That whether in any, and if in any, what work, Bishop Andrew be employed, is to be determined by his own decision and action, in relation to the previous action of this Conference in his case."

In view of the aforesaid proceedings of the General Conference, the undersigned, on the 11th of June, appended their names to a paper written in the words which follow:

"It is our opinion in regard to the action of the late General Conference in the case of Bishop Andrew, that it was designed by that body to devolve the responsibility of the exercise of the functions of his office exclusively on himself. In the absence of Bishop Andrew at the time of arranging the Plan of Episcopal Visitation for the ensuing four years, and he not having notified us of his desire, or purpose, with respect to it, we should regard ourselves as acting in contravention of the expressed will of the General Conference, if we apportioned to Bishop Andrew any definite portion thereof. But if he shall hereafter make a written application for a portion of the general oversight, we should feel ourselves justified in assigning it to him.

"After this paper was signed, and before the parting of the Superintendents, it was agreed to make out a reserved Plan of Episcopal Visitation, including Bishop Andrew in the apportionment of the work thereof, which was done, and intrusted to the safe keeping of Bishop Soule, with an explicit understanding, that if he should receive from Bishop Andrew a written application for his portion of the general superintendence, he was then, and in that event, to publish the second or reserved plan in immediate connection with the said application, that the reason for the substitution of the second plan might accompany its publication. Such was the action of the undersigned in the case presented, and such the ground on which it was based. At present, this is all that they feel themselves called to make public.

"Elijah Hedding,
"B. Waugh,
"Thomas A. Morris,
"L. L. Hamline."

CHAPTER VI.

Excitement along the Border—Rev. Joseph S. Tomlinson, D.D.—The Minerva Circuit, Kentucky Conference—Convention meets in Louisville, Kentucky, on the first day of May, 1845—Of whom composed—Bishops Soule, Andrew, and Morris present—Bishop Soule's address to the Convention—Committee appointed to consider the necessity of a Southern Organization—Resolutions offered by Dr. Winans—B. M. Drake's Resolution—Resolution offered by Drs. Smith and Pierce—Resolution offered by James E. Evans—Withdrawn—Dr. Smith's Resolution adopted—Report of the Committee on Organization—Its adoption—Resolutions requesting Bishops Soule and Andrew to unite with the Methodist Episcopal Church, South—Reply of Bishops Soule and Andrew—Pastoral Address—Adjournment of the Convention—Border Conferences.

WITH remarkable unanimity the Annual Conferences, throughout the slaveholding States, approved the course pursued by their delegates in the General Conference. Deprecating, as they did, the prospect of a division of the Church, they nevertheless preferred it to the surrender of rights and privileges which were a common heritage in a

Church, to the prosperity of which they had equally, with the North, contributed the wealth of their devotion and their lives. In language unmistakable, they declared that unless reparation should be made for past injury, and assurance given that the rights of both ministers and laymen could be effectually secured, according to the Discipline, against future aggressions, the contemplated division would be inevitable.

In the action of the several Annual Conferences provision was made for holding a Convention of delegates from the Conferences in the slaveholding States, in the city of Louisville, Kentucky, in compliance with "the recommendation of the Southern and South-western delegates in the late General Conference." To this Convention delegates were elected in the ratio of "one delegate for every eleven members of Conferences."

The question of a Convention not only elicited considerable discussion in the Northern Methodist press, but extraordinary efforts were made to defeat its object. The Plan of Separation had provided that "all the societies, stations, and Conferences adhering to the Church in the South, by a vote of a majority of the members of said societies, stations, and Conferences, shall remain under the unmolested pastoral care of the Southern Church; and the ministers of the M. E. Church shall in no wise attempt to organize

Churches or societies within the limits of the Church, South, nor shall they attempt to exercise any pastoral oversight therein; it being understood that the ministry of the South reciprocally observe the same rule in relation to stations, societies, and Conferences adhering, by vote of a majority, to the M. E. Church; provided, also, that this rule shall apply only to societies, stations, and Conferences bordering on the line of division, and not to interior charges, which shall, in all cases, be left to the care of that Church within whose territory they are situated."

This privilege, extended to "societies, stations, and Conferences" on the border, while it was intended to promote the harmony of the Churches embraced in the provision, opened the door for controversy and strife, which, in too many instances, resulted in the religious bankruptcy and ruin of societies on the border.

The Kentucky Conference embraced the entire State of Kentucky, with the exception of a small district lying South of the Tennessee River, which was included in the Memphis Conference. Its Northern and Western borders extended along the Ohio River from Catlettsburg to Smithland, a distance of nearly seven hundred miles. All along this border, on the Kentucky shore, were beautiful towns, in which Methodism had been planted, and where it had grown and prospered. On the opposite shore the Kentucky Conference was confronted by the Ohio, the Indiana, and the Illinois Conferences. To the Church in Kentucky, under the blessing of Heaven, these Conferences were indebted for the introduction of Methodism among them. The men who first bore the tidings of a Redeemer's love beyond the beautiful Ohio, to what are now the States of Ohio, Indiana, and Illinois, were sent out from Kentucky. The Rev. Joseph S. Tomlinson, D.D., was the abolition leader in Kentucky. He was the President of Augusta College, and resided in Augusta, a pleasant and flourishing village on the Ohio River. The College over which he presided had been patronized conjointly by the Ohio and Kentucky Conferences; the former, however, had turned its attention to an institution of learning in its own State, while the latter, unable to sustain Augusta College alone, had accepted a flattering invitation to the occupancy of the Transylvania University, located in Lexington.

In Augusta, Methodism was the synonym of all that was good. It had been planted there by Walter Griffith, and was watered by the labors of Finley, Trimble, McCown, Tomlinson, and Bascom, while the whole surrounding country was under its benign influence. The town of Augusta, as a preaching-place, was embraced in the Minerva Circuit. In the winter previous to the General

Conference of 1844, an extensive revival of religion, in which many hundreds were awakened and converted to God, spread over the Minerva Circuit. The work began at Mount Zion, a few miles south of Augusta, on Christmas-day. From Mount Zion it extended to Brooksville, to Minerva, the Stone Church, Dover, and Augusta. For ninety days and nights, without intermission, the work went on in this circuit, the revival influence spreading all over it.

On the 8th of February, previous to the meeting of the Convention, a quarterly-meeting was held at Mount Zion Church, and sundry resolutions were offered by Dr. Tomlinson, protesting against the division of the Church under any circumstances, and pledging, in case of division, the continuance of that circuit in the Methodist Episcopal Church. These resolutions failed, and the following were offered by the preacher in charge, and adopted:

"1. *Resolved*, That it is our deliberate judgment, that the action of the late General Conference of the Methodist Episcopal Church, virtually deposing Bishop Andrew, and also their action affirming the decision of the Baltimore Conference, in the case of the Rev. F. A. Harding, are not sustained by the Discipline of our Church, and that we consider these proceedings as constituting a highly dangerous precedent.

"2. *Resolved*, That we deeply regret the prospect of division, growing out of these proceedings, and do most sincerely and devoutly pray to the great Head of the Church, that some effectual means, not inconsistent with the cause of Christ or the honor of all concerned, may be suggested and devised, by which so great a calamity may be averted, and our long-cherished union preserved and perpetuated.

"3. *Resolved*, That unless we can be assured that the rights of our ministry and membership will be effectually secured, according to Discipline, against future aggression, and full reparation be made for past injury, we shall deem the contemplated division unavoidable.

"4. *Resolved*, That the manner in which Bishop Andrew sustained himself under his informal and lawless prosecution, characterized equally by Christian meekness and the firmness of conscious integrity, commands our admiration, and has given him, if possible, even a higher place than he already occupied in our esteem and affections.

"5. *Resolved*, That the members of the General Conference who so firmly and perseveringly resisted the unjust and extrajudicial proceedings against Bishop Andrew and the South, merit our warmest thanks.

"6. *Resolved*, That we have the most implicit confidence in the intelligence and piety of the delegates elected to the Convention to be held in Louisville in May next; and, knowing from their zeal and unflinching ardor in the service of God, that they will have nothing but the glory of God and the good of the Church in view, we most cheerfully commit our cause into their hands.

"7. *Resolved,* That in case of division, we cannot go with the North. We believe they have deserted the 'old landmarks' of our fathers, disregarded the Discipline of the Church, *and we cannot hesitate between a separation from the North, or a separation from our excellent Book of Discipline*—from our ministers, through whose pious instrumentality we were converted to God, and whose interests are identified with our own.

"8. *Resolved,* That we do not separate from the Methodist Episcopal Church, but from the jurisdiction of the General Conference of said Church.

"9. *Resolved,* That if the Church divide, the South is not responsible for it; but the whole weight of the responsibility rests with the North, whose lawless acts are driving us from their bosom."

The Rev. John C. Harrison was in the chair, being the Presiding Elder on the Maysville District, in which the Minerva Circuit was embraced.

From this hour the war in that circuit against the action of the Kentucky Conference was carried on by Dr. Tomlinson with a zeal which had never previously distinguished his labors in the Church. Day and night, through long months, with unremitting energy, he toiled to prevent the Minerva Circuit, in the bounds of which he lived, from adhering to the fortunes of the South. His labors were unavailing, except in the town of Augusta. All the other societies in the circuit, with the exception of a small minority at Mount Zion, sustained the action of the Kentucky Conference, and pledged themselves to adhere to the Southern division of the Church. Baffled in their expectations, the abolition party sought revenge by securing, from a packed Grand Jury, an indictment against the preacher in charge of the circuit, who had thwarted their designs. The indictment reads:

"We, the Grand Jury, now in session at Brooksville, the county seat of Bracken county, Kentucky, find a true bill against A. H. Redford, as a disturber of the peace; and if his principles were carried out, would lead to a dissolution of our happy union, according to the evidence before us."*

---

*The indictment was promptly dismissed by the Hon. Judge Reed, the Judge of the Circuit Court, and the Hon. Harrison Taylor, the Commonwealth's Attorney; the former a member of the Campbellite Church, and the latter not a member of any Church. A few days later, nearly every member of the Grand Jury asked the forgiveness of the preacher whom they had wronged.

In no district in Kentucky was the war waged with so much violence as in the Maysville. The Presiding Elder was in sympathy with the Northern Church, but performed the duties of his office in connection with this question with equal justice and impartiality.

While the disturbance in this part of Kentucky was more deeply felt in its results than on the border elsewhere, yet in other parts of the State, as also in Missouri and Virginia, controversies occurred which, in some instances, rent societies in twain.

The Convention of Delegates from the Southern and South-western Conferences of the Methodist Episcopal Church, viz., Kentucky, Missouri, Holston, Tennessee, North Carolina, Memphis, Arkansas, Virginia, Mississippi, Texas, Alabama, Georgia, South Carolina, Florida, and Indian Mission—elected on the basis of the Plan of Separation adopted by the General Conference, on the 8th June, 1844—assembled in the city of Louisville, Kentucky, on the 1st day of May, A.D. 1845.

The meeting was called to order at 9 o'clock A.M., by Dr. William Capers, and Dr. Lovick Pierce, of Georgia Conference, was elected President *pro tem.* This venerable minister opened the Convention by reading the second chapter of the Epistle to the Philippians; by singing a hymn, containing an appropriate invocation of the Holy Spirit—"Come Holy Spirit, heavenly Dove"—and by offering a suitable and impressive prayer to the throne of grace.

Thomas N. Ralston, of the Kentucky Conference, was then chosen Secretary *pro tem.* The Conferences represented in the Convention were then called over in the order in which they stand in the General Minutes; and the delegates presented their certificates of election—the Convention having decided that those members who are not furnished with certificates of election shall, nevertheless, take their seats; provided that the presiding officer of their respective Conferences, or some member present, attest their election.

The following brethren, having furnished the necessary vouchers, took their seats as members of the Convention, to wit:

Kentucky Conference.—H. B. Bascom, Edward Stevenson, Hubbard H. Kavanaugh, Benjamin T. Crouch, William Gunn, George W. Taylor, George W. Brush, John C. Harrison, Burr H. McCown, James King, John James, Thomas N. Ralston.

Missouri.—Andrew Monroe, Jesse Green, John Glanville, Wesley Browning, William Patton, John H. Linn, Joseph Boyle, Thomas Johnson.

Holston.—Thomas K. Catlett, Thomas Stringfield, Rufus M. Stevens, Timothy Sullins, Creed Fulton.

Tennessee.—Robert Paine, John B. McFerrin, Alexander L. P. Green, Fountain E. Pitts, Ambrose F. Driskill, John W. Hanner, Joshua Boucher, Thomas Maddin, Frederick G. Ferguson, Robert L. Andrews.

North Carolina.—Samuel S. Bryant, Hezekiah G. Leigh, Bennet T. Blake, Robert J. Carson, Peter Doub, John T. Brame.

Memphis.—Moses Brock, George W. D. Harris, William McMahon, Thomas Joyner, Asbury Davidson, Wilson L. McAlister, Thomas Smith.

Arkansas.—John Harrell, John F. Truslow, Jacob Custer.

Virginia.—John Early, Thomas Crowder, William A. Smith, Leroy M. Lee, Abraham Penn, David S. Doggett, Henry B. Cowles, Anthony Dibrell.

Mississippi.—William Winans, Lewell Campbell, John G. Jones, Green M. Rogers, Benjamin M. Drake, Samuel W. Speer, William H. Watkins.

Texas.—Littleton Fowler, Francis Wilson, R. Alexander.

Alabama.—Jefferson Hamilton, Jesse Boring, Thomas H. Capers, Eugene V. Levert, Elisha Calloway, Thomas O. Summers, Greenbury Garrett.

Georgia.—Lovick Pierce, George F. Pierce, James E. Evans, John W. Glenn, Samuel Anthony, Augustus B. Longstreet, Isaac Boring, James B. Payne, Thomas Samford.

South Carolina.—William Capers, William M. Wightman, Hugh A. C. Walker, Samuel Dunwody, Bond English, Samuel W. Capers, Whitefoord Smith, Robert J. Boyd.

Florida.—Peyton P. Smith, Thomas C. Benning.

Indian Mission.—Edward T. Peery, David B. Cumming.

On motion of Augustus B. Longstreet and William Capers, it was

Resolved, That the Bishops of the Methodist Episcopal Church, now in attendance, be requested to preside over the meeting, under such arrangements as they may make from day to day among themselves. This resolution was adopted unanimously, by a standing vote.

Bishop Soule being present, informed the Convention that he would express his views on the subject of this resolution, both on behalf of himself and his colleague, Bishop Andrew (who was also present), on to-morrow morning.

On motion of John Early, it was

Resolved, That all elections for officers be by ballot, when more than one is nominated; otherwise by nomination and election.

An election of Secretary then took place, and Thomas O. Summers was, on the first balloting, duly elected. Thomas N. Ralston was, in like manner, duly elected Assistant Secretary.

On the second day of the Convention, Bishop Soule addressed the body as follows:

I rise on the present occasion to offer a few remarks to this Convention of ministers, under the influence of feelings more solemn and impressive than I recollect ever to have experienced before. The occasion is certainly one of no ordinary interest and solemnity. I am deeply impressed with a conviction of the important results of your deliberations and decisions in relation to that numerous body of Christians and Christian ministers you here represent, and to the country at large. And knowing as I do the relative condition of the vast community where your acts must be extensively felt, I cannot but feel a deep interest in the business of the Convention, both as it respects yourselves, and the millions who must be affected by your decisions. With such views and feelings, you will indulge me in an expression of confident hope that all your business will be conducted with the greatest deliberation, and with that purity of heart and moderation of temper suitable to yourselves, as a body of Christian ministers, and to the important concerns which have called you together in this city.

The opinion which I formed at the close of the late General Conference, that the proceedings of that body would result in a division of the Church, was not induced by the impulse of excitement, but was predicated of principles and facts after the most deliberate and mature consideration. That opinion I have freely expressed. And however deeply I have regretted such a result, believing it to be inevitable, my efforts have been made, not to prevent it, but rather that it might be attended with the least injury, and the greatest amount of good which the case would admit. I was not alone in this opinion. A number of aged and influential ministers entertained the same views. And, indeed, it is not easy to conceive how any one, intimately acquainted with the facts in the case, and the relative position of the North and South, could arrive at any other conclusion. Nothing has transpired since the close of the General Conference to change the opinion I then formed; but subsequent events have rather confirmed it. In view of the certainty of the issue, and at the same time ardently desirous that the two great divisions of the Church might be in peace and harmony within their own respective bounds, and cultivate the spirit of Christian fellowship, brotherly kindness, and charity for each other, I cannot but consider it an auspicious event that sixteen Annual Conferences, represented in this Convention, have acted with such extraordinary unanimity in the measures they have taken in the premises. In the Southern Conferences which I have attended, I do not recollect that there has been a dissenting voice with respect to the *necessity* of a separate organization; and although their official acts in deciding the important question, have been marked with that clearness and decision which should afford satisfactory evidence that they have acted under a solemn conviction of duty to Christ, and to the people of their charge, they have been equally distinguished by moderation and candor. And as far as I have been informed, all the other Conferences have pursued a similar course.

It is ardently to be desired that the same unanimity may prevail in the counsels of this Convention as distinguished, in such a remarkable manner, the views, and deliberations, and decisions of your constituents. When it is recollected that it is not only for yourselves, and the present ministry and membership of the Conferences you represent, that you are assembled on this occasion, but that millions of the present race, and generations yet unborn, may be affected, in their most essential interest, by the results of your deliberations, it will occur to you how important it is that you should "do all things as in the immediate presence of God." Let all your acts, dear brethren, be accompanied with much prayer for that *wisdom which is from above.*

While you are thus impressed with the importance and solemnity of the subject which has occasioned the Convention, and of the high responsibility under which you act, I am confident you will cultivate the spirit of Christian moderation and forbearance; and that in all your acts you will keep strictly within the limits and provisions of the "Plan of Separation" adopted by the General Conference with great unanimity and apparent Christian kindness. I can have no doubt of the firm adherence of the ministers and members of the Church in the Conferences you represent, to the doctrines, rules, order of government, and forms of worship, contained in our excellent Book of Discipline. For myself, I stand upon the basis of Methodism as contained in this book, and from it I intend never to be removed. I cannot be insensible to the expression of your confidence in the resolution you have unanimously adopted, requesting me to preside over the Convention in conjunction with my colleagues. And after having weighed the subject with careful deliberation, I have resolved to accept your invitation, and discharge the duties of the important trust to the best of my ability. My excellent colleague, Bishop Andrew, is of the same mind, and will cordially participate in the duties of the chair.

I am requested to state to the Convention that our worthy and excellent colleague, Bishop Morris, believes it to be his duty to decline a participation in the presidential duties. He assigns such reasons for so doing as are, in the judgment of his colleagues, perfectly satisfactory; and it is presumed they would be considered in the same light by the Convention. In conclusion, I trust that all things will be done in that spirit which will be approved of God; and devoutly pray that your acts may result in the advancement of the Redeemer's kingdom, and the salvation of the souls of men.

Bishop Soule then took the chair, which was courteously vacated by Dr. Pierce.

On motion of J. Early and W. A. Smith, it was

"*Resolved,* That a committee of *two* members, from each Annual Conference represented in this Convention, be appointed, whose duty it shall be to take into consideration the propriety and necessity of a Southern organization, according to the Plan of Separation adopted by the late General Conference; together with the acts of the several Annual Conferences on this subject, and report the best method of securing the objects contemplated in the appointment of this Convention."

On motion of John Early and Thomas Crowder,

the foregoing committee was chosen by the respective delegations, and are as follows:

Kentucky Conference.—Henry B. Bascom and Edward Stevenson.

Missouri.—William Patton and Andrew Monroe.

Holston. — Thomas K. Catlett and Thomas Stringfield.

Tennessee.—Robert Paine and Fountain E. Pitts.

North Carolina.—Hezekiah G. Leigh and Peter Doub.

Memphis.—George W. D. Harris and Moses Brock.

Arkansas.—John Harrell and John F. Truslow.

Virginia.—John Early and William A. Smith.

Mississippi.—William Winans and Benjamin M. Drake.

Texas.—Francis Wilson and Littleton Fowler.

Alabama.—Jefferson Hamilton and Jesse Boring.

Georgia.—Lovick Pierce and Augustus B. Longstreet.

South Carolina.—William Capers and William M. Wightman.

Florida.—Thomas C. Benning and Peyton P. Smith.

Indian Mission.—Edward T. Peery and David B. Cumming.

Soon after the appointment of the Committee on Organization, religious exercises ensued, in which Dr. Capers, William Burke, Bishop Morris, and Bishop Soule, took the lead.

On Monday, the 5th, on motion of Dr. William Winans, it was

"*Resolved*, That the Committee on Organization be instructed to inquire whether or not any thing has transpired, during the past year, to render it possible to maintain the unity of the Methodist Episcopal Church, under the same General Conference jurisdiction, without the ruin of Southern Methodism."

On motion of Benjamin M. Drake, it was

"*Resolved*, That the Committee on Organization be, and are hereby, instructed to inquire into the propriety of reporting resolutions in case a division should take place, leaving the way open for re-union on terms which shall not compromise the interest of the *Southern*, and which shall meet, as far as may be, the views of the *Northern* portion of the Church."

Dr. William A. Smith and Dr. Lovick Pierce presented the following resolution, which at their request was laid on the table to be taken up to-morrow morning:

"*Resolved*, By the delegates of the several Annual Conferences in the Southern and South-western States, in General Convention assembled, That we cannot sanction the action of the late General Conference of the Methodist Episcopal Church, on the subject of slavery, by remaining under the ecclesiastical jurisdiction of that body, without deep and lasting injury to the interests of the Church and the country; we, therefore, hereby instruct the Committee on Organization, that if upon a careful examination of the whole subject, they find that there is no reasonable ground to hope that the Northern majority will recede from their position and give some safe guaranty for the future security of our civil and ecclesiastical rights, that they report in favor of a separation from the ecclesiastical jurisdiction of the said General Conference."

The resolution offered by Drs. Smith and Pierce was supported by speeches from Dr. Smith, Dr. Pierce, Dr. Capers, Lewell Campbell, Dr. Longstreet, Samuel Dunwody, Dr. Paine, G. F. Pierce, and Thomas Crowder.

On Tuesday, the 13th of May, the following resolution was offered by James E. Evans, of Georgia:

"*Resolved*, That in the judgment of the Convention, it is not necessary that the general causes and necessities for a separate organization should be discussed any longer—unless some members from the border Conferences should think it necessary to do so, in order to represent their portion of the Church correctly."

On this resolution speeches were made by

George W. Brush, H. H. Kavanaugh, Thomas Stringfield, William Patton, Andrew Monroe, and William Gunn.

On the 14th, the resolution of Mr. Evans was taken up, and speeches were made by Fountain E. Pitts, of the Tennessee Conference, Moses Brock, William McMahon, and George W. D. Harris, of the Memphis, William Gunn and Benjamin T. Crouch, of the Kentucky, Dr. Smith, of the Virginia, and Thomas K. Catlett, of the Holston.

The resolution of James E. Evans was then withdrawn, and the one offered by William A. Smith was again taken up, and supported in a few remarks by Joseph Boyle and Jesse Green, of Missouri, and Littleton Fowler, of Texas. The resolution was then adopted, with one dissenting vote.

On the 15th of May, it was announced that the Committee on Organization were prepared to make their report. They submitted the following, which was read by Rev. Henry B. Bascom, D.D., the Chairman of the Committee:

The committee appointed to inquire into the propriety and necessity of a separate organization of the Annual Conferences of the Methodist Episcopal Church, in the slaveholding States, for the purpose of a separate General Conference connection and jurisdiction, within the limits of said States and Conferences, having had the entire subject under careful and patient consideration, together with the numerous petitions, instructions, resolutions, and propositions for adjustment and compromise, referred to them by the Convention, offer the following as their

REPORT:

In view of the extent to which the great questions in controversy, between the North and the South of the Methodist Episcopal Church, have been discussed, and by consequence must be understood by the parties more immediately interested, it has not been deemed necessary by the committee to enter into any formal or elaborate examination of the general subject, beyond a plain and comprehensive statement of the facts and principles involved, which may place it in the power of all concerned to do justice to the convictions and motives of the Southern Church, in resisting the action of the late General Conference on the subject of slavery, and its unconstitutional assumption of right and power in other respects; and also presenting, in a form as brief and lucid as possible, some of the principal grounds of action, had in view by the South, in favoring the provisional Plan of Separation, adopted by the General Conference at its last session.

On the subject of the legitimate right, and the full and proper authority, of the Convention to institute, determine, and finally act upon the inquiry referred to the committee to deliberate and report upon, the committee entertain no doubt whatever. Apart from every other consideration which might be brought to bear upon the question, the General Conference of 1844, in the Plan of Jurisdictional Separation adopted by that body, gave full and express authority to "the Annual Conferences in the slaveholding States," to judge of the propriety, and decide upon the necessity, of organizing a "separate ecclesiastical connection" in the South. And not only did the General Conference invest this right in "the Annual Conferences in the slaveholding States," without limitation or reserve, as to the *extent* of the investment, and *exclusively* with regard to every other division of the Church, and all other branches or powers of the government, but left the method of official determination and the mode of action, in the exercise or assertion of the right, to the free and untrammeled discretion of the Conferences interested. These Conferences, thus accredited by the General Conference to judge and act for themselves, confided the right and trust of decision and action in the premises to delegates regularly chosen by these bodies respectively, upon a uniform principle and fixed ratio of representation, previously agreed upon by each, in constitutional session, and directed them to meet in general convention, in the city of Louisville, May, 1845, for this and other purposes, authorized by the General Conference, at the same time and in the same way. All the right and power, therefore, of the General Conference, in any way connected with the important decision in question, were duly and formally transferred to "the Annual Conferences in the slaveholding States," and exclusively invested in them. And as this investment was obviously for the purpose that such right and power might be exercised by them, in any mode they might prefer, not inconsistent with the terms and conditions of the investment, the delegates thus chosen, one hundred in number, and representing sixteen Annual Conferences, under commission of the General Conference, here and now assembled in Convention, have not only all the right and power of the General Conference, as transferred to "the Annual Conferences in the slaveholding States," but in addition, all the right and power of necessity inherent in these bodies, as constituent parties, giving birth and power to the General Conference itself, as the common federal council of the Church. It follows hence, that for all the purposes specified and understood in this preliminary view of the subject, the Convention possesses all the right and power both of the General Conference and the sixteen "Annual Conferences in the slaveholding States," jointly and severally considered. The ecclesiastical and conventional right, therefore, of this body to act in the premises, and act conclusively, irrespective of the whole Church—and all its powers of government beside —is clear and undoubted. As the *moral* right, however, to act as proposed in the General Conference Plan of Jurisdictional Separation, rests upon entirely different grounds, and will, perhaps, be considered as furnishing the only allowable warrant of action, notwithstanding constitutional right, it may be necessary at least to glance at the grave moral reasons creating the necessity, the high moral compulsions by which the Southern Conferences and Church have been impelled to the course of action, which it is the intention of this Report to explain and vindicate, as not only right and reasonable, but indispensable to the character and welfare of Southern Methodism.

The preceding statements and reasoning present no new principle or form of action in the history of the Church. Numerous instances might be cited, in the constitutional history of Church-polity, in which high moral necessity, in the absence of any recognized conventional right, has furnished the only and yet sufficient warrant for ecclesiastical movements and arrangements, precisely similar in character with that contemplated in the plan of a separate Southern Connection of the Methodist Episcopal Church, adopted by the late General Conference. Wesleyan Methodism, in all its phases and aspects, is a most pertinent illustration of the truth we assume, and the fitness and force of the example must go far to preclude the necessity of any other proof. It was on the specific basis of such necessity, without conventional right, that the great Wesleyan Connection arose in England. It was upon the same basis, as avowed by Wesley, that the American Connection became separate and independent; and this Connection again avows the same principle of action, in the separation and establishment of a Methodist Episcopal Church in Canada, whose organization took place by permission and direction of the same authority under which this Convention is now acting for a similar purpose.

Should it appear, in the premises of the action proposed, that a high moral and religious duty is devolved upon the ministry and membership of the Methodist Episcopal Church in the South—devolved upon us by the great Head of the Church, and the providential appointments of our social condition, which we cannot neglect without infidelity to a high moral trust, but which we cannot fulfill in connectional union with the Northern portion of the Church, under the same General Conference jurisdiction, owing to causes connected with the civil institutions of the country, and beyond the control of the Church, *then* a strong moral necessity is laid upon us, which assumes the commanding character of a positive duty, under sanction of divine right, to dissolve the ties and bonds of a single General Conference jurisdiction, and in its place substitute one in the South, which will not obstruct us in the performance of duty, or prevent us from accomplishing the great objects of the Christian ministry and Church-organization. From a careful survey of the entire field of facts and their relations—the whole range of cause and effect, as connected with the subject-matter of this Report—it is confidently believed that the great warrant of *moral necessity*, not less than unquestionable ecclesiastical right, fully justifies this Convention in the position they are about to take, as a separate organic division of the Methodist Episcopal Church, by authority of its chief synod, "the delegates of all the several Annual Conferences in General Conference assembled." One of the two main issues, which have decided the action of the Southern Conferences, relates, as all know, to the assumed right of the Church to control the question of slavery, by means of the ordinary and fluctuating provisions of Church-legislation, without reference to the superior control of State policy and civil law. From all the evidence accessible in the case, the great masses of the ministry and membership of the Methodist Episcopal Church, North and South, present an irreconcilable opposition of conviction and feeling on the subject of slavery, so far as relates to the rights of the Church to interfere with the question—the one claiming unlimited right of interference to the full extent the Church may, at any time, or from any cause, be concerned, and the other resisting alike the assumption or exercise of any such right, because, in nearly all the slave-holding States, such a course of action must bring the Church in direct conflict with the civil authority, to which the Church has pledged subjection and support in the most solemn and explicit forms, and from the obligations of which she cannot retreat without dishonoring her own laws, and the neglect and violation of some of the plain and most imperative requirements of Christianity. Under such circumstances of disagreement—in such a state of adverse conviction and feeling on the part of the North and South of the Church—it is believed that the two great sections of the Church, thus situated in relation to each other by causes beyond the control of either party, cannot remain together and successfully prosecute the high and common aims of the Christian ministry and Church-organization under the same General Conference jurisdiction. The manifest want of uniformity of opinion and harmony of coöperation must always lead, as heretofore, to struggles and results directly inconsistent with the original intention of the Church, in establishing a common jurisdiction, to control all its general interests. And should it appear that, by a division and future duality of such jurisdiction as authorized by the late General Conference, the original purposes of the Church can better be accomplished, or rather, that they can be accomplished in no other way, how can the true and proper unity of the Church be maintained except by yielding to the necessity, and having a separate General Conference jurisdiction for each division? By the Southern portion of the Church generally, slavery is regarded as strictly a civil institution, exclusively in custody of the civil power, and as a regulation of State beyond the reach of Church-interference or control, except as civil law and right may be infringed by ecclesiastical assumption. By the Northern portion of the Church, individuals are held responsible for the alleged *injustice* and *evil* of relations and rights, created and protected by the organic and municipal laws of the Government and country, and which relations and rights, in more than two-thirds of the slaveholding States, are not under individual control in any sense or to any extent.

Both portions of the Church are presumed to act from principle and conviction, and cannot, therefore, recede; and *how*, under *such* circumstances, is it possible to prevent the most fearful disunion, with all the attendant evils of contention and strife, except by allowing each section a separate and independent jurisdiction, the same in character and purpose with the one to which both have hitherto been subject? What fact, truth, or principle, not merely of human origin, and therefore of doubtful authority, can be urged as interposing any reasonable obstacle to a change of jurisdiction, merely *modal* in character, and simply designed to adapt a single principle of Church-government, not pretended to be of divine obligation or Scripture origin, to the character and features of the civil government of the country? Nothing essential to Church-organization—nothing essentially distinctive of Methodism—even American Methodism, is proposed to be disturbed, or even touched, by the arrangement. It is a simple division of general jurisdiction, for strong moral reasons, arising out of the civil relations and position of the parties, intended to accomplish for both what it is demonstrated by experiment cannot be accomplished by one common jurisdiction, as now constituted, and should therefore, under the stress of such moral necessity, be attempted in some other way.

The question of slavery, more or less intimately interwoven with the interests and destiny of nine millions of human beings in the United States, is certainly of sufficient importance, coming up as it has in the recent history of the Methodist Episcopal Church, and as it does in the deliberations of this Convention, to authorize any merely *modal* or even organic changes in the government of the Church, should it appear obvious that the original and avowed purposes of the Church will be more effectively secured and promoted by the change proposed, than by continuing the present or former system. The evidence before the committee establishes the fact in the clearest manner possible, that throughout the Southern Conferences, the ministry and membership of the Church, amounting to nearly 500,000, in the proportion of about ninety-five in the hundred, deem a division of jurisdiction indispensable to the welfare of the Church, in the Southern and South-western Conferences of the slaveholding States; and this fact alone must go far to establish the *right*, while it demonstrates the *necessity*, of the separate jurisdiction contemplated in the plan of the General Conference, and adopted by that body in view of such necessity as likely to exist. The interests of State, civil law, and public opinion, in the South, imperiously require that the Southern portion of the Church shall have no part in the *discussion* and agitation of this subject in the chief councils of the Church. In this opinion, nearly universal in the South, we *concur*.

Christ and his apostles—Christianity and its inspired and early teachers—found slavery in its most offensive and aggravated forms, as a civil institution, diffused and existing throughout nearly the entire field of their ministrations and influence; and yet, in the New Testament, and earlier records of the Church, we have no legislation—no interference—no denunciation with regard to it—not even remonstrance against it. They found it wrought up and vitally intermingled with the whole machinery of civil government and order of society—so implicated with "the powers that be," that infinite wisdom, and the early pastoral guides of the Church, saw just reason why the Church should not interfere beyond a plain and urgent enforcement of the various duties growing out of the peculiar relation of master and slave, leaving *the relation* itself, as a civil arrangement, untouched and unaffected, except so far as it seems obviously to have been the divine purpose to remove every form and degree of wrong and evil connected with the institutions of human government, by a faithful inculcation of the doctrines and duties of Christianity, without meddling in any way with the civil polity of the countries into which it was introduced. A course precisely similar to this, the example of which should have been more attractive, was pursued by the great founder of Methodism, in all slaveholding countries in which he established societies. Mr. Wesley never deemed it proper to have any rule, law, or regulation on the subject of slavery, either in the United States, the West Indies, or elsewhere. The effects of the early and unfortunate attempts of the Methodist Church to meddle and interfere, in the *legislation* and *practice* of government and discipline, with the institution of slavery in the United States, are too well known to require comment. Among the more immediate results of this short-sighted, disastrous imprudence, especially from 1780 to 1804, may be mentioned the watchful jealousy of civil government, and the loss of public confidence throughout a very large and influential portion of the whole Southern community. These, and similar developments, led the Church, by the most careful and considerate steps, to the adoption, gradually, of a medium compromise course of legislation on the subject, until the law of slavery, as it now exists in the *letter* of Discipline, became, by the last material act of legislation in 1816, the great compromise bond of union between the North and the South on the subject of slavery. The whole law of the Church, all there is in the statute-book to govern North and South on this subject, is the following: *First.* The general rule, which simply prohibits "the buying and selling of men, women, or children, with an *intention to enslave them.*" *Second.* "No slaveholder shall be eligible to any official station in our Church hereafter, where the laws of the State in which he lives admit of emancipation, and permit the liberated slave to enjoy freedom. When any traveling preacher becomes an owner of a slave, or slaves, by any means, he shall forfeit his ministerial character in our Church, unless he execute, if it be practicable, a legal emancipation of such slaves, conformably to the laws of the State in which he lives."

Here is the law, the *whole*, the *only*, law of the Church, containing first, a *prohibition*, and second, a *grant*. The prohibition is, that no member or minister of the Church is allowed to purchase or sell a human being, who is to be *enslaved*, or *reduced to a state of slavery*, by such purchase or sale. And farther, that no minister, in *any of the grades* of ministerial office, or other person, having official standing in the Church, can, if he be the owner of a slave, be allowed to sustain such official relation to the Church, unless he shall legally provide for the emancipation of such slave or slaves, if the laws of the State in which he lives will admit of legal emancipation, and permit the liberated slave to enjoy freedom. Such is the plain *prohibition* of law, binding upon all. The *grant* of the law, however, is equally plain and unquestionable. It is, that persons *may* purchase or sell men, women, or children, provided such purchase or sale does not involve the fact or intention of enslaving them, or of *reducing the subjects* of such purchase or sale *to a state of slavery*.

The intention of the law no doubt is, that this may be done from motives of humanity, and not by any means for the purpose of gain. But, farther, the law distinctly provides, that every minister, *in whatever grade of office*, and every person having *official standing of any kind*, in the Methodist Episcopal Church, being the owner or owners of slave property, shall be protected against any forfeiture of right, on this account, where the laws of the State do not admit of legal emancipation, and allow the liberated slave to enjoy freedom in the State in which he is emancipated. Here is the plain *grant of law* to which we allude. From the first agitation of the subject of slavery in the Church, the Northern portion of it has been disposed to insist upon farther *prohibitory* enactments. The South, meanwhile, has always shown itself ready to go as far, by way of prohibition, as the law in question implies, but has uniformly resisted any attempt to impair Southern rights under protection of the grant of law to which we have asked attention. Under such circumstances of disagreement and difficulty, the conventional and legislative adjustment of the question, as found in the General Rule, but especially the tenth section of the Discipline, was brought about, and has always been regarded in the South as a great compromise arrangement, without strict adherence to which the North and the South could not remain together under the same general jurisdiction. That we have not mistaken the character of the law, or misconstrued the intention and purposes of its enactment, at different times, we think entirely demonstrable from the whole history, both of the legislation of the Church and the judicial and executive administration of the Government. The full force and bearing of the law, however, were more distinctly brought to view, and authoritatively asserted, by the General Conference of 1840, after the most careful examination of the whole subject, and the judicial determination of that body, connected with the language of the Discipline just quoted, gives in still clearer light *the true and only law of the Church* on the subject of slavery. After deciding various other principles and positions incidental to the main question, the decision is summed up in the following words:

"While the general rule (or law) on the subject of slavery, relating to those States whose laws admit of emancipation, and permit the liberated slave to enjoy freedom, should be firmly and constantly enforced, the exception to the general rule (or law) applying to those States where emancipation, as defined above, is *not practicable*, should be recognized and protected with equal firmness and impartiality; therefore,

"*Resolved, by the several Annual Conferences in General Conference assembled,* That under the provisional exception of the general rule (or law) of the Church, on the subject of slavery, the simple holding of slaves, or mere ownership of slave property, in States or Territories where the laws do not admit of emancipation and permit the liberated slave to enjoy freedom, constitutes *no legal barrier* to the election or ordination of ministers to the various grades of office known in the ministry of the Methodist Episcopal Church, and cannot, therefore, be considered as operating *any forfeiture* of right, in view of such election and ordination."

This decision of the General Conference was not objected to or dissented from by a single member of that body. It was the unanimous voice of the great representative and judical council of the Church then acting in the character of a high court of appeals for the decision of an important legal question. It will be perceived how strikingly the language of this decision accords with *both* the features of the law of slavery which we have thought it important to notice, the *prohibition* and the *grant* of law in the case; what may *not* be done as the general rule, and at the same time what *may be done*, under the provisional exception to the general law, without forfeiture of right of any kind. It is also worthy of particular notice, that beside the plain assurance of the original law, that where emancipation is not legally practicable, and the emancipated slave allowed to enjoy freedom, or where it is practicable to emancipate, but the emancipated slave cannot enjoy freedom, emancipation is not required of any owner of slaves in the Methodist Episcopal Church, from the lowest officer up to the Bishop, but the rights of all thus circumstanced are protected and secured, notwithstanding their connection with slavery. Besides this, the full and elaborate decision of the General Conference as a grave and formal adjudication had upon all the issues involved in the question, published to all who were in, or might be disposed to enter, the Church, that the law of slavery applied to States where emancipation is impracticable, and the freed slave not allowed to enjoy freedom, this clear and unambiguous decision, by the highest authority of the Church, *leaves* the owner of slaves upon the ground—upon a basis of the most perfect equality with *other* ministers of the Church, having no connection with slavery. Such, then, is the law; such its construction; such the official and solemn pledge of the Church. And these had, to a great extent, restored the lost confidence and allayed the jealous apprehensions of the South, in relation to the purposes of the Church respecting slavery. There was in the South no disposition to disturb, discuss, or in any way agitate the subject. The law was not objected to or complained of, but was regarded as a settled compromise between the parties, a medium arrangement on the ground of mutual concession, well calculated to secure and promote the best interests of the Church, North and South.

That this law, this great compromise conservative arrangement, which had been looked to as the only reliable bond of jurisdictional union between the North and South for nearly half a century, was practically disregarded and abandoned by the last General Conference, in the memorable cases of Harding and Andrew, both by judicial construction and virtual legislation, manifestly inconsistent with its provisions and purposes, and subversive of the great objects of its enactment, has been too fearfully demonstrated by various forms of proof, to require more than a brief notice in this Report. The actual position of the Church was suddenly reversed, and its long-established policy entirely changed. The whole law of the Church, and the most important adjudications had upon it, were treated as null and obsolete, and that body proceeded to a claim of right and course of action amounting to a virtual repeal of all law, and new and capricious legislation on the most difficult and delicate question ever introduced into the councils of the Church or named upon its statute-book.

By no fair construction of the law of slavery, as given above, could the Church be brought in conflict with civil legislation on the subject. It is true, as demanded by the convictions and opinions of the Church, testimony was borne against the evil of slavery, but it was done without conflicting with the polity and laws of any portion of the country. No law, for example, affected the lay-membership of the Church with regard to slaveholding; the Church gave its full permission that the private members of the Church might own and hold slaves at discretion; and the inference is indubitable, that the Church did not consider simple slaveholding *as a moral evil,* personally attaching to the mere fact of being the owner or holder of slaves. The evil charged upon slavery must of necessity have been understood of other aspects of the subject, and could not imply moral obliquity, without impeaching the integrity and virtue of the Church. Moreover, where the laws precluded emancipation, the ministry were subjected to no disabilities of any kind, and the requirements of the Church, in relation to slavery, were not at least in any thing like direct conflict with civil law. In contravention, however, of the plain and long-established law of the Church, the action of the General Conference of 1844, in the well-known instances cited, brought the Church into a state of direct and violent antagonism with the civil authority and the rights of citizenship, throughout all the slaveholding States. This was not done by the repeal of existing law, or additional legislation by direct enactment, but in a much more dangerous form, by the simple process of resolution by an irresponsible majority, requiring Southern ministers, as slaveholders, in order to Church eligibility and equality of right with non-slaveholding ministers of the Church, to do what cannot be done without a violation of the laws of the States in which they reside, and is not required or contemplated, but expressly excepted, and even provided against, by the law of the Church.

It will thus appear that the entire action of the General Conference on the subject of slavery was in direct conflict with the law, both of the Church and the land, and could not have been submitted to by the South without the most serious detriment to the interests of the Church. The action in the instance of Bishop Andrew was, in the strongest and most exceptional sense, extrajudicial. It was not pretended that Bishop Andrew had violated any law of the Church; so far from this, the only law applicable to the case, gave, as we have seen, ample and explicit assurance of protection. So to construe law, or so proceed to act without reference to law, as to abstract from it its whole protective power, and deprive it of all its conservative tendencies in the system, is one of the most dangerous forms of legal injustice, and, as a principle of action, must be considered as subversive of all order and government. The late General Conference required of Bishop Andrew, the same being equally true in the case of Harding, as the condition of his being acceptable to the Church, the surrender of rights secured to him, both by civil and ecclesiastical law. The purposes of law were contravened and destroyed, and its prerogative and place usurped by mere opinion.

The requisition in the case was not only extra-judicial, being made in the absence of any thing like law authorizing the measure, but being made at the same time against law, it was usurpation; and so far as the proceeding complained of is intended to establish a principle of action with regard to the future, it gives to the General Conference all the attributes of a despotism, claiming the right to govern *without*, *above*, and *against law*. The doctrine avowed at the late General Conference, and practically indorsed by the majority, that that body may, by simple resolution, advisory, punitive, or declaratory, repeal an existing law in relation to a particular case, leaving it in full force with regard to other cases; or may enact a new and different law, and apply it judicially to the individual case, which led to the enactment, and all in a moment, by a single elevation of the hand, is a position—a doctrine—so utterly revolutionary and disorganizing, as to place in jeopardy at once, both the interests and reputation of the Church.

The action in the case of Bishop Andrew not only assumed the character and usurped the place of law, but was clearly an instance of *ex post facto* legislation, by making that an offense after the act which was not such before. The conduct charged as an offense was at the time, and continues to be, under the full protection of a well-understood and standing law of the Church; and yet this conduct was made criminal and punishable by the retrospective action of the Conference to which we allude. The officially expressed will of the General Conference intended to govern and circumscribe the conduct of Bishop Andrew, without reference to existing law, and indeed contrary to it, was made the rule of action, and he found guilty of its violation, by acts done before he was made acquainted with it. The conduct charged was in perfect consistency with the law of the Church, and could only be wrought into an offense by an *ex post facto* bearing of the after-action of the General Conference.

Bishop Andrew became the owner of slave property, involuntarily, several years before his marriage; and as the *fact*, and not the *extent*, of his connection with slavery constituted his offense, it follows that, for a relation in which he was placed by the action of others, and the operation of civil law, and in which, as a citizen of Georgia, he was compelled to remain, or be brought in conflict with the laws of the State, he *was*, in violation of the pledge of public law, as we have shown, arrested and punished by the General Conference. That body, by direct requirement, such at least by implication, commanded him to free his slaves, or suffer official degradation. The law of Georgia required him to hold his slaves, or transfer them to be held as such by others under heavy and painful penalties to master and slave. To avoid ecclesiastical punishment and disability, the Church required him either to leave the State of his residence, or violate its laws. In this way, taking the judicial decision in Harding's case, and the anomalous action in Bishop Andrew's, the Church is placed in most offensive conflict with the civil authority of the State. Can any country or government safely allow the Church to enforce disobedience to civil law, as a Christian duty? If such attempts are made to subordinate the civil interests of the State to the schemes and purposes of Church innovation, prompted and sustained by the bigotry and fanaticism of large masses of ignorant and misguided zealots engaged in the conflict in the name of God and conscience, and for the ostensible purposes of religious reform, what can be the stability of civil government, or the hopes of those seeking its protection? And what, we ask, must be the interest of the South in connection with such movements?

In the instance of slavery in this country, it is but too well known, that such antagonism as is indicated by the preceding facts and developments between the purposes of the Church and the policy of the State, must result in the most disastrous consequences to both. The slavery of the Southern States can never be reduced in amount or mitigated in form by such a state of things. The Southern States have the sole control of the question, under the authority and by contract of the Federal Constitution, and all hope of removing the evil of slavery, without destroying the national compact and the union of the States, must connect with the individual sovereignty of the Southern States, as parties to the Federal compact, and the independent policy of each State in relation to slavery, as likely to be influenced by moral and political reasons, and motives, brought to bear, by proper means and methods, upon the understanding and moral sense of the Southern people. All trespass upon right, whether as it regards the rights of property or of character—every thing like aggression, mere denunciation or abuse—must of necessity tend to provoke farther resistance on the part of the South, and lessen the influence the North might otherwise have upon the great mass of the Southern people, in relation to this great and exciting interest. The true character and actual relations of slavery in the United

States are *so predominantly civil and political* that any attempt to treat the subject, or control the question, upon purely moral and ecclesiastical grounds, can never exert any salutary influence South, except in so far as the moral and ecclesiastical shall be found strictly subordinate to the civil and political. This mode of appeal, it is believed, will never satisfy the North. The whole Northern portion of the Church, speaking through their guides and leaders, is manifesting an increasing disposition to form issues upon the subject, so utterly inconsistent with the rights and peace of the slaveholding States, that by how far the Methodist Episcopal Church in the South may contribute to the bringing about of such a state of things, or may fail to resist it, the influence of Methodism must be depressed, and the interest of the Church suffer. In addition, then, to the fact that we have already received an amount of injury beyond what we can bear, except under a separate organization, we have the strongest grounds of apprehension, that unless we place ourselves in a state of defense and prepare for independent action, under the distinct jurisdiction we are now authorized by the General Conference to resolve upon, and organize, we shall soon find ourselves so completely subjected to the adverse views and policy of the Northern majority, as to be left without right or remedy, except as a mere secession from the Church. Now, the case is entirely different, as we propose to do nothing not authorized in the General Conference Plan of Separation, either expressly or by necessary implication. The general view thus far taken of the subject is intended to show that "the Annual Conferences in the slaveholding States," embracing the entire Church, South, have found themselves placed in circumstances, by the action of the General Conference in May last, which, according to the declaration of the Southern delegates, at the time, render it impracticable to accomplish the objects of the Christian ministry and Church-organization, under the present system of General Conference control, and showing, by the most clear and conclusive evidence, that there exists the most urgent necessity for the "separate ecclesiastical connection," constitutionally provided for by the General Conference upon the basis of the Declaration just adverted to. At the date of the Declaration the Southern delegates were fully convinced that the frequent and exciting agitation and action in that body on the subject of slavery and abolition, as in Harding's case, and especially the proceedings in the case of Bishop Andrew—each being regarded as but a practical exposition of the principle of the majority—rendered a *separate organization* indispensable to the success of Methodism in the South. The truth of the Declaration, so far from being called in question by the majority, was promptly conceded in the immediate action the Conference had upon it, assigning the Declaration as the sole ground or reason of the action, which terminated in the adoption of the Plan of Separation, under which we are now acting as a Convention, and from the spirit and intention of which it is believed to be the purpose of the Convention not to depart in any of its deliberations or final acts. Although the action of this General Conference on the subject of slavery, and the relative adverse position of the parties North and South, together with the irritating and exasperating evils of constant agitation and frequent attempts at legislation, are made in the Declaration the grounds of the avowal, that a separate organization was necessary to the success of the ministry in the slaveholding States, it was by no means intended to convey the idea, or make the impression, that no other causes existed rendering a separate organization proper and necessary; but as the action of the Conference on the subject of slavery was certain to involve the Church in the South in immediate and alarming difficulty, and it was believed that this could be so shown to the majority as to induce them to consent to some course of action in remedy of the evil, the complaint of the Declaration was confined to the simple topic of slavery. It will be perceived that the case of Bishop Andrew, although prominently introduced, is not relied upon as exclusively furnishing the *data* of this conclusion at which we have arrived. The entire action the General Conference so frequently brought to view, and which is made the ground of dissent and action, both in the Protest and Declaration of the Southern Delegates, must be understood as belonging to the premises and language employed as including all the principles avowed, as well as the action had by the late General Conference on the subject of slavery. The attempt to disclaim the judicial character of the action in Bishop Andrew's case and show it to be merely advisory, cannot affect the preceding reasoning; for, first, the disclaimer is as equivocal in character as the original action; and, secondly, the reasoning in support of the disclaimer negatives the supposition of mere advice, because it involves issues coming legitimately within the province of judicial process and legal determination; and, thirdly, Bishop Andrew is, by the explanation of the disclaimer itself, held as responsible for his conduct, in view of the alleged advice, as he could have been held by the original action without the explanation. While, therefore, the explanation giving the original action an *advisory* character, notwithstanding the inconsistency involved, fully protects Bishops Soule and Andrew from even the shadow of blame in the course they have pursued, the entire action in the case, and especially when connected with the case of Harding, as alluded to in the Declaration, fully sustains the general view of the subject we have taken in this Report. The Southern delegates at the General Conference, in presenting to that body their Declaration and Protest, acted, and they continue to act, as the representatives of the South, under the full conviction that the principles and policy avowed by the Northern majority are such as to render their *public* and *practical renunciation* by the Southern Methodist ministry and people necessary to the safety, not less than the success, of the Church in the South.

Other views of the subject, however, must claim a share of our attention. Among the many weighty reasons which influence the Southern Conferences in seeking to be released from the jurisdiction of the General Conference of the Methodist Episcopal Church, as now constituted, are the novel, and, as we think, dangerous doctrines, practically avowed and indorsed by that body and the Northern portion of the Church generally, with regard to the *constitution* of the Church, and the constitutional rights and powers respectively of the EPISCOPACY and the General Conference. In relation to the first, it is confidently, although most unaccountably, maintained that the six short *Restrictive Rules* which were adopted in 1808, and first became obligatory, as an amendment to the constitution, in 1812, are in fact the *true* and *only* constitution of the Church. This single position, should it become an established principle of action to the extent it found favor with the last General Conference, must subvert the government of the Methodist Episcopal Church. It must be seen at once, that the position leaves many of the organic laws and most important institutions of the Church entirely unprotected and at the mercy of a mere and ever-fluctuating majority of the General Conference. Episcopacy, for example, although protected in the abstract, in general terms, may be entirely superseded or destroyed by the simple omission to elect or consecrate Bishops, neither of which is provided for in the Restrictive Articles. The whole itinerant system, except general superintendency, is without protection in the Restrictive Rules; and there is nothing in them preventing the Episcopacy from restricting their superintendency to *local* and *settled* pastors, rather than a traveling ministry, and thus destroying the most distinctive feature of Wesleyan Methodism. So far as the Restrictive Rules are concerned, the Annual Conferences are without protection, and might also be destroyed by the General Conference at any time. If the new constitutional theory be correct, class-leaders and private members are as eligible, upon the basis of the constitution, to a seat in the General Conference as any ministers of the Church. Societies, too, instead of Annual Conferences, may elect delegates, and may elect *laymen* instead of ministers, or local instead of traveling ministers. Very few indeed of the more fundamental and distinguishing elements of Methodism, deeply and imperishably imbedded in the affection and veneration of the Church, and vital to its very existence, are even alluded to in the Restrictive Articles. This theory assumes the self-refuted absurdity, that the General Conference is in fact the government of the Church, if not the Church itself. With no other constitution than these mere restrictions upon the powers and rights of the General Conference, the government and discipline of the Methodist Episcopal Church as a system of organized laws and well-adjusted instrumentalities for the spread of the gospel and the diffusion of piety, and whose living principles of energy and action have so long commanded the admiration of the world, would soon cease even to exist. The startling assumption that a Bishop of the Methodist Episcopal Church, instead of holding office under the constitution, and by tenure of law, and the faithful performance of duty, is nothing in his character of Bishop but a mere officer at will of the General Conference, and may accordingly be deposed at any time, with or without cause, accusation, proof, or form of trial, as a dominant majority may capriciously elect, or party interests suggest —and that the General Conference may do, by right, whatever is not prohibited by the Restrictive Rules, and, with this single exception, possess power, "supreme and all-controlling;" and this, in all possible forms of its manifestation, legislative, judicial, and executive—the same men claiming to be at the same time both the fountain and functionaries of all the powers of government, which powers, thus mingled and concentrated into a common force, may at any time be employed, at the prompting of their own interests, caprice, or ambition. Such wild and revolutionary assumptions, so unlike the faith and discipline of Methodism, as we have been taught them, we are compelled to regard as fraught with mischief and ruin to the best interests of the Church, and as furnishing a strong additional reason why we should avail ourselves of the warrant we now have, but may never again obtain, from the General Conference, to "establish an ecclesiastical connection," embracing only the Annual Conferences in the slaveholding States.

Without intending any thing more than a general specification of the disabilities under which the Southern part of the Church labors, in view of existing difficulties, and must continue to do so until they are removed, we must not omit to state, that should we submit to the action of the late General Conference, and decline a separate organization, it would be to place, and finally confirm, the whole Southern ministry in the relation of an *inferior caste,* the effect of which, in spite of all effort to the contrary, would be such a relation, if not (as we think) real degradation of the ministry, as to destroy its influence to a great—a most fearful—extent throughout the South. A practical proscription, under show of legal right, has long been exercised toward the South, with regard to the higher offices of the Church, especially the Episcopacy. To this, however, the South submitted with patient endurance, and was willing farther to submit in order to maintain the peace and unity of the Church, while the *principle* involved was disavowed, and decided to be unjust, as by the decision of the General Conference in 1840. But when, in 1844, the General Conference declared by their action, without the forms of legislative or judicial process, that the mere providential ownership of slave property, in a State where emancipation is legally prohibited under all circumstances, and can only be effected by special legislative enactment, was hereafter to operate as a forfeiture of right in all similar cases, the law of the Church and the decision of the preceding General Conference to the contrary notwithstanding, the Southern ministry were compelled to realize that they were deliberately fixed, by the brand of common shame, in the degrading relation of standing inferiority to ministers, not actually, nor yet liable to be, connected with slavery, and that they were published to the Church and the world as belonging to a *caste* in the ministry, from which the higher offices of the Church could never be selected.

To submit, under such circumstances, would have been a practical, a most humiliating recognition of the *inferiority of caste*, attempted to be fixed upon us by the Northern majority, and would have justly authorized the inference of a want of conscious integrity and self-respect, well calculated to destroy both the reputation and influence of the ministry in all the slaveholding States. It may be no virtue to avow it, but we confess we have no humility courting the grace of such a baptism. The higher objects, therefore, of the Christian ministry, not less than conscious right and self-respect, demanded resistance on the part of the Southern ministry and Church, and these unite with other reasons in vindicating the plea of necessity, upon which the meeting and action of this Convention are based, with the consent and approval of the General Conference of the Methodist Episcopal Church. The variety of interests involved, renders it necessary that the brief view of the subject we are allowed to take, be varied accordingly.

Unless the Southern Conferences organize as proposed, it is morally certain, in view of the evidence before the committee, that the gospel, now regularly and successfully dispensed by the ministers of these Conferences to about a million of slaves, in their various fields of missionary enterprise and pastoral charge, must, to a great extent, be withheld from them, and immense masses of this unfortunate class of our fellow-beings be left to perish, as the result of Church-interference with the civil affairs and relations of the country.

The committee are compelled to believe that the mere division of jurisdiction, as authorized by the General Conference, cannot affect either the moral or legal unity of the great American family of Christians, known as the Methodist Episcopal Church, and this opinion is concurred in by the ablest jurists of the country. We do nothing but what we are *expressly authorized to do* by the supreme, or rather highest, legislative power of the Church. Would the Church authorize us to do wrong? The division relates only to the power of general jurisdiction, which it is not proposed to destroy or even reduce, but simply to invest it in two great organs of Church-action and control, instead of one as at present. Such a change in the present system of general control cannot disturb the moral unity of the Church, for it is strictly an *agreed modification* of General Conference jurisdiction, and such agreement and consent of parties must preclude the idea of disunion. In view of *what* is the alleged disunion predicated? Is the purpose and act of becoming a separate organization proof of disunion, or want of proper Church-unity? This cannot be urged with any show of consistency, inasmuch as "the several Annual Conferences in General Conference assembled," that is to say, the Church through only its constitutional organ of action, on all subjects involving the power of legislation, not only agreed to the separate organization South, but made full constitutional provision for carrying it into effect. It is a separation by consent of parties, under the highest authority of the Church. Is it intended to maintain that the unity of the Church depends upon the modal uniformity of the jurisdiction in question? If this be so, the Methodist Episcopal Church has lost its unity at several different times. The general jurisdiction of the Church has undergone modifications, at several different times, not less vital, if not greatly more so, than the one now proposed. The high conventional powers, of which we are so often reminded, exercised in the organization of the Methodist Episcopal Church, were in the hands of a Conference of unordained lay-preachers, under the sole superintendence of an appointee of Mr. Wesley. This was the first General Conference type and original form of the jurisdiction in question. The jurisdictional power now proposed by the General Conference was for years exercised by small Annual Conferences, without any defined boundaries, and acting separately on all measures proposed for their determination. This general power of jurisdiction next passed into the hands of the Bishops' Council, consisting of some ten persons, where it remained for a term of years. Next it passed into the hands of the whole itinerant ministry, in full connection, and was exercised by them, in collective action, as a General Conference of the whole body, met together at the same time. The power was afterward vested in the whole body of traveling Elders, and from thence finally passed into the hands of Delegates, elected by the Annual Conferences, to meet and act quadrennially as a General Conference, under constitutional restrictions and limitations. Here are several successive reörganizations of General Conference jurisdiction, each involving a much more material change than that contemplated in the General Conference plan, by authority of which this Convention is about to erect the sixteen Annual Conferences in the slaveholding States into a separate organization. We change no principle in the existing theory of General Conference jurisdiction.

We distinctly recognize the jurisdiction of a delegated General Conference, receiving its appointment and authority from the whole constituency of Annual Conferences. The only change, in fact or in form, will be that the delegates of the "Annual Conferences in the slaveholding States," as authorized in the Plan of Separation, will meet in one General Conference assembly of their own, and act in behalf only of their own constituency, and in the regulation of their own affairs, consistently with the good faith and fealty they owe the authority and laws of the several States in which they reside, without interfering with affairs beyond their jurisdiction, or suffering foreign interference with their own. And in proceeding to do this, we have all the authority it was in the power of the Methodist Episcopal Church to confer. We have also farther example and precedent in the history of Methodism, to show that there is nothing irregular or inconsistent with Church-order or unity in the separation proposed. The great Wesleyan Methodist family, everywhere one in faith and practice, already exists under several distinct and unconnected jurisdictions—there is no jurisdictional or connectional union between them; and yet it has never been pretended that these several distinct organizations were in any sense inconsistent with Church-unity. If the Southern Conferences proceed, then, to the establishment of another distinct jurisdiction, without any change of doctrine or discipline, except in matters necessary to the mere economical adjustment of the system, will it furnish any reason for supposing that the real unity of the Church is affected by what all must perceive to be a simple division of jurisdiction? When the Conferences in the slaveholding States are separately organized as a distinct ecclesiastical connection, they will only be what the General Conference authorized them to be. Can this be irregular or subversive of Church-unity? Acting under the Provisional Plan of Separation, they must, although a separate organization, remain in essential union with, and be part and parcel of, the Methodist Episcopal Church, in every scriptural and moral view of the subject; for what they do is with the full consent, and has the official sanction, of the Church as represented in the General Conference. The jurisdiction we are about to establish and assert as separate and independent, is expressly declined and ceded by the General Conference as originally its own, to the Southern Conferences, for the specific purpose of being established and asserted in the manner proposed. All idea of secession, or an organization alien in right or relation to the Methodist Episcopal Church, is forever precluded by the terms and conditions of the authorized Plan of Separation. In whatever sense we are *separatists* or *seceders,* we are such by authority—the *highest* authority of the Methodist Episcopal Church. To whatever extent or in whatever aspect we are not true and faithful ministers and members of that Church, such delinquency or misfortune is authenticated by her act and approval, and she declares us to be "without blame." "Ministers of every grade and office in the Methodist Episcopal Church may, as they prefer, without blame, attach themselves to the Church, South." Bishops, Elders, and Deacons come into the Southern organization at their own election, under permission from the General Conference, not only accredited as ministers of the Methodist Episcopal Church, but with credentials *limiting* the exercise of their functions *within the Methodist Episcopal Church.* Is it conceivable that the General Conference would so act and hold such language in relation to an ecclesiastical connection which was to be regarded as a secession from the Church? Does not such act and language, and the whole Plan of Separation, rather show that as the South had asked, so the General Conference intended to authorize a simple division of its own jurisdiction, and nothing more?

All idea of secession, or schism, or loss of right or title, as ministers of the Methodist Episcopal Church, being precluded by the specific grant or authority under which we act, as well as for other reasons assigned, many considerations might be urged, strongly suggesting the *fitness* and *propriety* of the separate jurisdiction contemplated, rendered *necessary*, as we have seen, upon *other* and *different* grounds; and among these the increased value of the representative principle likely to be secured by the change, is by no means unworthy of notice. At the first representative General Conference, thirty-three years ago, each delegate represented five traveling ministers and about two thousand members, and the body was of convenient size for the transaction of business. At the late General Conference, each delegate was the representative of twenty-one ministers and more than five thousand members, and the body was inconveniently large for the purpose of deliberation and action. Should the number of delegates in the General Conference be increased with the probable growth of the Church, the body will soon become utterly unwieldy. Should the number be reduced, while the ministry and membership are multiplying, the representative principle would become to be little more than nominal, and, in the same proportion, without practical value. Beside that the proposed reörganization of jurisdiction will remedy this evil, at least to a great extent, it will result in the saving of much time and expense and useful services to the Church, connected with the travel and protracted sessions of the General Conference, not only as regards the delegates, but also the bench of Bishops, whose general oversight might become much more minute and pastoral in its character, by means of such an arrangement. When, in 1808, the Annual Conferences resolved upon changing the form of General Conference jurisdiction, the precise reasons we have just noticed were deemed sufficient ground and motive for the change introduced; and as we are seeking only a similar change of jurisdiction, although for other purposes as well as this, the facts to which we ask attention are certainly worthy of being taken into the estimate of advantages likely to result from a separate and independent organization, especially as the ministry and membership, since 1808, have increased *full seven hundred per centum;* and should they continue to increase, in something like the same ratio, for thirty years to come, under the present system of General Conference jurisdiction, some such change as that authorized by the late General Conference must be resorted to, or the Church resign itself to the virtual extinction of the representative principle, as an important element of government action.

In establishing a separate jurisdiction as before defined and explained, so far from affecting the moral oneness and integrity of the great Methodist body in America, the effect will be to secure a very different result. In resolving upon a separate Connection, as we are about to do, the one great and controlling motive is to restore and perpetuate the peace and unity of the Church. At present we have neither, nor are we likely to have, should the Southern and Northern Conferences remain in connectional relation, as heretofore. Inferring effects from causes known to be in existence and active operation, agitation on the subject of slavery is certain to continue, and frequent action in the General Conference is equally certain, and the result, as heretofore, will be excitement and discontent, aggression and resistance. Should the South retire and decline all farther conflict, by the erection of the Southern Conferences into a separate jurisdiction, as authorized by the General Conference plan, agitation in the Church cannot be brought in contact with the South, and the former irritation and evils of the controversy must, to a great extent, cease, or at any rate so lose their disturbing force as to become comparatively harmless. Should the Northern Church continue to discuss and agitate, it will be within their own borders and among themselves, and the evil effects upon the South must, to say the least, be greatly lessened. At present, the consolidation of all the Annual Conferences under the jurisdictional control of one General Conference, always giving a decided Northern majority, places it in the power of that majority to manage and control the interests of the Church, in the slaveholding

States, as they see proper, and we have no means of protection against the evils certain to be inflicted upon us, if we judge the future from the past. The whole power of legislation is in the General Conference, and as that body is now constituted, the Annual Conferences of the South are perfectly powerless in the resistance of wrong, and have no alternative left them but unconditional submission. And such submission to the views and action of the Northern majority on the subject of slavery, it is now demonstrated must bring disaster and ruin upon Southern Methodism, by rendering the Church an object of distrust on the part of the State. In this way, the assumed *conservative power* of the Methodist Episcopal Church, with regard to the *civil union* of the States, is to a great extent destroyed, and we are compelled to believe that it is the *interest,* and becomes the *duty,* of the Church in the South to seek to exert *such conservative influence* in some *other* form; and after the most mature deliberation and careful examination of the whole subject, we know of nothing so likely to effect the object as the jurisdictional separation of the great Church parties unfortunately involved in a religious and ecclesiastical controversy about an affair of State —a question of civil policy, over which the Church has no control, and with which, it is believed, she has no right to interfere. Among the nearly five hundred thousand ministers and members of the Conferences represented in this Convention, we do not know *one* not *deeply* and *intensely* interested in the *safety* and *perpetuity* of the *National Union,* nor can we for a moment hesitate to *pledge them all* against *any* course of *action* or *policy* not calculated, in their judgment, *to render that union as immortal as the hopes of patriotism would have it to be!*

Before closing the summary view of the whole subject taken in this Report, we cannot refrain from a brief notice of the relations and interests of Southern border Conferences. These, it must be obvious, are materially different from those of the more Southern Conferences. They do not, for the present, feel the pressure of the strong necessity impelling the South, proper, to immediate separation. They are, however, involved with regard to the subject-matter of the controversy, and committed to well-defined principles, in the same way, and to the same extent, with the most Southern Conferences. They have with almost perfect unanimity, by public official acts, protested against the entire action of the late General Conference on the subject of slavery, and in reference to the relative rights and powers of Episcopacy and the General Conference, as not only *unconstitutional,* but *revolutionary,* and, therefore, dangerous to the best interests of the Church. They have solemnly declared, by approving and indorsing the

Declaration, the Protest, and Address of the Southern delegates, that the objects of their ministry cannot be accomplished under the existing jurisdiction of the General Conference, without reparation for past injury and security against future aggression; and unless the border Conferences have good and substantial reason to believe such reparation and security not only *probable*, but so certain as to remove *reasonable* doubt, they have, so far as *principle* and pledge are concerned, the same motive for action with the Conferences South of them. Against the principles thus avowed by every one of the Conferences in question, the antislavery and abolition of the North have, through official Church-organs, declared the most open and undisguised hostility, and these Conferences are reduced to the necessity of deciding upon *adherence* to the principles they have officially avowed, or of a resort to expediency to adjust difficulties in some unknown form, which they have said could only be adjusted by substantial reparation for past injury, and good and sufficient warrant against future aggression. The question is certainly one of no common interest. Should any of the border Conferences, or Societies South, affiliate with the North, the effect, so far as we can see, will be to transfer the seat of war from the remoter South to these border districts; and what, we ask, will be the security of these districts against the moral ravages of such a war? What protection or security will the *discipline* or the *conservatism* of the Middle Conferences afford? Of what avail were *these* at the last General Conference, and has *either* more influence now than then? The controversy of a large and rapidly-increasing portion of the North is not so much with the *South* as with the *Discipline*, because it tolerates slavery *in any form* whatever; and should the Southern Conferences remain under the present common jurisdiction, or any slaveholding portions of the South unite in the Northern Connection in the event of division, it requires very little discernment to see that *this controversy* will never cease until every slaveholder or every abolitionist is out of the Connection. Beside, the border Conferences have a great and most delicate interest at stake in view of their *territorial* and *civil* and *political* relations, which it certainly behooves them to weigh well and examine with care in coming to the final conclusion, which is to identify them with the North or the South. Border districts going with the North, after and notwithstanding the action of the border Conferences, must, in the nature of things, as found in the Methodist Episcopal Church, affiliate, to a great extent, with the entire aggregate of Northern antislavery and abolition, as now embarked against the interests of the South—as also with all the recent official violations of right, of law, and discipline, against which the South is now contending. In doing this, they must of necessity, if we have reasoned correctly, elect and contribute their influence to retain in the Connection of their choice all the principles and elements of strife and discord which have so long and fearfully convulsed the Church. Will this be the election of Southern border sections and districts, or will they remain where, by location, civil and political ties and relations, and their own avowed principles, they properly belong, firmly planted upon the long and well-tried platform of the Discipline of our common choice, and from which the Methodism of the South has never manifested any disposition to swerve? To the Discipline the South has always been loyal. By it she has *abided* in every trial. Jealously has she cherished and guarded that "form of sound words"—the faith, the ritual, and the government of the Church. It was Southern defense against Northern invasion of the Discipline, which brought on the present struggle; and upon the Discipline, the whole Discipline, the South proposes to organize, under authority of the General Conference, a separate Connection of the Methodist Episcopal Church. This result, from first to last, has been consented to on the part of the South with the greatest reluctance.

After the struggle came on, at the late General

Conference, the Southern delegates, as they had often done before, manifested the most earnest desire, and did all in their power, to maintain jurisdictional union with the North, without sacrificing the interests of the South: when this was found impracticable, a *connectional* union was proposed, and the rejection of this by the North led to the *projection* and *adoption* of the present General Conference Plan of Separation. Every overture of compromise, every plan of reconciliation and adjustment, regarded as at all eligible, or likely to succeed, was offered by the South and rejected by the North. All subsequent attempts at compromise have failed in like manner, and the probability of any such adjustment, if not extinct, is lessening every day, and the Annual Conferences in the slaveholding States are thus left to take their position upon the ground assigned them by the General Conference of 1844, as a distinct ecclesiastical connection, ready and most willing to treat with the Northern division of the Church at any time, in view of adjusting the difficulties of this controversy, upon terms and principles which may be safe and satisfactory to both.

Such we regard as the *true position of the Annual Conferences* represented *in this Convention. Therefore, in view of all the principles and interests involved*, appealing to the *Almighty Searcher of hearts for the sincerity of our motives, and humbly invoking the Divine blessing upon our action,*

Be it Resolved, by the Delegates of the several Annual Conferences of the Methodist Episcopal Church, in the slaveholding States, in General Convention assembled, That it is right, expedient, and necessary to erect the Annual Conferences, represented in this Convention, into a distinct ecclesiastical connection, separate from the jurisdiction of the General Conference of the Methodist Episcopal Church, as at present constituted; and, accordingly, we, the Delegates of said Annual Conferences, acting under the Provisional Plan of Separation adopted by the General Conference of 1844, do solemnly *declare* the jurisdiction hitherto exercised over said Annual Conferences, by the General Conference of the Methodist Episcopal Church, *entirely dissolved;* and that said Annual Conferences shall be, and they hereby *are constituted,* a separate ecclesiastical connection, under the Provisional Plan of Separation aforesaid, and based upon the Discipline of the Methodist Episcopal Church, comprehending the doctrines, and entire moral, ecclesiastical, and economical rules and regulations of said Discipline, except only in so far as verbal alterations may be necessary to a distinct organization, and to be known by the style and title of the *Methodist Episcopal Church, South.*

Resolved, That while we cannot abandon or

compromise the principles of action upon which we proceed to a separate organization in the South; nevertheless, cherishing a sincere desire to maintain Christian union and fraternal intercourse with the Church, North, we shall always be ready kindly and respectfully to entertain, and duly and carefully consider, any proposition or plan having for its object the union of the two great bodies in the North and South, whether such proposed union be *jurisdictional* or *connectional.*

Resolved, That this Convention request the Bishops presiding at the ensuing sessions of the border Conferences of the Methodist Episcopal Church, South, to incorporate into the aforesaid Conferences any societies or stations adjoining the line of division, provided such societies or stations by the majority of the members, according to the provisions of the Plan of Separation aforesaid, request such an arrangement.

Resolved, That Answer the 2d of 3d Section, Chapter 1st, of the Book of Discipline, be so altered and amended as to read as follows: "The General Conference shall meet on the first of May, in the year of our Lord 1846, in the town of Petersburg, Va., and thenceforward, in the month of April or May, once in four years successively, and in such place and on such day as shall be fixed on by the preceding General Conference," etc.

Resolved, That the first answer in the same chapter be altered by striking out the word "*twenty-one,*" and inserting in its place the word "*fourteen,*" so as to entitle each Annual Conference to one delegate for every fourteen members.

Resolved, That a committee of three be appointed, whose duty it shall be to prepare and report to the General Conference of 1846 a revised copy of the present Discipline, with such changes as are necessary to conform it to the organization of the Methodist Episcopal Church, South.

On motion of William A. Smith and William Capers, the Report was accepted, and the Publishing Committee were instructed to print one hundred copies for the use of the Convention.

On Saturday morning, the 17th of May, on motion of John Early, of the Virginia Conference, the Report of the Committee on Organization was taken up, and the Convention resolved to act on it by *yeas* and *nays*—sick and absent members being permitted to enter their votes at some subsequent period during the session.

The first resolution was read, and, on motion of John Early, was adopted, William Gunn, George W. Taylor, and John C. Harrison, voting in the negative.

The remaining resolutions were then taken up, and adopted without a dissenting vote.

On the 19th of May, the Report of the Committee on Organization was taken up and adopted as a whole, only George W. Taylor and John C. Harrison voting in the negative.

On the same day the Committee on Organization reported the following resolutions, which were unanimously adopted:

"1. *Resolved,* That Bishops Soule and Andrew be, and they are hereby, respectfully and cordially requested by this Convention to unite with, and become regular and constitutional Bishops of, the Methodist Episcopal Church, South, upon the basis of the Plan of Separation adopted by the late General Conference.

"2. *Resolved,* That should any portion of an Annual Conference on the line of separation, not represented in this Convention, adhere to the Methodist Episcopal Church, South, according to the Plan of Separation adopted at the late General Conference, and elect delegates to the General Conference of the Church in 1846, upon the basis of representation adopted by this Convention, they shall be accredited as members of the General Conference.

"3. *Resolved,* That a committee of three be appointed, whose duty it shall be to prepare, and report to the General Conference of 1846, a revised copy of the present Discipline, with such changes as are necessary to conform it to the Organization of the Methodist Episcopal Church, South."

In reply to the invitation contained in the first resolution, the following letters were received from Bishops Soule and Andrew:

"Dear Brethren:—I feel myself bound in good faith to carry out the official plan of Episcopal Visitations as settled by the Bishops in New York, and published in the official papers of the Church, until the session of the first General Conference of the Methodist Episcopal Church, South; from which time it would be necessary that the plan should be so changed as to be accommodated to the jurisdiction of the two distinct General Conferences. That when such Southern General Conference shall be held, I shall feel myself fully authorized by the Plan of Separation, adopted by the General Conference of 1844, to unite myself with the Methodist Episcopal Church, South, and if received by the General Conference of said Church, to exercise the functions of the Episcopal office within the jurisdiction of said General Conference.

"Joshua Soule.

"Louisville, Ky., May 19, 1845."

"Dear Brethren: — I decidedly approve the course which the Convention has taken in establishing the Methodist Episcopal Church, South, believing as I do most sincerely that it will tend, under God's blessing, to the wider spread and more efficient propagation of the gospel of the grace of God. I accept the invitation of the Convention to act as one of the Superintendents of the Methodist Episcopal Church, South, and pledge myself, in humble dependence upon Divine grace, to use my best efforts to promote the cause of God in the interesting and extensive field of labor assigned me.

"May the blessing of God be upon us mutually in our laborious field of action, and finally may we all, with our several charges, be gathered to the home of God and the good in heaven!

"Affectionately your brother and fellow-laborer,

"JAMES O. ANDREW.

"LOUISVILLE, May, 1845."

The preparation of a Pastoral Address had been referred to a special committee, and on the 19th of May the following was submitted and adopted:

LOUISVILLE, KY., May 19, 1845.

To the ministers of the several Annual Conferences of the Methodist Episcopal Church, South, and to all the brethren of their pastoral oversight, the Convention of said Annual Conferences address this letter, with Christian salutation.

We gratefully regard it matter of congratulation, beloved brethren, for which our thanks should be offered at the throne of grace, that we have been enabled to conduct the business confided to us by you with great harmony, and except, perhaps, some inconsiderable shades of difference on points of minor import, with unexampled unanimity. Our agreement on all questions of importance has probably been as perfect as the weakness of human knowledge might allow or reason should require.

For full information of all that we have done, we refer you to the Journal of our proceedings and the documents which accompany it, particularly the Reports of the Committees on Organization and on Missions. This latter interest we have made the subject of a special letter, wishing to bring it immediately to the notice of all our Churches and congregations, (to whom we have requested the letter might be read,) to engage their instant liberality.

We made it a point of early inquiry, in the course of our proceedings, to ascertain with what unanimity the Annual Conferences represented by us, and the entire body of the ministry and membership within their general bounds, were known to have concurred in sustaining the Declaration of the Southern delegates in the late General Conference, and in approving of the plan provided by that Conference for our being constituted a distinct ecclesiastical connection, separate from the North. The Committee on Organization, being composed of two members from each of the Annual Conferences, were furnished with ample means of obtaining satisfactory information. The members of the committee held meetings with their several delegations apart, and on a comparison of their several reports, carefully made, it was found that, both as to the members of the Annual Conferences and the local ministry and membership of our entire territory, the declaration had been sustained, and a separate organization called for, by as great a majority as *ninety-five to five.* Nor did it appear that *even five in a hundred* were disposed to array themselves against their brethren, whose interests were identical with their own, but that part were Northern brethren sojourning in our borders, and part were dwelling in sections of the country where the questions involved did not materially concern their Christian privileges, or those of the slaves among them. So great appears to have been the unanimity of opinion prevailing, both among the pastors and the people, as to the urgent necessity of the great measure which we were deputed to effect, by organizing on the basis of the Discipline, and the plan provided by the late General Conference, THE METHODIST EPISCOPAL CHURCH, SOUTH.

That on so grave a question, concerning interests so sacred, and affecting so numerous a people, spread over the vast extent of the country from Missouri to the Atlantic Ocean, and from Virginia to Texas, there should be found some who dissent, is what we could not but expect. But that the number dissenting should have been so small, compared to the number of those who have required us to act, is, at least to our minds, conclusive proof of the absolute necessity of this action, as affording the only means left in our power to preserve the Church in the more Southern States from hopeless ruin. Indeed, the action of the late General Conference, without the intervention of the Declaration of the Southern delegates, and the Provisional Plan for a separate Southern Connection, must have immediately broken up all our missions to the people of color, and subjected their classes in most of the Southern circuits to ruinous deprivations. Of this the evidence has been unquestionable. And it must appear to you, brethren, that for whatever reason so great an evil was threatened for a cause which the Southern delegates did nothing to produce, but resisted in the General Conference, *that* evil could not fail of being inflicted with redoubled violence, and to a still greater extent, if we, having a platform legally furnished for a separate organization, should hesitate a moment to avail ourselves of it. It would be, in effect, to put ourselves, in relation to the laws and policy of the Southern people, in the same position which was so injuriously offensive in our Northern brethren, while it could not be pleaded in extenuation of the fault, that we were Northern men, and ignorant of the state of affairs at the South. Into such a position we could not possibly put ourselves; nor can we think that reasonable men would require us to do so.

We avow, brethren, and we do it with the greatest solemnity, that while we have thus been laid under the imperative force of an absolute necessity to organize the Southern and South-western Conferences into an independent ecclesiastical connection, whose jurisdiction shall be exclusive of all interference on the part of the North, we do not withdraw from the true Christian and catholic pale of the Methodist Episcopal Church. And that whilst we have complained, with grievous cause, of the power of the majority of the General Conference, as that power has been construed and exercised, we have not complained, and have no complaint, against the Church itself. The General Conference, or a majority thereof, is not the Church. Nor is it possible that that should be the Methodist Episcopal Church which withdraws the ministry of the gospel from the poor, and turns her aside from her calling of God "to spread Scripture holiness over these lands," in order to fulfill some other errand, no matter what.

We could not be Methodists at all—as we have been taught what Methodism is—if, with our knowledge of its nature, its aim, its constitution, its discipline, and of the ruin inevitable to the work of the ministry in most of the Southern States, if not in all of them, should we still cleave to a Northern jurisdiction; we nevertheless could not be persuaded to yield the gospel for a jurisdictional affinity with brethren who, we believe in our hearts, cannot govern us without great injury to the cause of Christ in most parts of our work. If we err, it is the spirit of Methodism which prompts us to the error. We "call God for a record" that, as far as we know our hearts, we intend nothing, we desire nothing, we do nothing, having any other object or aim but that the gospel may be preached, without let or hindrance, in all parts of our country, and especially to the poor. There is nothing belonging of right to the Church—her doctrines, her discipline, her economy, her usages, her efficiency—which we do not cherish in our inmost hearts. It is not the Church, not any thing proper to the Church, in her character as Christ's body, and consecrated to the promotion of his cause in the earth, which we would disown, or depart from, or oppose; but only such a position *in* the Church as some of her sons would force us into, antagonistic to her principles, her policy, and her calling of God. Nor yet can we be charged with any factious or schismatic opposition to the General Conference, for we have done nothing, and mean to do nothing, not authorized by express enactment of that body, in view of the very emergency which compels our action.

It had been too much to expect, considering the weakness of man, that, suddenly roused to resistance as the Southern Churches were by the unlooked-for action in the cases of Bishop Andrew and Brother Harding, there should not in some instances have escaped expressions of resentment and unkindness; or that, put to the defense of the majority of the General Conference, where the evil complained of was so serious, the advocates of that majority should not sometimes have expressed themselves in terms which seemed harsh and unjust. We deeply deplore it, and pray that for the time to come such exhibitions of a mortifying frailty may give place to Christian moderation. We invoke the spirit of peace and holiness. That brother shall be esteemed as deserving best who shall do most for the promotion of peace. Surely this is a time of all others, in our day, when we should seek and pursue peace. A continuance of strife between North and South must prove prejudicial on both sides. The separation is made—formally, legally made—and let peace ensue. In Christ's name, let there be peace. Whatever is needful to be done, or worth the doing, may be done in peace. We especially exhort brethren of the border Conferences and societies to forbear each other in love, and labor after peace. Let every one abide by the law of the General Conference with respect to our bounds, and choose for himself with Christian temper, and permit others to choose without molestation, between North and South. Our chief care should be to maintain "the unity of the Spirit in the bond of peace." Methodism preserved in what makes it one the world over—the purity of its doctrines, the efficiency of its discipline, its unworldliness, its zeal for God, its self-devotion—is of infinitely greater value than a question of boundary or General Conference jurisdiction merely.

And now, brethren, beseeching you to receive the word of exhortation which we have herein briefly addressed to you, and humbly invoking the blessings of God upon you, according to the riches of his grace in Christ our Lord, praying for you, as we always do, that you may abound in every good work, and confiding in your prayers for us, that we may be found one with you in faith and charity at the appearing of Jesus Christ, we take leave of you, and return from the work which we have now fulfilled, to renew our labors with you and among you in the Lord.

JAMES O. ANDREW, President.

THOMAS O. SUMMERS, Secretary.

Several questions of importance, to which we have not referred, claimed the careful consideration of the Convention, among which the missionary work and the subject of education were prominent.

On the 19th of May, on motion of Whitefoord Smith, it was

"*Resolved,* That we devoutly acknowledge the superintending providence of God over this Convention, and rejoice in the harmony which has prevailed in all its deliberations and decisions."

The Convention attracted no inconsiderable attention during its session. Distinguished ministers from all parts of the country were in attendance, and watched its progress with greatest anxiety. The large and spacious audience-room and galleries of the old Fourth-street Church were densely crowded, by members of the Church and others, who listened with breathless interest to all that was said. Full two hours were spent in the reading of the Report of the Committee on Organization, and frequently during this time the silence was painful, but was frequently broken with bursts of applause, while tears of joy coursed their way down many a cheek.

After the close of the Convention, every effort was made to induce the Southern Conferences on the Northern border to adhere to the Methodist Episcopal Church (North). It was affirmed that the Kentucky, Missouri, and Holston Conferences would each, by a large majority, decline any connection with the Methodist Episcopal Church, South.

The Kentucky Conference met in Frankfort, Ky., September 10, 1845. Bishops Soule and Andrew were both present. On the first day of the session the following preamble and resolutions were presented and adopted:

"Whereas, the long-continued agitation and excitement on the subject of slavery and abolition in the Methodist Episcopal Church, and especially such agitation and excitement in the last General Conference, in connection with the civil and domestic relations of Bishop Andrew, as the owner of slave property, by inheritance and marriage, assumed such form in the action had in the case of Bishop Andrew, as to compel the Southern and South-western delegates in that body to believe, and formally and solemnly to declare, that a state of things must result therefrom which would render impracticable the successful prosecution of the objects and purposes of the Christian ministry and Church-organization, in the Annual Conferences within the limits of the slaveholding States; upon the basis of which declaration the General Conference adopted a Provisional Plan of Separation, in view of which said Conferences might, if they found it necessary, form themselves into a separate General Conference jurisdiction; and whereas, said Conferences, acting first in their separate Conference capacity, as distinct ecclesiastical bodies, and then collectively, by their duly appointed delegates and representatives, in General Convention assembled, have found and declared such separation necessary, and have farther declared a final dissolution, in fact and form, of the jurisdictional connection hitherto existing between *them* and the General Conference of the Methodist Episcopal Church as heretofore constituted; and have organized the Methodist Episcopal Church, South, upon the unaltered basis of the doctrines and discipline of the Methodist Episcopal Church in the United States before its separation, as authorized by the General Conference; and whereas, said Plan of Separation, as adopted by the General Conference, and carried out by the late Convention of Southern delegates in the city of Louisville, Ky., and also recognized by the entire Episcopacy as authoritative and of binding obligation in the whole range of their administration, provides that Conferences bordering on the line of division between the two Connections—North and South—shall determine by vote of a majority of their members respectively, to which jurisdiction they will adhere; therefore, in view of all the premises, as one of the border Conferences, and subject to the above-named rule,

"*Resolved, by the Kentucky Annual Conference*

of the Methodist Episcopal Church, That in conforming to the General Conference Plan of Separation, it is necessary that this Conference decide by a vote of a majority of its members to which Connection of the Methodist Episcopal Church it will adhere, and that we now proceed to make such decision.

"*Resolved,* That any member or members of this Conference, declining to adhere to that Connection to which the majority shall by regular, official vote decide to adhere, shall be regarded as entitled, agreeably to the Plan of Separation, to hold their relation to the other ecclesiastical connection—North or South—as the case may be, without blame or prejudice of any kind, unless there be grave objections to the moral character of such member or members, before the date of such formal adherence.

"*Resolved,* That agreeably to the provisions of the General Conference Plan of Separation, and the decisions of the Episcopacy with regard to it, any person or persons, from and after the act of non-concurrence with the majority, as above, cannot be entitled to hold membership, or claim any of the rights or privileges of membership in this Conference.

"*Resolved,* That as a Conference, claiming all the rights, powers, and privileges of an Annual Conference of the Methodist Episcopal Church, we *adhere* to the Methodist Episcopal Church, South, and that all our proceedings, records, and official acts hereafter, be in the name and style of the Kentucky Annual Conference of the Methodist Episcopal Church, South.

"FRANKFORT, KY., September 10, 1845."

The vote on the fourth resolution was taken by ayes and noes, and stood, ayes 77, noes 6, and four of the six voting in the negative afterward adhered personally to the M. E. Church, South. The action of the Conference, almost unanimous, contributed much in promoting harmony in the Churches throughout Kentucky. With a line of border of several hundred miles, there was but a single society that adhered North, while in nearly all the others scarcely a voice of dissent was heard.

In Missouri, Northern Methodists were equally baffled in their expectations. The resolutions adopted by the Kentucky Conference were, in substance, introduced and adopted by the Missouri, only fourteen voting in the negative.

The Holston Conference, at its annual meeting, adopted the following preamble and resolutions, offered by Samuel Patton, with only one vote in the negative; the person voting afterward adhered to the M. E. Church, South, and took work in the Conference:

"Whereas, the long-continued agitation on the subject of slavery and abolition in the Methodist

Episcopal Church did, at the General Conference of said Church, held in the city of New York, in May, 1844, result in the adoption of certain measures by that body which seriously threatened a disruption of the Church; and to avert this calamity, said General Conference did devise and adopt a plan contemplating the peaceful separation of the South from the North; and constituting the Conferences in the slaveholding States the sole judges of the necessity for such separation; and, whereas, the Conferences in the slaveholding States, in the exercise of the right accorded to them by the General Conference, did, by their representatives in Convention at Louisville, Ky., in May last, decide that separation was necessary, and proceeded to organize themselves into a separate and distinct ecclesiastical connection, under the style and title of the Methodist Episcopal Church, South, basing their claim to a legitimate relation to the Methodist Episcopal Church in the United States upon their unwavering adherence to the Plan of Separation adopted by the General Conference of said Church in 1844, and their devotion to the doctrines, discipline, and usages of the Church as they received them from their fathers.

"And as the Plan of Separation provides that the Conferences bordering on the geographical line of separation shall decide their relation by the votes of the majority—as also that ministers of every grade shall make their election North or South without censure—therefore,

"1. *Resolved,* That we now proceed to determine the question of our ecclesiastical relation by the vote of the Conference.

"2. That we, the members of the Holston Annual Conference, claiming all the rights, powers, and privileges of an Annual Conference of the Methodist Episcopal Church in the United States, do hereby make our election with, and adhere to, the Methodist Episcopal Church, South.

"3. That while we thus declare our adherence to the Methodist Episcopal Church, South, we repudiate the idea of secession in any schismatic or offensive sense of the phrase, as we neither give up nor surrender any thing which we have received as constituting any part of Methodism, and adhere to the Southern ecclesiastical organization, in strict accordance with the provisions of the Plan of Separation, adopted by the General Conference of the Methodist Episcopal Church at its session in New York in May, 1844.

"4. That we are satisfied with our Book of Discipline as it is on the subject of slavery, and every other vital feature of Methodism, as recorded in that Book; and that we will not tolerate any changes whatever, except such verbal or unimportant alterations as may, in the judgment of the General Conference, facilitate the work in which we are engaged, and promote uniformity and harmony in our administration.

"5. That the journals of our present session, as well as all our official business, be henceforth conformed in style and title to our ecclesiastical relations.

"6. That it is our desire to cultivate and maintain fraternal relations with our brethren of the North. And we do most sincerely deprecate the continuance of paper warfare, either by editors or correspondents, in our official Church-papers, and devoutly pray for the speedy return of peace and harmony in the Church, both North and South.

"7. That the Holston Annual Conference most heartily commend the course of our beloved Bishops, Soule and Andrew, during the recent agitations which have resulted in the territorial and jurisdictional separation of the Methodist Episcopal Church, and that we tender them our thanks for their steady adherence to principle and the best interests of the slave population.

"David Adams."

Similar action was taken by all the border Conferences in the slaveholding States.

At the several Annual Conferences delegates were elected, as provided for by the Convention, to the first General Conference of the Methodist Episcopal Church, South, to meet on the first day of May, 1846, in Petersburg, Virginia.

CHAPTER VII.

The first General Conference of the Methodist Episcopal Church, South—Bishops Soule and Andrew present—Bishop Soule's Communication—Referred to a Committee—Report of Committee—Dr. Pierce appointed Fraternal Messenger to the General Conference of the Methodist Episcopal Church—Dr. Dixon from the British Conference, Dr. Richey, and Revs. J. Ryerson and A. Green from the Canada Conference—Fraternal intercourse with the Methodist Episcopal Church, South, declined—Dr. Pierce's popularity in Pittsburgh—His Report to the General Conference of the Methodist Episcopal Church, South, in 1850—The Property Question—The Lawsuits—Decisions in favor of the Methodist Episcopal Church, South—Position, duty, and prospects of the Methodist Episcopal Church, South.

THE first General Conference of the Methodist Episcopal Church, South, met in Petersburg, Virginia, on the first day of May, 1846.

Bishop Andrew not having arrived, and Bishop Soule not having, as yet, formally adhered to the Methodist Episcopal Church, South, the delegates were called to order at nine o'clock A.M., by Dr. William Winans, of Mississippi Conference. The

Rev. John Early, of Virginia Conference, was elected President *pro tem;* whereupon he took the chair, and General Conference was opened—religious service conducted by Dr. Winans.

The Secretary of the Louisville Convention being absent, the President called on the Assistant Secretary to receive and read the certificates of election, as presented by the delegates.

The General Conference was composed of the following delegates, viz.:

Kentucky Conference.—Henry B. Bascom, Hubbard H. Kavanaugh, Benjamin T. Crouch, Jonathan Stamper, George W. Brush, Edward Stevenson, Thomas N. Ralston, Charles B. Parsons, John C. Harrison, Napoleon B. Lewis.

Holston.—Samuel Patton, David Fleming, Timothy Sullins, Thomas K. Catlett, Elbert F. Sevier.

Missouri.—William Patton, Andrew Monroe, Thomas Wallace, William W. Redman, John H. Linn, Joseph Boyle.

Tennessee.—John B. McFerrin, Robert Paine, Fountain E. Pitts, Alexander L. P. Green, John W. Hanner, Edmund W. Sehon, Samuel S. Moody, Frederick G. Ferguson, Ambrose F. Driskill.

Virginia. — William A. Smith, John Early, Thomas Crowder, Abraham Penn, Leroy M. Lee, Henry B. Cowles, Anthony Dibrell.

North Carolina.—Hezekiah G. Leigh, James Jamieson, Samuel S. Bryant, Peter Doub.

Indian Mission.—Wesley Browning, Jerome C. Berryman.

Memphis.—Moses Brock, George W. D. Harris, William McMahon, William M. McFerrin, Arthur Davis, John T. Baskerville.

South Carolina.—William Capers, Charles Betts, Nicholas Talley, William M. Wightman, Hugh A. C. Walker, Samuel W. Capers.

Mississippi.—William Winans, Benjamin M. Drake, John Lane, Lewel Campbell, Green M. Rogers, Andrew T. M. Fly, John G. Jones.

East Texas.—Francis Wilson.

Texas.—Robert Alexander, Chauncey Richardson.

Florida.—Alexander Martin, R. H. Luckey.

Alabama.—Thomas H. Capers, Elisha Callaway, Eugene V. Levert, Jesse Boring, Jefferson Hamilton, Greenbury Garrett, Thomas O. Summers.

Georgia.—Lovick Pierce, William J. Parks, John W. Glenn, Samuel Anthony, James E. Evans, George F. Pierce, Isaac Boring, Augustus B. Longstreet.

Arkansas.—John F. Truslow, William P. Ratcliffe, Andrew Hunter.

Thomas N. Ralston, of the Kentucky Conference, was elected Secretary, and Thomas O. Summers, of the Alabama Conference, Assistant Secretary.

On the 2d of May, Bishop Andrew arrived and took the chair.

On the same day Bishop Soule presented the following communication to the Conference:

PETERSBURG, May 2, 1846.

REV. AND DEAR BRETHREN:—I consider your body, as now organized, as the consummation of the organization of the Methodist Episcopal Church, South, in conformity to the "Plan of Separation," adopted by the General Conference of the M. E. Church in 1844. It is therefore in strict agreement with the provisions of that body, that you are vested with full power to transact all business appropriate to a Methodist General Conference.

I view this organization as having been commenced in the "Declaration" of the delegates of the Conferences in the slaveholding States, made at New York in 1844; and as having advanced in its several stages in the "Protest"—"the Plan of Separation"—the appointment of delegates to the Louisville Convention—in the action of that body—in the subsequent action of the Annual Conferences, approving the acts of their delegates at the Convention, and in the appointment of delegates to this General Conference.

The organization of the M. E. Church, South, being thus completed in the organization of the General Conference with a constitutional President, the time has arrived when it is proper for me to announce my position. Sustaining no relation to one Annual Conference which I did not sustain to every other, and considering the General Conference as the proper judicatory to which my communication should be made, I have declined making this announcement until the present time. *And now, acting with strict regard to the Plan of Separation, and under a solemn conviction of duty, I formally declare my adherence to the Methodist Episcopal Church, South.* And if the Conference receive me in my present relation to the Church, I am ready to serve them according to the best of my ability. In conclusion, I indulge the joyful assurance that although separated from our Northern brethren by a distinct Conference jurisdiction, we shall never cease to treat them as "brethren beloved," and cultivate those principles and affections which constitute the essential unity of the Church of Christ.

(Signed) JOSHUA SOULE.

So soon as the above communication from Bishop Soule was read, Drs. Bascom and Winans were appointed a committee to respond to it, and on the 7th of May submitted the following, which was unanimously adopted:

PETERSBURG, VA., May 6, 1846.

Whereas, the Rev. Joshua Soule, D.D., senior

Bishop of the Methodist Episcopal Church, has addressed a communication to the General Conference of the M. E. Church, South, now in session in Petersburg, Va., bearing date the 2d inst., in which he *formally declares his adherence to the M. E. Church, South*, in accordance with the right secured to him by the Plan of Separation, adopted by the General Conference of the M. E. Church at its last session in 1844; therefore,

Resolved, (by the delegates of the several Annual Conferences of the M. E. Church, South, in General Conference assembled,) That, fully agreeing with Bishop Soule, as it regards his right of action in the premises, by authority of the General Conference of 1844, we cheerfully and unanimously recognize him as Bishop of the M. E. Church, South, with all the constitutional rights and privileges pertaining to his office as Bishop of the M. E. Church.

H. B. BASCOM,
WM. WINANS.

It does not belong to our design to trace the proceedings of the General Conference of 1846. The consideration of a few questions that came before that body, lies properly within the range of our work.

The Methodist Episcopal Church was now divided into two separate and distinct ecclesiastical jurisdictions, known as the Methodist Episcopal

Church (North), and the Methodist Episcopal Church, South. Whether the North or the South was responsible for the legislation which led to this result, our readers must determine for themselves. Notwithstanding the division between the two Methodisms, there were many things in common. For seventy years the Methodist Episcopal Church had dispensed its blessings all over our land. From a small beginning it had grown and spread until its genial rays penetrated every portion of the country. The history of all sections was one history. The Churches, at whose altars thousands had bowed and worshiped God, were the common property of Methodism. We preached the same blessed gospel, and taught the same doctrines and precepts. The names of Wesley, of Coke, of Asbury, and McKendree, were alike dear to every Methodist heart.

Since the action of the General Conference in the case of Bishop Andrew, two years had elapsed, and on both sides the line of division an opportunity had been afforded for calm deliberation. The ministers and members of the Methodist Episcopal Church, South, had proclaimed to the world that their object in a separate organization was the promotion of Christianity; and launching their bark upon the sea, they unfurled the white flag of peace.

Among the resolutions adopted by the Convention at the time of the organization of the M. E. Church, South, it was

"*Resolved,* That while we cannot abandon or compromise the principles of action upon which we proceed to a separate organization in the South, nevertheless, cherishing a sincere desire to maintain Christian union and fraternal intercourse with the Church, North, we shall always be ready kindly and respectfully to entertain and duly and carefully consider any proposition or plan having for its object the union of the two great bodies in the North and South, whether such proposed union be *jurisdictional* or *connectional.*"

Desirous that all strife should cease, and that the two branches of American Methodism should live in harmony, and thus accomplish more readily their mission of good, the General Conference of the Methodist Episcopal Church, South, in 1846, among the last acts of that body,

"*Resolved,* by a rising and unanimous vote, That Dr. Lovick Pierce be, and is hereby, delegated to visit the General Conference of the M. E. Church, to be held in Pittsburgh, May 1, 1848, to tender to that body the Christian regards and fraternal salutations of the General Conference of the Methodist Episcopal Church, South. In case of the inability of Dr. Pierce to attend the session of the aforesaid Conference, the Bishops are respectfully requested to appoint a substitute."

The Bishops were "requested to prepare an Address on behalf of the Conference, to be presented by Dr. Pierce to the General Conference of the M. E. Church (North) at his visit to that body in May, 1848."

Dr. Pierce was eminently qualified to perform the duties with which he was intrusted. He was no ordinary man, but took rank with the most distinguished preachers of the age. Since 1802 he had been a member of the Methodist Church, and had entered the South Carolina Conference as an itinerant preacher in 1804. He was a member of the General Conference of 1812, and had frequently served the Church since then in its highest councils. In the State of Georgia, where he resided, no man exerted a more potent influence; and in the Georgia Conference, of which he was a member, no preacher was more beloved. He not only brought into the ministry talents of the first order, but with a commanding and thrilling eloquence he enforced the sublime truths of Christianity. To these he added a sound judgment, a sweet and gentle spirit, and a heart sanctified by grace. Such was the man selected by the first General Conference of the M. E. Church, South, to bear to the General Conference of the M. E. Church (North) its "Christian regards and fraternal salutations."*

---

*Dr. Pierce is still living. He is this day (March 24, 1871,) eighty-six years of age. His mental powers are unimpaired, and he is able to preach three times every Sunday.

That the mission of Dr. Pierce would meet with favor in the body to which he was sent as a fraternal messenger, no member of the General Conference appointing him doubted for a moment. The majority in the General Conference of 1844, recognizing the necessities of the Church in the South, had met the emergency in a spirit of enlarged liberality, and had provided for an amicable division of the Church. The Northern press, it is true, had indulged in words of bitterness toward the South, but time had been given for reflection, and the cessation of hostilities was due to a common Methodism and a common Christianity.

It was eminently proper, too, that any proposition looking to the existence between the two Churches of fraternal relations, should be inaugurated by the Methodist Episcopal Church, South. That Church had established a separate ecclesiastical organization, and its General Conference was the first to convene.

Two years would elapse before the meeting of the General Conference of the Methodist Episcopal Church (North), and if any "roots of bitterness" remained, they would have time to die out.

On the first day of May, 1848, the General Conference of the Methodist Episcopal Church (North) assembled in the city of Pittsburgh. We miss from the body many of the men who were leaders in 1844; but John A. Collins, John P. Durbin, Jesse T. Peck, James B. Finley, and Charles Elliott, are present.

Among the distinguished ministers from abroad, the name of the Rev. Dr. Dixon deserves to be mentioned. He was a member of the Wesleyan Conference in Great Britain, and appointed by that body as their representative to bear to the General Conference of the Methodist Episcopal Church (North) their fraternal salutations. Dr. Dixon was introduced to the Conference, and "by general consent the rules of the Conference were suspended, and the credentials of Dr. Dixon, representative from England, were presented and read."

Dr. Dixon submitted the following Address of the British Conference:

To the Bishops of the Methodist Episcopal Church in the United States of North America, and to the Ministers in Conference assembled.

VERY DEAR BRETHREN:—At our last Annual Conference held in Liverpool, it was resolved, That as it is desirable to maintain that fraternal and Christian affection which has long subsisted between your Church and the British Methodists, a representative should be appointed from among us to attend your next General Conference.

The Rev. James Dixon, D.D., was affectionately

requested to undertake this important mission, and the Rev. Joseph Stinson was desired to accompany him. We presume that Dr. Dixon, the bearer of this letter, is not altogether unknown to you. Among us he has lived for many years in the highest esteem and veneration. His Christian simplicity, the meekness of his spirit, his manly and effective eloquence in preaching the gospel, as well as the ability and fidelity with which he has maintained our ecclesiastical polity, have pointed him out as well fitted to undertake this mission. The British Conference has deputed him to visit you with the utmost confidence in his integrity and ability. His companion, the Rev. Joseph Stinson, also visits you in compliance with our earnest desire, and with our entire confidence and growing esteem.

A lengthened epistle is rendered unnecessary by the presence among you of our representatives. They will convey to you our fraternal salutations. We respectfully refer you to them for any such information respecting our affairs as it may be agreeable to them to communicate.

Our earnest prayer is that the Holy Spirit may pour upon your approaching assembly his choicest influences, and conduct your deliberations to such results as shall promote the glory of Christ and the maintenance and spread of scriptural holiness through your extended country.

We are, dear brethren, in behalf of the British Conference, SAMUEL JACKSON, *President.*

ROBERT NEWTON, *Secretary.*

After a brief address from Dr. Dixon, on motion of Jesse T. Peck, it was

"*Resolved,* by the delegates of the Annual Conferences of the Methodist Episcopal Church in the United States of America, in General Conference assembled, 1st. That the cordial thanks of this body be presented to the Rev. Dr. Dixon, and through him to the Conference he represents, for the honor conferred on us in his presence and address, and that he be affectionately invited to take such part in our deliberations as may be agreeable to him. 2d. That the communication from the British Conference, presented by him, be referred to a select committee of three, with instructions to report the reply of the Conference."

The committee appointed "to respond to the communication from the Wesleyan Conference, England," consisted of J. P. Durbin, C. Elliott, and C. Pitman. On the 29th of May the committee presented the following report:

To the British Conference of the Wesleyan Methodist Church.

FATHERS AND BRETHREN:—Nothing gives us more pleasure than to receive your fraternal salutations at a session of our General Conference;

and this pleasure is heightened when we receive them at the hands and in the words of one of your own body. It affords us much happiness to bear testimony to the excellent spirit and amiable deportment of your representative, the Rev. Dr. Dixon; and we should have been pleased to receive with him the Rev. Joseph Stinson, whom you requested to accompany him. We avail ourselves of your kind and confiding reference to your representative, and consider his address to us as the voice of our British brethren.

Through him you express the continuance of your cordial affection toward us, and your earnest desire for our increased prosperity. We receive this expression as in some degree a manifestation of paternal feeling on your part, which in our judgment has somewhat of a divine blessing connected with it. And, in return, we declare the unabated admiration and love which we bear your body, and our desire to prove ourselves worthy of our sacred spiritual relations with you. We have good hope that we shall be able to do so, as well from our own knowledge of the true Wesleyan character of our doctrines, services, and Discipline, as from the frank and clear declaration of your representative, that the Methodist Episcopal Church appeared to him to exhibit essentially pure Wesleyan Methodism.

Your representative was pleased to allude to the

unhappy separation of our beloved Church, growing out of the connection of one of our Superintendents with slavery, prior to the General Conference of 1844; and expressed his deep regret that any such cause of separation should have arisen.

The true cause of the difficulty in our beloved Zion was our refusal to admit, under any circumstances, a connection of our Episcopacy with slavery. True, your honored representative took occasion to say farther (declaring at the same time that he expressed the sentiments of the whole body of Methodists in England, both ministers and people), that your sympathies were entirely on the side of liberty.

On our part we would say that, while our sympathies lie in the same direction, and it is our purpose still, as heretofore, to bear steadily our testimony against the great evil of slavery, and, within our legitimate sphere as a Church, to discountenance it and seek its removal, we, nevertheless, have long been satisfied that our brethren in other countries, occupying a distant stand-point, and, therefore, not clearly comprehending the complicated conditions of this extremely difficult subject, have not been able to do full justice to our policy and conduct as a Church in regard to this matter, they may have thought that we should have acted with more directness and decision. Feeling ourselves within the complications of this great evil, whose effects are felt throughout the sacred, social, and political relations of this country, it becomes us to act prudently and in the fear of God, and strive to consider well, and settle all things on the surest and best foundations for the promotion of his glory, and the peace and prosperity of the Church.

Your representative took occasion to express to us the high satisfaction he felt in visiting our country, and conversing with the most distinguished and intelligent of its citizens, both in the government and in private life. And we acknowledge a sense of unfeigned gratification on our part, while we listened to his frank and candid avowal of his astonishment at the mellowing influences of our institutions, in inspiring our great men with striking condescension and courtesy, and in elevating the lowly. And we were edified with the direct and fervent prayers which he offered up for our government and nation in his public administrations; while, at the same time, he as frankly and fervently mingled therewith his prayers for your beloved queen, your government, and nation, which found a warm response from our hearts.

We will take this occasion to say, we have great pleasure in observing that you have distinctly assumed all the titles, forms, and functions of a true Church of Christ, which, indeed, we have regarded you always to have been. The present condition of Protestantism in Europe, and particularly in England, renders this position on your part very important to the interests of Christ's Church.

Your systematic and efficient organization, not only for a regular and abundant supply of the word of life to the people, but also for your foreign missionary work, commands our admiration and moves us to action. We behold you planting the standard of the cross in the islands of every ocean, and on the coasts and plains of every continent, provoking us thereby to enter more largely into the same great work.

It gives us pleasure to assure you that in this respect we are steadily advancing. Though our movements are not so striking as yours, yet they are vast and important. Our own country stretches westward over the Rocky Mountains to the Pacific Ocean, a distance of thousands of miles, through which is dispersed a sparse population from all the nations of Europe, together with the numerous and populous tribes of the native Indians of its unbroken forests.

These elements of vast empires must be taught the principles, imbued with the spirit, and provided with the institutions, of our holy Christianity. This immense domain is our domestic field of missionary operations, and it is a cause of devout thankfulness to God that we see it yearly blossoming as the rose. As a specimen, we mention our German missions. Hundreds of thousands of native Germans flock to our land, bringing with them the cold and heartless Rationalism, or ignorant and fanatical Roman Catholicism, of Germany. In their new and strange circumstances they become easily accessible to us, and within ten years past, five thousand have been converted to God, of whom about two thousand were Roman Catholics. These have been formed into regular societies, which have been reduced to regular circuits, stations, and Districts, and well appointed by German preachers, amounting in all to eighty-five. The work is still rapidly advancing, and we are taking measures to insure its increase and purity. Arrangements are being made to compile and publish an Evangelical Commentary on the New Testament, also Sunday-school books for our German Sunday-schools, and to translate additional works from our General Catalogue into German. Already this great light, kindled among the natives of Germany now residing in this country, is beginning to illumine their fatherland, by means of letters, books, and visitors from the members of this new evangelical German Church. God is sending Germany to us to be evangelized; and indeed, in some degree, all the nations of Europe; and we doubt not but the reaction of this great domestic missionary work among us will be great and salutary on the Old World. But we are not content within this domestic field—we are extending our missionary operations to Oregon, California, portions of Mexico, and to China. And, aided by the bright example of your brilliant missionary resources and operations, we hope shortly to fill up the measure of the missionary work which God may be pleased to assign us.

And while we are thus endeavoring to extend the kingdom of God wider in the world, we are not unmindful of the population he hath given us at home. And believing that education is one great means of advancing and fortifying his kingdom among us, we have, within the last twenty years, given much attention to this matter. While we have not thought it best to have theological seminaries proper, and have judged that a proper course of study which our young men are required to accomplish in four years, while they are actively engaged in preaching the gospel and taking care of souls, will make them able ministers of the New Testament, we have been careful to provide universities, colleges, and academies for the education of our own people, as well as the public at large. And in this department of our work we may congratulate ourselves as having been successful. We have now seven colleges fully organized, and affording academic education to thousands of our younger sons, and also of our daughters, who are thus prepared to diffuse the essence and odor of piety in the more private and sacred walks of life.

We take pleasure in naming, as additional means of education, the vast capital and appliances of our General Book Concern, and the numerous excellent works which issue from it. In the General Catalogue there are two hundred and seventy-five distinct works, some of them extending to six heavy volumes. In the list are commentaries, dictionaries, Church-histories, and many excellent ecclesiastical and theological works. We should be wanting in honor did we not acknowledge that many of them have been derived from your Connection. Our Sunday-school publications also are very numerous; the Youth's Library already amounts to four hundred and eleven volumes, and our Tract publications to three hundred and sixty. It would be difficult to state the many thousands of these works that are annually distributed throughout our vast country.

Our periodical literature is also immense. The weekly issue from our various presses in newspaper form amount to not less than forty-five thousand copies. We have one monthly magazine, entitled "The Ladies' Repository," with about seven thousand subscribers. It is conducted with taste and ability, and the mechanical execution and embellishments are very creditable.

Our Quarterly Review is conducted with ability, and affords a medium of presenting to our ministers and principal friends the graver topics in theology, and in general science and literature. Our childreu in our thousands of Sunday-schools are supplied, semi-monthly, with the Sunday-school Advocate, in quarto form. It has now eighty thousand subscribers, and is rapidly advancing to one hundred thousand. We have also a monthly Missionary Advocate, with a subscription-list of at least twenty thousand, which distributes throughout our Church general missionary intelligence from various parts of the world. We trust that these vast issues of books and periodicals from our various presses and agencies are deeply imbued with the doctrines and spirit of genuine Christianity.

We did not think it necessary in the earlier part of this address to allude to the only little matter of uneasiness between us; that is, the liberty which some of our ministers (we say *some*, although we are advised of but one case) have taken to visit England, and make appointments for preaching and public services without the regular approbation or concurrence of the proper authorities among you. It gives us pleasure to testify our disapprobation of this course, and to say it has never been done with our sanction; and that we will see that hereafter the proper restraint is put upon all our traveling ministers in this matter. As it respects local preachers, we have no direct authority in the premises; but we wish distinctly to declare our disapprobation of any conduct on their part, as preachers in your country, which has not your special sanction, and is not under your direction.

We have been gratified to observe that the cause of temperance, on the principle of total abstinence from intoxicating liquors, is attracting attention in England; and we respectfully ask your attention to it, and your kind consideration of it, as intimately connected with the best interests of society in general, and greatly conducive to the success of the gospel. Such is our experience in America, particularly when the Church enters heartily into the cause.

In conclusion, it gives us great pleasure to renew to you the expression of our fraternal affection; and to say that it is now in our minds, at some suitable time hereafter, to reciprocate the favor you have done us by sending us your excellent representative to refresh our spirits by his holy ministry, and to edify us by your Christian fellowship which we enjoy through him.

Wishing you all prosperity and peace as a Church, through the abounding grace of God in our Lord Jesus Christ, we are, dear fathers and brethren, yours in the bonds of the gospel.

It is gratifying to know that every courtesy due the distinguished representative of the British Conference was shown to him during his stay in Pittsburgh. On the 8th of May he was requested, by a resolution of the General Conference, to preach a sermon to the Conference on Wednesday, the 10th of May, at half-past 10 o'clock A.M.; and on Thursday, the 11th, the order of the day was suspended, that the following resolution might be offered:

"*Resolved,* That the cordial thanks of this General Conference be presented to the Rev. Dr. Dixon for his excellent and evangelical sermon, and that we respectfully and earnestly request Rev. Dr. Dixon to furnish the substance of the sermon he delivered before the General Conference yesterday for publication, and that he expand his remarks in any part of it as he may judge proper, and write out his last proposition, of which he only presented us with the outline."

"The Methodists in Upper Canada were formerly under the jurisdiction of the Methodist Episcopal Church in the United States, but, from political considerations chiefly, it was deemed advisable that they should be transferred to the jurisdiction of the British Conference," which was done in 1830.

The Rev. Dr. Richey and Rev. Messrs. Ryerson and Green, members of the Wesleyan Methodist Conference in Canada, were delegated to bear the fraternal greetings of that body to the Methodist Episcopal Church (North). On the 9th of May they presented the following address:

To the Bishops and Members of the General Conference of the Methodist Episcopal Church.

REVEREND FATHERS AND BRETHREN:—With undiminished feelings of regard for our brethren of the Methodist Episcopal Church in general, and particularly for the Bishops and ministers who labor in word and doctrine within its pale, we avail ourselves of the occasion of the assembling of the General Conference to renew the testimony of our esteem and affection.

We are aware that very important topics were discussed at your last General Conference, and since that period some of these subjects have engrossed the attention and excited the feelings of ministers and people throughout your extensive country. In the serious difficulties by which you have been surrounded, and the troubles in which you have been involved, we have felt the deepest concern, and cherished the liveliest sympathy. But "God is the hope of Israel, the Saviour thereof in time of trouble." That he may overrule all things for his own glory, and the ultimate benefit and salvation of your venerated and beloved Church, is our devout and earnest prayer.

Your success in the midst of these trials and conflicts awakens our gratitude and joy. We notice with unmixed pleasure your extensive operations in the diffusion of education, in the circulation of useful and religious books and tracts, in the establishment and support of Sunday-schools, and in the preaching of the gospel as far as your population extends. We rejoice to learn that the great Head of the Church has poured out his Holy Spirit on various parts of your great field of labor, and that thousands by your instrumentality have been brought to the knowledge of Christ. May these tokens of Divine presence and favor be perpetuated among you to the latest generation!

The Wesleyan Church in Canada, as in the United States, has had its times of sorrow and seasons of joy. Since the year 1840, we have had to lament over serious difficulties existing between ourselves and the English Conference. Happily, upon a review of the whole, both parties were led to the conclusion that misapprehension had existed on several points, and that events which gave rise to differences in former years no longer existed. To the English Conference of 1846 we sent our esteemed brethren, the Rev. Messrs. Ryerson and Green, as our representatives, that, if practicable, peace and unity might be restored and promoted between the two legitimate Wesleyan bodies in Western Canada. Under the peculiar guidance of Divine Providence, their mission was signally successful. Our English brethren have promptly joined us in mutual agreement to bury in oblivion the record of the painful past, to reünite our separated bodies on terms generous and just, and to go forward as a united host in the defense and maintenance of the glorious gospel of the ever-blessed God. We are certain your earnest prayers will spontaneously blend with our own, that this union may be perpetual.

We are still endeavoring to assist in promoting the great object of useful and religious education in this country. Our college has its embarrassments, but we are gradually surmounting them. Our Book Room is in a state of efficiency. The mission work among us is increasing, and the funds are increasing with the work. Our other connectional funds are also on the advance, through the liberality of our people. Our united bodies make the statistics of the Connection in Western Canada as follows: Circuits and missions, 98; preachers, 189; members, 24,882.

Considering the hostilities we have had to combat in past years, we are truly thankful that our situation at present is so favorable, and shall enter upon the duties of another year high in hope and full of expectation that the blessing of the great

Head of the Church will be upon us and our beloved people, prospering us more and more in our work of faith and labor of love.

We have appointed our esteemed brethren, the Rev. Messrs. M. Richey, A.M., J. Ryerson, and Anson Green, as our representatives to your General Conference, to whom we refer you for any additional information respecting us which you may desire.

Signed by order and on behalf of the Conference of the Wesleyan Methodist Church in Canada, this 16th day of June, in the year of our Lord one thousand eight hundred and forty-seven. R. ALDER, *President*.

JAMES MUSGROVE, *Secretary*.

The same committee appointed to respond to the Address from the British Conference, was intrusted with the duty of preparing a response to the brethren in Canada, and on the 29th of May they presented the following:

DEAR BRETHREN:—We have received your very kind and agreeable address by the hands of your worthy and esteemed representatives, the Rev. Mr. Richey, D.D., Rev. J. Ryerson, and Rev. A. Green, conveying to us your warm Christian salutations. Your excellent representatives also took occasion to add thereto farther expressions of your fraternal regards, and of your personal esteem and affection for us. We accept all these expressions as tokens of your sincere love toward us, and of your earnest desire to cultivate the same in future. Allow us, dear brethren, to reciprocate from our hearts the affection you bear us, and to render thanks to God for the manifestations of his goodness to you, especially in restoring peace and concord between you and our common parent Connection in England. We rejoice that you have found in the British Connection, and we believe you will continue to find in it, counsel and support; and that, aided by its general and liberal fostering care, your own industry and enterprises will be abundantly fruitful.

In your address you allude to the interests of education among you, and of the prosperity of your Book Concern, which we regard as a spiritual handmaid of secular learning. It is a matter of real joy to us that you have a fair prospect of permanently endowing a college for the liberal education of your youth, and the youth of your province, under the salutary influence of your own Church. It is wise and good to take care of the people born to you in the bosom of your community, and also to expand and advance the kingdom of our Lord Jesus Christ in the midst of the world by means of a healthy, sanctified education; an education sound in its elements, and made vital by the personal spirituality of the professors and teachers who dispense it.

Your address also, as did your representatives, alluded to the difficulties which for the last four years have distressed our Zion; and although it appeared to us that they did not fully comprehend them, yet they kindly and properly expressed a hope that these troubles would pass away. They encouraged us by setting forth your own case as one of long-continued and great difficulty, yet happily adjusted at last. We also abide in hope that these difficulties may pass away from us, and our Zion be as tranquil and prosperous as formerly. But we do not now see the end, and have some apprehensions, as it is believed that both the Methodist Episcopal Church and the Methodist Episcopal Church, South, claim that essential principles of morals and policy are involved. But in the Lord we put our trust.

It gives us great pleasure to have no occasion for a lengthy epistle to you, on account of any misunderstandings between us. We are of one heart and one mind, and rejoice mutually in each other's prosperity. Let us continue to be of the same mind, and to walk by the same rule. It is now in our minds to send to you one of our own body, at a suitable time, to express to you, face to face, the love we bear you, and our fellowship with you.

And now, dear brethren, we commend you to God, and to the word of his grace; and we renew to you the assurance of our fraternal affection in Jesus Christ, our common Lord and Saviour.

These gentlemen were invited to address the Conference. Indeed, the same courtesy that was shown to Dr. Dixon was also shown to Dr. Richey, and Messrs. Ryerson and Green.

It was not only due these distinguished strangers, and the branches of Methodism they represented, but also the body to whom they were delegated to bear the Christian love of their respective Churches, to extend to them every courtesy and attention. The responses to the British Conference and the Wesleyan Church in Canada are replete with Christian sentiments that do honor to the Methodism from whence they emanated.

On the same day in which Dr. Dixon presented the communication from the British Conference, the Rev. Lovick Pierce, D.D., the accredited representative of the Methodist Episcopal Church, South, presented the following communication:

To the Bishops and Members of the Methodist Episcopal Church, in General Conference assembled:

Reverend and Dear Brethren:—The General Conference of the Methodist Episcopal Church,

South, appointed me as their delegate to beaı to you the Christian salutations of the Church, South, and to assure you that they sincerely desire that the two great bodies of Wesleyan Methodists, North and South, should maintain at all times a warm, confiding, and brotherly, fraternal relation to each other; and that through me they make this offer to you, and very ardently desire that you, on your part, will accept the offer in the same spirit of brotherly love and kindness.

The acceptance or rejection of this proposition, made by your Southern brethren, is entirely at your disposal; and as my situation is one of painful solicitude until this question is decided, you will allow me to beg your earliest attention to it.

And I would farther say, that your reply to this communication will most gratify me if it is made officially in the form of resolutions.

I have the honor to be, very respectfully, yours in the unity of Wesleyan Methodism,

L. Pierce,

Delegate from the M. E. Church, South.

Pittsburgh, May 3, 1848.

The communication of Dr. Pierce was referred to the Committee on the State of the Church. This committee was a large one, consisting of two members from each delegation, and of which the Rev. George Peck, of the New York Conference, was the Chairman. On the 5th of May the committee presented the following report:

"'That they have had under consideration the letter from the Rev. Dr. Pierce, and that they recommend to the General Conference the adoption of the following preamble and resolution:

"'Whereas, a letter from Rev. L. Pierce, D.D., delegate of the Methodist Episcopal Church, South, proposing fraternal relations between the Methodist Episcopal Church and the Methodist Episcopal Church, *South*, has been presented to this Conference; and whereas, there are serious questions and difficulties existing between the two bodies; therefore,

"'*Resolved*, That while we tender to the Rev. Dr. Pierce all personal courtesies, and invite him to attend our sessions, this General Conference does not consider it proper, at present, to enter into fraternal relations with the Methodist Episcopal Church, South. GEORGE PECK, *Chairman*.'

"Moved to adopt the report.

"John A. Collins moved to amend, so that the consideration of the report be delayed until the questions of division of Church-property and of the division line are settled.

"Voted to lay Brother Collins's motion to amend on the table.

"J. Holdich moved the following substitute to the original resolution in the report:

"'1. *Resolved,* That this General Conference invite Dr. Pierce, of the Methodist Episcopal Church, South, to take a seat in the house and address us on the subject of his mission.

"'2. *Resolved,* That as to fraternization, we are not prepared at present to give any decision, but shall leave that point open to farther consideration, under whatever light or information we may receive bearing upon that question.'

"J. D. Bridge moved to lay Brother Holdich's substitute on the table. Carried.

"Dr. Tomlinson moved to amend the report by adding the following, namely: 'Provided, however, that nothing in this resolution shall be so construed as to operate as a bar to any proposition from Dr. Pierce, or any other representative of the Methodist Episcopal Church, South, toward the settlement of existing difficulties between that body and this.'

"Dr. Durbin moved as a substitute to Dr. Tomlinson's amendment as follows, namely:

"'*Resolved,* That in so far as Dr. Pierce may come with authority to adjust the difficulties between the two bodies, we will cordially confer with him.'

"Dr. Durbin's substitute failed, and the question recurred on Dr. Tomlinson's amendment.

"Brother Walker moved to lay the amendment on the table. Not carried.

"Moved by Brother Holmes, that the vote be taken by yeas and nays. Carried.

"Moved by Brother Collins to amend, by inserting instead of 'to attend our sessions,' to take a seat within the bar. On motion, laid on the table.

"The yeas and nays were called, and the vote stood, yeas 147—no nays: three absent. So the report, as amended, was unanimously adopted."

On the 9th of May the following letter, replete with manly and Christian sentiments, was addressed to the Conference by Dr. Pierce:

Reverend and Dear Brethren:—I have received two extracts from your Journal of the 4th and 5th instant. From these extracts I learn you decline receiving me in my proper character, as the accredited delegate of the M. E. Church, South, and only invite me to a seat within the bar as due to me on account of my private and personal merits. These considerations I shall appreciate, and will reciprocate them in all the private and social walks of life; but within the bar of the General Conference I can only be known in my official character.

You will therefore regard this communication as final on the part of the M. E. Church, South. She can never renew the offer of fraternal relations between the two great bodies of Wesleyan

Methodists in the United States. But the proposition can be renewed at any time, either now or hereafter, by the M. E. Church. And if ever made upon the basis of the Plan of Separation, as adopted by the General Conference of 1844, the Church, South, will cordially entertain the proposition.

With sentiments of deep regret, and with feelings of disappointed hopes, I am yours, in Christian fellowship, L. PIERCE,

Delegate from the M. E. Church, South.

PITTSBURGH, May 9, 1848.

The student of Methodist history will ever feel surprised no less at the action of the General Conference in declining to receive Dr. Pierce as the accredited representative of the Methodist Episcopal Church, South, bearing tidings of good-will to those with whom they had once been so closely identified, and whose history was interwoven one with the other, than at the reason they assigned for this refusal, namely, that "there are serious questions and difficulties existing between the two bodies."

The "serious questions and difficulties" have reference to the claim of the South for their proportion of the property of the Church, to which they were entitled as provided for in the Plan of Separation. While an impartial verdict might admit that this would have been a valid reason why the Methodist Episcopal Church, South, should have hesitated to make fraternal propositions, it can find no plausible pretext on the part of the Methodist Episcopal Church (North) for their refusal to accept the kindly offer. We make no remarks on the action of the General Conference of the M. E. Church (North). It would be improper to do so.

Although entirely ignored by the body to whom he was appointed, other denominations sought the ministry of Dr. Pierce. The briefness of his stay, however, only allowed him to preach in a single pulpit, where a crowded audience was charmed with his eloquence, and blessed by his fervor and zeal for his Master's cause.

At the subsequent General Conference of the Methodist Episcopal Church, South, held in St. Louis, in 1850, Dr. Pierce made a full report of his visit to Pittsburgh, and of the failure of his mission. In this report he takes occasion to refer to the kind sentiments expressed by the representatives of the British and Canadian Conferences in reference to the M. E. Church, South. He says:

"On my way to Pittsburgh, I had the happiness to meet in Baltimore that Christian gentleman, and eminent minister of Christ, the Rev. Dr. Dixon. It having been assumed, as a thing of course, that a Wesleyan minister from England would indorse every abolition act of the majority, and knowing as I did that almost every Englishman was committed on the subject of slavery, I could but feel that caution and reserve were called for. My private feelings and almost involuntary confidence in his well-matured judgment still urged me to commune fearlessly with him on the points in dispute between the North and South. His attention, however, when his ear could be gained, was called mainly by one of the delegates, who also had fallen in with the Doctor in Baltimore. While descending the river from Brownsville, in a steamer, the Doctor and myself had some talk upon the subject of the division of the Church, and the cause which had led to it, to all which he listened as one whose heart sympathized with every interest of the great Wesleyan family.

"When in full view of the city, and knowing we would soon be separated, I remarked to him that, although we were delegates sent to the same body from different portions of one great family, I feared a very different fate awaited us. 'You will be received and welcomed as a messenger of the Church, while I shall be refused and rejected.'

"To these remarks he warmly said, 'I hope not;' adding, 'If you are rejected, it will be the occasion of everlasting regret to me.'

"Here we parted, and were but little together

until our departure for Cincinnati, when a gracious Providence brought us together again on another fine steamer.

"While on this passage, I found the Doctor intensely engaged reading the books which had been given him by the Southern preachers on the cause of division between the North and South. The facts contained in these records made a deep impression on his mind, and led him to converse more freely on this, to him, painful occurrence. He was a man, however, of such finely-balanced feeling, and well-disciplined mind, that no opinion was openly expressed. But permit me to say this much: I believe Dr. Dixon to be a man toward whom the Church, South, should cherish a high appreciation.

"On this trip to Cincinnati, I had the pleasure of the company of Brother Ryerson, one of the delegates from Canada, and the traveling companion of Dr. Dixon. His more natural and close relation to the Doctor contributed no little to the assurance I felt, that he sympathized with us in feelings of tender regard. The opportunity was so good, and the pleasure which fraternal intercourse with any and every legitimate organization of Wesleyan Methodists would impart, that I could not fail to ask Brother Ryerson how he thought an offer from us of friendly relations with the Canada Conference would be received. To which he replied: 'Most cordially. Our sympathies are all with the South.'

"In view of these very cordial words, and prompted, as we ever ought to be, by a pure fraternal love for all the children of Wesley, I would respectfully suggest the propriety of this General Conference directing, by resolution, the Bishops, or a committee created for the purpose, to send to the next British Conference a letter declaratory of our firm attachment to Methodism as we received it from Mr. Wesley in the days of Bishop Asbury, and of the pleasure it would afford us to be recognized by them as a worthy and true-hearted portion of the great Methodist family. And also, that the same course be pursued toward the Canada Conference, asking from each Conference an answer at their earliest convenience."

The General Conference accepted the report of their representative, and adopted the following resolution:

"*Resolved*, by the delegates of the Annual Conferences of the M. E. Church, South, in General Conference assembled, That we will steadfastly adhere to the ground taken in the last communication of our delegate to the General Conference of the M. E. Church, in Pittsburgh, May, 1848, to wit: That we cannot, under their act of rejection and refusal, renew our offer of fraternal relations and intercourse; but will at all times entertain any proposition coming from the M. E. Church to us, whether it be by written communication, or by delegation, having for its object friendly relations, and predicated of the rights granted to us by the Plan of Separation adopted in New York, 1844."

The spirit of charity and Christian forbearance shown on this occasion by the Methodist Episcopal Church, South, in their highest representative body, is worthy of all commendation, and will command the admiration of the Church of Christ in all the ages to come. Their proposal of fraternal intercourse refused—their messenger rejected—instead of returning "railing for railing," animated by the highest interests of Christianity, and the conquests to which the energies of Methodism were invited, they declare that while they cannot renew their offer of fraternal intercourse, they "will at all times entertain any proposition coming from the M. E. Church (North) to us, whether it be by written communication, or by delegation, having for its object friendly relations, and predicated of the rights granted to us by the Plan of Separation."

With the facts as presented before them, the M. E. Church, South, could not do more, and were not willing to do less.*

* Almost twenty-three years have elapsed since the General Conference of the M. E. Church (North) rejected the

The property question, however, had not been settled. This question embraced the interest held by the South in the Book Concerns in New York and Cincinnati, including "a common right to the use of all the copyrights in possession of the Book Concerns" in these cities, as well as their proportion of the Chartered Fund in Philadelphia. It also included the transfer "of the printing-presses in Charleston, Richmond, and Nashville," and "all the property of the Methodist Episcopal Church in meeting-houses, parsonages, colleges, schools, Conference Funds, cemeteries, and of every kind, within the limits of the Southern Organization," which had previously been claimed by the M. E. Church.

To accomplish the transfer of this property with the greatest facility, Nathan Bangs, George Peck, and James B. Finley, had been appointed Commissioners on the part of the M. E. Church (North) "to act in concert with the same number of Commissioners appointed by the Southern Organization."

It was thought by some Northern members of the General Conference of 1844, that the sixth restrictive article might possibly prevent the claims

proffer of friendly relations with the M. E. Church, South, and up to this date no proposition has come from them looking to fraternal intercourse between the two bodies of Methodists. (See Appendix C.)

of the South on the Book Concerns and Chartered Fund from being met with even-handed justice; and in order to guard against this possible contingency, so anxious were they at that time to deal fairly with the South, that "the Annual Conferences, at their approaching sessions," were recommended by the General Conference "to authorize a change" of this article, by which all barriers to a speedy and just settlement might be removed.

The failure to procure the requisite number of votes by which the sixth restrictive article might be changed, was not attributable to the South, nor could it in any way vitiate their claims to a *pro rata* division of the property.

In 1846, the General Conference of the Methodist Episcopal Church, South, adopted the following report:

Appointment of Commissioners by the General Conference of the M. E. Church, South, with instructions.

1. *Resolved*, (by the delegates of the several Annual Conferences of the Methodist Episcopal Church, South, in General Conference assembled,) That three Commissioners be appointed in accordance with the "Plan of Separation" adopted by the General Conference of the Methodist Episcopal Church in 1844, to act in concert with the Commissioners appointed by the said M. E. Church, to estimate the amount due to the South, according

to the aforesaid "Plan of Separation," and to adjust and settle all matters pertaining to the division of the Church-property and funds, as provided for in the "Plan of Separation," with full powers to carry into effect the whole arrangement with regard to said division.

2. *Resolved,* That the Commissioners of the M. E. Church, South, shall forthwith notify the Commissioners and Book Agents of the Methodist Episcopal Church of their appointment as aforesaid, and of their readiness to adjust and settle the matters aforesaid; and should no such settlement be effected before the session of the General Conference of the Methodist Episcopal Church in 1848, said Commissioners shall have power and authority for, and in behalf of, this Conference, to attend the General Conference of the M. E. Church to settle and adjust all questions involving property or funds which may be pending between the M. E. Church and the M. E. Church, South.

3. *Resolved,* That should the Commissioners appointed by this General Conference, after proper effort, fail to effect a settlement as above, then, and in that case, they shall be, and are hereby, authorized to take such measures as may best secure the just and equitable claims of the M. E. Church, South, to the property and funds aforesaid.

4. *Resolved,* That John Early be, and he is

hereby, authorized to act as the Agent or Appointee of the M. E. Church, South, in conformity to the "Plan of Separation" adopted by the General Conference of 1844, to receive and hold in trust for the use and benefit of the M. E. Church, South, all property and funds, of every description, which may be paid over to him by the agents of the M. E. Church.

5. *Resolved*, That the Commissioners, Appointee, and Book Agent, report to the next General Conference of the M. E. Church, South.

6. *Resolved*, That should a vacancy occur in the Board of Commissioners, or in the office of Appointee, herein provided for, by death or otherwise, in the interim of the General Conference, then, and in that case, the remaining members of the Board shall have power to fill such vacancy, with the approbation of one or more of the Bishops. W. A. SMITH, *Chairman.*

Immediately after the adoption of the report, the Conference proceeded to the election of the Commissioners by ballot, and "on the first balloting, H. B. Bascom, A. L. P. Green, and S. A. Latta were elected."

From the conciliatory spirit in which the General Conference of 1844 had met the necessities of the South, and from the anxiety expressed to do them ample justice, it would be readily supposed that the appointment of Commissioners was only necessary, that authority to receive the proportion of the property due the South might be somewhere invested.

On the 25th of August, 1846, Messrs. Bascom, Green, and Latta met in Cincinnati, and addressed the following communication to the Commissioners who had been appointed by the M. E. Church (North):

The undersigned Commissioners, appointed by the late General Conference of the Methodist Episcopal Church, South, in accordance with the Plan of Separation, adopted by the General Conference of the Methodist Episcopal Church in 1844, to act in concert with the Commissioners of said Methodist Episcopal Church, specially appointed for the purpose, in estimating the amount of property and funds due to the Methodist Episcopal Church, South, according to the Plan of Separation aforesaid, and to adjust and settle all matters pertaining to the division of the Church-property and funds as agreed upon and provided for in said plan, with full powers at the same time to carry into effect the whole arrangement with regard to said division of property, would respectfully give notice to the Rev. Dr. Bangs, Dr. Peck, and Rev. James B. Finley, Commissioners, and the Rev. George Lane and C. B. Tippett, Book Agents of the Methodist Episcopal Church, that they are prepared to act in concert with them, as the Plan of Separation contemplates, and requests in an amicable attempt to settle and adjust all the matters and interests to which the appointment of each Board of Commissioners relates—that is to say, all questions involving property and funds which may be pending between the Methodist Episcopal Church, and the Methodist Episcopal Church, South. And as necessary to such a result, in the judgment of the Commissioners, South, they would respectfully suggest and urge the propriety and necessity of a joint meeting of the Board of Commissioners, North and South, at a period as early as practicable, that the intention of the Plan of Separation, in this respect, may not be defeated by unnecessary delay. It has been the aim of the General Conference of the Methodist Episcopal Church, South, to see that all the terms and stipulations of the Plan of Separation be strictly complied with on their part, and provision has been accordingly made that the Rev. John Early, Book Agent of the Methodist Episcopal Church, South, and its appointee to receive the property and funds falling due to the South, be duly and properly clothed with the legal and corporate powers required by the Plan of Separation. And the undersigned Commissioners are not able to perceive any valid reason or reasons why the negotiation respecting the division of property should not proceed in the hands of the joint Commissioners without delay, and hence request the joint meeting of the Commissioners of the bodies they represent to judge and determine whether the Annual Conferences have authorized the change of the sixth restrictive rule; and as no such decision can be had until given by them, it seems important that such decision should be given by them as soon as practicable, and we know of no mode of conclusive action in the case, except by a joint meeting of the Commissioners. The Plan of Separation provides for no intermediate action between that of the Annual Conferences and that to be had by the Commissioners, and unless the Commissioners *North* are in possession of information, clear and satisfactory, that the action of the Annual Conferences, in the aggregate *vote* given by them, is adverse to the recommendation of the General Conference, it is obviously made their duty, by the Plan of Separation, to meet and decide the question. From all the information in our possession, we see no reason why we should not act upon the assumption that the proposed change in the restrictive rule has been authorized. The language of the Discipline is, "Upon the concurrent recommendation of three-fourths of all the members of the several Annual Conferences, who shall be present *and vote* upon such recommendations." The language of the Plan of Separation is, "Whenever the Annual Conferences, by a vote of three-fourths of all their members *voting* on the third resolution." It follows, hence, that both by the language of the Discipline, and that of the Plan of Separation, the question was to be settled by the aggregate vote of those members of the several Annual Conferences who were present in their annual sessions when the question came up, and *actually voted* upon it. If any refused or failed to vote, with such we have nothing to do; they cannot be regarded as either for or against the measure. They declined the right of suffrage by refusing to act, and the determination of the question rests with those who were present *and voted* in accordance with the law. In the instance of several Annual Conferences the vote was contingent, and future events, now to be judged of by the Commissioners, were to give an *affirmative* or *negative* character to their votes. In the instance of two of these at least, (and we believe it to be equally true of four,) it is susceptible of the clearest proof, that by their *own official showing*, their votes must, beyond all doubt, be counted in the affirmative, or not at all; and in either case, and indeed without reference to either, taking no account of the Conferences which refused to vote, it is believed the constitutional majority of all the votes given was in favor of the change; and it will, it seems to us, devolve upon the Commissioners of the Methodist Episcopal Church to make the contrary appear before they can, in good faith, refuse to carry into effect the Plan of Separation. To settle this question fairly and honorably, and in accordance with the facts in the case, it is believed that a meeting of the Commissioners is indispensable. To this we may add, that the most weighty considerations, both of justice and humanity, demand alike that the question be settled as early as possible, as the dividends to which we are declared entitled by the Plan of Separation, and which that plan pledges shall be paid to us, until the division of property shall actually take place, have already been withheld, and our "traveling, supernumerary, superannuated, and worn-out preachers, their wives, widows, and children, are literally suffering for the want of funds given in trust for their support —funds to which the General Conference of 1844 not only declared them entitled, but solemnly stipulated to divide with them upon principles of 'Christian kindness and strictest equity.'"

The division of property and funds stipulated contemplates no gratuity to the South, for it is well known that in receiving all the Plan of Separation accords to us, we are receiving but a part of what the South has contributed to the common fund in question.

There is another view of this subject which, in

our judgment, should not be overlooked by the Commissioners. The proposed change in the restrictive rule was regarded by all who favored the Plan of Separation in the General Conference of 1844, merely as means to an end. The end aimed at was an equitable division of the Church-property; and the more certainly and securely to effect this, within the established forms of law and order, the change in question was proposed; such change, however, or the want of it, cannot possibly affect, in any form, the question of right or the true issue in a legal process, should it be found necessary to institute such process.

The Methodist Episcopal Church, South, intends a most sacred appropriation of the funds they may receive, exclusively to the purposes specified in the sixth restrictive article, and not intending to divert them in any way to any other object or purpose, the change recommended by the General Conference can only be regarded as a matter of form, subordinate, in every high moral and legal sense, to the end had in view by the body in the adoption of the Plan of Separation. The object in calling attention to this view of the subject is not in any way to supersede the Plan of Separation, but to insist, as we shall always continue to do, that unless the letter of the plan shall interpose insuperable difficulties, its spirit and intention plainly and imperatively demand, at the hands of the Commissioners, that they carry it into effect, and that they cannot fail to do so without a grave abuse of the trust reposed in them. Hence, again, we urge that a meeting of the Commissioners at any early day is necessary to settle this preliminary question, which, it appears to us, can be conclusively settled in no other way.

It certainly cannot be necessary that we remind the Commissioners and Book Agents of the Methodist Episcopal Church, that the peace and quiet, not less than the character and hopes of the Church, North and South, urgently require that this great property question be settled as soon as practicable; and we are most anxious that it should be done amicably and with good feeling, and especially that it may be done without an appeal to the civil tribunals of the country; and the General Conference of the Methodist Episcopal Church, South, have accordingly instructed their Commissioners to look to such an issue as the last resort, in view of the adjustment aimed at.

In conclusion, the Commissioners of the Methodist Episcopal Church, South, in view of the facts and considerations to which they have adverted in this communication, would respectfully and urgently call upon Dr. Bangs, as Chairman of the Commissioners of the Methodist Episcopal Church, to call a meeting of the joint Board of Commissioners, as herein before indicated, and we cheerfully concede to him the right, so far as we are concerned, of fixing *the time* and *place* at any period between the last of October and the first of March next.

Very respectfully,

H. B. BASCOM,
A. L. P. GREEN,
S. A. LATTA.

CINCINNATI, OHIO, August 25, 1846.

P. S.—We would respectfully ask and claim, upon the ground of justice and right, that the Commissioners and Book Agents of the Methodist Episcopal Church make a direct call, by authority of the General Conference of 1844, upon the Secretaries of all the Annual Conferences of the Methodist Episcopal Church for an authentic, attested statement of the vote or action of each Conference in relation to the change of the sixth restrictive rule, and the Commissioners of the Methodist Episcopal Church, South, will do the same within the limits of the Southern Organization.

H. B. BASCOM,
A. L. P. GREEN,
S. A. LATTA.

To this communication the following reply was made:

To H. B. Bascom, A. L. P. Green, and S. A. Latta, Commissioners of the Methodist Episcopal Church, South.

Dear Brethren:—We have received your communication, dated the 25th August, 1846, requesting us to call a joint meeting of the Commissioners appointed by the General Conference of 1844 of the Methodist Episcopal Church, and the Commissioners appointed by the General Conference of 1845 of the Methodist Episcopal Church, South, in order to adjust the property question, as provided for in the Provisional Plan of Separation, adopted by the General Conference of 1844.

In reply to this, we have to say that, in our judgment, we have no authority to act in the premises, as we have never been officially notified that the requisite number of votes in the several Annual Conferences has been given in favor of the alteration in the sixth restrictive rule in the constitution of the Church, nor have we any authority to call on the Secretaries of the several Annual Conferences to give us the requisite information as you have suggested.

On these accounts we must respectfully decline to act in the premises, as our action would, in our opinion, be null and void.

N. Bangs,
Geo. Peck,
J. B. Finley.

New York, October 14, 1846.

From this period until the subsequent meeting of the General Conference of the M. E. Church (North), no farther steps were taken by the Southern Commissioners. The General Conference met in Pittsburgh on the first day of May, 1848, and on the 12th the Commissioners of the M. E. Church, South, submitted to that body the following communication:

PITTSBURGH, May 11, 1848.

REV. AND DEAR BRETHREN:—The undersigned Commissioners and Appointee of the Methodist Episcopal Church, South, respectfully represent to your body that, pursuant to our appointment, and in obedience to specific instructions, we notified the Commissioners and Agent of the Methodist Episcopal Church of our readiness to proceed to the adjustment of the property question according to the Plan of Separation adopted by the General Conference of 1844. And we furthermore state, that the Chairman of the Board of Commissioners of the Methodist Episcopal Church informed us they would not act in the case, and referred us to your body for the settlement of the question as to the division of the property and funds of the Church. And being furthermore instructed by the General Conference of the Methodist Episcopal Church, South, in case of a failure to settle with your Commissioners, to attend the session of your body in 1848, for the "settlement and adjustment of all questions involving property and funds, which may be pending between the Methodist Episcopal Church and the Methodist Episcopal Church, South," take this method of informing you of our presence, and of our readiness to attend to the matters committed to our trust and agency by the Methodist Episcopal Church, South; and we desire to be informed as to the time and manner in which it may suit your views and convenience to consummate with us the division of the property and funds of the Church, as provided for in the Plan of Separation, adopted with so much unanimity by the General Conference of 1844. And for our authority in the premises, we respectfully refer you to the accompanying document, marked A.

A. L. P. Green,
C. B. Parsons, } *Commissioners.*
L. Pierce,

John Early, *Appointee.*

This communication was accompanied with a document, properly authenticated, showing the authority under which the Southern Commissioners were acting.

To this communication no reply was made, nor was it even referred to a committee.

On the 18th the following letter was addressed

by the Commissioners of the M. E. Church, South, to the Commissioners of the M. E. Church (North):

PITTSBURGH, 18th May, 1848.

The undersigned, Commissioners of the M. E. Church, South, appointed by the General Conference of said Church, in accordance with the Plan of Separation, adopted by the General Conference of the M. E. Church in 1844, would respectfully represent to Rev. Nathan Bangs, George Peck, and James B. Finley, Commissioners on the part of the M. E. Church, that it is important their stay in the city should not be prolonged beyond the period necessary to accomplish, as far as may be found practicable, the objects of their commission. And with a view to a correct decision in the case, the undersigned beg leave to inquire—1st. Whether, as Commissioners, appointed by the General Conference of 1844, to act in concert with a similar Board of Commissioners in behalf of the Church, South, provided for in the Plan of Separation, you regard yourselves as authorized to act in the premises, under the authority above; and if so, in what form? 2d. Should your answer to this inquiry be in the negative, we would respectfully ask, Have you any thing to propose to us, as Commissioners of the M. E. Church, South, designed to carry into effect the provisions of the Plan of Separation, having reference to the division of the Church-property?

Very truly and respectfully,

H. B. BASCOM,
A. L. P. GREEN,
C. B. PARSONS.

Rev. N. Bangs, Geo. Peck, and Jas. B. Finley.

On the 20th of the month Mr. Finley presented this letter to the General Conference, and moved its reference to the Committee on the State of the Church. He afterward withdrew the motion to refer, when it was renewed by Mr. Creagh, of the New York Conference. To prevent its reference, however, Mr. Finley withdrew the paper.

On the same day Messrs. Peck and Finley replied as follows to the communication of Messrs. Bascom, Green, and Parsons:

PITTSBURGH, May 20, 1848.

Rev. Messrs. H. B. Bascom, D.D., A. L. P. Green, and C. B. Parsons:

GENTLEMEN:—The undersigned have the honor to acknowledge the receipt of your communication of the 18th inst., and would respectfully reply:

1. That the conditions upon which their powers, as "Commissioners" appointed by the General Conference at its session in 1844, were made to

depend, having failed, they have not, and never had, power to act in the matter in question.

2. In accordance with the above view, they would respectfully say that they have nothing to "propose" to you touching these matters.

With sentiments of esteem, yours,

GEORGE PECK,
JAMES B. FINLEY.

It will be borne in mind that the reason given by the General Conference for declining to receive Dr. Pierce as a fraternal messenger from the M. E. Church, South, was, that "serious questions and difficulties" existed "between the two bodies." It has already been stated that these "serious questions and difficulties" had reference to the property in which the South had an interest. The question will naturally occur, Why, if the M. E. Church (North) was willing to deal justly with the South, and to settle the points at issue, did the General Conference refuse to entertain the communication from the Southern Commissioners? The South asked for nothing to which they were not entitled, and which had not been conceded by the Plan of Separation. To the building up of the Book Concerns in New York and Cincinnati, as well as the Chartered Fund, the South had labored with untiring energy, as well as contributed their money. When the Book Concern in New

York, in 1834, was destroyed by fire, the Church in the South, as well as in the North, aided with large contributions to raise it from its ruins.

The duties of the Southern Commissioners, so far as they referred to the General Conference of the M. E. Church (North), having been performed, they left for their homes. Their presence in Pittsburgh, however, had excited extraordinary interest, and its influence was felt in the General Conference. This body was not content with its own action, or rather its want of action, and hence it gave evidence of unrest.

On the 18th of May, two days previous to the date of the letter addressed by the Southern Commissioners to Messrs. Peck and Finley, Mr. Finley offered the following preamble and resolution, which was laid on the table for the present:

"Whereas, the division of the Book Concern, and other Church-property, with the Church, *South,* has not been authorized by the vote of the Annual Conferences, as provided for in the Plan of Separation; and, whereas, they still claim that we owe them, which involves questions of great magnitude and importance; therefore,

"*Resolved,* That the Committee on the State of the Church be instructed to inquire into the propriety and expediency of offering to refer the above question to disinterested arbiters, to be chosen by the parties, for amicable adjustment, and report thereon."

On the 26th of the month the General Conference declared the Plan of Separation "null and void."

On the following day George Peck, the Chairman of the Committee on the State of the Church, presented so much of their report as referred to the "property question." It reads as follows:

The Committee on the State of the Church beg leave farther to report, in part—

That they have had under consideration the claims preferred by the Church, South, to a portion of the property of the Book Concern and Chartered Fund; and, pending the discussion of the subject, the question of proposing to refer the whole matter to disinterested arbiters was proposed and considered. Whereupon the committee agreed to recommend to the General Conference for adoption the following resolutions:

"*Resolved*, 1. That it is the sense of this Conference that we have no authority, independently of the Annual Conferences, to enter into arbitration with the Commissioners of the Methodist Episcopal Church, South, in relation to the claims set up by them to a division of the vested funds of the Methodist Episcopal Church.

"*Resolved*, 2. That this General Conference recommend to the Annual Conferences so far to suspend the sixth restrictive rule of the Discipline as to allow the appointment of Commissioners, for the purpose of arbitrating what is technically called the Property Question with the Commissioners of the Methodist Episcopal Church, South.

"By order of the committee.

"Respectfully submitted,

"GEORGE PECK, *Chairman.*"

This report was supported by a long speech from Mr. Peck, at the close of which the following substitute was offered by John F. Wright, of Ohio:

"Whereas, it is now ascertained that the recommendation of the General Conference of 1844, to change the sixth restrictive article, so as to allow of a division of the property of the Book Concern, with distinct ecclesiastical connection, which might be formed by the thirteen Annual Conferences in the slaveholding States, has not been concurred in by a vote of three-fourths of all the members of the several Annual Conferences present and voting on said recommendations;

"And, whereas, the thirteen protesting Annual Conferences in the slaveholding States, having formed themselves into a separate and distinct ecclesiastical organization, under the title or name of the Methodist Episcopal Church, South, and their General Conference in May, 1846, did authorize their Commissioners (whose credentials have been received by this General Conference) to present and adjust their claim on the funds of the Book Concern of the Methodist Episcopal Church;

"And, whereas, our common and holy Christianity prescribes and enjoins the most pacific measures for the settlement of all matters in dispute between individuals, as well as associations of professing Christians; and the whole Christian world expect ministers of the Lord Jesus Christ to adopt the most peaceful and conciliatory measures for the settlement of any claim that may be urged against them; therefore,

"*Resolved,* (by the delegates of the several Annual Conferences in General Conference assembled,) That we propose to the Commissioners of the Church, South, to refer the question of their claim on our Book Concern to *five* arbiters, neither of whom shall be a member of either Church, who shall be chosen in the manner here prescribed, namely:

" The Commissioners of the M. E. Church, *South,* shall choose two arbiters; and three Commissioners, to be appointed by this General Conference, shall choose other two; and the four arbiters thus chosen shall choose a fifth, each party being solemnly bound to abide by the decision such arbiters shall make on the questions of such claims."

This substitute was laid on the table.

Dr. Holdich offered and moved the following substitute, stating it to be a paper presented by the Bishops in response to a written request of several delegates that they would communicate their opinions in regard to the Property Question:

"Whereas, H. B. Bascom, D.D., A. L. P. Green, and C. B. Parsons, Commissioners of the M. E. Church, South, have visited the seat of this Conference to urge a claim to a portion of the funds of the Book Concern, based, it is understood, on an act of the last General Conference, known as the 'Report of the Committee of Nine;'

"And, whereas, the non-concurrence of the Annual Conferences in that part of said report which bears on the division of said funds, leaves this General Conference without any authority to recognize or adjust said claim in any voluntary way;

"And, whereas, it is understood from the periodicals of the M. E. Church, *South,* and from conversations with some of said Commissioners, that a suit at law will be resorted to for the recovery of said claim;

"And, whereas, the commencement of this suit will change the form of this difficulty, rendering it a mere business transaction, so as to throw it within the constitutional control of the General Conference;

"And, whereas, it is understood that the Commissioners would accept none but a strictly legal arbitration;

"And, whereas, this Conference desires to advance as far as its constitutional power will authorize toward an amicable adjustment of this difficulty; therefore,

"*Resolved*, (by the General Conference of the M. E. Church,) 1. That should such lawsuit be commenced by the Commissioners, our Book Agents at New York and Cincinnati be, and are hereby, authorized and advised to tender to said Commissioners an adjustment of the claim, based on the report aforesaid by arbitration, under such legal sanctions as shall render the award final, and of binding effect on the M. E. Church, and the M. E. Church, *South*.

"*Resolved*, 2. That inasmuch as the General Conference is not formally assured that such suit will be commenced, and inasmuch as an amicable settlement of the difficulty is in any event exceedingly desirable, and inasmuch as this General Conference has no power or authority to act at discretion in this matter, either to allow or arbitrate said claim, if not prosecuted in court, unless the Annual Conferences authorize it by a change of the constitution, it is hereby recommended to the Annual Conferences, if said suit is not commenced, so far to suspend the sixth 'restrictive article' of the Discipline as to authorize our Book Agents at New York and Cincinnati to submit to arbitrate what is technically called the Property Question.

"*Resolved*, 3. That in case said suit is not commenced, the Bishops are requested to lay the last resolution before the Annual Conferences for their concurrence."

The substitute offered by Dr. Holdich met the same fate as the one proposed by Mr. Wright.

The General Conference was evidently greatly perplexed. They were in a dilemma, from the meshes of which extrication was by no means easy. All over the Methodist Episcopal Church (North) were to be found men of sound judgment and enlightened piety, in communion with the Church, who regarded the claims of the Southern Division to a *pro rata* proportion of the property as not only beyond dispute, but as too sacred to be denied them.

The verdict of popular opinion throughout the Northern States was in favor of the Southern claims, while in the General Conference were ministers eminent for their learning and piety, who, though in the minority, were unwilling to compromise their honor by an act of repudiation. In the midst of the confusion Jesse T. Peck offered the following substitute, which was seconded by James B. Finley:

"Whereas, the Methodist Episcopal Church, *South*, having in due form preferred claims against the vested funds and other property of the Methodist Episcopal Church; and, whereas, the General Conference has no power officially to respond to, or in any way adjust, said preferred claims; and, whereas, we are anxious that an amicable and strictly equitable disposition may be made of them; therefore,

"1. *Resolved*, (by the delegates of the several Annual Conferences of the Methodist Episcopal Church in General Conference assembled,) That we hereby advise the Book Agents at New York and Cincinnati, immediately, in due form, and under such instructions as this Conference shall hereafter give them, to offer *to submit said preferred claims to the full and final decision of judicious and disinterested arbiters.*

"2. *Resolved*, That a committee of —— be appointed to report in detail to this Conference suitable instructions to be communicated to the said Agents for the government of their action in the premises."

The morning session closed without any action on the substitute of Messrs. Peck and Finley. On the afternoon of the same day Mr. Finley advocated the preamble and resolutions in a speech of considerable length, and was followed by Peter Akers, of the Illinois Conference.

The evening session, however, adjourned without reaching any conclusion. In the meantime the Sabbath intervened, and on Monday the following was offered by Mr. Akers, and referred to the Committee on the Book Concern:

"*Resolved,* That the Book Agents at New York be, and they are hereby, instructed to pay over to such person or persons as the said Book Agents may judge to be authorized to receive and receipt for the same in behalf of the several claimants narrated below, so much of the disciplinary allowances as may be due from year to year to the widows and orphans of such traveling, supernumerary, superannuated, and worn-out preachers, as have died in the service of the Methodist Episcopal Church before the organization of the Methodist Episcopal Church, *South;* also the superannuated preachers who still adhere to the Methodist Episcopal Church, so that such widows and orphans, and superannuated and supernumerary preachers aforesaid, living within the bounds of the several Annual Conferences of the Methodist Episcopal Church, *South,* may receive what may be equal in amount to that which widows and orphans in the Methodist Episcopal Church may have received, or shall hereafter receive, from the dividends made annually from the Book Concern."

On the afternoon of Monday, the 29th, Mr. Brenton, of North Indiana Conference, offered the following, which was presented by D. Curry and M. Simpson:

"Whereas, it is now ascertained that the recommendation of the General Conference, at its session in 1844, to change the sixth restrictive article so as to allow of a division of the property of the Book Concern, with a distinct ecclesiastical connection, which might be formed by the thirteen Annual Conferences in the slave States, has not been concurred in by a vote of three-fourths of all the members of the several Annual Conferences present and voting on said recommendation;

"And, whereas, the thirteen protesting Annual Conferences in the slaveholding States have formed themselves into a separate and distinct ecclesiastical connection, under the title and name of the 'Methodist Episcopal Church, *South*,' and their General Conference in 1846 did authorize three Commissioners (whose credentials have been received by this General Conference) to present and adjust their claim on the funds of the Book Concern of the Methodist Episcopal Church;

"And, whereas, our *common* and *holy* Christianity prescribes and enjoins the most pacific measures for the settlement of all matters in dispute between individuals, as well as associations of professing Christians, and the whole Christian world will expect ministers of the Lord Jesus Christ to adopt the most peaceful and conciliatory measures for the settlement of any claim that may be urged against them;

"And, whereas, this Conference desires to advance, as far as its constitutional powers will authorize, toward an amicable adjustment of this difficulty; therefore,

"1. *Resolved,* (by the delegates of the several Annual Conferences of the Methodist Episcopal Church in General Conference assembled,) That we hereby authorize the Book Agents at New York and at Cincinnati to offer to submit said claims to the decision of disinterested arbiters, provided that if said Agents, on the advice of eminent legal counsel, shall be satisfied that when clothed with all the authority which the General Conference can confer, their corporate powers will not warrant them to submit said claims to arbitration, this resolution shall not be binding upon them.

"2. *Resolved,* That should the Agents find, upon taking such legal counsel, that they have not the power to submit the case to voluntary arbitration, and should a suit at law be commenced by the Commissioners of the Methodist Episcopal Church, *South,* said Agents are hereby authorized, then and in that case, to tender to said Commissioners an adjustment of their preferred claims by a legal arbitration, under the authority of the court.

"3. *Resolved,* That should the Agents find that they are not authorized to tender a voluntary arbitration, and should no suit be commenced by the Commissioners aforesaid, then and in that case the General Conference being exceedingly desirous of effecting an amicable settlement of said claim, recommend to the Annual Conferences so far to suspend the 'sixth restrictive article' of the Discipline, as to authorize our Book Agents at New York and Cincinnati to submit said claim to arbitration.

"4. *Resolved,* That in the occurrence of the above specified contingencies, the Bishops are requested to lay the foregoing resolutions before the several Annual Conferences for their concurrence."

The first resolution was adopted by a majority of *three* votes; the second by a majority of *forty-nine;* the third by a majority of *fifty-seven;* on the fourth resolution the vote was not counted, being taken by lifting the hand.

It will always be a source of regret that the Methodist Episcopal Church (North) refused to comply with the Plan of Separation in reference to the division of the property, which belonged in common to the two branches of Methodism. The action of the General Conference of 1848, in declaring the agreement entered into between the North and South in 1844 to be null and void, and withholding from the minority what was justly theirs, can find justification nowhere.

The substitute adopted by that body must always be regarded as an evasion of the question, by no means creditable to so august an assembly as a General Conference.

In referring to this action, the Commissioners of the Methodist Episcopal Church, South, in their "Appeal to Public Opinion," thus speak:

"This 'so-called' proposition to arbitrate is uniquely curious in nearly all its aspects. It is so completely made up of conditions, shifts, and evasions, it is difficult to keep it in the mind long enough to analyze and detect its falsehoods. 'If' legal advice should so decide—'if' the Agents themselves are 'satisfied'—'if' their 'corporate powers will warrant'—'if' they find they have not power —'if' legal advice be against it—'if' suit be commenced, then, 'if' they choose, they can offer a legal arbitration—or of course let it alone, and with the warrant of indemnity before them, declare the whole movement 'null and void!' The chances of escape, however, are not exhausted. It is found the General Conference cannot do what they had seemed to do: with no right themselves to arbitrate, they can confer none, and hence new difficulties—'should' the Agents find they are not authorized—'should' the South not commence suit—'then, and in that case, they recommend the

Annual Conferences, not to authorize settlement and payment according to contract, but to permit arbitration—the arbitrators to say whether the General Conference shall keep faith and contract with the South, as pledged and conditioned in 1844!

"Finally, 'in the occurrence of the above specified *contingencies'—all* of them, of course—when even the mathematical improbabilities in the case must have amounted to an indefinite postponement of the whole question in the minds of the body thus legislating—then the Bishops are 'requested' to bring the matter before the Annual Conferences! And suppose the Annual Conferences consented to an arbitration, and 'eminent legal counsel' advised against it, in that event, of course, Agents would not act upon the permission of the Annual Conference, and the whole would be a nullity. Or, suppose counsel and Agents went for arbitration under the *quasi* grant of the General Conference, without consulting the Annual Conferences, then by the declared judgment of the General Conference, we should have a nullity again, as the right is assumed to be in the Annual Conferences exclusively. There is no ground of trust in any respect in which the subject is presented, upon which the South can repose without the fair probability of being farther deceived. Say that the Annual Conferences consent to arbitration in 1349, what reason have we to believe they would not reverse the decision in 1850? They promised an equitable division of the property with us through their 'supreme' representative council in 1844, and denied the obligation in 1845, and how far will this go to show they are likely to keep faith in future? Or if *they* should, what security have we that the next Northern General Conference would not undo the whole, and declare it 'null and void,' should the arbitration be favorable to the South? We had their public pledge in 1844, and have found it good for nothing; and what is going to make it any better in 1848, or subsequently? Must the fact that we have been deceived by them once, be received as a good reason why we shall not be a second time? What can be seen or found in all this to give us confidence? We contend with a party 'doubly armed.' If they pledge and promise us, as a General Conference, they release themselves in Annual Conference, where the same men reäppear as a separate disinterested party! The constituents refuse to be bound by the official acts of their representatives. The representatives repudiate their own acts, by resolving themselves, in Annual Conference, into the common constituency! We cannot trust men or movements of this description, and do not intend to be deceived by either any farther. The General Conference repudiate because, as they tell us, the Annual

Conferences so decided; and when we remind them of their dishonored faith, they refer us for remedy to the Annual Conferences! The nullification force at Pittsburgh has not alarmed us so much as to induce us to concede important rights in order to be informed by arbitrators whether we have any! So far from this, we intend the movement shall be of service to our cause. By declaring the Plan 'null and void,' *because* 'violated' by the South, they admit the *compact* character and *treaty* rights of the instrument, and the nullifiers are thus held to the responsibility of the original contract, unless they make good their charge of fundamental violation by the South, of the probability of which the reader by this time will be able to judge pretty correctly."

There were leading men in the North, among whom the Hon. Judge McLean was prominent, who deprecated the course pursued by this General Conference. In one of his letters to the Chairman of the Board of Southern Commissioners he said: "My wish is to *recognize* the South as *the same Church*, under a *distinct* organization, which results from their *local* institutions—that there be an *equitable division* of the Church-property, and that the *same feeling* of Christian fellowship and love shall be cherished as before the separation."

There was no wish on the part of the South to

appeal to the civil court, while there remained a vestige of hope of settlement without such appeal. It had, however, become evident that unless redress was sought through this medium, the claims of justice would never be met.

On the 9th of September, 1848, a meeting of the Commissioners of the Methodist Episcopal Church, South, was held, and the following explanatory statement and resolution were unanimously adopted—Bishops Soule, Andrew, Capers, and Paine, and the Rev. John Early, Book Agent, being present and consenting:

The Commissioners having been strongly impressed for the last four years with the apprehension that no fair and equitable settlement of the property question between the Northern and Southern divisions of the Church could be had without an appeal to legal process, had purposed bringing suit in conformity with the instructions under which they acted, early after the adjournment of the late Northern General Conference, should that body fail to take any conclusive action in the premises, and were only deterred from doing so by the attempt of that body to secure the sanction of the Church and public opinion to a mode of settlement in contravention of the Plan of Separation, and to which the Southern Commissioners could not consent without admitting the invalidity of that instrument; and having waited nearly four months, in deference to what public opinion might require of us, and in courtesy to the adverse party, without having received any proposition from the Church, North, the Northern General Conference having avowed want of authority to act in the case, and having failed to secure the constitutional majority of two-thirds preparatory to a change of the restriction, pleaded as a barrier to action, and without which no change of the restriction can be even recommended by the General Conference; and action having been had by several of the Northern Annual Conferences authorizing the opinion that the requisite three-fourths majority of their members would never consent to any mode of settlement to which the South could consent without the forfeiture of important rights; these Conferences, moreover, having failed at their recent sessions to make any movement toward a change of the sixth restriction, and several Annual Conferences, South, as well as individual claimants, having intimated a determination to seek legal redress independently of the Commissioners unless they proceed to bring suit—the long-neglected claims of the superannuated ministers, their wives, widows, and children, upon which many of them have to rely for subsistence almost exclusively, being extremely urgent—the Church, South, being unwilling to create another similar fund until it is known, after fair legal trial, that our equitable share of the existing fund cannot be recovered; and as arbitration is spoken of *not in fulfillment* of the contract between the parties, but as a consequence of its *denial and repudiation*, the adverse party thus seeking to avail themselves of a *false issue* deeply injurious to the South as a mode of settlement, and to which the Southern Commissioners had explicitly informed them they could not submit; and having informed the Rev. George Lane, the principal Book Agent, North, at his own request in May last, that we could not under our instructions consistently delay bringing suit to a period later than the date of the action now had; and believing the late General Conference had no authority or control of any kind over the property question, except in accordance with the conditions of the contract, as they had by special provision and transfer at the session of 1844 placed the entire settlement of the whole question in the hands of Agents and Commissioners; and regarding the action of the late General Conference in their attempt at the destruction of the Plan of Separation, and the substitution of a new and adverse mode of settlement, placing in jeopardy rights and claims previously admitted and provided for, as a gross, unlawful trespass, and, therefore, null and void in all its aspects and bearings—for these reasons, in connection with the facts and reasonings of the foregoing Appeal, of which this brief statement and the accompanying resolution form a part — therefore, deeply regretting the necessity of the measure, but deeming it important to the interests involved,

Resolved, That it is expedient and necessary, in view of the rights and interests in controversy, that the necessary suits be instituted as soon as practicable, for the recovery of the funds and property falling due to the Methodist Episcopal Church, South, under the contract of the Plan of Separation, adopted by the General Conference of 1844.

H. B. BASCOM,
A. L. P. GREEN,
S. A. LATTA.*

We have already referred to the property to which the South would be entitled under the Plan of Separation. The first suit was brought in the city of New York, against George Lane and others, for a division of the Book Concern in that

*As H. B. Bascom did not reach Pittsburgh until the 13th of May, Dr. Pierce was in due form substituted in his place *ad interim*, and his name accordingly appended to a communication addressed to the General Conference. Dr. Latta being prevented by extreme illness from meeting the Commissioners in Pittsburgh in May, 1848, the Rev. C. B. Parsons was duly appointed *ad interim* in his stead.

city. The ablest counsel was employed on both sides—for the plaintiffs, D. Lord, Hon. Reverdy Johnson, and Mr. Johnson, Jr.; and for the defendants, Hon. Rufus Choate, George Wood, and E. L. Fancher.

The case was tried before the Hon. Judges Nelson and Betts. It was opened on the 19th of May, 1851, by Mr. Lord. The speeches on both sides of the question were distinguished for their clearness and logical force. Every argument that could be brought to bear was employed, every proof was marshaled. The pleadings were closed on the 29th of May by Mr. Johnson, Jr. The whole country felt an interest in the decision, yet no one doubted the result.

On the 26th of November, 1851, the United States Circuit Court for the Southern District of New York caused the decree to be entered, ordering to be transferred to the Agents of the Methodist Episcopal Church, South, their *proportion* of the property of the New York Book Concern, including both capital and property, and the Clerk of the Court was instructed to ascertain the amount and value of the property. Exceptions were taken to his report, the Court not agreeing on some points, and the case was certified to the Supreme Court of the United States for decision.

The suit for a division of the Book Concern in Cincinnati was brought in the city of Columbus, in the United States Circuit Court for the District of Ohio. The Hon. Mr. Stanberry was employed by the plaintiffs, and Messrs. Badger and Ewing by the defendants. The Court was presided over by the Hon. Judge Leavitt, who rendered a decision in favor of the defendants. The Southern Commissioners appealed from the decision of Judge Leavitt to the Supreme Court of the United States. This Court was composed of Chief Justice Taney, and Associate Justices McLean,* Wayne, Catron, Daniel, Nelson, Greer, Curtis, and Campbell. The cause was heard in Washington City in April, 1854, and was decided in favor of the M. E. Church, South, without any dissent from any of the Justices. The opinion of the Court was delivered by Judge Nelson, April 25, 1854.†

The M. E. Church, South, also claimed an interest in the Chartered Fund, which was located in Philadelphia, which was paid over to the Agents without recourse at law.

From these several sources the Methodist Episcopal Church, South, received over three hundred thousand dollars, namely, from the New York Book Concern, one hundred and ninety-one thousand dollars; from the Cincinnati Book Concern, ninety-

---

* Judge McLean did not sit in the case.

† See Appendix D, for the Decision of the Court.

three thousand dollars; and from the Chartered Fund, seventeen thousand seven hundred and twelve dollars and ninety-five cents.

Before we close this chapter, we propose to invite attention to the Methodist Episcopal Church, South, and briefly to view its position, duty, and prospects. Forming a new ecclesiastical organization, the Southern Methodists published to the world the grounds on which they had separated from the Northern Division. They believed that an impartial tribunal would justify the course they had pursued, and that the faithful chronicler of the history of Methodism would accord to them purity of purpose. They established no new Church, but simply brought the Church of which they were members under a separate jurisdiction, making no change in doctrines, and taking the same Discipline, changing it only so far as to conform it to the new organization.

A vast field, already white unto the harvest, spread out before them, commanding their untiring energies and earnest devotion.

At the time of the division of the Methodist Episcopal Church, fifteen Annual Conferences, embracing all the Southern and South-western States, with the exception of Maryland, and comprising a membership of 329,057 white and 118,904 colored, making a total of 447,961 persons, adhered to the fortunes of the M. E. Church,

South. In addition to these, the Indian Mission Conference, embracing the Cherokee, Choctaw, Chickasaw, and Creek tribes, occupying a territory bounded by Kansas on the North, by Texas on the South, by Arkansas on the East, and on the West by the grand prairies which stretch away to the Rocky Mountains, with an aggregate population of fifty thousand, and a membership of two thousand nine hundred and seventy-eight, identified themselves with the Southern branch of Methodism. Provision was also made in the General Conference of 1846 for the establishment of a mission in China.

These were the fields which, under the blessing of Heaven, the Methodist Episcopal Church, South, was pledged to cultivate. The work was vast, and the responsibility that assumed it was great.

No department of the work of the Christian ministry has ever been more difficult than the planting of the gospel of Jesus Christ among the Indians. They had been so often and so cruelly wronged by the white man, who traded with their tribes, that they looked with distrust on the men who went among them to dispense the word of life.

If the task of implanting the great truths of Christianity in the mind of the Indian was difficult, it was not more so than the religious instruction of the negro was delicate and important. No work was ever intrusted to the Christian ministry that required greater devotion and skill. Scattered throughout the territory occupied by the M. E. Church, South, and predominating in numerical strength in some of the Gulf States, the negro had peculiar claims on the sympathy of the Church, South. It ought not to be forgotten that the Methodist ministry were not responsible for the existence of slavery in the Southern and South-western States. It antedated Methodism in the South, and owed its existence there to New England. Negro slavery was introduced into the colonial government by Great Britain previous to the Revolutionary war. Subsequent to that event, the African slave-trade was carried on, by the enterprising Puritan, until the meeting of the Convention in 1789, at which time a Constitution was secured to the United States Government. Previous to this period, all the Northern States recognized the right to ownership in slaves, and, with a single exception, were slave States. During the Convention, before the Constitution was adopted, the question of slavery was freely discussed in that body, and the African slave-trade condemned in no unmistakable terms. A majority of the representatives from the Southern States advocated the abolition of the slave-trade at once, as at war with every feeling of humanity; but the far-seeing Puritans, holding the balance of power in that body, pleaded and voted for the continuance of the inhuman practice. They succeeded in their efforts, and secured the passage of an act authorizing the continuance of the traffic until 1808. Language cannot portray the energy displayed by New England during these nineteen years, in the prosecution of this work of human misery. Vessel after vessel was fitted up, manned and sent out on its merciless cruise, and landing on the coast of Africa, the unsuspecting negro was decoyed on board, fettered with irons, subjected to every cruelty and torture, and in the most heartless manner was torn from country, and kindred, and home. The tears, the groans, the agony of these poor sufferers failed to find one chord of sympathy in the hearts of their cruel captors. The upturned faces of the suffering negro, pleading for pity, could find no echo in the bosom of the New Englander. During all the years allowed for this unholy traffic to be carried on, their vessels plowed the seas, burdened with human groans and laden with human woes. The traffic, however, brought wealth, and money was their god. In the meantime it was discovered that slave labor was not remunerative in the Northern States, and provision was made by legislative enactments for the gradual emancipation of the negro. The cotton States, however, presented a market, and instead of receiving the benefits of emancipation, in too many instances the negro was sold by his owner into perpetual servitude, who, putting into his pocket "the price of blood," walked through the halls of his palatial home, or reclined in his cushioned pew in the house of God, and said, "God, I thank thee, that I am not as other men!"

These negroes in the South had increased to millions, and to them the M. E. Church, South, had a special mission. In the Northern States no attention had been bestowed on their religious instruction. Pagans in their native land, under Puritan tutelage they remained pagans. In the North they had been subjected to a discipline remarkably severe, and, under the rigors of cruel masters, they had droned away an existence scarcely worth preserving. Without religious instruction, they had never been told of a higher destiny, of an immortality of bliss beyond the grave. They were simply used to increase the wealth of their masters, and when no longer profitable to Northern capitalists, they were sold to the South.

In the South, too, the master, in many places, had serious apprehensions from the efforts to impart religious instruction to his slaves. The Northern man had so frequently endeavored, under the guise of a religious teacher, to decoy the slave from his owner, that the ministers and the gospel were alike distrusted. To save this unfortunate race the Methodist Episcopal Church, South, was specially called.

Methodism occupied a most commanding position within the territory of the Southern Organization. A reference has been made already to a white membership of more than three hundred thousand who worshiped at its altars. To care for these, and to bring others into the fold, belonged to its mission. At home the field to be occupied was large and important, while abroad the Celestial Empire was commanding its energies. For the fidelity with which these trusts have been guarded, the thousands who have crowded its altars, many of whom have safely passed over the "last river," are its witnesses.

APPENDIX.

A.

LIST OF DELEGATES OF THE GENERAL CONFERENCE OF 1844.

New York Conference.—Nathan Bangs, Stephen Olin, Phineas Rice, Charles W. Carpenter, George Peck, John B. Stratton, Peter P. Sandford, Fitch Reed, Samuel D. Ferguson, Stephen Martindale, Marvin Richardson.

Providence Conference.—John Lovejoy, Frederick Upham, Sanford Benton, Paul Townsend.

New England Conference.—James Porter, Dexter S. King, Phineas Crandall, Charles Adams, George Pickering.

Maine Conference.—Moses Hill, Ezekiel Robinson, Daniel B. Randall, Charles W. Morse, John Hobart, Heman Nickerson, George Webber.

New Hampshire Conference.—Elihu Scott, Jared Perkins, Samuel Kelly, Schuyler Chamberlain, John G. Dow, Justin Spaulding, Charles D. Cahoon, William D. Cass.

Troy Conference.—Truman Seymour, John M. Wever, James Covel, Tobias Spicer, Seymour Coleman, James B. Houghtaling, Jesse T. Peck.

Black River Conference.—Albert D. Peck, Aaron Adams, Gardner Baker, W. W. Ninde.

Oneida Conference.—John M. Snyder, Silas Comfort, Nelson Rounds, David A. Shepherd, Henry F. Row, Elias Bowen, David Holmes, Jr.

Genesee Conference.—Glezen Fillmore, Samuel Luckey, Allen Steele, Freeborn G. Hibbard, Schuyler Seager, Asa Abell, William Hosmer, John B. Alverson.

Erie Conference.—John J. Steadman, John Bain, George W. Clarke, John Robinson, Timothy Goodwin.

Pittsburgh Conference.—William Hunter, Homer J. Clark, John Spencer, Simon Elliott, Robert Boyd, Samuel Wakefield, James Drummond.

Ohio Conference.—Charles Elliott, William H. Raper, Edmund W. Sehon, Joseph M. Trimble, James B. Finley, Leonidas L. Hamline, Zechariah Connell, John Ferree.

North Ohio Conference.—Edward Thompson, John H. Power, Adam Poe, Elmore Yocum, William Runnells.

Michigan Conference.—George Smith, Elijah Crane, Alvan Billings, John A. Baughman.

Indiana Conference.—Matthew Simpson, Allen Wiley, E. R. Ames, John Miller, Calvin W. Ruter, Aaron Wood, Augustus Eddy, James Havens.

Rock River Conference.—Bartholomew Weed, John Sinclair, Henry W. Reed, John T. Mitchell.

Illinois Conference.—Peter Akers, Peter Cartwright, Jonathan Stamper, John Vancleve, Newton G. Berryman.

Missouri Conference.—William W. Redman, William Patton, Jerome C. Berryman, James M. Jameson.

Kentucky Conference.—Henry B. Bascom, William Gunn, Hubbard H. Kavanaugh, Edward Stevenson, Benjamin T. Crouch, George W. Brush.

Holston Conference.—Elbert F. Sevier, Samuel Patton, Thomas Stringfield.

Tennessee Conference.—Robert Paine, John B. McFerrin, A. L. P. Green, Thomas Maddin.

Memphis Conference.—George W. D. Harris, Samuel S. Moody, Wm. McMahon, Thomas Joyner.

Arkansas Conference.—John C. Parker, William P. Ratcliffe, Andrew Hunter.

Texas Conference.—Littleton Fowler, John Clark.

Mississippi Conference.—William Winans, Benjamin M. Drake, John Lane, Green M. Rogers.

Alabama Conference.—Jesse Boring, Jefferson Hamilton, William Murrah, Greenbury Garrett.

Georgia Conference.—George F. Pierce, William J. Parks, Lovick Pierce, John W. Glenn, James E. Evans, A. B. Longstreet.

South Carolina Conference.—William Capers, William M. Wightman, Charles Betts, Samuel Dunwody, Hugh A. C. Walker.

North Carolina Conference.—James Jameson, Peter Doub, Bennett T. Blake.

Virginia Conference.—John Early, Thomas Crowder, William A. Smith, Leroy M. Lee.

Baltimore Conference.—Henry Slicer, John A. Collins, John Davis, Alfred Griffith, John A. Gere, John Bear, Nicholas J. B. Morgan, Thomas B. Sargent, Charles B. Tippett, George Hildt.

Philadelphia Conference.—John P. Durbin, Thomas J. Thompson, Henry White, Ignatius T. Cooper, Levi Scott, William Cooper.

New Jersey Conference.—Isaac Winner, John S. Porter, John K. Shaw, Thomas Neal, Thomas Sovereign.

B.

ACTION OF THE SOUTHERN CONFERENCES IN REGARD TO THE DIVISION OF THE CHURCH.

KENTUCKY CONFERENCE.

THE committee to whom was referred the subject of the division of the Church into two separate General Conference jurisdictions and kindred subjects, have had the same under serious consideration, and beg leave to report:

That, enlightened as the Conference is presumed to be on the merits of the very important subject upon which your committee have been called to act, it was not deemed expedient to delay this report by an elaborate and argumentative investigation of the matters committed to them, in their various relations, principles, and bearings; they, therefore, present the result of their deliberations to the Conference by offering for adoption the following resolutions:

1. *Resolved*, That it is the deliberate judgment of this Conference that the action of the late General Conference, virtually deposing Bishop Andrew, and also their action in confirming the decision of the Baltimore Conference, in the case of the Rev. F. A. Harding, are not sustained by the Discipline of our Church, and that we consider those proceedings as constituting a highly dangerous precedent.

2. *Resolved*, That we deeply regret the prospect of division growing out of these proceedings, and that we do most sincerely hope and pray that some effectual means, not inconsistent with the interests and honor of all concerned, may be suggested and devised by which so great a calamity may be averted, and to this end we recommend that our societies be freely consulted on the subject.

3. *Resolved*, That we approve the holding of a Convention of delegates from the Conferences in the slaveholding States in the city

of Louisville, on the first day of May next, agreeably to the recommendation of the Southern and South-western delegates in the late General Conference; and that the ratio of representation proposed by said delegates—to wit, one delegate for every eleven members of Conference—be, and the same is hereby, adopted; and that this Conference will elect delegates to the proposed Convention upon said basis.

4. *Resolved,* That should a division be found to be indispensable, the delegates of this Conference are hereby required to act under the following instructions, to wit: that the Southern and South-western Conferences shall not be regarded as a secession from the Methodist Episcopal Church, but that they shall be recognized in law, and to all intents and purposes, as a coördinate branch of the Methodist Episcopal Church in the United States of America, simply acting under a separate jurisdiction. And farther, that being well satisfied with the Discipline of the Church as it is, this Conference instruct its delegates not to support or favor any change in said Discipline by said Convention.

5. *Resolved,* That unless we can be assured that the rights of our ministry and membership can be effectually secured according to Discipline, against future aggressions, and reparation be made for past injury, we shall deem the contemplated division unavoidable.

6. *Resolved,* That we approve the course of our delegates in the late General Conference in the premises, and that we tender them our thanks for their faithful and independent discharge of duty in a trying crisis.

7. *Resolved,* That the Secretary of this Conference be directed to have these resolutions published in such of our Church-papers as may be willing to insert them.

All of which is respectfully submitted.

M. M. HENKLE, *Chairman.*

FARTHER ACTION IN REFERENCE TO THE CONTEMPLATED CONVENTION.

Resolved, by the Kentucky Annual Conference, That should the proposed Convention, representing the Annual Conferences of the Methodist Episcopal Church in the slaveholding States, appointed to assemble in the city of Louisville, the first of May, 1845, proceed to a separate organization, as contingently provided for in the resolutions of this body on yesterday, then, and in that event, the Convention shall be regarded as the regular General Conference, authorized and appointed by the several Annual Conferences of the Southern division of the Church, and as possessing all the rights, powers, and privileges of the General Conference of the Methodist Episcopal Church in the United States, and subject to the same restrictions, limitations, and restraints.

Resolved, That in order to secure the constitutional character and action of the Convention as a General Conference proper, should a separate organization take place, the ratio of representation as now found in the second restrictive rule, one for every twenty-one, shall prevail and determine the number of constitutional delegates, taking and accrediting as such the proper number from each Annual Conference first elected in order, and that the supernumerary delegates be regarded as members of the Convention to deliberate, etc., but not members of the General Conference proper, should the Convention proceed to a separate organization in the South. *Provided,* nevertheless, that should any delegate or delegates, who would not be excluded from the General Conference proper, by the operation of the above regulation be absent, then any delegate or delegates present, not admitted by said regulation as member or members of the constitutional General Conference, may lawfully take the seat or seats of such absent delegates, upon the principle of the selection named above.

Resolved, by the Kentucky Annual Conference, That we respectfully invite the Bishops of the Methodist Episcopal Church, who may feel themselves disposed to do so, to be in attendance at the contemplated Convention, to be held in the city of Louisville, Ky., in May, 1845.

Resolved, by the Kentucky Annual Conference, That we appoint the Friday immediately preceding the day fixed for the meeting of the proposed General Convention of the delegates of the Conferences, as a day of fasting and prayer for the blessing of Almighty God on the said Convention.

MISSOURI CONFERENCE.

The committee to whom was referred the subject of a division of the Church into two separate General Conference jurisdictions, together with the causes and circumstances connected with the same, have bestowed upon it, in the most prayerful and religious manner, all the time and attention they could command for the purpose, and beg leave to present the following as their report:

That, inasmuch as the Conference is presumed to be well informed on the merits of the very important subject upon which the committee has been called to act, it was not deemed necessary to delay this report by an extended and argumentative investigation of the matters committed to them, in their various relations, principles, and bearings; they would, therefore, present the result of their deliberations to the Conference by offering for adoption the following resolutions:

Resolved, That we have looked for many years with painful apprehension and disapproval upon the agitation of the slavery and abolition subject in our General Conference, and now behold with sorrow and regret the disastrous results which it has brought about.

Resolved, That while we accord to the great majority of our Northern brethren the utmost purity of intention, and while we would carefully refrain from all harsh denunciations, we are compelled to pronounce the proceedings of the late General Conference against Bishop Andrew extrajudicial and oppressive.

Resolved, That we deeply regret the prospect of separation growing out of these proceedings, and that we do most sincerely hope and pray that some effectual means, not inconsistent with the interests and honor of all concerned, may be suggested and devised by which so great a calamity may be averted; and to this end we recommend that our societies be freely consulted on this subject.

Resolved, That we approve the holding of a Convention of delegates from the Conferences in the slaveholding States, in the city of Louisville, Ky., on the first day of May next, agreeably to the recommendation of the delegates from the Southern and South-western Conferences, in the late General Conference; and that the ratio of representation proposed by said delegates—to wit, one delegate for every eleven members of the Conference—be, and the same is hereby, adopted; and that this Conference will elect delegates to the proposed Convention upon said basis.

Resolved, That our delegates act under the following instructions, to wit: to oppose the division of the Church, unless such division, under all the circumstances of the case, be found to be indispensable (and consequently unavoidable); and should such necessity be found to exist, and the division be determined on, then and in that event, that the Southern and South-western Conferences shall not be regarded as a secession from the Methodist Episcopal Church, but that they shall be recognized in law, and to all intents and purposes, as a coördinate branch of the Methodist Episcopal Church in the United States of America, simply acting under a separate jurisdiction. And farther, that being well satisfied with the Discipline of the Church as it is, this Conference instruct its delegates not to support or favor any change in said Discipline by said Convention.

Resolved, That unless we can be assured that the rights of our ministry and membership can be effectually secured according to the Discipline, against future aggressions, we shall deem the contemplated division as unavoidable.

Resolved, That should the proposed Convention, representing the Annual Conferences of the Methodist Episcopal Church in the slaveholding States, appointed to assemble at the city of Louisville, Ky., the first of May, 1845, proceed to a separate organization, as contingently provided for in the foregoing resolutions, then, in that event, the Convention shall be regarded as the regular General Conference, authorized and appointed by the several Annual Conferences of the Southern division of the Church, and as possessing all the rights, powers, and privileges of the General Conference of the Methodist Episcopal Church in the United States of America, and subject to the same restrictions, limitations, and restraints.

Resolved, That in order to secure the constitutional character and action of the Convention as a General Conference proper, should a separate organization take place, the ratio of representation as now found in the second restrictive rule, one for every twenty-one, shall prevail and determine the constitutional delegates, taking and accrediting as such the proper number from each Annual Conference, first elected in order, and that the supernumerary delegates be regarded as members of the Convention to deliberate, but not members of the General Conference proper, should the Convention proceed to a separate organization in the South. *Provided*, nevertheless, that should any delegate or delegates who would not be excluded from the General Conference proper, by the operation of the above regulation, be absent, then any delegate or delegates present, not admitted by said regulations as a member or members of the constitutional General Conference, may lawfully take the seat or seats of such absent delegates, upon the principle of selection named above.

Resolved, That we have read with deep regret the violent proceedings of some of our Southern brethren, in their primary meetings, against some of our Bishops and others; and that we do most cordially invite to our pulpits and firesides all our Bishops and Northern brethren who, in the event of a division, shall belong to the Northern Methodist Episcopal Church.

Resolved, That the preachers shall take up public collections in all their circuits and stations, some time before the first day of March next, for the purpose of defraying the expenses of the delegates to the above-named Convention, and pay over the same to the delegates, or the respective Presiding Elders, so that the delegates may receive the same before starting to the Convention.

WM. PATTON,	E. PERKINS,
ANDREW MONROE,	T. W. CHANDLER,
J. BOYLE,	JAS. G. T. DUNLEAVY,
W. W. REDMAN,	JOHN THATCHER.
JOHN GLANNVILLE,	

The following resolutions were offered, and immediately adopted by the Conference:

Resolved, That we approve the course of our delegates in their action at the late General Conference, in the case of Bishop Andrew, and the part they took in the subsequent acts of the Southern delegates, growing out of the proceedings of the majority, and they are hereby entitled to our hearty thanks for their manly course in a trying crisis.

Resolved, That we invite the Bishops of our Church, who may feel free to do so, and they are hereby invited, to attend the contemplated Convention at Louisville, Ky.

J. H. LINN,
R. BOYD.

HOLSTON CONFERENCE.

The committee to whom was referred the subject of Church-separation and other matters connected therewith, would respectfully submit the following report:

In common with our brethren all over our widely-extended Zion, our hearts are exceedingly pained at the prospect of disunion, growing out of the action of the late General Conference in the case of Bishop Andrew. Your committee believe this action to be extrajudicial, and forming a highly dangerous precedent. The aspect of affairs at the close of the General Conference was indeed gloomy; and while we have sought for light from every possible source, we cannot believe that our Church-papers are the true exponents of the views and feelings of the whole South, or of the whole North. We would respect the opinions of our brethren everywhere, but we feel that we shall not be doing justice to ourselves, the Church, or the world, if we do not express independently and in the fear of God, our own sentiments on this important subject. We are not prepared to see the Church of our love and choice, which has been so signally blessed of God, and cherished by the tears, prayers, and untiring efforts of our fathers, lacerated and torn asunder, without one more effort to bind up and heal her bleeding wounds; therefore,

Resolved, That we approve of the proposed Convention to be holden at Louisville, Ky., May 1st, 1845; and will elect delegates to said Convention, according to the ratio agreed upon at the last General Conference by the Southern delegates.

Resolved, That the Conferences in the non-slaveholding States and Territories be, and they are hereby respectfully requested to elect one delegate from each Annual Conference (either in Conference capacity or by the Presiding Elders), to meet with one delegate from each of the slaveholding Conferences, in the city of Louisville, Ky., on the first day of May, 1845, to devise some plan of compromise. And in the event that the non-slaveholding Conferences, or any number of them, which, with the slaveholding Conferences, shall make a respectable majority of all the Annual Conferences, shall so elect delegates; then, and in that case, the delegates which we will elect from this Conference to the Louisville Convention, shall appoint one of their number on said Committee of Compromise. And the Southern and South-western Conferences are respectfully requested to agree to and act upon this plan.

Resolved, That if nothing can be effected on the foregoing plan, then the delegates from this Conference are instructed to propose to the Louisville Convention the following or some similar plan, as the basis of connection between the two General Conferences, proposed in case of separate organization: The said General Conferences shall appoint an equal number of delegates (say ten), who shall meet together in the interim of the General Conferences, to whom shall be referred for adjustment all matters of difference between the two General Conferences, or those Churches over which they exercise jurisdiction, their decisions or propositions for adjustment to be referred for ultimate action to the General Conferences before mentioned; and when both General Conferences have confirmed their decision, it shall be final and binding on both parties.

Resolved, That if both the foregoing propositions should fail, then the delegates from this Conference are instructed to support the Plan of Separation proposed by the late General Conference. And in so doing, we positively disavow secession, but declare ourselves, by the act of the General Conference, a coördinate branch of the Methodist Episcopal Church. And in the event of either the second or third proposition obtaining, the delegates from this Conference are instructed not to favor any—even the least—alteration of our excellent Book of Discipline, except in so far as may be necessary to form a separate organization.

Resolved, That our delegates to the late General Conference merit the warmest expression of our thanks, for their prudent, yet firm, course in sustaining the interests of our beloved Methodism in the South.

Resolved, That we warmly commend the truly Christian and impartial course of our Bishops at the late General Conference, and we affectionately invite all our Superintendents to attend the Convention to be holden at Louisville, Ky.

All which is respectfully submitted,

T. SULLINS,
E. E. WILEY,
C. FULTON,
JAS. CUMMING,
T. K. CATLETT,
A. H. MATHES,
DAVID FLEMING,
R. M. STEVENS,
O. F. CUNNINGHAM.

TENNESSEE CONFERENCE.

The committee to whom was referred the proposed division of the Methodist Episcopal Church into two separate and distinct General Conference jurisdictions, and kindred subjects, having had the same under mature consideration, beg leave to submit the following:

Apprised, as we are, that the actions of the late General Conference, together with the entire merits of the proceedings of that body, leading to the contemplated separation of the Church, have been fully and fairly presented to our people, and that both the ministry and membership within our bounds have, with great solicitude and prayerful anxiety, investigated the subject in its various relations, principles, and bearings, we deem it entirely inexpedient at present to enter into detail or to prepare an elaborate investigation of the very important matters committed to us; therefore your committee present the result of their deliberations to the Conference by the offering for your consideration and adoption the following resolutions:

1. *Resolved*, That it is the candid and deliberate judgment of this Conference that the action of the late General Conference, by which Bishop Andrew was virtually deposed, as well as their action in confirming the decision of the Baltimore Conference in the case of the Rev. F. A. Harding, is not sustained by the Discipline of our Church, and that we consider such extrajudicial proceeding as constituting a highly dangerous precedent.

2. That under the great affliction caused by these unfortunate pro-

ceedings, we did most ardently hope and pray that the calamitous consequences might have been averted. But since the only plausible plan of reconciliation, the proposition unanimously recommended by our beloved Superintendents, was put down by the majority in the late General Conference, we honestly confess we see at present no prospect to avoid a separation.

3. That we approve the holding a Convention of delegates from all the Conferences in the slaveholding States, in the city of Louisville, on the first day of May next, agreeably to the recommendation of the Southern and South-western delegates in the late General Conference; and that the ratio of representation proposed by said delegates—to wit, one delegate for every eleven members of Conference—be, and the same is hereby adopted; and this Conference will elect delegates to the proposed Convention upon said basis.

4. That should a division be found to be indispensable, the delegates of this Conference are required to act under the following instruction, to wit: that the Southern and South-western Conferences shall not be regarded as a secession from the Methodist Episcopal Church, but that they shall be recognized in law, and to all intents and purposes, as a coördinate branch of the Methodist Episcopal Church in the United States of America, simply acting under a separate jurisdiction. And farthermore, as we are well satisfied with the Discipline of our Church as it is, this Conference instruct its delegates not to support or favor any change in said Discipline by said Convention, except in so far as may be necessary to conform it in its economical arrangements to the new organization.

5. That unless we can be well assured that the rights of our ministry and membership can be effectually secured according to Discipline against future aggression, and full reparation be made for past injury, we shall deem the contemplated division unavoidable.

6. That should the proposed Convention, representing the Annual Conferences of the Methodist Episcopal Church in the slaveholding States, appointed to assemble in the city of Louisville, the first of May next, proceed to a separate organization, as contingently provided for in the foregoing resolutions, then and in that event the Convention shall be regarded as the regular General Conference, authorized and appointed by the several Annual Conferences of the Southern division of the Church in the United States, and as possessing all the rights and privileges of the General Conference of the Methodist Episcopal Church in the United States of America, and subject to the same constitutional limitations and restrictions.

7. That in order to secure the constitutional character and action of the Convention, as a General Conference proper, should a separate organization take place, the ratio of representation, as now found in the second restrictive rule, one for every twenty-one, shall prevail and determine the number of constitutional delegates, taking and accrediting as such the proper number from the Annual Conference first elected in order; and that the supernumerary delegates be regarded as members of the Convention to deliberate, but not members of the General Conference proper, should the Convention proceed to a separate organization in the South. *Provided*, nevertheless, that should any delegate or delegates, who would not be excluded from the General Conference proper, by the operation of the above regulation, be absent, then any delegate or delegates present, not admitted by said regulation as member or members of the constitutional General Conference, may lawfully take the seat or seats of such absent delegates, upon the principle of selection named above.

8. That we do most cordially approve the course of our delegates in the late General Conference, in the premises, and that we tender them our sincere thanks for their faithful and independent discharge of duty in a trying crisis.

9. That the Secretary of this Conference be directed to have the foregoing preamble and resolutions published in the South-western Christian Advocate.

All which is respectfully submitted,

JOSHUA BOUCHER,
G. W. DYE,
W. D. F. SAWRIE,
A. F. DRISKILL,
F. E. PITTS,
F. G. FERGUSON,
P. P. NEELY,
JNO. W. HANNER,
R. L. ANDREWS.

MEMPHIS CONFERENCE.

The committee to whom was referred the subject of the division of the Church into two separate General Conference jurisdictions, and all matters connected therewith, after solemnly and prayerfully deliberating upon the same, present the following report. Inasmuch as the Conference is presumed to be well informed on the merits of the subject, we deem it unnecessary to consume time by entering into an extended and argumentative investigation of the various relations, principles, and bearings of the same, but proceed at once to offer the following resolutions for the action of the Conference.

Resolved, 1. That it is the deliberate judgment of this Conference, that the action of the late General Conference of the Methodist

Episcopal Church, virtually deposing Bishop Andrew, and also their action in affirming the decision of the Baltimore Annual Conference in the case of the Rev. F. A. Harding, are not sustained by the Discipline of our Church, and that we consider these proceedings as constituting a highly dangerous precedent.

2. That we deeply regret the prospect of division growing out of these proceedings, and do most sincerely and devoutly pray to the great Head of the Church that some effectual means, not inconsistent with the interests of the cause of Christ, or the honor of all concerned, may be suggested and devised, by which so great a calamity may be averted, and our long-cherished union preserved and perpetuated.

3. That we approve the holding a Convention of delegates from the Conferences in the slaveholding States, in the city of Louisville, Ky., on the first day of May next, agreeably to the recommendation of the Southern and South-western delegates in the late General Conference; and that the ratio of representation proposed by said delegates—to wit, one delegate for every eleven members of Conference—be, and the same is hereby adopted; and that this Conference will elect delegates to the proposed Convention on said basis.

4. That should a division be found to be indispensable, the delegates of this Conference are hereby required to act under the following instructions, to wit: That the Southern and South-western Conferences shall not be regarded as having, by such division, *seceded* from the Methodist Episcopal Church; but they shall be recognized in law, and to all intents and purposes, as a coördinate branch of the Methodist Episcopal Church in the United States of America, simply acting under a separate jurisdiction. And farther, that being well satisfied with the Discipline of the Church as it now is, this Conference instructs its delegates not to support or favor any change in said Discipline, by said Convention, only so far as necessary to perfect a Southern Organization.

5. That unless we can be assured that the rights of our ministry and membership will be effectually secured, according to Discipline, against future aggressions, and full reparation be made for past injury, we shall deem the contemplated division unavoidable.

6. That should the proposed Convention, representing the Annual Conferences of the Methodist Episcopal Church in the slaveholding States, appointed to assemble at the city of Louisville, on the first day of May, 1845, proceed to a separate organization, as contingently

provided for in the foregoing resolutions; then, and in that event, the Convention shall be regarded as the regular General Conference, authorized and appointed by the several Annual Conferences of the Southern division of the Church, and as possessing all the rights, powers, and privileges of the General Conference of the Methodist Episcopal Church in the United States of America, and subject to the same restrictions, limitations, and restraints.

7. That in order to secure the constitutional character and action of the Convention as a General Conference proper, should a separate organization take place, the ratio of representation, as it now stands in the second restrictive rule, one for every twenty-one, shall prevail and determine the constitutional delegates, taking as such the proper number from each Annual Conference, first elected in order, and that the remaining delegates be regarded as members of the Convention to deliberate, but not members of the General Conference proper, should the Convention proceed to a separate organization in the South. *Provided*, nevertheless, that should any delegate or delegates who would not be excluded from the General Conference proper, by the operation of the foregoing regulation, be absent, then, any delegate or delegates present, not admitted by said regulation as a member or members of the constitutional General Conference, may lawfully take the seat or seats of such absent delegates upon the principles of selection before named.

8. That we have witnessed with sorrow and disapprobation alike, the violence manifested by some at the South, and the ultraism displayed by others at the North, and that we regret exceedingly that any Annual Conference should have deemed it necessary to refuse to concur in the recommendation of the late General Conference to alter the sixth restrictive article; nevertheless, we shall entertain for our brethren of the North the feelings of Christian kindness and brotherly love.

9. That we heartily approve the entire course pursued by our delegates at the late General Conference.

10. That we cordially invite such of our Bishops, as may deem it proper, to be present at the contemplated Convention in Louisville.

11. That it be made the duty of each preacher to take up a public collection in every congregation under his charge, for the purpose of defraying the expenses of the delegates to the Convention, and that such collections be taken up previous to the first Sabbath in April next, and immediately transmitted to some one of the delegates.

And that the delegates be required to report to the next Annual Conference the sums received by them for this purpose, together with the amount expended by them in attending said Convention.

12. That the Secretary of this Conference be instructed to forward the foregoing to the South-western Christian Advocate for publication, with a request that all other Church-papers copy.

Moses Brock,
Thomas Smith,
J. T. Baskerville,
B. H. Hubbard,
A. T. Scruggs,
Joseph Travis,
M. J. Blackwell,
D. J. Allen,
William Pearson.

MISSISSIPPI CONFERENCE.

The committee to whom was referred the subject of the contemplated division of the Methodist Episcopal Church, have endeavored to examine the subject carefully, and in a spirit of reliance upon the teachings of the word of God for direction.

Your committee can but deplore the existence of such causes as compel the Church of our choice to meditate a severance of that union which has so long existed, and which, under God, has contributed so efficiently to the spread of scriptural holiness through these lands. But we are fully convinced that justice to ourselves, as well as compassion for the slaves, demand an unqualified disapproval of the action of the late General Conference; first, in confirming the decision of the Baltimore Conference in the case of Rev. F. A. Harding; and secondly, in virtually suspending Bishop Andrew from the Episcopacy, not only without law or usage, but in direct contravention of all law, and in defiance of a resolution adopted by the General Conference of 1840, which provides "that under the provisional exception of the general rule of the Church on the subject of slavery, the simple holding of slaves, or mere ownership of slave-property, in the States or Territories where the laws do not admit of emancipation and permit the liberated slave to enjoy freedom, constitutes no legal barrier to the election or ordination of ministers to the various grades of office known in the ministry of the Methodist Episcopal Church, and cannot, therefore, be considered as operating any forfeiture of right in view of such election and ordination."

With the abstract question of slavery we are not now concerned, nor do we regard it as a subject on which the Church has a right to legislate; neither are we disposed in this report to state the full extent of our grievances, or to investigate the reasons which impose upon us the necessity of planning an amicable separation. Your committee deeply regret the injury which may be inflicted upon our beloved Zion by the intemperate and unjust denunciation of the *whole North* by those who have occasion to complain of the illegal and oppressive course pursued by the majority of the late General Conference, and most earnestly recommend the exercise of that charity which "suffereth long and is kind." As the result of our prayerful examination of the subject in all its bearings, we offer the following resolutions for your consideration and adoption:

Resolved, 1. That the decision of the late General Conference in the cases of Rev. F. A. Harding and Bishop Andrew, was unauthorized by the Discipline of the Methodist Episcopal Church, and that a tame submission to them, upon the part of the Church in the slave-holding States, would prevent our access to the slaves, and expose us to suspicions destructive to our general usefulness.

Resolved, 2. That as no authorized plan of compromise has been suggested by the North, and as all the propositions made by the Southern delegates were rejected, we regard a separation as inevitable, and approve the holding of a Convention, to meet in Louisville, Ky., on the first day of May next, agreeably to the recommendation of the Southern and South-western delegates to the late General Conference; and that the ratio of representation proposed by said delegates—to wit, one delegate for every eleven members of the Annual Conferences—be, and the same is hereby adopted; and that this Conference will elect delegates to the proposed Convention upon said basis. *Provided*, however, that if, in the providence of God, any plan of compromise which, in the judgment of our delegates, will redress our grievances and effectually secure to us the full exercise and peaceable enjoyment of all our Disciplinary rights should be proposed in time to prevent disunion, we will joyfully embrace it.

Resolved, 3. That our delegates to said Convention shall be empowered to coöperate with the delegates to said Convention from the other Conferences, in adopting such measures as they shall deem necessary for the complete organization of a Southern Church, provided that it conform in all its essential features to the Discipline of the Methodist Episcopal Church.

Resolved, 4. That the course pursued by our immediate representatives in the late General Conference, was and is approved by us.

Resolved, 5. That the conciliatory spirit evinced by our General Superintendents entitles them to the unqualified approbation of the whole Church, and that we do most cordially invite them to attend the proposed Convention.

All of which is respectfully submitted,

Wm. H. Watkins,
B. Pipkin,
Jno. N. Hamill,
David M. Wiggins,
D. O. Shattuck,
Jno. G. Jones,
L. Campbell,
A. T. M. Fly,
W. G. Gould.

ARKANSAS CONFERENCE.

The committee to whom was referred the several subjects connected with the prospective division of the Methodist Episcopal Church, have had the same under calm and prayerful consideration, and beg leave to present the following as the result of their honest deliberations:

Being well convinced that the members of this body have not been inattentive to the proceedings of the late General Conference, and that they have not failed to derive some information from the numerous addresses and communications that have appeared in our periodicals, your committee have not been disposed to waste their time, nor insult your judgments, by detailing the many circumstances which, were you differently situated, would require amplification; they, therefore, present to your minds, for consideration and action, the subjoined resolutions:

1. *Resolved*, That it is the decided opinion of this Conference that the Discipline of the Methodist Episcopal Church does not sustain the action of the late General Conference in the cases of Rev. F. A. Harding and Bishop Andrew.

2. *Resolved*, That we approve the suggestions of the Bishops, as well as the request of several Southern delegates, which contemplated the postponing of the action of the General Conference, until the wishes of the whole Church could be consulted.

3. *Resolved*, That, as we see no probability that reparation will be made for past injuries, and no security given that the rights and privileges of the ministry and membership in the slaveholding Conferences will be equally respected, we believe it is the imperative duty, if not the only alternative, of the South to form a separate organization. Nevertheless, should honorable and satisfactory propositions for pacification be made by the North, we shall expect our delegates to favor the perpetuation of the union.

4. *Resolved*, That we approve the holding of a Convention of delegates from the Conferences in the slaveholding States, in the city of

Louisville, Ky., on the first day of May, 1845, agreeably to the recommendation of the delegates from the Southern and South-western Conferences in the late General Conference.

5. *Resolved*, That should the proposed Convention, representing the Methodist Episcopal Church in the slaveholding States, appointed to assemble at Louisville, Ky., the first day of May, 1845, proceed to a separate organization, as contingently provided for in the foregoing resolutions, then, in that event, the Convention shall be regarded as the regular General Conference, authorized and appointed by the several Annual Conferences in the Southern division of the Church, and as possessing all the rights, powers, and privileges of the General Conference of the Methodist Episcopal Church in the United States of America, and subject to the same restrictions, limitations, and restraints.

6. *Resolved*, That in order to secure the constitutional character and action of the Convention as a General Conference proper, should a separate organization take place, the ratio of representation, as now found in the second restrictive rule, one for every twenty-one, shall prevail and determine the constitutional delegates, taking and accrediting as such the proper number from each Annual Conference, first elected in order; and that the supernumerary delegates be regarded as members of the Convention to deliberate, but not members of the General Conference proper, should the Convention proceed to a separate organization in the South. *Provided*, nevertheless, that should any delegate or delegates, who would not be excluded from the General Conference proper by the operation of the above regulation, be absent, then any delegate or delegates present, not admitted by said regulation as a member or members of the constitutional General Conference, may lawfully take the seats of such absent delegates, upon the principle of selection named above.

7. *Resolved*, That, as we are well satisfied with the Discipline of the Methodist Episcopal Church as it is, we hereby instruct our delegates to said Convention not to favor any change therein.

8. *Resolved*, That, though we feel ourselves aggrieved, and have been wounded, *without cause*, in the house of our friends, we have no disposition to impute wrong motives to the majority in the late General Conference, and no inclination to indorse those vindictive proceedings had in some portions of the South, believing it to be the duty of Christians, under all circumstances, to exercise that *charity* which *beareth all things*.

9. *Resolved*, That the preachers take up collections on their several

circuits and stations at an early period, and hand the money collected to their Presiding Elders, that the delegates may receive the whole amount collected before they shall be required to start for Louisville.

10. *Resolved*, That we tender our warmest thanks to our representatives in the late General Conference for the stand which they took, with others, in defense of our disciplinary rights.

11. *Resolved*, That the Bishops generally be, and they hereby are requested, if it be congenial with their feelings, to attend the Convention at Louisville.

12. *Resolved*, That we recommend to our people the observance of the first of May next as a day of humiliation and prayer, that the divine presence may attend the deliberations of the Convention.

JOHN HARRELL, FOUNTAIN BROWN,
J. B. ANNIS, JACOB CUSTER,
ALEXANDER AVERY, J. F. TRUSLOW.

VIRGINIA CONFERENCE.

The committee to whom was referred the resolutions of the late General Conference, recommending to all the Annual Conferences at their first approaching sessions to authorize a change of the sixth restrictive article, so that the first clause shall read, "They shall not appropriate the produce of the Book Concern nor of the Chartered Fund to any purpose other than the traveling, supernumerary, superannuated, and worn-out preachers, their wives, widows, and children, and to such other purposes as may be determined on by the votes of two-thirds of the members of the General Conference," and to whom was also referred the Address of the Southern delegates in the late General Conference, recommending a Southern Convention, to be held in Louisville, Ky., on the first day of May, 1845, together with the proceedings of various primary and Quarterly Conference meetings within the bounds of the Virginia Conference on the subject of a separation from the ecclesiastical jurisdiction of the General Conference of the Methodist Episcopal Church, beg leave to report:

That, having maturely considered these subjects, they do not deem it necessary to present an argument upon the various topics submitted to them; but that the duty assigned them will probably be more satisfactorily accomplished in the following series of resolutions, viz.:

Resolved, 1. That we concur in the recommendation of the late General Conference to change the sixth restrictive article of the Discipline of our Church.

Resolved, 2. That from the ample sources of information before your committee in numerous primary meetings which have been held in various charges within our pastoral limits, and the proceedings of Quarterly-meeting Conferences, which we have the most sufficient reason to regard as a fair and full exponent of the mind and will of the membership upon the subject of the action of the recent General Conference, and the propriety of division, we are of opinion that it is the mind of the laity of the Church, with no exception sufficient to be regarded as the basis of action, that whilst they seriously deprecate division, considered relatively, and most earnestly wish that some ground of permanent union could have been found, they see no alternative, and therefore approve of a peaceable separation in the present circumstances of our condition; and in *this opinion* and *this determination* your committee unanimously concur.

Resolved, 3. That we concur in the recommendation of the Southern delegates in the late General Conference, that there be a Southern Convention, to be held in Louisville, Ky., on the first day of May, 1845; and *in the objects of this Convention, as is contemplated in the Address of the Southern delegates.*

Resolved, 4. That while we do not propose to dissolve our connection with the Methodist Episcopal Church, but only *with the General Conference* of the Methodist Episcopal Church, we are, therefore, entitled to our full portion of all the rights and privileges appertaining to the property of the Church. Nevertheless, our delegates to the Convention to be held in Louisville, Ky., in May, 1845, are hereby instructed not to allow the question of property to enter into the calculation whether or not we shall exist as a separate organization.

Resolved, 5. That the action of the late General Conference in the case of Bishop Andrew was in violation of the provisional rule of the Discipline on the subject of slavery, and in derogation of the dignity and authority of the Episcopal office; it was, therefore, equally opposed to the rights of the Southern portion of the Church, and of those of the incumbents of the Episcopal office. But more than this: it was an effort to accomplish, by legislative action, what it was only competent for them to do, *if at all*, by regular judicial process; the very attempt was an acknowledgment that there was no rule of Discipline under which he could either be deposed or censured, and that the General Conference, being unrestrained by the authority of law, was supreme. Thus both the Episcopal office and its incumbents were taken from under the protection of the constitutional restriction, and the provisional rule of Discipline, by which it was made a coördinate branch of the government, and placed at the caprice of a majority, which claims that its mere will is the law of the Church.

Bishop Andrew, therefore, in refusing to resign his office, or otherwise yield to this unwarranted assumption of authority on the part of the General Conference, has taken a noble stand upon the platform of constitutional law, in defense of the Episcopal office and the rights of the South, which entitles him to the cordial approbation and support of every friend of the Church; and we hereby tender him the unanimous expression of our admiration of his firmness in resisting the misrule of a popular majority.

Resolved, 6. That we cordially approve the course of the Southern and South-western delegates of the late General Conference, in resisting with so much constancy and firmness the encroachments of the majority upon the rights of the South; and for so faithfully warning them against the tendency of those measures, which we fear do inevitably draw after them the dissolution of our ecclesiastical union.

JOHN EARLY,	THOMAS CROWDER, JR.,
WM. A. SMITH,	ABRAM PENN,
GEO. W. NOLLEY,	ANTHONY DIBRELL,
H. B. COWLES,	D. S. DOGGETT.
JOS. H. DAVIS,	

The recommendation to change the sixth restrictive article was concurred in—eighty-one in favor, and none against it—and the whole Report of the committee was unanimously adopted by the Conference.

NORTH CAROLINA CONFERENCE.

The committee to whom the resolution of the late General Conference respecting the alteration of the sixth restrictive rule, the Report of the Select Committee of Nine on the Declaration of the Southern delegates, and the Reports of numerous voluntary meetings, both of ministers and people, within the bounds of North Carolina Conference, were referred, beg leave to report:

Your committee deeply regret the division of the Methodist Episcopal Church, which the course of the majority in the late General Conference renders not only necessary but inevitable. The unity of the Church, so long the boast and praise of Methodism, was a feature greatly admired, and more than esteemed, by Southern Methodists. For its promotion and preservation they were willing to surrender any thing but principle—vital principle. *This* they could not do! *this* they dare not do! The course of the late General Conference demanded a submission on the part of the ministers in the slaveholding Conferences, which the Discipline did not require, and the institutions of the South absolutely forbade. To have yielded, therefore, would have opened a breach in Methodism wholly subversive of the Church and greatly mischievous to the civil community—to have yielded would have been ruin. This, therefore, they *refused to do;* absolutely refused! With the Discipline in their hands, sustained and upheld by it, they protested against the proceedings of the majority, with an unfaltering and manly voice, declaring them to be not only unauthorized, but unconstitutional. The protestation, however, just and legal as it was, authorized and borne out by the Discipline, was altogether unavailing. Nothing was left for the South to do but to pass from under the jurisdiction of so wayward a power to the regulations and government of our old, wholesome, and scriptural Discipline. This, we sorrow when we say it, has opened a great gulf—we fear an impassable gulf—between the North and the South. This consolation, however, if no other, they have—the good Book of Discipline, containing the distinctive features of the Methodist Episcopal Church, shall still lie on the South side. Compelled by circumstances which could neither be alleviated nor controlled—which neither the entreaties of kindness nor the force of truth could successfully resist—we hesitate not to decide on being forever separate from those whom we not only esteem, but love. Better far that we should suffer the loss of union, than that thousands—yea, millions—of souls should perish.

From the reports of Quarterly-meeting Conferences, and numerous voluntary meetings within the bounds of the North Carolina Conference, both of ministers and people, we feel assured that it is the mind of our people and preachers fully to sustain the action of the Southern and South-western delegates, as set forth in the Declaration and Protest; and therefore,

1. *Resolved,* That the time has come for the ministers of the Methodist Episcopal Church in the slaveholding States to refuse to act in union with the North.

2. *Resolved,* That we concur in the proposed alteration of the sixth restrictive rule of the Discipline.

3. *Resolved,* That we concur in the recommendation to hold a Convention in Louisville, Ky., in May, 1845.

4. *Resolved*, That this Conference elect delegates to said Convention according to the basis of representation recommended.

5. *Resolved*, That the action of the late General Conference, in the case of Bishop Andrew, was a violation of the rule of Discipline on the subject of slavery, and derogatory to the dignity of the Episcopal office, by throwing it from under the protection of law, and exposing it to the reproach and obloquy of misrule and lawless power. The Bishop, therefore, acted justly and honorably in resisting such action and declining obedience to the resolution of said Conference; and for thus guarding and respecting the rights of the South, both of ministers and people, he is entitled to our highest regards.

All which is respectfully submitted.

S. S. Bryant, H. G. Leigh,
P. Doub, Jas. Jameson,
James Reid, Bennet T. Blake,
R. I. Carson, D. B. Nicholson,
Wm. Carter.

The above report was *unanimously* adopted by the Conference. On the question of concurrence in altering the sixth restrictive rule, the vote was—ayes 58, nays none.

SOUTH CAROLINA CONFERENCE.

The committee to whom was referred the general subject of the difficulties growing out of the action of the late General Conference on the case of Bishop Andrew and Brother Harding, and, in particular, the Report of the Select Committee on the Declaration of the Southern and South-western delegates of the General Conference, as adopted by the Conference, and the proceedings of numerous Quarterly Conferences, and other meetings, in all parts of our Annual Conference District, respectfully offer the following Report:

It appears to your committee, on the evidence of numerous documents, and the testimony of the preachers in open Conference, that in all the circuits and stations of this Conference District, the people have expressed their minds with respect to the action of the General Conference, and the measures proper to be adopted in consequence of that action. Resolutions to that effect have been adopted by the Quarterly Conferences of all the circuits and stations, without any exception; and in many, perhaps in most of them, by other meetings also, which have been called expressly for the purpose; and in some of them, by meetings held at every preaching-place where there was a society. And on all these occasions, there has been but one voice uttered—one opinion expressed—from the seaboard to the mountains, as to the unconstitutionality and injurious character of the action in the cases above named; the necessity which that action imposes for a separation of the Southern from the Northern Conferences, and the expediency and propriety of holding a Convention at Louisville, Ky., and of your sending delegates to it, agreeably to the proposition of the Southern and South-western delegates of the late General Conference.

Your committee also have made diligent inquiry, both out of Conference and by calling openly in Conference, for information from the preachers, as to the number, if any, of local preachers, or other official members, or members of some standing among us, who should have expressed, in the meetings or in private, a different opinion from that which the meetings have proclaimed. And the result of this inquiry has been, that, in the whole field of our Conference District, one individual only has been heard to express himself doubtfully as to the expediency of a separate jurisdiction for the Southern and South-western Conferences; not even one as to the character of the General Conference action. Nor does it appear that this unanimity of the people has been brought about by popular harangues, or any schismatic efforts of any of the preachers, or other influential persons; but that it has been as spontaneous as universal, and, from the time that the final action of the General Conference became known, at every place. Your committee state this fact thus formally, that it may correct certain libelous imputations which have been cast on some of our senior ministers, in the Christian Advocate and Journal; as well as for the evidence which it furnishes of the necessity of the measures which are in progress for the relief of the Church in the South and South-west.

Your committee also consider it due to state, that it does not appear that the action of the General Conference, in the cases of the Bishop and of Brother Harding, proceeded of ill-will, as of purpose to oppress us, nor of any intended disregard of the authority of the Scriptures or of the Discipline, as if to effect the designs of a politico-religious faction, without warrant of the Scriptures, and against the Discipline and the peace of the Church; but they consider that action as having been produced out of causes which had their origin in the fanatical abolitionism of Garrison and others; and which, being suffered to enter and agitate the Church, first in New England and afterward generally at the North, worked up such a revival of the antislavery spirit as had grown too strong for the restraints of either Scripture or Discipline, and too general through the Eastern, Northern, and North-western Conferences, to be resisted any longer by the easy, good-natured prudence of the brethren representing those Conferences in the late General Conference. Pressed beyond their strength, whether little or much, they had to give way; and, reduced (by the force of principles which, whether by their own fault or not, had obtained a controlling power) to the alternative of breaking up the Churches of their own Conference Districts, or adopting measures which they might hardly persuade themselves could be endured by the South and South-west, they determined on the latter. The best of men may have their judgments perverted; and it is not wonderful that, under such stress of circumstances, the majority should have adopted a new construction of both Scripture and Discipline, and persuaded themselves that in pacifying the abolitionists they were not unjust to their Southern brethren. Such, however, is unquestionably the character of the measures they adopted; and which the Southern Churches cannot possibly submit to, unless the majority who enacted them could also have brought us to a conviction that we ought to be bound by their judgment, against our consciences and calling of God, and the warrant of Scripture, and the provisions of the Discipline. But while we believe that our paramount duty in our calling of God positively forbids our yielding the gospel in the Southern States to the pacification of abolitionism in the Northern—and the conviction is strong and clear in our own minds that we have both the warrant of Scripture and the plain provisions of the Discipline to sustain us—we see no room to entertain any proposition for compromise, under the late action in the cases of Bishop Andrew and Brother Harding, and the principles avowed for the maintenance of that action, short of what has been shadowed forth in the Report of the Select Committee which we have had under consideration, and the measures recommended by the Southern and South-western delegates at their meeting after the General Conference had closed its session.

Your committee do, therefore, recommend the adoption of the following resolutions:

1. *Resolved*, That it is necessary for the Annual Conferences in the slaveholding States and Territories, and in Texas, to unite in a distinct ecclesiastical connection, agreeably to the provisions of the Report of the Select Committee of Nine of the late General Conference, adopted on the 8th day of June last.

2. *Resolved*, That we consider and esteem the adoption of the Re-

port of the aforesaid Committee of Nine by the General Conference (and the more for the unanimity with which it was adopted) as involving the most solemn pledge which could have been given by the majority to the minority, and the Churches represented by them, for the full and faithful execution of all the particulars specified and intended in that Report.

3. *Resolved*, That we approve of the recommendation of the Southern delegates, to hold a Convention in Louisville, on the first day of May next, and will elect delegates to the same on the ratio recommended in the Address of the delegates to their constituents.

4. *Resolved*, That we earnestly request the Bishops, one and all, to attend the said Convention.

5. *Resolved*, That while we do not consider the proposed Convention competent to make any change or changes in the Rules of Discipline, they may nevertheless indicate what changes, if any, are deemed necessary under a separate jurisdiction of the Southern and South-western Conferences. And that *it is necessary* for the Convention to resolve on, and provide for, a separate organization of these Conferences under a General Conference to be constituted and empowered in all respects *for the government of these Conferences*, as the General Conference hitherto has been with respect to *all* the Annual Conferences—according to the provisions and intention of the late General Conference.

6. *Resolved*, That as, in common with all our brethren of this Conference District, we have deeply sympathized with Bishop Andrew in his afflictions, and believe him to have been blameless in the matter for which he has suffered, so, with them, we affectionately assure him of our approbation of his course, and receive him as not the less worthy, or less to be honored in his Episcopal character, for the action which has been had in his case.

7. *Resolved*, That we recognize in the wisdom and prudence, the firmness and discretion, exhibited in the course of Bishop Soule, during the General Conference—as well as in former instances wherein he has proved his devotion to the great principles of constitutional right in our Church—nothing more than was to be expected from the bosom friend of Asbury and McKendree.

8. *Resolved*, That in common with the whole body of our people, we approve of the conduct of our delegates, both during the General Conference and subsequently.

9. *Resolved*, That we concur in the recommendation of the late General Conference for the change of the sixth article of the restric-

tive rules in the Book of Discipline, so as to allow an equitable *pro rata* division of the Book Concern.

W. Capers,
W. Smith,
H. Bass,
N. Talley,
H. A. C. Walker,
C. Betts,
S. W. Capers,
S. Dunwody,
R. J. Boyd.

INDIAN MISSION CONFERENCE.

The committee to whom was referred the action of the late General Conference relating to an amicable division of the Methodist Episcopal Church in the United States, beg leave to report the following resolutions for adoption by the Conference:

1. *Resolved*, That we concur in the proposed alteration of the sixth restrictive article of the Discipline.

2. *Resolved*, That we approve the course pursued by the minority of the late General Conference.

3. *Resolved*, That we elect delegates to represent the Indian Mission Conference in the contemplated Convention to be held in Louisville, Ky., in May next.

4. *Resolved*, That this Conference do deeply deplore the necessity for division of any kind in the Methodist Episcopal Church; and that we will not cease to send up our prayers to Almighty God for his gracious interposition, and that he may guide the affairs of the Church to a happy issue. J. C. Berryman, *Chairman.*

The above report having been read, was taken up section by section, and disposed of as follows: The first resolution was adopted—ayes 14, nays 1. The second resolution was adopted—ayes 11, nays 3; declined voting, 4. The third resolution was adopted—ayes 17. The fourth resolution was adopted—ayes 17. The preamble and resolutions were then adopted by the Conference as a whole.

The Conference then proceeded, in accordance with the third resolution, to elect delegates to attend the proposed Convention in Louisville, in May next. On counting the votes, it appeared that the whole number of votes given was twenty-one, of which number William H. Goode had received twenty, Edward T. Peery eighteen, scattering four. Whereupon, W. H. Goode and E. T. Peery having received a majority of all the votes given, were declared duly elected. D. B. Cumming was then elected reserve delegate.

The following resolutions were on the next day unanimously adopted at the request of the delegates elect:

Resolved, That in view of the condition of the Church at the present trying crisis, the members of this Conference will, when practicable, as near as may be at the hour of twilight, in the evening of each day, until the close of the approaching Convention at Louisville, meet each other at a throne of grace, and devoutly implore the blessing of God upon our assembled delegates in the discharge of their important duties.

Resolved, That the Friday preceding the opening of said Convention be set apart as a day of fasting and supplication to Almighty God for the continued unity, peace, and prosperity of the Methodist Episcopal Church; and that our members throughout this Conference be requested to join us in the devotions of that day.

WM. H. GOODE,
E. T. PEERY.

GEORGIA CONFERENCE.

The committee appointed to take into consideration the difficulties of the Church as growing out of the action of the General Conference in the case of Bishop Andrew, and to submit some recommendations to the Annual Conference for their adoption, beg leave to report:

The action of the majority in the last General Conference of the Methodist Episcopal Church, in the cases of Bishop Andrew and the Rev. Mr. Harding, has rendered it *indispensable* that the Conferences within whose limits slavery exists should cease to be under the jurisdiction of that body. They must either abandon the people collected under their ministry, and committed to their pastoral care, and the vast and widening field of missionary labor among the slaves—a field to which their attention is imperatively called by their sympathies as Christians, their sense of ministerial obligation as preachers of the gospel, and their interests and duties as citizens—or they must live under the control of an ecclesiastical body separate and distinct from and independent of the Conferences lying within the States and Territories where slavery is not allowed by law. In view of the relations before stated, that distinct organization is required by a *necessity* strict and *absolute*, and upon that issue we place it before the Church and the world. The exigence which brings it upon us, arose not out of our acts or designs; no collateral considerations of expedience abated our zeal in withstanding it; no collateral issues upon points involved affected our determination to maintain the unity of the Church under one organization as heretofore existing;

no pride of opinion, speculative differences, nor personal motives have conducted us to this conclusion. We did not seek to effect any changes in the doctrine or discipline of our Church; we did not ask any boon at the hands of the General Conference, nor any exemption from the operation of the laws which were common to the whole Connection; and whatever consequences affecting the Church, or the civil community, may result from our movement, we confidently look for acquittal to the judgment of posterity, and the decision of the sober and unprejudiced among our contemporaries. The General Conference violated the law of the Church, first, by confirming the decision of the Baltimore Conference, suspending the Rev. Mr. Harding from his connection with that Conference as a traveling preacher therein, because he would not give freedom to slaves, which by the laws of the land he could not manumit; and secondly, by passing a resolution intended to inhibit Bishop Andrew from the exercise of his Episcopal functions for the same reasons; in both cases contrary to the express provisions of the Discipline, which allow preachers to hold slaves wherever they are not permitted by the laws of the land to enjoy freedom when manumitted, and in both cases striking an effective blow at the fundamental principle of the economy of Methodism, as it destroys that general itinerancy of the preachers which is its most distinguished peculiarity; for under their decision, preachers holding slaves in Conferences where by the law of the Discipline they are allowed so to do, may not be transferred to Conferences within whose limits slavery does not exist. By the same decision, both preachers and lay-members holding slaves are thrown into an odious and dishonored caste, the first deprived of office therefor, and the religious character of both impeached and thrown under suspicion thereby; to which must be added, as an evil not lightly to be regarded, nor slightly overlooked, that, in connection with the fanatical movements of abolitionists in the North, East, and West, it is well fitted to excite slaves to disaffection and rebellion, making it imperative upon governments and citizens to prohibit all communication between slaves and preachers who either teach such doctrine or impliedly admit it to be true by submitting to such dishonor and deprivation. Secondly. That in the case of Bishop Andrew, the General Conference have violated the Discipline of the Church and invaded personal rights, which are secured by the laws of every enlightened nation, if not by the usages of every savage people on earth. They tried and sentenced Bishop Andrew without charges preferred, or a cognizable offense stated. If it is even admitted that they intended to charge him with "improper conduct," as a phrase used in the Discipline to embrace every class of offenses for which a Bishop is amenable to the General Conference, and, on conviction, liable to be expelled, they did not *formally* prefer that charge; if they intended to specify his "connection with slavery" as the substantive offense under that charge, a "connection with slavery" is not a cognizable offense, under any law of our Church, written or unwritten, statutory or prescriptive; and the only "connection with slavery" attempted to be established in his case, is expressly permitted by the Discipline, in section 10, part ii., on Slavery. If they claimed the right to declare in their legislative capacity, that "such a connection with slavery" was an offense in a Bishop, they could only extend it to him *retroactively by ex post facto enactment*, and even then it was never *promulgated* until the very moment in which they pronounced his sentence by a majority vote. But we cannot admit that the framers of our Discipline ever intended to subject a Bishop to the monstrous injustice of being liable to be *expelled* by the General Conference, exercising original jurisdiction, for an *impropriety* short of immorality or official delinquency, whilst they so cautiously secured his official and personal rights in all cases where that body has appellate cognizance of charges for positive immoralities; and we are confident that a fair and rational construction of the 4th and 5th questions and their answers, in the 4th section of the 1st chapter of the Discipline, will make "improper conduct," in the answer to the 4th question, and "immorality," in the 5th, descriptive of the same class of offenses in the mind of the law-maker, who could never have intended to subject that venerable officer to expulsion for offenses so light that they could not be considered either immoralities or official delinquencies, and so entirely dependent for their very existence upon the caprice or varying notions of every General Conference, that they could not either be classified or designated.

The foregoing views we consider the embodiment of public opinion throughout our Conference. The sentiments of our people in primary meetings, in Quarterly Conferences, as expressed in the most solemn forms, sustain the course of our delegation in the General Conference, and approve, and even demand, an organization which shall transfer the slaveholding Conferences from the jurisdiction of the North. The unanimity of the people we verily believe to be without a parallel in the history of Church action, and therefore feel ourselves perfectly justified in recommending to your body the adoption of the following resolutions, viz.:

1. *Resolved*, That we will elect delegates to the Convention to be held in Louisville, Ky., on the 1st of May next, upon the basis of representation proposed and acted on by the other Conferences—viz., one delegate for every eleven members of our Conference.

2. *Resolved*, That our delegates be instructed to coöperate with the delegates from other Southern and South-western Conferences, who shall be represented in the Convention, in effecting the organization of a General Conference, which shall embrace those Annual Conferences, and in making all necessary arrangements for its going into operation, as soon as the acts of the said Convention shall have been reported by the several delegations to their constituents, and accepted by them, according to such arrangements as may be made by the Convention for carrying the same into effect.

3. *Resolved*, That our delegates be instructed to use all prudent precautions to secure that portion of the Book Concern and Chartered Fund of the Methodist Episcopal Church to which the Annual Conferences represented in the Convention shall be unitedly entitled, and all the property to which the several Annual Conferences are entitled, to them severally, and that to this end they be requested to obtain the written opinions of one or more eminent lawyers; but that, in the event they must either abandon the property or remain under the jurisdiction of the General Conference of the Methodist Episcopal Church, constituted as it now is, they be left to the exercise of a sound discretion in the premises.

4. *Resolved*, That our delegates make a report to this body at its next session, of all their acts and doings in the aforesaid Convention, and this body shall not be bound by any arrangements therein made, until after it shall have accepted and approved them in Conference assembled.

5. *Resolved*, That our delegates be, and they are hereby instructed not to agree to any alterations in the Discipline of the Methodist Episcopal Church, but that the Discipline adopted under the new organization shall be that known and recognized as the Discipline of the Methodist Episcopal Church in the United States, with such modifications only as are necessary formally to adapt it to the new organization.

6. *Resolved*, That we consider ourselves as an integral part of the Methodist Episcopal Church in the United States, and that we have done no act, nor do we authorize any act to be done in our name, by which our title to be so considered shall be forfeited, unless in the event contemplated in the last clause of the third resolution it becomes necessary so to do.

7. *Resolved*, That we highly appreciate the devotion of our venerable senior Bishop to the Constitution and Discipline of the Church, and his uncompromising firmness in maintaining both the one and the other, and hereby assure him of our increased confidence and affection.

8. *Resolved*, That our beloved Bishop Andrew has endeared himself to the preachers and people of the Southern Church, by resisting the constitutional dictation of the majority of the late General Conference, and that we cordially approve his whole action in the case and welcome him to the unrestricted exercise of his Episcopal functions among us.

9. *Resolved*, That the course of our delgates in the trying circumstances by which they were surrounded during the last session of the General Conference, meets our entire approbation.

10. *Resolved*, That we concur in the alteration of the sixth restrictive rule, as recommended by the resolution of the General Conference.

11. *Resolved*, That we do not concur with the Holston Conference in the resolution proposed by them, regarding it as tending only to embarrass the action of the Convention, without the slightest promise of good to either division of the Church.

L. Pierce, Thomas Samford,
Samuel Anthony, Ignatius A. Few,
Geo. F. Pierce, Isaac Boring,
W. D. Matthews, John W. Talley,
Josiah Lewis, J. B. Payne.

FLORIDA CONFERENCE.

The committee to whom was referred the subject of the action of the late General Conference in the cases of Bishop Andrew and F. A. Harding—also the Report of the Committee of Nine in the late General Conference on the subject of a peaceable separation of the Church—also the resolution of the Holston Conference on the same subject—submit the following resolutions, to wit:

1. *Resolved*, That we disapprove of the course of the late General Conference in the cases of Bishop Andrew and F. A. Harding.

2. That we heartily approve the proposed Plan of Separation as adopted by the General Conference, under which the Southern and South-western Conferences are authorized to unite in a distinct ecclesiastical connection.

3. That we are satisfied that the peace and success of the Church in the South demand a separate and distinct organization.

4. That we commend and admire the firm and manly course pursued by Bishop Andrew under the trials he has had to encounter, and that we still regard him as possessing all his Episcopal functions.

5. That the course pursued by our venerable senior Superintendent, Bishop Soule, in defending the Discipline of our Church, has served but to endear him to us more and more, and we heartily approve his course in inviting Bishop Andrew to assist him in his Episcopal visitations.

6. That we tender our warmest thanks to all those brethren who voted in the minority in Bishop Andrew's case.

7. That we approve of the proposed Convention to be held in Louisville the 1st of May next, and will proceed to elect delegates to said Convention.

8. That *we do not* concur in the resolutions of the Holston Conference, proposing the election of delegates for forming a Plan of Compromise.

9. That *we do* concur in the recommendation of the late General Conference for the change of the sixth article in the restrictive rules in the Book of Discipline, allowing an equitable *pro rata* division of the Book Concern.

P. P. Smith,
T. C. Benning,
J. W. Yarbrough,
W. W. Griffin,
A. Martin,
S. P. Richardson,
R. H. Luckey,
R. H. Howren,
A. Peeler.

TEXAS CONFERENCE.

The committee to whom were referred certain acts of the late General Conference, causing and providing for a division of the Methodist Episcopal Church, or the General Conference thereof, and sundry communications pertaining thereto, have had the same under solemn and prayerful consideration, and beg leave to present the following Report:

In view of the numerous expositions and arguments, *pro* and *con*, with which the Christian Advocates have teemed for some months, on the merits of the highly important subject upon which your committee have been called to act, they presume that the Conference is too well enlightened to need an elaborate and argumentative investigation of them, in their multifarious relations and bearings; they therefore respectfully present the following resolutions, as the result of their deliberations:

Resolved, 1. That we approve of the course of the Southern and South-western delegates in the late General Conference; and that their independent and faithful discharge of duty, in a trying crisis, commands our admiration and merits our thanks.

2. That we deeply deplore the increasingly fearful controversy between the Northern and Southern divisions of the Methodist Episcopal Church on the institution of domestic slavery, and that we will not cease to pray most fervently to the great Head of the Church for his gracious interposition in guiding this controversy to a happy issue.

3. That we approve the appointment of a Convention of delegates from the Conferences in the slaveholding States, in the city of Louisville, on the 1st of May next, by the Southern and South western delegates in the late General Conference; and also the ratio of representation proposed by said delegates—to wit, one delegate for every eleven members of the Conference—and that we will elect delegates to the proposed Convention upon said basis, to act under the following instructions, to wit: To endeavor to secure a compromise between the North and South; to oppose a formal division of the Church before the General Conference of 1848, or a general Con vention, can be convened to decide the present controversy. But should a division be deemed unavoidable, and be determined on by the Convention, then, being well satisfied with the Discipline of the Church as it is, we instruct our delegates not to support or favor any change in said Discipline, by said Convention, other than to adapt its fiscal economy to the Southern organization.

4. That we approve of the dignified and prudent course of the bench of Bishops who presided in the late General Conference.

5. That it is the sense of this Conference that the Rev. John Clarke, one of our delegates to the late General Conference, entirely misrepresented our views and sentiments in his votes in the cases of Rev. F. A. Harding and Bishop Andrew.

6. That we appoint the Friday immediately preceding the meeting of the proposed general Convention of the delegates of the Southern and South-western Conferences, as a day of fasting and prayer for the blessing of Almighty God on said Convention—that it may be favored with the healthful influence of his grace, and the guidance of his wisdom.

CHAUNCEY RICHARDSON,
ROBERT ALEXANDER,
SAMUEL A. WILLIAMS.

ALABAMA CONFERENCE.

The committee appointed by the Conference to take into consideration the subject of a separate jurisdiction for the Southern Conferences of the Methodist Episcopal Church, beg leave to report that they have meditated with prayerful solicitude on this important matter, and have solemnly concluded on the necessity of the measure. They suppose it to be superfluous to review formally all the proceedings which constitute the unhappy controversy between the Northern and Southern portions of our Church, inasmuch as their sentiments can be expressed in one sentence: They indorse the unanswerable Protest of the Minority in the late General Conference. They believe that the doctrines of that imperishable document cannot be successfully assailed. They are firm in the conviction that the action of the majority in the case of Bishop Andrew was unconstitutional. Being but a delegated body, the General Conference has no legitimate right to tamper with the office of a General Superintendent—his amenableness to that body and liability to expulsion by it, having exclusive reference to maladministration, ceasing to travel, and immoral conduct. They are of opinion that Bishop Andrew's connection with slavery can come under none of these heads. If the entire Eldership of the Church, in a conventional capacity, were to constitute non-slaveholding or even abolitionism a tenure by which the Episcopal office should be held, or if they were to abolish the office, they doubtless could plead the abstract right thus to modify or revolutionize the Church in its supreme executive administration. But before the General Conference can justly plead this right, it must show when and where such plenary power was delegated to it by the *only fountain of authority—the entire Pastorate of the Church.* Your committee are, therefore, of opinion that the General Conference has no more power over a Bishop, except in the specified cases of maladministration, ceasing to travel, and immorality, than over the Episcopacy, as an integral part of our ecclesiastical polity. It can no more depose a Bishop for slaveholding than it can create a new Church.

Your committee deeply regret that these "conservative" sentiments did not occur to the majority in the late General Conference, and that the apologists of that body, since its session, have given them no place in their ecclesiastical creed, but, on the contrary, have given fearful evidence that the proceedings in the case of Bishop Andrew are but the incipiency of a course which, when finished, will leave not a solitary slaveholder in the communion which shall be, unfortunately, under their control. The foregoing sentiments and opinions embody the general views expressed most unequivocally throughout the Conference District since the late General Conference, by the large body of the membership, both in *primary meetings* and Quarterly Conferences.

The committee, therefore, offer to the calm consideration and mature action of the Alabama Annual Conference, the following series of resolutions:

1. *Resolved*, That this Conference deeply deplores the action of the late General Conference of the Methodist Episcopal Church in the case of our venerable Superintendent, Bishop Andrew, believing it to be unconstitutional, being as totally destitute of warrant from the Discipline as from the word of God.

2. That the almost unanimous agreement of Northern Methodists with the majority, and Southern Methodists with the minority of the late General Conference, shows the wisdom of that body in suggesting a duality of jurisdiction to meet the present emergency.

3. That this Conference agrees to the proposition for the alteration of the sixth restrictive rule of the Discipline.

4. That this Conference approves of the projected Convention at Louisville in May next.

5. That this Conference most respectfully invites all the Bishops to attend the proposed Convention at Louisville.

6. That this Conference is decided in its attachment to Methodism as it exists in the Book of Discipline, and hopes that the Louisville Convention will not make the slightest alteration, except so far as may be absolutely necessary for the formation of a separate jurisdiction.

7. That every preacher of this Conference shall take up a collection in his station or circuit, as soon as practicable, to defray the expenses of the delegates to the Convention, and the proceeds of such collection shall be immediately paid over to the nearest delegate or Presiding Elder; and the excess, or deficit of the collection for the said expenses shall be reported to the next Conference, which shall take action on the same.

8. That the Friday immediately preceding the session of the Convention shall be observed in all our circuits and stations as a day of fasting and prayer for the blessings of God upon its deliberations.

9. That whilst this Conference fully appreciates the commendable motives which induced the Holston Conference to suggest another

expedient to compromise the differences existing between the Northern and Southern divisions of the Church, it nevertheless cannot concur in the proposition of that Conference concerning that matter.

10. That this Conference fully recognizes the right of our excellent Superintendent, Bishop Soule, to invite Bishop Andrew to share with him the responsibilities of the Episcopal office, and while the Conference regrets the absence of the *former*, it rejoices in being favored with the efficient services of the *latter*—it respectfully tenders these "true yoke-fellows" in the superintendency the fullest approbation, the most fervent prayers, and the most cordial sympathies.

THOS. O. SUMMERS,	A. H. MITCHELL,
E. V. LEVERT,	J. HAMILTON,
E. HEARN,	W. MURRAH,
J. BORING,	GEO. SHAEFFER.
C. MCLEOD,	

C.

CORRESPONDENCE CONCERNING UNION.

It has frequently been stated, and believed by some, that the Methodist Episcopal Church (North) has made propositions of fraternal relations to the Methodist Episcopal Church, South. We publish in this Appendix all the official correspondence that has taken place between the two branches of Methodism, since the General Conference of 1848, at which time fraternal intercourse was declined by the Methodist Episcopal Church (North).

At the meeting of the Bishops of the Methodist Episcopal Church, South, in the city of St. Louis, in May, 1869, the following correspondence took place between the Bishops of the Methodist Episcopal Church (North) and the Bishops of the Methodist Episcopal Church, South.

412 Locust St., St. Louis, May 7, 1869.

To the Bishops of the Methodist Episcopal Church, South:

Rev. and Dear Brethren:—We have been deputed to convey to you a communication from the Board of Bishops of the Methodist Episcopal Church.

We are ready to wait upon you at such time and place as may suit your convenience.

With assurances of Christian regard,

Yours truly,

E. S. Janes,
M. Simpson.

St. Louis, May 7, 1869.

To Bishops Janes and Simpson:

Rev. and Dear Brethren:—Your note of this date to the College of Bishops of the Methodist Episcopal Church, South, informing them that you have been deputed to convey to them a communication from the Board of Bishops of the Methodist Episcopal Church, and of your readiness to wait upon them for this purpose, has been received.

I have been instructed to reply that they will be pleased to receive you to-morrow, at 10 o'clock A.M., at their room, 1406 Lucas Place.

Very respectfully and truly yours,

H. N. McTyeire, Sec'y.

Accordingly, at 10 o'clock A.M., Bishops Janes and Simpson, having been announced, were introduced, and, after some general conversation, made the following communications:

Meadville, Pa., April 23, 1869.

Dear Brethren:—It seems to us, that as the division of those Churches of our country which are of like faith and order has been productive of evil, so the reunion of them would be productive of good.

As the main cause of the separation has been removed, so has the chief obstacle to the restoration.

It is fitting that the Methodist Church, which began the disunion, should not be the last to achieve the reunion; and it would be a reproach to the chief pastors of the separated bodies, if they waited until their flocks prompted them to the union, which both the love of country and of religion invoke, and which the providence of God seems to render inevitable at no distant day.

We are aware that there are difficulties in the way, growing out of the controversies of the past and the tempers of the present.

We have, therefore, deputed our colleagues, Morris and Janes, to confer with you, alike as to the propriety, practicability, and methods of reunion, hoping that they, having been elected to their high office by the Church before its severance, and endeared to all its parts by their apostolic labors, may live to see the several parts united upon a foundation honorable to all, stable as truth, and harmonious with the fundamental law of our religion.

In behalf of the Bishops of the Methodist Episcopal Church.

Respectfully yours, etc., T. A. Morris, President.

D. W. Clark, Sec'y.

To the Reverends, the Bishops of the Methodist Episcopal Church, South.

P. S.—Bishop Morris having stated that it was doubtful whether he would be able to fulfill the duties of the Commission, it was resolved that Bishop Simpson be added to the delegation above described.

T. A. Morris.

At this stage of the interview the following letter from Bishop Morris was read:

SPRINGFIELD, OHIO, May 4, 1869.

Rev. Bishop E. S. Janes, D.D.:

DEAR BROTHER:—If I remember rightly, this is the week in which you expect to visit St. Louis on important business of the Church. I regard it as complimentary to myself that I was appointed to accompany you on that benevolent mission, and regret that it is not convenient for me to execute that mission in person, but trust that my alternate will more than supply my lack of service.

For three weeks past our family have all had enough to fill our heads and hands and hearts to overflowing; one result is, the health of Mrs. Morris is more feeble and precarious than usual. This is the chief cause of my failure to appear.

Please accept this explanation and excuse my absence.

The official letter of the Bishops of the Methodist Episcopal Church to the Rev. Bishops of the Methodist Episcopal Church, South, not only bears my official signature, but it has my personal approval. I believe it accords with the action of our last General Conference. I also think it judicious and opportune, and trust that beneficial results may follow.

If you have any opportunity to address the Reverend Episcopal Board in St. Louis in person, please present them collectively with my fraternal greetings.

Praying that the Lord may direct them and us in all things to his glory and the general good of all concerned, I am, dear colleague, respectfully and fraternally yours ever, T. A. MORRIS.

Bishop Janes then presented the following communication:

To the Bishops of the Methodist Episcopal Church, South, convened in St. Louis, Mo.:

REV. AND DEAR BRETHREN:—At a meeting of the Board of Bishops of the Methodist Episcopal Church, held in Erie, Pa., in June, 1865, we made and published the following declaration:

"That the great cause which led to the separation from us of both the Wesleyan Methodists of this country and of the Methodist Episcopal Church, South, has passed away, and we trust the day is not far distant when there shall be but one organization, which shall embrace the whole Methodist family in the United States."

This declaration was made in good faith, and shows what were then our sentiments and feelings, and was deemed by us as the utmost we were authorized to say or do on the subject at that time.

Although our late General Conference did not directly authorize us to take farther specific action in the matter, yet we judge that some of its acts justify advanced steps on our part.

In our Quadrennial Address to the General Conference we referred to the declaration above quoted, and no exception was taken to it by that body.

The General Conference, to promote the union of Methodistic Churches, appointed a Commission, consisting of eight members of that body and the Bishops of the Church, who were "empowered to treat with a similar Commission from any other Methodist Church," that may desire a union with us.

We have understood that there were in the minds of many of the members and ministers of the Methodist Episcopal Church, South, reasons why they consider it unsuitable for them to initiate measures to effect a reunion of the two Churches.

Believing as we do that if they were one in both spirit and organization, much more could be accomplished for the interests of humanity and the glory of God, we are desirous of doing all we consistently can to promote a reunion on terms alike honorable to both Churches and in the spirit of our Divine Lord.

We therefore ask your attention to the Commission above referred to, and we express to you the opinion, that should your approaching General Conference see proper to appoint a similar Commission, they will be promptly met by our Commission, who we doubt not will be happy to treat with them, and to report the result to our next General Conference.

Praying that Infinite Wisdom may guide both you and us in this important matter, so that our Redeemer's kingdom may be advanced and his name be glorified, we are yours in the bonds of the gospel of Christ,

E. S. Janes,
M. Simpson.

In behalf of the Bishops of the Methodist Episcopal Church.

St. Louis, Mo., May 8, 1869.

The Bishops of the M. E. Church, South, a few days afterward, made the following reply to the foregoing:

To the Bishops of the Methodist Episcopal Church:

Rev. and Dear Brethren:—It has afforded us pleasure to receive in person your respected colleagues, Bishops Janes and Simpson, deputed by you to confer with us; and we cannot forbear to express our regret that one of the delegation appointed by you to us—the venerable Bishop Morris—was not able to be present. We desired to see him again face to face, to enjoy his society, and to renew to him the assurances of our affection and regard. Our own senior Superintendent, Bishop Andrew, though in the city, was hindered by the feebleness and infirmities incident to age from being present at the reception of your colleagues, and enjoying with us the interview.

Your communication, together with that laid before us by your Commission, has been considered, and we entirely agree in your estimate of the responsibility in the premises resting on the chief pastors of the separated bodies of Methodism.

We would approach, dear brethren, the matter of your communication with the utmost candor and love, and so meet the advanced steps on your part that nothing shall be wanting on ours to bring about a better state of things, becoming and beneficial to us both. We deplore the unfortunate controversies and tempers that have prevailed, and that still prevail; and our earnest desire and prayer to God is, that they may give place, and that speedily, to peace. In evidence of this, we are ready not only to respond to, but to go farther than your communication, and from our point of view to suggest what may help to remove the difficulties and obstacles that are in the way.

Pemit us, then, to say, in regard to "reunion," that in our opinion there is another subject to be considered before that can be entertained, and necessarily in order to it: we mean the establishment of fraternal feelings and relations between the two Churches. They must be one in spirit before they can be one in organization. Concord must be achieved before any real union. Heart divisions must be cured before corporate divisions can be healed.

You will not consider it as unfriendly to the freest flow of Christian sympathy evoked by your overture, if we remind you that we initiated the measure to effect fraternal relations some years ago; and, as was declared then, and as we do now declare, in good faith and with most Christian purposes. Our General Conference sent one of its most honored Elders to your General Conference to convey their Christian salutations, and through him to "offer to you the establishment of fraternal relations and intercourse." It pains us to refer to the fact, but it is matter of history, that he was not received.

The closing words of Dr. Pierce to your General Conference, upon being notified of the failure of his mission, are in your possession:

"You will therefore regard this communication as final on the part of the M. E. Church, South. She can never renew the offer of fraternal relations between the two great bodies of Wesleyan Methodists in the United States. But the proposition can be renewed at any time, either now or hereafter, by the M. E. Church. And if ever made upon the basis of the Plan of Separation, as adopted by the General Conference of 1844, the Church, South, will cordially entertain the proposition."

His language to our General Conference in submitting his report was:

"Thus ended the well-intended Commission from your body. Upon this noble effort I verily believe the smile of Divine approbation will rest, when the heavenly bodies themselves will have ceased to shine. We did affectionately endeavor to make and preserve peace, but our offer was rejected as of no deserving."

The evils that have followed this rejection we suffer in common with you. We lament them in common with you; and, notwithstanding all that has since occurred, we are ready, on terms honorable to all, to join heart and hand with you to stay, and, as far as practicable, to remedy them. But you could not expect us to say less than this—that the words of our rejected delegate have been ever since, and still are, our words.

It may help to the more speedy and certain attainment of the ends we both desire, to keep distinctly in mind our mutual positions, and to hold the facts involved in our common history in a clear light.

You say, "that the great cause which led to the separation from us of both the Wesleyan Methodists of this country and of the Methodist Episcopal Church, South, has passed away." If we understand your reference, we so far differ from you in this opinion, that it may help any negotiations hereafter taking place to restate our position. Slavery was not, in any proper sense, the cause, but the occasion only, of that separation, the necessity of which we regretted as much as you. But certain principles were developed in relation to the political aspects of that question, involving the right of ecclesiastical bodies to handle and determine matters lying outside of their proper jurisdiction, which we could not accept; and, in a case arising, certain constructions of the constitutional powers and prerogatives of the General Conference were assumed and acted on, which we considered oppressive and destructive of the rights of the numerical minority represented in that highest judicatory of the Church. That which you are pleased to call—no doubt sincerely thinking it so—"the great cause" of separation, existed in the Church from its organization, and yet for sixty years there was no separation. But when those theories, incidentally evolved in connection with it, began to be put into practice, then the separation came.

We cannot think you mean to offend us when you speak of our having separated from you, and put us in the same category with a small body of schismatics who were always an acknowledged secession. Allow us, in all kindness, brethren, to remind you, and to keep the important fact of history prominent, that we separated from you in no sense in which you did not separate from us. The separation was by compact and mutual; and nearer approaches to each other can be conducted, with hope of a successful issue, only on this basis.

It is our opinion that the controversies and tempers which so disturb the Churches, and are so hurtful to the souls of those for whom Christ died, are due, in a large measure, to irritating causes which are not entirely beyond the control of the chief pastors of the separated bodies. To this end we invite your concurrence and coöperation.

And we take this occasion frankly to say, that the conduct of some of your missionaries and agents who have been sent into that portion of our common country occupied by us, and their avowed purpose to disintegrate and absorb our societies that otherwise dwell quietly, have been very prejudicial to that charity which we desire our people to cultivate toward all Christians, and especially those who are called by the endeared name of Methodists; and their course in taking possession of some of our houses of worship has inflicted both grief and loss on us, and bears the appearance, to disinterested men of the world, of being not only a breach of charity, but an invasion of the plainest rights of property. Thus the adversary has had occasion to speak reproachfully, and the cause of our Master has been wounded by its professed friends.

Brethren, these things ought not so to be; and we propose, until some action more formal, and authoritative, and advanced in this direction, can be taken by our highest judicatories, to unite with you in preventing them. We do not say that our own people have been, in every instance of these unhappy controversies and tempers, without blame as toward you. But this we say, if any offenses against the law of love, committed by those under our appointment, any aggressions upon your just privileges and rights, are properly represented to us, the representation will be respectfully considered, and we shall stand ready, by all the authority and influence we have, to restrain and correct them.

These are our views; and we are sure that we represent the sentiments of our ministers and people. We have no authority to determine any thing as to the "propriety, practicability, and methods" of reunion of the Churches represented by you and ourselves.

With sentiments of Christian regard, we are, dear brethren, very truly yours, R. PAINE, Chairman.

H. N. McTYEIRE, Sec'y.

ST. LOUIS, MO., May 11, 1869.

Nothing farther transpired on this subject previous to the General Conference of the M. E. Church, South, which convened in the city of Memphis, Tenn., in May, 1870.

Bishop Janes and the Rev. William L. Harris, D.D., of the M. E. Church (North), reached the city of Memphis during the session of the General Conference, and on the 11th of May sent the following communication to the Conference, which was read:

To the Bishops and General Conference of the Methodist Episcopal Church, South, in Conference assembled:

DEAR BRETHREN:—The Commissioners appointed by the General Conference of the Methodist Episcopal Church, in 1868, to treat with similar Commissioners from other Methodist Churches, on the subject of union, at a meeting held in Philadelphia, Nov. 23, 1868, appointed the Rev. Bishop Janes and the Rev. John McClintock, D.D., a deputation to bear to you a communication from them. Since then Dr. McClintock has deceased, and, by the authority of the Commission, the Rev. William L. Harris, D.D., has been appointed to serve in his stead.

The undersigned, now constituting the deputation, are present at the seat of your session for the purpose of presenting to you the communication of the Commission, which we will be happy to do, either in person or by letter, as may best accord with your convenience and pleasure. Though we had proposed to ourselves the satisfaction of spending several days in witnessing the proceedings of your Conference, and enjoying the society of its members, the recent severe bereavement of our Church, in the death of several of her chief ministers, makes it necessary for us to return as soon as we can fulfill the simple duty assigned us.

Truly and affectionately yours, E. S. JANES,
W. L. HARRIS.

OVERTON HOTEL, MEMPHIS, May 11, 1870.

On motion of J. E. Evans, a Committee of Three was appointed to wait on Bishop Janes and Dr. Harris, and invite them to the Conference-room. The Chair appointed Bishop Wightman, Trusten Polk, and L. M. Lee, on this committee.

Bishop Wightman, Governor Polk, and Dr. Lee, immediately called on Bishop Janes and Dr. Harris, and accompanied them to the Conference-room, where they were introduced to the Conference by Bishop Doggett.

The following communication was presented by Bishop Janes, and read by the Secretary. It is as follows:

To the Bishops and General Conference of the Methodist Episcopal Church, South, in Conference assembled:

DEAR BRETHREN:—By the action and authority of the General Conference of the Methodist Episcopal Church, held in Chicago in May, 1868, the undersigned were appointed a Commission, in behalf of said Church, to treat with a similar Commission from any other Methodist Church, on the subject of union.

The Bishops of the Methodist Episcopal Church, who also constitute a part of this Commission, in May, 1869, communicated to the Bishops of the Methodist Episcopal Church, South, the fact that such a Commission had been appointed, and expressed to them the conviction that the Commission would be happy to meet a similar one from the Methodist Episcopal Church, South, for the purpose contemplated in its appointment.

At a meeting of this Commission, held in Philadelphia, November 23, 1869, a resolution was unanimously adopted, approving the aforesaid action of the Bishops. Nevertheless, the Commission, as such, and as constituted by the General Conference, being desirous of discharging its duties in the fullest and most acceptable manner, deemed it proper to make a farther communication on this subject, addressed to the Bishops and General Conference of the Methodist Episcopal Church, South, to meet in Memphis, in May, 1870.

The fact that the General Conference of the Methodist Episcopal Church appointed this Commission, shows that, in the judgment of that body, there are now no sufficient reasons why a union may not be effected on terms equally honorable to all, and that the realization of such union is very important and desirable.

Hoping that you may see this subject in the same light, and that it may be your pleasure to appoint a similar Commission to confer with us previous to the meeting of our next General Conference in 1872; and praying that you may be prospered in all that pertains to the welfare of a Christian Church, and desiring your prayers in behalf of the Church we represent, that we may share a like prosperity, we are, dear brethren, yours in Christ Jesus,

EDMUND S. JANES,	LEVI SCOTT,
MATTHEW SIMPSON,	EDWARD R. AMES,
DAVIS W. CLARK,	EDWARD THOMSON,
LUKE HITCHCOCK,	DANIEL CURRY,
JOHN MCCLINTOCK,	JOHN LANAHAN,
JOHN G. BRUCE,	THOMAS M. EDDY,
JAMES PIKE,	WILLIAM L. HARRIS,

PHILADELPHIA, Nov. 23, 1869. Commissioners.

After the reading of the communication, Bishop Janes came forward and thus addressed the Conference:

"Having presented that document, we consider that our official duty is performed. There is one incident, however, in connection with this matter, to which I think it proper to refer. When that document was provided for, it was not intended to be made public until it was presented here at this time. Its being made public is not by the action or approval of this Commission. It was its intention, in a dignified and delicate manner, to make this communication, and it was not intended to be heralded in the papers, that there should be any discussion over it that it could be made use of to the advantage or the disadvantage of any party. I think it due this Commission to say that this has not been done by our action or approval. I deem it proper to say farther, that I believe that the General Conference has acted with Christian impulse and candor.

"I am sure that this Commission acts from religious convictions and with perfect candor. The action of the General Conference was limited, and you can interpret it as wisely as I can. This Commission was appointed to treat with similar Commissions from other Methodist Churches. I do not understand that it is authorized to take any definite action, but only that it might learn what embarrassments are in the way of union, and ascertain in what manner union may be effected. In being deputed to bear this document, I was not authorized to negotiate on any question, but I judge that we can confer together with the view to receive or give any information on this subject. I believe this is a simple and true explanation, so far as respects the Church which we represent. I do not think that any of us can expect that perfect organic union can be effected at once without much negotiation. The history of the past five years will not justify us in entertaining such a hope, and yet we do believe that the prayer of Christ will be heard, and the day will come when his people shall be one. I am not willing to lead this Conference to any action but what is justified by the action of the Conference I represent. I would do great injustice to my own feelings did I not add that it affords me great pleasure to look upon my brethren whom I have known in years gone by. I thank God for his preserving kindness, and for his blessings conferred upon you. It also gives me pleasure to be present at your deliberations, and I pray that grace may be with all them that love our Lord Jesus Christ in sincerity."

Dr. Harris being invited to address the Conference, said: "It is impossible for me to add any thing to what has already been said, except that I *most* cordially agree with the Bishop touching the feeling of the Church and the purpose of the Commission which we represent."

Dr. Keener said: "I have listened, together with the rest of my brethren, with great pleasure to the Christian and very earnest spirit of our brethren of the Methodist Episcopal Church. Coming to us as they do, across a period of disaster and division, they are especially grateful to us. As to this proposition which comes to us with the prestige of their Church, I think we should pause for a moment to examine into its meaning. If I understand the Journal of the M. E. Church on this point, this Commission extends to the African M. E. Zion Church, and to all other Methodist Churches wishing to seek union with them. I will read the resolution adopted by them on this question from the Journal of the last General Conference of the M. E. Church, which I hold in my hand:

"'*Resolved*, That the Commission ordered by the General Conference to confer with a like Commission from the African M. E. Zion Church, to arrange for the union of that body with our own, be also empowered to treat with a similar Commission from any other Methodist Church that may desire a like union.'

"If I understand that, this Commission is to treat with any Churches that may be knocking for admission at the door of the M. E. Church, and not to knock for admission at the door of any other Church. If this be the condition of things, then there is a great difficulty in entertaining any proposition looking to union, because of the original instructions of their Conference. But if they come before us desiring fraternal intercourse, another difficulty presents itself—they do not come authorized to negotiate for union. I therefore offer the following resolutions, which I move to be referred to a special committee to be appointed on this question:

"*Resolved*, 1. That gratefully recognizing that Providence which has hitherto guided us, multiplied us, and strengthened our hands under trying conditions, both of war and peace, as a Church of Jesus Christ, we earnestly desire to cultivate true Christian fellowship with every other branch of the Christian Church, and especially with our brethren of the several branches of Methodism in this country and in Europe.

"2. That the action of our Board of Bishops at their last annual meeting in St. Louis, in response to the Message from the Board of Bishops of the M. E. Church, has the full indorsement of this General Conference, and accurately defines our position in reference to any overtures which may proceed from that Church, having in them an official and proper recognition of this body.

"3. That the distinguished Commission now present, of the General Conference of the M. E. Church at Chicago in May, 1868, appointed by it specifically, to confer with Commissioners from the African M. E. Zion Church, to arrange for union with that body, and to treat with a similar Commission from any other Church which may desire a like union, cannot, in our judgment, be construed, without great violence, as having been constituted by that General Conference, a committee to bear its fraternal expressions to the General Conference of the M. E. Church, South.

"4. That we are highly gratified at the visit of the Commission as indicative of the return of proper Christian sentiments and relations between the two great branches of Northern and Southern Methodism, and that we extend to them personally our highest regards as brethren beloved in the Lord."

J. E. Evans moved to appoint a Committee of Nine to take this subject under consideration.

Bishop Janes said: "It is proper for me to say, before that motion is put, that of course we abide by what is said in the Journal of the General Conference, and yet I think it does not correctly represent the object of the appointment of this Commission. It was not appointed with the sole object of conferring with the Commission of the African M. E. Zion Church, but before its appointment this subject in question came up, and this Commission was appointed with the understanding that it was alike to the Methodist Churches throughout the country. Perhaps we have transcended our bounds in thus coming at the present time, and not waiting to be first approached on this subject. But we did not esteem ourselves so highly as to think that all these Churches should first knock for admission. We judged it proper to inform these Churches of the appointment of this Commission, and that it would give us pleasure to meet them. I think this explanation is due. Dr. Keener's remarks were justified by what he has read from the Journal."

The motion of J. E. Evans prevailed.

Bishop Janes rose and said: "My colleague thinks that I have made a mistake in my remarks concerning the Journal of the General Conference. I meant to say that I do not think the Journal represents fully the action of the Conference. The Commission was provided for in that resolution, but not appointed at that time."

A. L. P. Green, Trusten Polk, J. C. Keener, L. C. Garland, Robert Alexander, James Jackson, A. W. Wilson, G. W. Williams, and E. K. Miller, were appointed the committee to which the subject was referred.

In their first communication to the Conference, Bishop Janes and Dr. Harris informed the body that they could only remain in Memphis for a short time. On the 12th of May they appeared in the Conference-room, before leaving, and were invited to address the Conference. Bishop Janes said:

"I very much regret that circumstances make it necessary for me to leave your Conference and your city this afternoon. It would have been a very high gratification to me to have enjoyed your society; especially am I interested in witnessing your proceedings, as this is the first Conference in which I have seen the action of lay delegation, and I confess that what I have witnessed has given me much pleasure. I think I can say that I anticipate, though it is not positively certain, that the laity will be associated with us in the highest legislations of our Church. I especially regret the necessity of leaving at this time, since the Committee on Public Worship has invited us to preach. I wish it understood that I do not decline from any other reason but that I am compelled to be absent on other important business. I hope it will be understood. It would certainly be a pleasure to me to remain and to listen as I have done to others of you.

"I desire to acknowledge thankfully the generous hospitality extended to me by the committee, and I wish to acknowledge the official and personal courtesy extended to me as a body, and by a very large part of the Conference as individuals. I think that I can say, in behalf of those whom we represent, that it will give us pleasure to reciprocate it at any time. I again invoke the blessing of our common Parent and our one Saviour upon the individuals of this Conference, and the Church you represent. May the blessing of God be and abide with you all! Amen."

The Bishop having taken his seat, Dr. Harris arose and said:

"I desire to say that I have spent the last two days with great personal satisfaction. I came here a stranger, acquainted with only two of your body, and they received me as old friends, and I reciprocate the feelings which they expressed; and now, in leaving, I desire to express to you, and through you to the committee, my profound thanks for the Christian courtesy which you have extended to me. I shall bear it ever in mind. And I unite with the Bishop in invoking the richest blessings upon you and upon your Church."

The committee to whom the subject was intrusted was large and influential, and was composed of ministers and laymen. They submitted their report on the 14th of May, which is as follows:

The committtee to whom were referred the papers relating to the proposals of union made by the Commission from the Methodist Episcopal Church, having carefully considered the subject, recommend the adoption of the following resolutions:

Resolved, 1. That gratefully recognizing that Providence which has hitherto guided us, multiplied us, strengthened our hands, and preserved our integrity as a Church of Jesus Christ under the trying conditions both of war and peace, we earnestly desire to cultivate true Christian fellowship with every other branch of the Christian Church, and especially with our brethren of the several branches of Methodism in this country and in Europe.

2. That the action of our Bishops in their last annual meeting in St. Louis, in response to the message from the Bishops of the Methodist Episcopal Church, has the full indorsement of this General Conference, and accurately defines our position in reference to any overtures which may proceed from that Church, having in them an official and proper recognition of this body.

3. That the distinguished Commission now present, of the General Conference of the Methodist Episcopal Church, met at Chicago in May, 1868, appointed by it for the specific purpose expressed in the following resolution, viz., "*Resolved*, That the Commission ordered by the General Conference to confer with a like Commission from the African M. E. Zion Church to arrange for the union of that body with our own, be also empowered to treat with similar Commissions from any other Methodist Church that may desire a like union," can-

not, in our judgment, without great violence in construing the language of said resolution, be regarded as having been constituted by that General Conference a Commission to make proposals of union to the General Conference of the Methodist Episcopal Church, South.

4. *Resolved, moreover*, That if this distinguished Commission were fully clothed with authority to treat with us for union, it is the judgment of this Conference that the true interests of the Church of Christ require and demand the maintenance of our separate and distinct organization.

5. That we tender to the Rev. Bishop E. S. Janes, and the Rev. W. L. Harris, D D., the members of the Commission now with us, our high regards as brethren beloved in the Lord, and express our desire that the day may soon come when proper Christian sentiments and fraternal relations between the two great branches of Northern and Southern Methodism shall be permanently established.

A. L. P. GREEN, J. C. KEENER,
A. W. WILSON, L. C. GARLAND,
JAMES JACKSON, GEO. W. WILLIAMS,
E. K. MILLER, TRUSTEN POLK.
R. ALEXANDER,

The action of the General Conference reflected the sentiments of the entire M. E. Church, South, both in the ministry and laity. No discordant note came up from any quarter to disturb the harmony of sentiment.

D.

DECISION OF THE SUPREME COURT OF THE UNITED STATES.

WILLIAM A. SMITH and others, *v.* LEROY SWORMSTEDT and others.
16 H. 288.

Upon a bill in equity by several traveling preachers of the Methodist Episcopal Church, South, in behalf of themselves and the other traveling preachers of that organization, *held,*

1. That as numerous parties had a common interest in the fund in controversy, a few might sue, representing the others.
2. That the General Conference, in 1844, had power to consent to the division of the Methodist Episcopal Church into two bodies, and that the separation was not a secession of a part of the traveling preachers from that Church, but a division, in pursuance of proper authority.
3. That this division carried with it, as matter of law, a division of the common property, which belonged to the traveling preachers, as such.
4. That the removal of the sixth restrictive article, was not a condition to the enjoyment by the Church, South, of its share of the common fund, but to enable the General Conference to make the division.
5. That as the complainants not only represent the other traveling preachers South, but the "Book Concern" there, the share of the fund they thus represent may properly be paid over to them.

THE case is stated in the opinion of the court.

Stanberry, for the appellants.

Badger and *Ewing*, contrà.

NELSON, J., delivered the opinion of the court.

This is an appeal from a decree of the Circuit Court of the United States for the District of Ohio.

The bill is filed by the complainants, for themselves, and in behalf of the traveling and worn-out preachers in connection with the society of the Methodist Episcopal Church, South, in the United States, against the defendants, to recover their share of a fund called the Book Concern, at the city of Cincinnati, consisting of houses, machinery, printing-presses, book-bindery, books, etc., claimed to be of the value of some $200,000.

The bill charges that, at and before the year 1844, there existed in the United States a voluntary association unincorporated, known as the Methodist Episcopal Church, composed of seven Bishops, four thousand eight hundred and twenty-eight preachers belonging to the traveling connection, and in Bishops, ministers, and members, about one million one hundred and nine thousand nine hundred and sixty, united and bound together in one organized body by certain doctrines of faith and morals, and by certain rules of government and discipline.

That the government of the Church was vested in one body called the General Conference, and in certain subordinate bodies called Annual Conferences, and in Bishops, traveling ministers, and preachers.

The bill refers to a printed volume, entitled "The Doctrines and Discipline of the Methodist Episcopal Church," as containing the constitution, organization, form of Government, and rules of discipline, as well as the doctrines of faith of the association.

The complainants farther charge, that differences and disagreements had sprung up in the Church between what was called the Northern and Southern members, in respect to the administration of the government with reference to the ownership of slaves by the ministers of the Church, of such a character and attended with such consequences as threatened greatly to impair its usefulness, as well as permanently to disturb its harmony; and it became and was a question of grave and serious importance whether a separation ought not to take place, according to some geographical boundary to be agreed upon, so as that the Methodist Episcopal Church should thereafter constitute two separate and distinct organizations. And that, accordingly, at a session of the General Conference held in the city of New York in May, 1844, a resolution was passed by a majority of over three-fourths of the body, by which it was determined, that if the Annual Conferences of the slaveholding States should find it necessary to unite in a distinct ecclesiastical connection, the following rule should be observed with regard to the Northern boundary of such connection—all the societies, stations, and Conferences adhering to the Church in the South, by a vote of a majority of the members, should remain under the pastoral care of the Southern Church; and all adhering to the Church, North, by a like vote, should remain under the pastoral care of that Church. This Plan of Separation contains eleven other resolutions, relating principally to the mode and terms of the division of the common property of the association between the two divisions, in case the separation contemplated should take place; and which, in effect, provide for a *pro rata* division, taking the number of the traveling preachers in the Church, North and South, as the basis upon which to make the partition.

The complainants farther charge that, in pursuance of the above resolutions, the Annual Conferences in the slaveholding States met and resolved in favor of a distinct and independent organization, and erected themselves into a separate ecclesiastical connection, under the provisional Plan of Separation, based upon the Discipline of the Methodist Episcopal Church, and to be known as the Methodist Episcopal Church, South. And they insist that, by virtue of these proceedings, this Church, as it had existed in the United States previous to the year 1844, became and was divided into two separate Churches, with distinct and independent powers, and authority composed of the several Annual Conferences, stations, and societies, lying North and South of the aforesaid line of division. And also, that by force of the same proceedings, the division of the Church, South, became and was entitled to its proportion of the common property, real and personal, of the Methodist Episcopal Church, which belonged to it at the time the separation took place; that the property and funds of the Church had been obtained by voluntary contributions, to which the members of the Church, South, had contributed more than their full share, and which, down to the time of the separation, belonged in common to the Methodist Episcopal Church, as then organized.

The complainants charge that they are members of the Church, South, and preachers, some of them supernumerary, and some superannuated preachers, and belonged to the traveling connection of said Church; and that, as such, have a personal interest in the property, real and personal, held by the Church, North, and in the hands of the defendants; and, farther, that there are about fifteen hundred preachers belonging to the traveling connection of the Church, South, each of whom has a direct and personal interest in the same right with the complainants in the said property, the large number of whom make it inconvenient and impracticable to bring them all before the court as complainants.

They also charge that the defendants are members of the Methodist Episcopal Church, North; and that each, as such, has a personal interest in the property; and, farther, that two of them have the custody and control of the fund in question; and that, in addition to these defendants, there are nearly thirty-eight hundred preachers belonging to the traveling connection of the Church, North, each of whom has an interest in the fund in the same right, so that it is impossible, in view of sustaining a just decision in the matter, to make them all parties to the bill.

The complainants also aver that this bill is brought by the authority, and under the direction, of the General and Annual Conferences of the Church, South, and for the benefit of the same, and for themselves, and all the preachers in the traveling connection, and all other ministers and persons having an interest in the property.

The defendants, in their answer, admit most of the facts charged in the bill, as it respects the organization, government, discipline, and faith of the Methodist Episcopal Church as it existed at and previous to the year 1844. They admit the passage of the resolutions, called the Plan of Separation, at the session of the General Conference of that year, by the majority stated; but deny that the resolutions were duly and legally passed; and also deny that the General Conference possessed the competent power to pass them, and submit that they were therefore null and void. They also submit that, if the General Conference possessed the power, the separation contemplated was made dependent upon certain conditions, and among others a change of the sixth restrictive article in the constitution of the Church, by a vote of the Annual Conferences, which vote the said Conferences refused.

The defendants admit the erection of the Church, South, into a distinct ecclesiastical organization; but deny that this was done agreeably to the Plan of Separation. They deny that the Methodist Episcopal Church, as it existed in 1844, or at any time, has been divided into two distinct and separate ecclesiastical organizations; and submit that the separation and voluntary withdrawal from this Church of a portion of the Bishops, ministers, and members, and organization into a Church, South, was an unauthorized separation; and that they have thereby renounced and forfeited all claim, either in law or equity, to any portion of the property in question. The defendants admit that the Book Concern at Cincinnati, with all the houses, lots, printing-presses, etc., is now, and always has been, beneficially the property of the preachers belonging to the traveling connection of the Methodist Episcopal Church; but insist that, if such preachers do not, during life, continue in such traveling connection, and in the communion, and subject to the government of the Church, they forfeit for themselves and their families all ownership in, or claim to, the said Book Concern, and the produce thereof; they admit that the Book Concern was originally commenced and established by the traveling preachers of this Church, upon their own capital, with the design, in the first place, of circulating religious knowledge, and that, at the General Conference of 1796, it was determined that the profits derived from the sale of books should in future be devoted wholly to the relief of traveling preachers, supernumerary and worn-out preachers, and the widows and orphans of such preachers—and the defendants submit that the Methodist Episcopal Church, South, is not entitled at law or in equity to have a division of the property of the Book Concern, or the produce, or to any portion thereof; and that the ministers, preachers, or members, in connection with such Church, are not entitled to any portion of the same; and farther, that, being no longer traveling preachers belonging to the Methodist Episcopal Church, they are not so entitled, without a change of the sixth restrictive article of the constitution of 1808, provided for in the Plan of Separation, as a condition of the partition of said fund.

The proofs in the case consist chiefly of the proceedings of the General Conference of 1844, relating to the separation of the Church and of the proceedings of the Southern Conferences, in pursuance of which a distinct and separate ecclesiastical organization South took place.

There is no material controversy between the parties, as it respects the facts. The main difference lies in the interpretation and effect to be given to the acts and proceedings of these several bodies and authorities of the Church. Our opinion will be founded almost wholly upon facts alleged in the bill, and admitted in the answer.

An objection was taken, on the argument, to the bill for want of proper parties to maintain the suit. We think the objection not well founded.

The rule is well established, that where the parties interested are numerous, and the suit is for an object common to them all, some of the body may maintain a bill on behalf of themselves and of the others; and a bill may also be maintained against a portion of a numerous body of defendants, representing a common interest. Story's Eq. Pl. §§ 97, 98, 99, 103, 107, 110, 111, 116, 120; 2 Mitf. Pl. (Jer. Ed.) 167; 2 Paige, 19; 4 Mylne & Cr. 134, 619; 2 De Gex & Smale, 102, 122.

Story, J., in his valuable treatise on Equity Pleadings, after discussing this subject, with his usual research and fullness, arranges the exceptions to the general rule as follows: 1. Where the question is one of a common or general interest, and one or more sue or defend for the benefit of the whole. 2. Where the parties form a voluntary association for public or private purposes, and those who sue or defend may fairly be presumed to represent the rights and interests of the whole; and, 3. Where the parties are very numerous, and though they have or may have separate and distinct interests, yet it is impracticable to bring them all before the court.

In this latter class, though the rights of the several persons may be separate and distinct, yet there must be a common interest or a common right, which the bill seeks to establish or enforce. As an illustration, bills have been permitted to be brought by the lord of a manor against some of the tenants, and *vicè versa*, by some of the tenants, in behalf of themselves and the other tenants, to establish some right—such as suit to a mill, or right of common, or to cut turf. So by a parson of a parish against some of the parishioners to establish a general right to tithes—or conversely, by some of the parishioners, in behalf of all, to establish a parochial modus.

In all cases where exceptions to the general rule are allowed, and a few are permitted to sue and defend on behalf of the many, by representation, care must be taken that persons are brought on the record fairly representing the interest or right involved, so that it may be fully and honestly tried.

Where the parties interested in the suit are numerous, their rights and liabilities are so subject to change and fluctuation by death or otherwise, that it would not be possible, without very great inconvenience, to make all of them parties, and would oftentimes prevent the prosecution of the suit to a hearing. For convenience, therefore, and to prevent a failure of justice, a court of equity permits a portion of the parties in interest to represent the entire body, and the decree binds all of them the same as if all were before the court. The legal and equitable rights and liabilities of all being before the court by representation, and especially where the subject-matter of the suit is common to all, there can be very little danger but that the interest of all will be properly protected and maintained.

The case in hand illustrates the propriety and fitness of the rule. There are some fifteen hundred persons represented by the complainants, and over double that number by the defendants. It is manifest that to require all the parties to be brought upon the record, as is required in a suit at law, would amount to a denial of justice. The right might be defeated by objections to parties, from the difficulty of ascertaining them, or, if ascertained, from the changes constantly occurring by death or otherwise.

As it respects the persons into whose hands the fund in question should be delivered for the purpose of distribution among the beneficiaries, in case of a division of it, we shall recur to the subject in another part of this opinion.

We will now proceed to an examination of the merits of the case.

The Book Concern, the property in question, is a part of a fund which had its origin at a very early day, from the voluntary contributions of the traveling preachers in the connection of the Methodist Episcopal Church. The establishment was at first small, but at present, is one of very large capital, and of extensive operations, producing great profits. In 1796, the traveling preachers, in General Conference assembled, determined that these profits should be thereafter devoted to the relief of the traveling preachers, and their families; and, accordingly, resolved that the produce of the sale of the books, after the debts were paid, and sufficient capital provided for carrying on the business, should be applied for the relief of distressed traveling preachers, for the families of traveling preachers, and for supernumerary and worn-out preachers, and the widows and orphans of preachers.

The establishment was placed under the care and superintendence of the General Conference, the highest authority in the Church, which was composed of the traveling preachers; and it has grown up to its present magnitude, its capital amounting to nearly a million of dollars, from the economy and skill with which the concern has been managed, and from the labors and fidelity of the traveling preachers, who have always had the charge of the circulation and sale of the books in the Methodist connection throughout the United States, accounting to the proper authorities for the proceeds. The agents who have the immediate charge of the establishment make up a yearly account of the profits, and transmit the same to the several Annual Conferences, each an amount in proportion to the number of traveling preachers, their widows and orphans comprehended within it, which bodies distribute the fund to the beneficiaries individually, agreeably to the design of the original founders. These several Annual Conferences are composed of the traveling preachers residing or located within certain districts assigned to them, and comprehended, in the aggregate, the entire body in connection with the Methodist Episcopal Church. The fund has been thus faithfully administered since its foundation down to 1846, when the portion belonging to the complainants in this suit, and those they represent, was withheld, embracing some thirteen of the Annual Conferences.

In the year 1844, the traveling preachers, in General Conference assembled, for causes which it is not important particularly to refer to, agreed upon a plan for division of the Methodist Episcopal Church in case the Annual Conferences in the slaveholding States should deem it necessary; and to the erection of two separate and distinct ecclesiastical organizations. And according to this plan, it was agreed that all the societies, stations, and Conferences adhering to the Church, South, by a majority of their respective members, should remain under the pastoral care of that Church; and all of these several bodies adhering, by a majority of its members, to the Church, North, should remain under the pastoral care of that Church; and, farther, that the ministers, local and traveling, should, as they might prefer, attach themselves, without blame, to the Church North or South. It was also agreed that the common property of the Church, including this Book Concern, that belonged specially to the body of traveling preachers, should, in case the separation took place, be divided between the two Churches in proportion to the number of traveling preachers falling within the respective divisions. This was in 1844. In the following year the Southern Annual Conferences met in Convention, in pursuance of the Plan of Separation, and determined upon a division, and resolved that the Annual Conferences should be constituted into a separate ecclesiastical connection, and based upon the Discipline of the Methodist Episcopal Church, comprehending the doctrines and entire moral, ecclesiastical, and economical rules and regulations of said Discipline, except only so far as verbal alterations might be necessary; and to be known by the name of the Methodist Episcopal Church, South.

The division of the Church, as originally constituted, thus became complete; and from this time two separate and distinct organizations have taken the place of the one previously existing.

The Methodist Episcopal Church having been thus divided, with the authority and according to the plan of the General Conference, it is claimed on the part of the complainants, who represent the traveling preachers in the Church, South, that they are entitled to their share of the capital stock and profits of this Book Concern; and that the withholding of it from them is a violation of the fundamental law prescribed by the founders, and consequently of the trust upon which it was placed in the hands of the defendants.

The principal answer set up to this claim is, that, according to the original constitution and appropriation of the fund, the beneficiaries must be traveling preachers, or the widows and orphans of traveling preachers, in connection with the Methodist Episcopal Church, as organized and established in the United States at the time of the foundation of the fund; and that, as the complainants, and those they represent, are not shown to be traveling preachers in that connection, but traveling preachers in connection with a different ecclesiastical organization, they have forfeited their right, and are no longer within the description of its beneficiaries.

This argument, we apprehend, if it proves any thing, proves too much; for if sound, the necessary consequences is that the beneficiaries connected with the Church, North, as well as South, have forfeited their right to the fund. It can no more be affirmed, either in point of fact or of law, that they are traveling preachers in connection with the Methodist Church as originally constituted, since the division, than of those in connection with the Church, South. Their organization covers but about half of the territory embraced within that of the former Church; and includes within it but a little over two-thirds of the traveling preachers. Their General Conference is not the General Conference of the old Church, nor does it represent the interest, or possess territorially the authority of the same; nor are they the body under whose care this fund was placed by its founders. It may be admitted that, within the restricted limits, the organization and authority are the same as the former Church. But the same is equally true in respect to the organization of the Church, South.

Assuming, therefore, that this argument is well founded, the consequence is that all the beneficiaries of the fund, whether in the Southern or Northern division, are deprived of any right to a distribution, not being in a condition to bring themselves within the description of persons for whose benefit it was established; in which event the foundation of the fund would become broken up, and the capital revert to the original proprietors, a result that would differ very little in its effect from that sought to be produced by the complainants in their bill.

It is insisted, however, that the General Conference of 1844 possessed no power to divide the Methodist Episcopal Church as then organized, or to consent to such division; and hence, that the organization of the Church, South, was without authority, and the traveling preachers within it separated from an ecclesiastical connection which is essential to enable them to participate as beneficiaries. Even if this were admitted, we do not perceive that it would change the relative position and rights of the traveling preachers within the divisions North and South, from that which we have just endeavored to explain. If the division under the direction of the General Conference has been made without the proper authority, and for that reason the traveling preachers within the Southern division are wrongfully separated from their connection with the Church, and thereby have lost the character of beneficiaries; those within the Northern division are equally wrongfully separated from that connection, as both divisions have been brought into existence by the same authority. The same consequence would follow in respect to them, that is imputable to the traveling preachers in the other division, and hence each would be obliged to fall back upon their rights as original proprietors of the fund.

But we do not agree that this division was made without the proper authority. On the contrary, we entertain no doubt but that the General Conference of 1844 was competent to make it; and that each division of the Church, under the separate organization, is just as legitimate, and can claim as high a sanction, ecclesiastical and temporal, as the Methodist Episcopal Church first founded in the United States. The same authority which founded that Church in 1784 has divided it, and established two separate and independent organizations, occupying the place of the old one.

In 1784, when this Church was first established, and down till 1808, the General Conference was composed of all the traveling preachers in that connection. This body of preachers founded it by organizing its government, ecclesiastical and temporal, established its doctrines and discipline, appointed its Superintendents, or Bishops, its ministers and preachers, and other subordinate authorities, to administer its polity, and promulgate its doctrines and teachings throughout the land.

It cannot, therefore, be denied—indeed, it has scarcely been denied—that this body, while composed of all the traveling preachers, possessed the power to divide it, and authorize the organization and establishment of the two separate independent Churches. The power must necessarily be regarded as inherent in the General Conference. As they might have constructed two ecclesiastical organizations over the territory of the United States originally, if deemed expedient, in the place of one, so they might, at any subsequent period, the power remaining unchanged.

But it is insisted that this power has been taken away or given up by the action of the General Conference of 1808. In that year the constitution of this body was changed so as to be composed thereafter by traveling preachers, to be elected by the Annual Conferences, in the ratio of one for every five members. This has been altered from time to time, so that, in 1844, the representation was one for every twenty-one members. At the time of this change, and as part of it, certain limitations were imposed upon the powers of this General Conference, called the six restrictive articles: 1. That they should not alter or change the articles of religion, or establish any new standard of doctrine. 2. Nor allow of more than one representative for every fourteen members of the Annual Conferences, nor less than one for every thirty. 3. Nor alter the government so as to do away with Episcopacy, or destroy the plan of itinerant superintendencies. 4. Nor change the rules of the united societies. 5. Nor deprive the ministers or preachers of trial by a committee, and of appeal; nor members before the society, or lay committee, and appeal. And 6. Nor appropriate the proceeds of the Book Concern, nor the Charter Fund, to any purpose other than for the benefit of the traveling, supernumerary, superannuated, and worn-out preachers, their wives, widows, and children. Subject to these restrictions, the delegated Conference possessed the same powers as when composed of the entire body of preachers. And it will be seen that these relate only to the doctrine of the Church, its representation in the General Conference, the Episcopacy, discipline of its preachers and members, the Book Concern and Charter Fund. In all other respects, and in every thing else that concerns the welfare of the Church, the General Conference represents the sovereign power the same as before. This is the view taken by the General Conference itself, as exemplified by the usage and practice of that body. In 1820, they set off to the British Conference of Wesleyan Methodists the several circuits and societies in Lower Canda. And in 1828, they separated the Annual Conference of Upper Canada from their jurisdiction, and erected the same into a distinct and independent Church. These instances, together with the present division, in 1844, furnish evidence of the opinions of the eminent and experienced men of this Church in these several Conferences, of the power claimed, which, if the question was otherwise doubtful, should be regarded as decisive in favcr of it. We will add, that all the Northern Bishops, five in number, in council in July, 1845, acting under the Plan of Separation, regarded it as of binding obligation, and conformed their action accordingly.

It has also been urged, on the part of the defendants, that the division of the Church, according to the Plan of the Separation, was made to depend not only upon the determination of the Southern Annual Conferences, but also upon the consent of the Annual Conferences, North, as well as South, to a change of the sixth restrictive article; and as this was refused, the division which took place was unauthorized. But this is a misapprehension. The change of this article was not made a condition of the division. That depended alone upon the decision of the Southern Conferences.

The division of the Methodist Episcopal Church having thus taken place, in pursuance of the proper authority, it carried with it, as matter of law, a division of the common property belonging to the ecclesiastical organization, and especially of the property in this Book Concern, which belonged to the traveling preachers. It would be strange if it could be otherwise, as it respects the Book Concern, inasmuch as the division of the association was effected under the authority of a body of preachers who were themselves the proprietors and founders of the fund.

It has been argued, however, that, according to the Plan of Separation, the division of the property in this Book Concern was made to depend upon the vote of the Annual Conferences to change the sixth restrictive article, and that, whatever might be the legal effect of the division of the Church upon the common property otherwise, this stipulation controls it, and prevents a division till the consent is obtained.

We do not so understand the Plan of Separation. It admits the right of the Church, South, to its share of the common property, in case of a separation, and provides for a partition of it among the two divisions, upon just and equitable principles; but, regarding the sixth restrictive article as a limitation upon the power of the General Conference, as it respected a division of the property in the Book Concern, provision is made to obtain a removal of it. The removal of this limitation is not a condition to the right of the Church, South, to its share of the property, but is a step taken in order to enable the General Conference to complete the partition of the property.

We will simply add that, as a division of the common property followed, as matter of law, a division of the Church-organization, nothing short of an agreement or stipulation of the Church, South, to give up their share of it, could preclude the assertion of their right; and, it is quite clear, no such agreement or stipulation is to be found in the Plan of Separation. The contrary intent is manifest from a perusal of it.

Without pursuing the case farther, our conclusion is, that the complainants, and those they represent, are entitled to their share of the property in this Book Concern. And the proper decree will be entered to carry this decision into effect.

The complainants represent not only all the beneficiaries in the division of the Church, South, but also the General Conference and the Annual Conferences of the same. The share, therefore, of this Book Concern belonging to the beneficiaries in that Church, and which its authorities are entitled to the safe keeping and charge of, for their benefit, may be properly paid over to the complainants as the authorized agents for this purpose.

We shall accordingly direct a decree to be entered, reversing the decree of the court below, and remanding the proceedings to that court, directing a decree to be entered for the complainants against the defendants; and a reference of the case to a master to take an account of the property belonging to the Book Concern, and report to the court its cash value, and to ascertain the portion belonging to the complainants, which portion shall bear to the whole amount of the fund the proportion that the traveling preachers in the division of the Church, South, bore to the traveling preachers in the Church, North, at the time of the division of said Church. And on the coming in of the report, and confirmation of the same, a decree shall be entered in favor of the complainants for that amount.

Order. This cause came on to be heard on the transcript of the record, from the Circuit Court of the United States for the District of Ohio, and was argued by counsel. On consideration whereof it is ordered, adjudged, and decreed by this court that the decree of said Circuit Court in this cause be, and the same is hereby, reversed and annulled. And this court doth farther find, adjudge, and decree:

1. That, under the resolutions of the General Conference of the Methodist Episcopal Church, holden at the city of New York, according to the usage and Discipline of said Church, passed on the eighth day of June, in the year of our Lord one thousand eight hundred and forty-four (in the pleadings mentioned), it was, among other things, and in virtue of the power of the said General Conference, well agreed and determined by the Methodist Episcopal Church in the United States of America, as then existing, that, in case the Annual Conferences in the slaveholding States should find it necessary

to unite in a distinct ecclesiastical connection, the ministers, local and traveling, of every grade and office, in the Methodist Episcopal Church, might attach themselves to such new ecclesiastical connection, without blame.

2. That the said Annual Conferences in the slaveholding States did find and determine that it was right, expedient, and necessary to erect the Annual Conferences last aforesaid into a distinct ecclesiastical connection, based upon the Discipline of the Methodist Episcopal Church aforesaid, comprehending the doctrines and entire moral and ecclesiastical rules and regulations of the said Discipline (except only in so far as verbal alterations might be necessary to, or for a distinct organization), which new ecclesiastical connection was to be known by the name and style of the Methodist Episcopal Church, South; and that the Methodist Episcopal Church, South, was duly organized under said resolutions of the said General Conference, and the said decision of said Annual Conferences last aforesaid, in a Convention thereof held at Louisville, in the State of Kentucky, in the month of May, in the year of our Lord one thousand eight hundred and forty-five.

3. That, by force of the said resolutions of June the eighth, eighteen hundred and forty-four, and of the authority and power of the said General Conference of the Methodist Episcopal Church as then existing, by which the same were adopted, and by virtue of the said finding and determination of the said Annual Conferences in the slaveholding States therein mentioned, and by virtue of the organization of such Conferences into a distinct ecclesiastical connection as last aforesaid, the religious association known as the Methodist Episcopal Church in the United States of America as then existing, was divided into two associations or distinct Methodist Episcopal Churches, as in the bill of complaint is alleged.

4. That the property denominated the Methodist Book Concern at Cincinnati, in the pleadings mentioned, was, at the time of said division, and immediately before, a fund subject to the following use —that is to say, that the profits arising therefrom, after retaining a sufficient capital to carry on the business thereof, were to be regularly applied toward the support of the deficient traveling, supernumerary, superannuated, and worn-out preachers of the Methodist Episcopal Church, their wives, widows, and children, according to the rules and discipline of said Church; and that the said fund and property are held under the act of incorporation in the said answer, mentioned by the said defendants, Leroy Swormstedt and John H.

Power, as agents of said Book Concern, and in trust for the purposes thereof.

5. That, in virtue of the said division of said Methodist Episcopal Church in the United States, the deficient traveling, supernumerary, superannuated, and worn-out preachers, their wives, widows, and children comprehended in, or in connection with, the Methodist Episcopal Church, South, were, are, and continue to be, beneficiaries of the said Book Concern to the same extent, and as fully as if the said division had not taken place, and in the same manner and degree as persons of the same description who are comprehended in, or in connection with, the other association, denominated* since the division of the Methodist Episcopal Church; and that as well the principal as the profits of said Book Concern, since said division, should of right be administered and managed by the respective General and Annual Conferences of the said two associations and Churches, under the separate organizations thereof, and according to the shares or proportions of the same as hereinafter mentioned, and in conformity with the rules and discipline of said respective associations, so as to carry out the purposes and trusts aforesaid.

6. That so much of the capital and property of said Book Concern at Cincinnati, wherever situate, and so much of the produce and profits thereof as may not have been heretofore accounted for to said Church, South, in the New York case hereinafter mentioned, or otherwise, shall be paid to said Church, South, according to the rate and proportions following—that is to say, in respect to the capital, such share or part as corresponds with the proportion which the number of the traveling preachers in the Annual Conferences which formed themselves into the Methodist Episcopal Church, South, bore to the number of all the traveling preachers of the Methodist Episcopal Church before the division thereof, which numbers shall be fixed and ascertained as they are shown by the minutes of the several Annual Conferences next preceding the said division and new organization in the month of May, A.D. eighteen hundred and forty-five.

And in respect to the produce or profits, such share or part as the number of Annual Conferences which formed themselves into the Methodist Episcopal Church, South, bore, at the time of said division, in May, A.D. 1845, to the whole number of Annual Conferences

---

*We presume there is an omission in the Report of the words, "the Methodist Episcopal Church."—A. H. R.

then being in the Methodist Episcopal Church, excluding the Liberia Conference; so that the division or apportionment of said produce and profits shall be had by Conferences, and not by numbers of the traveling preachers.

7. That said payment of capital and profits, according to the ratios of apportionment so declared, shall be made and paid to the said Smith, Parsons, and Green, as commissioners aforesaid, or their successors, on behalf of said Church, South, and the beneficiaries therein, or to such other person or persons as may be thereto authorized by the General Conference of said Church, South, the same to be subsequently managed and administered so as to carry out the trusts and uses aforesaid, according to the Discipline of said Church, South, and the regulations of the General Conference thereof.

8. And in order more fully to carry out the matters hereinbefore settled and adjudged, it is farther ordered and decreed that this cause be remanded to the said Circuit Court for farther proceedings—that is to say,

That the same be referred to a master to take and state an account as follows:

1. Of the amount and value of the said Book Concern at Cincinnati, on the first day of May, 1845, and of what specific property and effects (according to a general description or classification thereof) the same then consisted, whether composed of real or personal estate, and of whatever nature or description the same may have been; and a similar account as of the date or time when the said master shall take this account.

2. Of the produce and profits of said Book Concern from the time of the General Conference of May, 1844, as reported thereto (if so reported), up to the time of the said division in May, 1845, and from the last-mentioned date down to the time of making up his report: specifying how much of said profits and produce have been transferred to said Book Concern at New York, and accounted for to said Church, South, in the settlement of the case there; and how much remains to be accounted for to said Church, South, on the basis settled by this decree.

And in taking said accounts, and in the execution of said reference, the said defendants shall produce, on oath, all deeds, accounts, books of account, instruments, reports, letters, and copies of letters, memoranda, documents, and writings whatever, pertinent to said reference, in their possession or control, and the said defendants may be examined, on oath, on the said reference; and each party may produce evidence before the master, and have process to compel the attendance of witnesses.

And the said master is farther directed, in respect to any annual profits of said Concern, not heretofore accounted for to said Church, South, to allow to said Church, South, interest at the rate of 6 per cent. upon such unpaid balances from the date at which the same ought to have been paid.

And in respect to all the costs in this case, including the costs of the reference, and all other costs from the commencement of the case until its conclusion, and in respect to the fees of counsel and solicitors therein, of both parties, so far as the same may be reasonable, and in respect of just and necessary expenses, as well of plaintiffs as of defendants in conducting the suit, the same ought to be paid out of said Book Concern, and a common charge thereon, before apportionment and division, and the master is accordingly directed to allow and pay the same to the respective parties entitled thereto, and then to apportion the residue according to the principles fixed in this decree.

And the master is farther directed to return his report to the said Circuit Court with all convenient dispatch, which court shall then proceed to enforce the payment of whatever sum or sums may be found due to said Church, South, on the confirmation of the master's report, in such installments as may be by said court adjudged reasonable, each party having due opportunity of excepting to the master's report; and all questions arising upon said report, and not settled by this decree, may be moved before said Circuit Court, to which court either party shall be at liberty to apply on the footing of this decree.

17 H. 591; 18 H. 480.

THE END.

www.ingramcontent.com/pod-product-compliance
Lightning Source LLC
LaVergne TN
LVHW021052110826
845150LV00001B/57

9781425567378